remaining 19 papers, 14 are presented in this volume. Three additional papers have been added to balance topical coverage, making a total of 17 papers.

The 17 papers are arranged into three categories:

Part 1, Process, includes 9 papers which describe or interpret mechanisms initiating or operating during a debris flow or debris avalanche.

Part 2, Recognition, includes 6 papers which discuss different ways of dating and identifying potential debris flow and debris avalanche hazard areas.

Part 3, Mitigation, contains 2 papers which describe the state-of-the-art in debris flow hazard controls and flow characteristics prediction.

These 17 papers present a fair representation of where debris flow and debris avalanche work is being conducted in North America and by whom. Seven papers cover field areas in California, three papers are devoted to the Appalachians, three to British Columbia, one to Mount St. Helens, and one to Japan. First authors of these papers represent a remarkably even balance between government agencies (8), academic institutions (5), and private industry (4).

REVIEWS IN ENGINEERING GEOLOGY
VOLUME VII

DEBRIS FLOWS/AVALANCHES: PROCESS, RECOGNITION, AND MITIGATION

Edited by
JOHN E. COSTA
AND
GERALD F. WIECZOREK

The Geological Society of America
3300 Penrose Place, P.O. Box 9140
Boulder, Colorado 80301
1987

Published by The Geological Society of America, Inc.
3300 Penrose Place, P.O. Box 9140, Boulder, Colorado 80301

Printed in U.S.A.

GSA Science Editor Campbell Craddock

Library of Congress Cataloging-in-Publication Data

Debris flows/avalanches.

    (Reviews in engineering geology ; v. 7)
    Papers from a symposium co-sponsored by the
Engineering Geology and Quaternary Geology and
Geomorphology Divisions of the Geological Society of
America, at the annual meeting in Reno, Nev. on
Nov. 5, 1984.
    Includes bibliographies.
    Includes index.
    1. Mass-wasting—Congresses.   2. Avalanches—
Congresses. I. Costa, John E.   II. Wieczorek, Gerald F.
III. Geological Society of America. Division of
Engineering Geology.   IV. Geological Society of
America. Quaternary Geology and Geomorphology Division.
V. Series.
TA705.R4 vol. 7 [QE598]   624.1'51 s [551.3]   87-19657
ISBN 0-8137-4107-6

Contents

Contents

Part 3. Mitigation

Preface

Debris flows and debris avalanches are among the most dangerous and destructive natural hazards that affect humans and human works. Worldwide, these mass movements claim hundreds of lives and millions of dollars in property losses every year. The past two decades have been a time of great scientific and engineering advances in the understanding of the processes, the recognition of debris flow and debris avalanche potential, and the finding of ways to mitigate loss of life and property.

Recognizing the timely need to pull together some of the recent research results, the Engineering Geology Division and the Quaternary Geology and Geomorphology Division of the Geological Society of America co-sponsored a symposium on debris flows and debris avalanches at the annual meeting in Reno, Nevada, on November 5, 1984. Twenty papers were presented during that symposium. One of the "papers" was the premier showing of the U.S. Geological Survey's videotape entitled "Debris-flow dynamics" (U.S. Geological Survey Open-File Report 84-606). Of the remaining 19 papers, 14 are presented in this volume. Three additional papers have been added to balance topical coverage, making a total of 17 papers.

The 17 papers are arranged into three categories:

Part 1, Process, includes 9 papers which describe or interpret mechanisms initiating or operating during a debris flow or debris avalanche.

Part 2, Recognition, includes 6 papers which discuss different ways of dating and identifying potential debris flow and debris avalanche hazard areas.

Part 3, Mitigation, contains 2 papers which describe the state-of-the-art in debris-flow hazard controls and flow characteristics prediction.

These 17 papers present a fair representation of where debris flow and debris avalanche work is being conducted in North America and by whom. Seven papers cover field areas in California, three papers are devoted to the Appalachians, three to British Columbia, one to Mount St. Helens, and one to Japan. First authors of these papers represent a remarkably even balance between government agencies (8), academic institutions (5), and private industry (4).

The cooperative spirit between the two GSA Divisions which led to the organization of the symposium in Reno has been sustained in this more permanent record of the symposium, and we are happy that the Engineering Geology Division agreed to publish it as a part of their series "Reviews in Engineering Geology."

We would like to thank several people who made the symposium, as well as the production of this volume, an enjoyable and worthwhile experience. Robert L. Schuster and Donald F. Eschman, former chairmen respectively of the Engineering Geology Division and the Quaternary Geology and Geomorphology Division, provided constant guidance and support, and Jeffrey R. Keaton and Garnett P. Williams supplied support and encouragement.

John E. Costa
Gerald F. Wieczorek

Geological Society of America
Reviews in Engineering Geology, Volume VII
1987

A rheologic classification of subaerial sediment-water flows

Thomas C. Pierson
John E. Costa
U.S. Geological Survey
David A. Johnston Cascades Volcano Observatory
5400 MacArthur Boulevard
Vancouver, Washington 98661

ABSTRACT

Classifications of flowing sediment-water mixtures have, in the past, been based primarily on relative, qualitative differences in the style and rate of movement as well as on morphology and sedimentology of deposits. A more quantitative and physically relevant classification is presented here, based on thresholds in rheologic behavior. The classification is constructed on a two-dimensional matrix in which flows are located according to deformation rate (mean velocity) and sediment concentration, with composition of the mixture constant. Three major rheologic boundaries are crossed as sediment concentration increases from 0 (clear water) to 100 percent (dry sediment): (1) the acquisition of a yield strength—the transition from liquid "normal streamflow" to plastic "hyperconcentrated streamflow"; (2) an abrupt increase in yield strength coinciding with the onset of liquefaction behavior—the transition to "slurry flow"; and (3) the loss of the ability to liquefy—the transition of "granular flow." These three rheologic boundaries shift according to particle-size distribution and composition of the mixture.

Processes controlling flow behavior depend on deformation rate (velocity). Rate-independent frictional and viscous forces dominate at lower velocities and in finer grained mixtures; rate-dependent inertial forces dominate at higher velocities and in coarser grained mixtures. As velocity increases, grain-support mechanisms change from low-energy varieties (buoyancy, cohesion, structural support) to progressively higher energy mechanisms (turbulence, dispersive stress, fluidization).

Existing nomenclatures of geologic flow phenomena can fit within this rheologic classification. The morphology and sedimentology of flow deposits commonly can be used to deduce rheologic behavior, but caution needs to be exercised in inferring processes from deposits.

INTRODUCTION

The earth scientist interested in surficial processes commonly encounters process terminologies based on relative, qualitative differences in style and rate of movement, as well as on morphology and sedimentology of deposits. For those interested in the mechanics of flow, such terminologies are inadequate. As increasing numbers of studies involve direct observations and quantification of both natural phenomena and physical models, the need grows for a terminology with classification criteria based on the rheologic behavior of the material, with well-defined boundaries. The current use of terminology is inconsistent and

often misleading. For example, a term such as "mudflow" can connote vastly different geologic processes ranging from very slow plastic deformation of clay slopes (Skempton and Hutchinson, 1969) to very rapid, turbulent flow of muddy water transporting coarse sediment (including boulders) as bedload (Kurdin, 1973). Conversely, a single process such as channelized flow of a liquefied, structurally coherent mixture of poorly sorted sediment may be identified by a confusing number of terms (debris flow, mudflow, debris torrent, mud flood, debris avalanche). The nomenclature problem is particularly acute because of the large

1

variety of geomorphic processes involving the flow of sediment-water mixtures that seem to grade from one to another without obvious boundaries. The confusion is compounded further by the fact that dynamic analysis of such flows is centered between the two disciplines of fluid mechanics and rheology (Fisher, 1971).

OBJECTIVES

This chapter proposes a useful, process-oriented classification of types or styles of movement of water and earth materials (at above-freezing temperatures) that involve flow. Therefore, rock glaciers, for example, that may have an ice core or ice glaciers are not included. Our purpose is not to displace other classifications, but rather to develop a set of process descriptors that are reflective of rheologic behavior, and to constrain existing mass movement and flow nomenclature within an objective framework based on the dynamics of flows that do not consider flow-initiation mechanisms or deposit morphology and sedimentology. The type of sediment carried in the flows is assumed to be a coarse, poorly sorted hypothetical mixture typical of hillslope colluvium. A sufficient number of first-hand measurements, observations, or eye-witness accounts of the different kinds of subaerial sediment-water flows presently exists so that the rheologic behavior of the flows can be inferred (e.g., Costa and Williams, 1984).

FLUIDS AND FLOWS

When a physical substance is subjected to an applied stress of sufficient magnitude, that substance will deform. If the deformation is irreversible, it is called flow. Response to stress is not solely intrinsic to the material, but it is also a function of other factors such as time, temperature, and deformation history (Van Wazer and others, 1963).

When considering the macroscopic hydrologic and geologic processes that occur at the earth's surface, flow may be defined as the continuous, irreversible deformation of a geologic material that occurs in response to applied stress. The applied stress in most geomorphic situations is gravity, and it is usually applied as a shear stress. The material is usually some mixture of particulate solids (rock, soil, organic debris), water, and air. By the most general definition, a fluid is considered to be simply a material that flows (Van Wazer and others, 1963).

The viscosity of a fluid is the ratio of applied shear stress to rate of shear. Water will flow under any applied shear stress, and viscosity is constant at a constant temperature. These properties make water, by definition, a Newtonian fluid (Fig. 1). A fluid having a viscosity that decreases with increasing rate of shear (a shear-thinning fluid) is termed a pseudoplastic fluid (Fig. 1). Conversely, a fluid that exhibits an increase in viscosity with shear rate (shear-thickening) is termed a dilatant fluid (Fig. 1). The term liquid which defines a material of fixed volume at constant temperature and pressure that spontaneously assumes

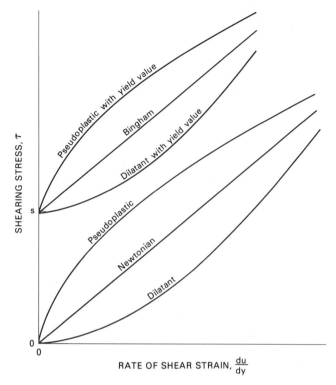

Figure 1. Flow curves for idealized liquid and plastic rheologic bodies, with names of flow models indicated. Liquids exhibit no shear strength; plastic bodies begin to deform only after yield stress, *s,* is exceeded.

the shape of its container, may be applied to Newtonian, pseudoplastic, and dilatant fluids.

Some naturally occurring materials will not flow until a minimum shear stress (variously termed the yield stress, yield strength, or yield value) has been exceeded. If shear rate is proportional to shear stress, the material is called a plastic fluid or Bingham fluid (Fig. 1). A pseudoplastic fluid with a yield value or a dilatant fluid with a yield value (Fig. 1) may also be encountered. Yield strength is not present in true single-phase liquids, only in fluids where bubbles or solid particles are suspended in a continuous (liquid) phase (Van Wazer and others, 1963). In addition, some non-Newtonian fluids exhibit time-dependent flow effects, both reversible and irreversible. Certain substances become more fluid (less viscous) with time of flow under steady-flow conditions. Such materials are termed "thixotropic."

The rheology of fluids naturally occurring at above-freezing temperatures at the earth's surface is primarily a function of composition, such as chemistry, and solids content. Temperature and pressure effects are comparatively minor. With the exception of clear water and air, fluids encountered in nature are multiphase systems. They involve some combination of solid (sediment), liquid (water), and gas (air). Flow behavior in response to applied shear stress is a function of (1) the relative proportions of these components; (2) the grain-size distribution of the solid component; and (3) the physical and chemical properties of the solid component, assuming the properties of the liquid and gas phases are relatively constant.

CLASSIFICATION: A PERSPECTIVE

Previous classifications of sediment-water flows have been based on a number of criteria obtained either through direct observation and measurement of the processes, or through inference based on morphology and sedimentology of deposits, on physical models, or on theory. Although classification efforts have been divided largely between subaerial and subaqueous flow processes, many of the physical mechanisms involved appear to be similar, despite the obvious differences in ambient fluids.

Subaerial Flows

Many of the subaerial terminologies followed an early, comprehensive landslide classification by Sharpe (1938) where two primary parameters—relative velocity and relative sediment concentration—were used to differentiate a suite of flow processes categorized as debris avalanche, mudflow, earthflow, solifluction, creep, and streamflow. However, this classification did not define concisely the boundaries between these processes. Nevertheless, this classification has been widely used, and the classification presented in this paper is similar conceptually to Sharpe's.

Twenty years later another important landslide classification was published by Varnes (1958). That classification and its slightly revised edition (Varnes, 1978) have become, probably, the most widely used reference for mass-movement terminology. Varnes' classification is based on two main characteristics: (1) type of material (bedrock, coarse debris, and fine earth), and (2) type of movement (falls, topples, slides, lateral spreads, flows, and complex). Velocity (using a quantified scale) and moisture content are used for second-order subdivisions. Within Varnes' classification, subdivisions of flow include: block stream, debris avalanche, debris flow, solifluction, and soil creep for coarse material; and dry sand or silt flows, wet sand or silt flows, rapid earth flow, and earth flow for fine materials. The term "mudflow" is a subcategory of debris flow with less than 50 percent gravel. Varnes' classification, however, does not deal with the most fluid end of the sediment-water spectrum.

The fluid flows at the watery end of the sediment-water spectrum were addressed by Beverage and Culbertson (1964), who divided streamflow sediment concentrations into normal, high, extreme, hyperconcentrated, and mudflow categories. Although specific sediment concentration boundaries were designated for these classes of flow, the limits appear to be arbitrary with the exception of the hyperconcentrated-mudflow boundary. In China, the term "hyperconcentrated" is generally used for any mixture that possesses a measurable yield strength. Debris flow is viewed as a special homogeneous type of hyperconcentrated flow (Qian and others, 1980; Wang and others, 1983).

Subaerial classifications also have been focused on the flow process itself and have expanded the number of criteria to differentiate flow types. Based on many years of field and laboratory investigations in the Soviet Union, Gagoshidze (1969) divided flows into flash floods, turbulent mudflow (mud flood), and structural mudflow based on sediment concentration. Kurdin (1973) expanded on this classification, using genesis, type of material, material properties, and size as classifying criteria. British landslide terminology, exemplified by Skempton and Hutchinson (1969), reflected the predominance of clay in slope stability problems in England. The categories of earthflow, mudflow, solifluction, and creep are differentiated, but "mudflow" is a much slower, more viscous mass movement in this discussion than the term implies for the American or Soviet authors cited previously.

Many of the more recent discussions of flow terminology have attempted to "lump" or "split" the terms already established, and most discussions have included more quantitative criteria. Coates (1977) devised a classification scheme based on type of material and type of movement. In essence his scheme is a simplified version of Varnes' classification. Takahashi (1981) classified four types of subaerial mass movement—fall, landslide, creep (avalanche); *sturzstrom*; pyroclastic flow; and debris flow— based on grain-support mechanisms, properties of the interstitial fluid, velocity, and travel distance.

In the United States, the Committee on Methodologies for Predicting Mudflow Areas (1982) classified flows as clear-water floods, mud floods, mudflows, and other landslides. The difference between clear-water floods and mud floods is the relative amount of sediment load. Mud floods and mudflows are distinguished during an event by the velocity, flow patterns, and characteristics of particle support. Mudflows are distinguished from other landslides by the latter moving as discrete blocks or groups of blocks by sliding, falling, or toppling. The Committee on Methodologies for Predicting Mudflow Areas (1982) also indicated that the different flow processes can be identified on the basis of characteristics of deposits. Lawson (1982) described and sampled four types of subaerial sediment-water flows at the Matanuska Glacier, Alaska. He measured water content and several engineering properties including Atterberg limits and shear strength. Lawson (1982) demonstrated that as water content increased, maximum flow rate, erosiveness, and fabric development of the sediment-water flows increased, and mean grain size, maximum thickness, density, and shear strength decreased.

More recently, O'Brien and Julien (1985) conducted laboratory experiments on natural mudflow sediments from Colorado. They divided the flow results into four categories based on flow properties controlled by sediment concentration: water flood, mud flood, mudflows, and landslides. VanDine (1985) classified floods, mudflows, debris torrents, debris flows, debris slides, and debris avalanches based on the type of materials involved, mechanics of movement, locations of movement, and relative water content. Smith (1986) used sedimentology to differentiate between normal streamflow, hyperconcentrated flood flow, and debris flow.

Other work, while not classification attempts per se, has addressed characteristics of flow phenomena that are relevant to classification. Four such papers have examined the properties or deposits of high-concentration streamflow. Bull (1962) proposed that texture of sedimentary deposits could be used to differentiate among water flows, intermediate flows, and mudflows on alluvial fans in California. Scott and Dinehart (1985) and Pierson and Scott (1985) examined the measured flow characteristics of a hyperconcentrated flood surge that occurred at Mount St. Helens in 1982, the sedimentologic evidence for a progressive transition from debris flow to hyperconcentrated flow, and the probable grain-support mechanisms at work. Bradley and McCutcheon (1985) summarized the effect of large sediment loads on transport phenomena and flow behavior in streams.

Two other papers clarified the rheologic behavior of deforming bulk solids. Savage (1984) investigated granular flows and proposed three flow regimes: (1) macroviscous, in which viscous effects of interstitial fluids and interactions of solid particles determine stresses; (2) quasi-static, in which dry friction and interlocking between particles are important and inertial effects are negligible; and (3) grain-inertia, in which inertia associated with individual particles is fundamental. Each flow regime is characterized by the relative magnitudes of interstitial viscosity, solids fraction, and rate of deformation. Iverson (1985), in developing a generalized constitutive equation for idealized mass-movement behavior, mathematically connected a suite of rheologic models, linear and nonlinear, ranging from purely plastic to purely viscous. This equation provides a powerful analytical tool for interrelating and contrasting different types of sediment-water flows.

Subaqueous Flows

A substantial amount of work attempting to interpret flow processes from sedimentary deposits in subaqueous environments has been published. It forms much of the basis for the interpretation of subaerial flows. Efforts to classify subaqueous mass movements have included attempts to link deposits with process. This is necessary because the deposits are virtually the only record of the processes in this environment. Because of this link, considerable attention has been given to the rheologic characteristics of the sediment-water mixtures involved in such mass movements (Kuenen, 1951; Dott, 1963; Sanders, 1965; Middleton, 1970; Fisher, 1971; Hampton, 1972).

Dott (1963) classified flow-type movements as either mass flows or turbidity flows on the basis of rheologic behavior—plastic versus viscous fluid. He also identified the rheologic boundaries of yield limit and liquid limit as fundamentally important. Carter (1975) discussed rheologic criteria for mass flow classification in detail. He differentiated between sediment creep, slurry flow, grain flow, and turbidity flow using type of movement, rate, and rheologic properties of the mixture as criteria. Specifically, he considered whether the flow state is laminar or turbulent and whether the dominant grain interaction is vis-

TABLE 1. CONVERSION OF ORDER-OF-MAGNITUDE RATES AND MORE EASILY VISUALIZED APPROXIMATE EQUIVALENTS

Order of Magnitude Velocities (m/sec)	Approximate Equivalents	
10^2	360 km/hr	(225 mph)
10^1	36 km/hr	(23 mph)
10^{-2}	0.6 m/min	(2.0 ft/min)
10^{-3}	3.6 m/hr	(11.8 ft/hr)
10^{-5}	0.9 m/day	(3.0 ft/day)
10^{-7}	3.1 m/yr	(10.2 ft/yr)
10^{-10}	3.1 mm/yr	(0.12 in/yr)

cous or inertial. Middleton and Hampton (1976) identified four types of subaqueous sediment gravity flows based on the way particles are supported above the bed as interpreted from the sedimentary textures and structures in deposits. They included turbidity currents, in which particles are supported by turbulence; fluidized sediment flow, in which the upward flow of fluid escaping between grains supports particles as they try to settle; grain flows, in which sediment is supported by grain-to-grain interactions; and debris flows, in which larger particles are supported by a fine-grained matrix with finite yield strength. Middleton and Hampton (1976) acknowledged that distinguishing between deposits formed from the different types of flows is difficult. Lowe (1979) followed the classification of Middleton and Hampton (1976) by separating flows based on fluid and plastic behavior. They are further subdivided on the basis of dominant coarse-particle support mechanism. Fluid-flow behavior includes turbidity currents, fluidized flows, and some liquefied flows. Plastic-flow behavior includes some other liquefied flows, grain flows, and debris flows.

Numerous other landslide classifications exist, including some of the types of flows covered in this chapter. Many of these classifications were summarized by Hansen (1984).

RHEOLOGIC CLASSIFICATION OF FLOW

A classification of distinct flow types (Fig. 2) can be constructed using a two-dimensional matrix based on mean flow velocity and sediment concentration. The rheology of a sediment-water mixture can be roughly inferred from the velocity of sustained flow on slopes or in channels. Velocity is a surrogate for rate of shear when the material is subjected to an applied shear stress (gravity). Over the range of slope and channel angles encountered in natural landscapes, identified flow processes move at characteristic rates, which frequently are possible to measure or estimate in the field. Conversion of order-of-magnitude rates used in Figure 2 to more easily visualized rates is shown in Table 1.

Rheologic response of a sediment-water mixture at a given strain rate is governed primarily by sediment concentration (or water content) and is affected to a lesser extent by the grain-size distribution of the solids and the physical and chemical properties

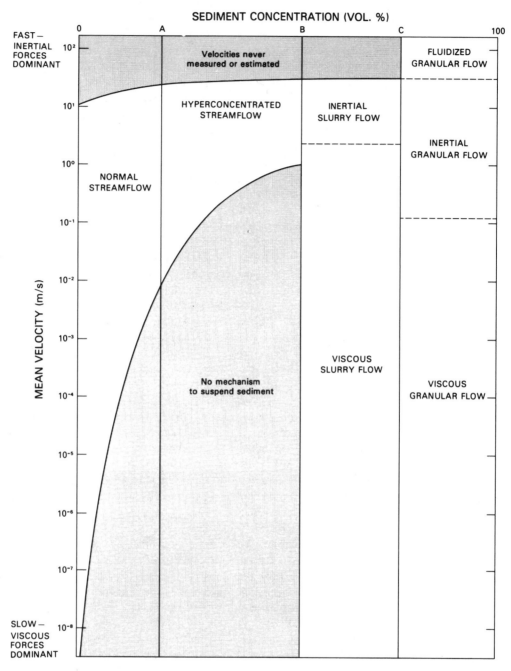

Figure 2. Rheologic classification of sediment-water flows. Vertical boundaries A, B, and C are rheologic thresholds and are a function of grain-size distribution (here assumed to be coarse, poorly sorted mixture) and sediment concentration. Moving from left to right, boundary A marks onset of yield strength; boundary B marks sudden, rapid increase in yield strength that permits static suspension of gravel and onset of liquefaction behavior; boundary C marks cessation of liquefaction behavior. Horizontal velocity boundaries, also function of grain-size distribution and sediment concentration as well as particle density, are determined by how stress is transmitted between particles during flow.

of the particles. In a particular geographic area, the latter two variables would tend to be more constant than sediment concentration. Sediment concentration might therefore be considered a more sensitive parameter. For this reason, it was chosen as the second variable for the classification matrix (Fig. 2). No numbers are shown on the horizontal sediment-concentration axis except pure water (0%) and dry sediment (100%) because exact values depend on grain-size distribution and physical-chemical composition. The positions of the vertical boundary lines between processes shift to the right or to the left, depending on the values of these compositional variables. The positions of the vertical boundary lines in Figure 2 assume that the flowing sediment is a coarse, poorly sorted, noncohesive mixture of particles, exemplified by the kind of physically weathered, colluvial soils typically found in mountainous regions. For sediments that are cohesive or that contain more fines, the vertical boundary lines shift to the left. For coarser, better sorted, non-cohesive sediment, the vertical boundary lines shift to the right.

The boundaries in the classification diagram (Fig. 2), both horizontal and vertical, are only approximate, and, to a large degree, inferred. Field measurements of both composition (including water content) and velocity of actual flow events are relatively few. As more field measurements are carried out, boundaries will be better defined.

The shaded "off-limits" areas in the classification diagram involve combinations of velocity and sediment concentration not believed to occur under natural conditions. The shaded zone at the top of the diagram connotes an upper velocity limit due to viscous and frictional forces for all but the rapid inertial granular flows. This type of flow may experience reduced rates of energy dissipation due to other mechanisms such as fluidization. Some empirical data exist to define the boundaries of this upper shaded zone. At the left side of this upper zone, streamflows exceeding 10 m/sec in natural channels are unlikely to be free of sediment. The shape of the right-hand side of this zone is determined by historic measurements or estimates of flows. In the United States, the fastest streamflow velocity ever measured by current meter is about 9.1 m/sec (Leopold, 1974), the fastest mean velocity ever computed from an indirect discharge measurement is about 30 m/sec (Baker, 1978), and the fastest velocities estimated for inertial slurry flows and granular flows (debris flows and "small" debris avalanches) are about 35 to 40 m/sec (Nakamura, 1926; Janda and others, 1981; Kadomura and others, 1983; Pierson, 1985). The zone ends at boundary C because rapid inertial granular flows (large rock avalanches) have achieved velocities greater than 100 m/s (Plafker and Ericksen, 1978). The larger shaded zone at the bottom of Figure 2 involves velocities inferred to be too slow to permit dynamic suspension in streamflow of the material making up the bulk of the hypothetical sediment mixture.

Apparent Liquid Flow

When observed in the field, two types of flows with relatively small sediment concentrations at the left side of the classification proposed in Figure 2 appear to flow as liquids. These dilute sediment-water flows are referred to as normal streamflow and hyperconcentrated streamflow.

Streamflow. In most natural streams, most of the time water is the continuous phase of a multiphase fluid. Fine-grained sediment (organic and inorganic solids) and bubbles (air) are commonly dispersed in (suspended in) the water. As long as the dispersion is relatively dilute, the sediment particles and/or bubbles do not interact, and the fluid maintains the rheologic characteristics of the continuous phase (Van Wazer and others, 1963). Normal streamflow is defined here as flowing water with a sufficiently small sediment concentration that its flow behavior is unaffected by the presence of sediment in transport. It is a Newtonian fluid.

As the concentration of suspended particles (discussion hereinafter limited to solid particles) increases, a point is reached at which these particles begin to interact. In clay-water mixtures, the interference between particles is the result of the electrochemical attractions of positively charged clay-platelet edges to negatively charged platelet faces (Lambe, 1960; Van Wazer and others, 1963) and also the result of atomic bonding (Mitchell and others, 1969). Unless the surface changes are satisfied by cations in solution, clay particles will clump together with bound water to form small clusters (flocs), which in turn form more weakly bonded large aggregates and networks of flocs (Michaels and Bolger, 1962). When particle interaction occurs, the fluid acquires a yield strength and becomes a non-Newtonian fluid. The suspended-sediment concentration at which this threshold is crossed (boundary A, Fig. 2) is highly dependent on the grain-size distribution, degree of clay dispersion, and clay mineralogy. For flocculated suspensions of smectite, yield values appear at concentrations as low as 3 percent by volume (Hampton, 1972). However, a dispersed suspension of kaolinite does not acquire yield strength until a concentration of about 13 percent by volume is reached (Hampton, 1972). In the absence of fines, a suspension of coarse neutrally buoyant particles at low strain rates can remain a Newtonian fluid until frictional interaction begins—at volume concentrations as high as 50 percent by volume (Rodine, 1974).

Hyperconcentrated streamflow. Hyperconcentrated flow originally was defined by Beverage and Culbertson (1964) as streamflow with sediment concentrations between 40 and 80 percent by weight (20 to 60 percent by volume). Here we are defining "hyperconcentrated streamflow" as a flowing mixture of water and sediment that possesses a measurable yield strength but that still appears to flow like a liquid (i.e., yield strength is low, probably less than 400 dynes/cm^2) (Kang and Zhang, 1980). Although hyperconcentrated streamflow will appear very similar to muddy normal streamflow in the field, one noticeable difference is the marked dampening of turbulence (Wang and others, 1983; van Rijn, 1983; Yang and Zhao, 1983; Pierson and Scott, 1985). Although Beverage and Culbertson (1964) did not use yield strength as a criterion for defining hyperconcentrated streamflow originally, it is used by many Chinese hydrologists (Qian and others, 1980; Wang and others, 1983). However, the

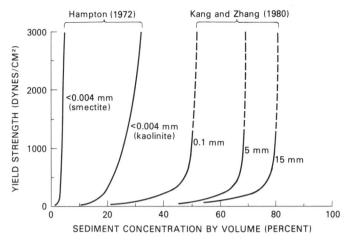

Figure 3. Yield strength of various sediment-water mixtures (average grain size indicated) plotted against sediment concentration (from Pierson and Scott, 1985). Intersection of each curve with abscissa marks transition from normal streamflow to hyperconcentrated streamflow (boundary A, Fig. 2). Abrupt steepening of slope in each curve marks approximate transition from hyperconcentrated streamflow to slurry flow (boundary B, Fig. 2). Data from Hampton (1972) are from artificial clay-water mixtures; data from Kang and Zhang (1980) are interpolated from actual debris flow samples.

Chinese usage does not limit the term to fluids that appear to be liquid.

Flow of Plastic Fluids

Two types of plastic fluid flows are included in this classification: slurry flow and granular flow.

Slurry Flow. As the sediment concentration of a sediment-water dispersion increases still further, yield strength increases slowly until another transition point (or zone) is crossed, after which yield strength increases rapidly (boundary B, Fig. 2). This transition can be identified by the sharp bend in plots of yield strength versus sediment concentrations (Fig. 3). The change in the rate of increase in yield strength is more abrupt in coarse mixtures than in fine. This increase in resistance to flow is attributed to the onset of internal friction (Rodine, 1974). Electro-chemical bonding still may be dominant in clay-rich mixtures, but in coarser mixtures, sliding friction between grains and grain interlocking appear to be the principal mechanisms (Rodine, 1974).

The flow of sediment-water mixtures having sufficient yield strength to exhibit plastic flow behavior in the field (that is, to form steep, lobate fronts and lateral levees, and to carry gravel-sized particles in suspension) and yet to become partially liquefied as they are remolded, is termed here slurry flow (after Carter, 1975). Such a mixture is saturated, pore water is trapped to some degree (depending on sorting) in the framework of grains, and the liquidity index (in fine-grained mixtures, the ratio of natural mois-

ture content to the liquid limit of the sediment) is greater than 1.0 (Carson, 1976). The pore fluid is at pressures in excess of hydrostatic pressure because part of the weight of the solid phase is carried by the pore water (i.e., the mixture is partially liquefied). Such a mixture will flow as a coherent, homogeneous mass when the yield strength is exceeded. The trapped water is transported by the flowing granular mass, and entrained air probably does not exceed a few percent by volume. Depending on the shear strength of the mixtures and the dynamic particle-support mechanisms operating, particles to the size of large boulders can be suspended in slurry flows. Boulders exceeding the suspension competence of the slurry can be rolled along by the flow. When the flowing slurry comes to a stop, it consolidates at the rate at which the pore fluid can drain out. With the exception of some of the clay and silt that escapes with the pore water, fine and coarse particles settle together without any interparticle movement. This is in contrast to hypercontentrated flow, where particles settle out of suspension and are deposited separately, depending on their fall velocities (Qian and others, 1980).

Viscous forces can control the flow behavior of slurries when the silt-clay content of the mixture is relatively high or the shear rate, mean grain diameter, grain density, and water content are relatively low (Bagnold, 1954). Under these conditions, the Bingham plastic model often is chosen to be the constitutive equation for predicting flow behavior (Thomas, 1963; Johnson, 1970; Bird and others, 1982), although some experimental results have shown a nonlinear relation between shear stress and strain rate for clay-water slurries (Michaels and Bolger, 1962; Howard, 1963). Flows of this type are termed here viscous slurry flows. When the viscosity of the pore fluid is relatively low and shear rates, mean grain diameter, density, and water content are sufficiently high, the dominating effect of viscous forces is supplanted by inertial forces wherein momentum is transferred through particle collisions. Flows in which this mechanism is dominant are termed here inertial slurry flows, and the dilatant fluid model can be used to model behavior (Takahashi, 1978). If shear sorting takes place because of the effect of dispersive stress (Bagnold, 1954) or some other mechanism, flow behavior may become thixotropic (Denlinger and others, 1984). Use of the Bagnold number, the ratio of inertial stress over viscous stress (Bagnold, 1954; Hill, 1966), would be a rigorous means of determining the transition from viscous flow to inertial flow. However, measuring the parameters necessary to make such a calculation would be very difficult. Therefore, an intuitive estimate of the critical velocity separating the viscous and inertial mechanisms is about 2 m/sec for our hypothetical coarse-sediment mixture, but this estimate would change according to the composition of the mixture.

Note that the yield strength of a slurry may cause the formation of a rigid plug during flow, a zone in which the yield strength is generally not exceeded, and the material behaves more as a solid (Johnson, 1970; Rodine, 1974; Bird and others, 1982). If a rigid plug grows in cross-sectional dimensions, the shear zone (zone of actual flowage) shrinks. As more and more shear is concentrated in a thinner and thinner zone near the lower boundary, flow becomes transitional to sliding. In some earthflows, for example, sliding is recognized as the principal mode of movement (Keefer and Johnson, 1983).

Granular Flow. Granular flow begins when the sediment concentration of the material increases to the point where the mass is no longer partially liquefied when remolded (boundary C, Fig. 2). In other words, pore-water pressures are no longer in excess of hydrostatic pressures, and the full weight of the flowing granular mass is borne by grain-to-grain contact or collisions. Liquidity index is less than 1.0 (Keefer and Johnson, 1983). The mixture may be partly dried with air filling some of the pore space, or it may still be saturated but with a grain-size distribution (well sorted) and shear rate (low) that allow pore water to escape readily during remolding (i.e., a free-draining mixture). Our use of the term granular flow here is very similar to grain flow as defined by Middleton (1970), but that term was avoided here because of its wide and ambiguous use in the literature. Savage's (1984) use of "granular flow" is adopted here, where volume concentration of grains is high, direct interaction between individual grains is frequent, and bulk behavior is governed largely by interparticle forces, namely friction and collisions.

At low rates of shear, rate-independent sliding friction and interlocking among the grains, combined with viscous effects of the interstitial fluid, determine the bulk stresses within the deforming mass. Grain inertia effects are negligible. Flow of this type is termed here frictional granular flow, and it encompasses Savage's (1984) quasi-static and macroviscous flow regimes. We infer this to be the case for our hypothetical mixture at mean velocities less than about 0.1 m/sec. This value probably is lower than the velocity separating inertial and viscous slurry flows because of the lower viscosity of the fluid phase.

At moderate rates of shear, rate-dependent grain inertial effects begin to dominate, but frictional effects are still significant. This corresponds to Savage's (1984) grain-inertia flow regime. Grain collisions transfer momentum between particles, resulting in a measurable dispersive stress (Bagnold, 1954). Flow of this type is called here inertial granular flow, and mean flow velocities bounding this type of flow are believed to be approximately 0.1 and 35 m/sec.

Flowing debris masses in excess of about 1 million m^3 (Scheidegger, 1973) are able to achieve extremely high shear rates, with mean flow velocities ranging as high as 50 to 100 m/sec (Hsu, 1978; Plafker and Ericksen, 1978; Voight and others, 1983). Under these conditions, momentum transfer by energetic interparticle collisions primarily determines how the flow behaves; frictional effects are minimal. Many such large debris avalanches, or *sturzstroms,* also appear to achieve excessively long runout distances in proportion to volume relative to smaller debris avalanches (Hsu, 1975; Voight and others, 1985). Such mass movements are termed here rapid inertial granular flows.

The proposed mechanisms of rapid inertial granular flows are varied. They include fluidization (the reduction of effective normal stress and a decrease in interparticle friction resulting from the upward motion of a fluid supporting part of the sediment weight) involving dust and air (Hsu, 1975; Kent, 1966); mechanical dilation under shear and separation of particles through collision and rebound (Heim, 1882; McSaveney, 1978; Davies, 1982); vacuum-induced upward flow of air from the airfoil shape of the upper flow surface (Krumdieck, 1984); steam from frictional heating of entrained moisture (Habib, 1975); grain separation through vibrational (acoustic) energy from the noise of the flow itself (Melosh, 1979; Melosh, this volume); frictional melting of a thin layer of rock debris at the base of the flow (Erismann, 1979); and air layer lubrication (Shreve, 1968).

Another type of rapid inertial granular flow is dry pyroclastic flow, although such flow is not considered directly in this classification of sediment-water flows. These highly mobile granular flows generally are considered to be fluidized by hot gases exsolving from pumice particles (Brown, 1962; Sparks, 1978) and/or escaping heated air entrained by the flow (McTaggart, 1960; Wilson and Walker, 1982).

For frictional granular flows, pure flow is probably the exception. The increasing yield strength of the moving material acquired with decreasing water content promotes the formation of discrete failure or shear zones along the boundaries of the flows, and sliding begins to become a significant mechanism for movement. This increased role of sliding is expressed as narrow shear zones in many earthflow velocity profiles, and as slickensides along the boundaries of frictional granular flows (Keefer and Johnson, 1983; Iverson, 1985). In effect, at low strain rates, the sediments on the far right side of the classification in Figure 2 are beginning to act as Coulomb substances, not just as viscous fluids.

RHEOLOGIC BOUNDARIES FOR EXISTING FLOW NOMENCLATURE

The names of the individual flow classes in Figure 2 are based on our interpretation of the dominant forces involved in the flow (inertial, viscous, or frictional), on whether the flow mixtures have yield strength, and on whether sediments in the flow are liquefied (slurry flow) or not (granular flow). While the categories in Figure 2 are an attempt to classify flows on the basis of rheologic behavior alone, the categories also can be used to put rheologically based boundaries on better known geomorphic-process terms as shown in Figure 4.

"Streamflow" is used in both Figures 2 and 4 because this term implies the flow of water or a sediment-water mixture that acts like water, i.e., a liquid, to the casual observer. Streamflow is a widely used term with sufficient rheologic meaning. "Hyperconcentrated" is chosen to modify streamflow when the fluid becomes slightly plastic in the rheologic sense but still appears to flow like water. The onset of yield strength has significant implications, however, for stream hydraulics and sediment transport (Bradley and McCutcheon, 1985). The term mud flood recently has been applied to flows of this type (Committee on Methodologies for Predicting Mudflow Areas, 1982; O'Brien and Julien,

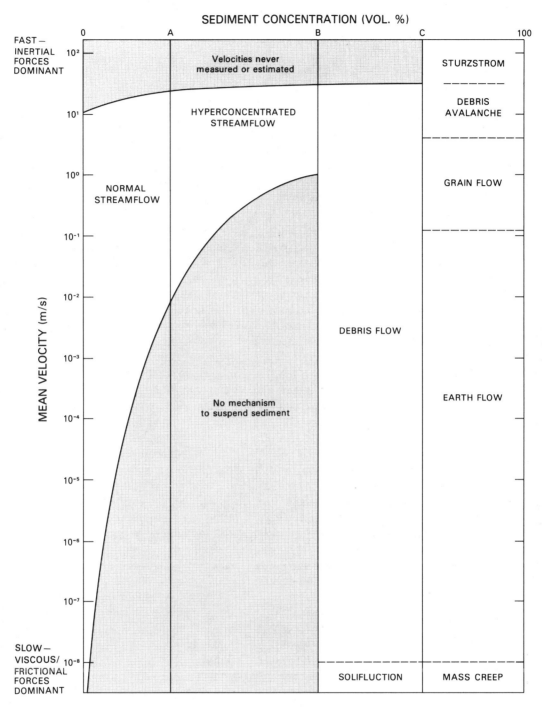

Figure 4. Fitting appropriate existing flow nomenclature into proposed rheologic classification.

1985), but this label has compositional implications that are not necessarily true. For example, the sediment transported during a hyperconcentrated streamflow event at Mount St. Helens in 1982 was predominantly sand (Pierson and Scott, 1985).

"Debris flow" seems to be the most appropriate term for slurry flows of both the inertial and viscous variety, except for the extremely slow flows of saturated regolith that are appropriately called solifluction (Flint, 1971). Although viscous slurry flow often is termed mudflow, and mud-rich mixtures often are dominated by viscous forces, we maintain that this differentiation between inertial and viscous flow ought to be based on shear rate, not on composition. Predominantly coarse- or predominantly fine-grained mixtures can be either viscous or inertial flows, depending on the driving force (slope steepness), grain density, and water content. Therefore, we believe that the use of the term "mudflow" is misleading from a process point of view. The term "debris torrent," which is in wide use, particularly in the forestry literature of the northwestern United States and Canada, is also a misleading term for two reasons. First, "mountain torrent" or "debris torrent" is used in European and Japanese literature to mean a very steep channel, not the material that flows in it (Eisbacher, 1982). Second, the term was coined to differentiate between coarse debris flows occurring in channels and flows occurring on open slopes (Swanston, 1974; VanDine, 1985), a criterion that has no rheologic or other process-specific basis. We suggest that usage of the term "debris torrent" be discontinued and that the more general term "debris flow" be used instead, with appropriate descriptive adjectives when specifics are required.

Inertial granular flows including sturzstroms appropriately can be called debris avalanches (Sharpe, 1938; Varnes, 1958, 1978). *Sturzstrom* (Hsu, 1975) is a useful, more specific term for large, rapid inertial granular flows. We suggest that "grain flow," a widely applied term for both subaerial and subaqueous mass movements, be limited to inertial granular flow, such as flowing lobate sheets of gravel that occur on oversteepened talus cones or in gravel pits, or lobate flows of sand down the front of dune faces.

The term earthflow is used in Figure 4 for frictional granular flows in the velocity range of 10^{-8} to 10^{-1} m/sec, even though some basal sliding also may be occurring. Earthflows described in the literature (summarized in Keefer and Johnson, 1983) typically have velocities restricted to the slow end of the assigned velocity range. Higgins (1982) cited a paucity of reported velocities in the range of 10^{-5} to 10^{-1} m/sec and suggested that the velocity spectrum may not be continuous because of inherent differences in the mechanics of different types of mass movement. Nevertheless, we have attempted to include all possibilities. "Mass creep" (Carson and Kirkby, 1972) is a term that connotes very slow, nonliquefied, frictional granular flow.

Any sediment-water flow process can be classified with Figure 2 under the following conditions: (1) if the approximate velocity of movement is known; and (2) if it is known whether the flowing mixture has shear strength, whether it has enough shear strength to suspend gravel, and whether it is liquefied (in the zone of flowage). These characteristics might be determined from landform and sediment deposits (Middleton and Hampton, 1976; Scott and Dinehart, 1985; Smith, 1986; Crozier, 1973; Desloges and Gardner, 1984; Pierson, 1985) as well as from direct observations and measurements.

CONCLUSIONS

A sufficiently large number of observations and measurements of different kinds of sediment-water flows have been made by trained scientists that it is possible to propose a quantitative and physically relevant classification based on the actual properties and characteristics of the moving flows. Although much of the information about different kinds of sediment-water flows comes from direct observations and measurements, laboratory experiments, theory, and indirect evidence, erosional and depositional patterns and deposit sedimentology also contribute to the understanding of flow behavior.

The classification in this report is based on the rheologic response of coarse, poorly sorted sediment-water mixtures to applied shear stress. Vertical process boundaries change as the texture or composition of the sediment in transport changes. For example, they move to the left for finer grained, cohesive sediments, and to the right for coarser, less cohesive, better sorted sediments. Future adjustments of the horizontal process boundaries must be based on additional observations or measurements of sediment-water flows, or on new developments in the mechanical theory of sediment-water flows.

All types of subaerial sediment-water flows (excluding ice) can be categorized with this classification. As such, this classification provides a useful basis for understanding about a suite of earth-surface flow phenomena that occur nearly everywhere and occasionally cause catastrophic property damage and loss of life.

ACKNOWLEDGMENTS

We thank David Varnes and David Keefer, U.S. Geological Survey, for their guidance and direction during the formative stages of this paper. Many thanks also to Gerald Wieczorek, Donald Lowe, and Thomas Drake for their thoughtful and insightful reviews of the manuscript, and to numerous other colleagues for interesting discussions.

REFERENCES CITED

Bagnold, R. A., 1954, Experiments on a gravity-free dispersion of large solid spheres in a Newtonian fluid under shear: Proceedings of the Royal Society of London, series A, v. 225, p. 49–63.

Baker, V. R., 1978, Paleohydraulics and hydrodynamics of Scablands floods, *in* Baker, V. R., and Nummedal, D., eds., The Channeled Scablands, A guide to the geomorphology of the Columbia Basin, Washington: Washington, D.C., National Aeronautics and Space Administration, p. 59–79.

Beverage, J. P., and Culbertson, J. K., 1964, Hyperconcentrations of suspended sediment: Journal of the Hydraulics Division, American Society of Civil Engineers, v. 90, no. HY6, p. 117–126.

Bird, R. B., Dai, G. C., and Yarusso, B. J., 1982, The rheology and flow of viscoplastic materials: Reviews in Chemical Engineering, v. 1, no. 1, p. 1–70.

Bradley, J. B., and McCutcheon, S. C., 1985, The effects of high sediment concentrations on transport processes and flow phenomena, *in* Takei, A., ed., Proceedings of the International Symposium on Erosion, Debris Flow, and Disaster Prevention, Tsukuba, Japan: Tokyo, Toshindo Printers, p. 219–225.

Brown, M. C., 1962, Discussion: Nuées ardentes and fluidization: American Journal of Sciences, v. 260, p. 467–470.

Bull, W. B., 1962, Relation of textural (CM) patterns to depositional environment of alluvial-fan deposits: Journal of Sedimentary Petrology, v. 32, p. 211–216.

Carson, M. A., 1976, Mass-wasting, slope development, and climate, *in* Derbyshire, E. D., ed., Geomorphology and climate: London, John Wiley, p. 101–136.

Carson, M. A., and Kirkby, M. J., 1972, Hillslope form and process: London, Cambridge University Press, 475 p.

Carter, R. M., 1975, A discussion and classification of subaqueous mass-transport with particular application to grain-flow, slurry-flow, and fluxoturbidites: Earth Science Reviews, v. 11, p. 145–177.

Coates, D. R., 1977, Landslide perspectives, *in* Coates, D. R., ed., Landslides: Geological Society of America, Reviews of Engineering Geology, v. 3, p. 3–28.

Committee on Methodologies for Predicting Mudflow Areas, 1982, Selecting a methodology for delineating mudslide hazard areas for the National Flood Insurance Program: Washington, D.C., National Research Council, National Academy Press, 35 p.

Costa, J. E., and Williams, G. P., 1984, Debris-flow dynamics (videotape): U.S. Geological Survey Open-File Report 84-606, 22½ min.

Crozier, M. J., 1973, Techniques for the morphometric analysis of landslips: Zeitschrift für Geomorphologie, v. 17, p. 78–101.

Davies, T.R.H., 1982, Spreading of rock avalanche debris by mechanical fluidization: Rock Mechanics, v. 15, p. 9–24.

Denlinger, R. P., Scott, K. M., and Pierson, T. C., 1984, Granular resorting and its effects on resistance to flow in grain-supported lahars [abs.]: EOS Transactions of the American Geophysical Union, v. 65, p. 1142.

Desloges, J. R., and Gardner, J. S., 1984, Process and discharge estimation in ephemeral channels, Canadian Rocky Mountains: Canadian Journal of Earth Science, v. 21, p. 1050–1060.

Dott, R. H., Jr., 1963, Dynamics of subaqueous gravity depositional processes: American Association of Petroleum Geologists Bulletin, v. 47, p. 104–128.

Eisbacher, G. H., 1982, Mountain torrents and debris flows: Episodes, v. 1982 no. 4, p. 12–17.

Erismann, T. H., 1979, Mechanisms of large landslides: Rock Mechanics, v. 12, p. 15–46.

Fisher, R. V., 1971, Features of coarse-grained, high-concentration fluids, and their deposits: Journal of Sedimentary Petrology, v. 41, p. 916–927.

Flint, R. F., 1971, Glacial and Quaternary Geology: New York, John Wiley, 892 p.

Gagoshidze, M. S., 1969, Mudflows and floods and their control: Soviet Hydrology, no. 4, p. 410–422.

Habib, P., 1975, Production of gaseous pore pressure during rockslides: Rock Mechanics, v. 7, p. 193–197.

Hampton, M. A., 1972, The role of subaqueous debris flow in generating turbidity currents: Journal of Sedimentary Petrology, v. 42, p. 775–793.

Hansen, M. J., 1984, Strategies of classification of landslides, *in* Brunsden, D., and Prior, D. B., eds., Slope instability: London, John Wiley, p. 1–25.

Heim, A., 1882, Der Bergsturz von Elm: Zeitschrift der Deutscher Geologischer Gesellschaft, v. 34, p. 74–115.

Higgins, C. G., 1982, Discontinuity in rates of downslope movement: Geological Society of America Abstracts with Programs, v. 14, no. 7, p. 514.

Hill, H. M., 1966, Bed forms due to fluid stream: American Society of Civil Engineers Proceedings, v. 92, no. HY2, p. 127–143.

Howard, C.D.D., 1963, Flow of clay-water suspensions: Journal of the Hydraulics Division, American Society of Civil Engineers, v. 89, no. HY5, p. 89–97.

Hsu, K. J., 1975, Catastrophic debris streams *(sturzstroms)* generated by rockfalls: Geological Society of America Bulletin, v. 86, p. 129–140.

—— , 1978, Albert Heim; Observations on landslides and relevance to modern interpretations, *in* Voight, B., ed., Rockslides and avalanches, v. 1: Amsterdam, Elsevier, p. 71–93.

Iverson, R. M., 1985, A constitutive equation for mass-movement behavior: Journal of Geology, v. 93, p. 143–160.

Janda, R. J., Scott, K. M., Nolan, K. M., and Martinson, H. A., 1981, Lahar movement, effects, and deposits, *in* Lipman, P. W., and Mullineaux, D. R., eds., The 1980 eruptions of Mount St. Helens, Washington: U.S. Geological Survey Professional Paper 1250, p. 461–478.

Johnson, A. M., 1970, Physical processes in geology: San Francisco, Freeman and Cooper, 577 p.

Kadomura, H., Okada, H., Imagawa, T., Moriya, I., and Yamamoto, H., 1983, Erosion and mass movements on Mt. Usu accelerated by crustal deformation that accompanied its 1977-1982 volcanism: Journal of Natural Disaster Science, v. 5, p. 33–62.

Kang, Z., and Zhang, S., 1980, A preliminary analysis of the characteristics of debris flow, *in* Proceedings of the International Symposium on River Sedimentation: Beijing, Chinese Society for Hydraulic Engineering, p. 225–226.

Keefer, D. K., and Johnson, A. M., 1983, Earth flows; Morphology, mobilization, and movement: U.S. Geological Survey Professional Paper 1264, 56 p.

Kent, P. E., 1966, The transport mechanism in catastrophic rockfalls: Journal of Geology, v. 74, p. 79–83.

Krumdieck, M. A., 1984, On the mechanics of large landslides, *in* Proceedings, 4th International Symposium on Landslides, Toronto: Canadian Geotechnical Society, p. 539–544.

Kuenen, Ph. H., 1951, Properties of turbidity currents of high density, *in* Hough, J. L., ed., Turbidity currents and the transportation of coarse sediments to deep water: Society of Economic Paleontologists and Mineralogists Special Publication No. 2, 107 p.

Kurdin, R. D., 1973, Classification of mudflows: Soviet Hydrology, no. 4, p 310–316.

Lambe, T. W., 1960, A mechanistic picture of shear strength in clay, *in* Proceedings of Conference on Shear Strength of Cohesive Soils: American Society of Civil Engineers, p. 555–580.

Lawson, D. E., 1982, Mobilization, movement, and deposition of active subaerial sediment flows, Matanuska Glacier, Alaska: Journal of Geology, v. 90, p. 279–300.

Leopold, L. B., 1974, Water, a primer: San Francisco, W. H. Freeman and Company, 172 p.

Lowe, D. R., 1979, Sediment gravity flows; Their classification and some problems of application to natural flows and deposits, *in* Doyle, L. J., and Pilkey, O. H., eds., Geology of continental slopes: Society of Economic Paleontologists and Mineralogists Special Publication No. 27, p. 75–82.

McSaveney, M. J., 1978, Sherman Glacier rock avalanche, Alaska, USA, *in* Voight, B., ed., Rockslides and avalanches, v. 1: Amsterdam, Elsevier, p. 197–258.

McTaggart, K. C., 1960, The mobility of nuées ardentes: American Journal of Science, v. 258, p. 369–382.

Melosh, H. J., 1979, Acoustic fluidization; A new geologic process?: Journal of Geophysical Research, v. 84, p. 7513–7520.

Michaels, A. S., and Bolger, J. C., 1962, The plastic flow behavior of flocculated kaolin suspensions: Industrial Engineering and Chemical Fundamentals, v. 1, no. 3, p. 153–162.

Middleton, G. V., 1970, Experimental studies related to problems of flysch sedimentation: Geological Association of Canada Special Paper 7, p. 253–272.

Middleton, G. V., and Hampton, M. A., 1976, Subaqueous sediment transport and deposition by sediment gravity flows, *in* Stanley, D. J., and Swift, J. P., eds., Marine sediment transport and environmental management: New York, John Wiley, p. 197–218.

Mitchell, J. K., Singh, A., and Campanella, R. G., 1969, Bonding, effective stresses, and strength of soils: Journal, Soil Mechanics and Foundation Division, American Society of Civil Engineers, v. 95, no. SM5, p. 1219–1246.

Nakamura, S., 1926, On the velocity of recent mud-flows in Japan, *in* Proceedings of the Third Pan-Pacific Congress: Tokyo, p. 788–800.

O'Brien, J. S., and Julien, P. Y., 1985, Physical properties and mechanics of hyperconcentrated sediment flows, *in* Bowles, D. S., ed., Proceedings of a Specialty Conference on Delineations of Landslide, Flash Flood, and Debris Flow Hazards in Utah: Logan, Utah State University, p. 260–279.

Pierson, T. C., 1985, Initiation and flow behavior of the 1980 Pine Creek and Muddy River lahars, Mount St. Helens, Washington: Geological Society of America Bulletin, v. 96, p. 1056–1069.

Pierson, T. C., and Scott, K. M., 1985, Downstream dilution of a lahar; Transition from debris flow to hyperconcentrated streamflow: Water Resources Research, v. 21, p. 1511–1524.

Plafker, G., and Ericksen, G. E., 1978, Nevados Huascarán Avalanches, Peru, *in* Voight, B., ed., Rockslides and avalanches, v. 1: Amsterdam, Elsevier, p. 277–314.

Qian, Y., Yang, W., Zhao, W., Cheng, X., Zhang, L., and Xu, W., 1980, Basic characteristics of flow with hyperconcentrations of sediment, *in* Proceedings of the International Symposium on River Sedimentation: Beijing, Chinese Society of Hydraulic Engineering, p. 175–184.

Rodine, J. D., 1974, Analysis of mobilization of debris flows [Ph.D. thesis]: Stanford, California, Stanford University, 226 p.

Sanders, J. E., 1965, Primary sedimentary structures formed by turbidity currents and related resedimentation mechanisms, *in* Middleton, G. V., ed., Primary sedimentary structures and their hydrodynamic interpretation: Society of Economic Paleontologists and Mineralogists Special Publication 12, p. 192–219.

Savage, S. B., 1984, The mechanics of rapid granular flows: Advances in Applied Mechanics, v. 24, p. 289–366.

Scheidegger, A. E., 1973, On the prediction of the reach and velocity of catastrophic landslides: Rock Mechanics, v. 5, p. 231–236.

Scott, K. M., and Dinehart, R. L., 1985, Sediment transport and deposit characteristics of hyperconcentrated streamflow evolved from lahars at Mount St. Helens, Washington: Proceedings, International Workshop on Flow at Hyperconcentrations of Sediment, Beijing, China, 33 p.

Sharpe, C.F.S., 1938, Landslides and related phenomena: New York, Columbia University Press, 137 p.

Shreve, R. L., 1968, The Blackhawk landslide: Geological Society of America Special Paper 108, 47 p.

Skempton, A. W., and Hutchinson, J. N., 1969, Stability of natural slopes and embankment foundations: Proceedings of the 7th International Conference on Soil Mechanics, Mexico City, Mexico, p. 291–340.

Smith, G. A., 1986, Coarse-grained nonmarine volcaniclastic sediment; Terminology and depositional process: Geological Society of America Bulletin, v. 97, p. 1–10.

Sparks, R.S.J., 1978, Gas release rates from pyroclastic flows; An assessment of the role of fluidization in their emplacement: Bulletin Volcanologique, v. 41, p. 1–9.

Swanston, D. N., 1974, Slope stability problems associated with timber harvesting in mountainous regions of the western United States: U.S. Forest Service General Technical Report PNW-21, 14 p.

Takahashi, T., 1978, Mechanical characteristics of debris flows: Journal of the Hydraulics Division, American Society of Civil Engineers, v. 104, no. HY8, p. 1153–1169.

—— , 1981, Debris flow: Annual Reviews of Fluid Mechanics, v. 13, p. 57–77.

Thomas, D. G., 1963, Non-Newtonian suspensions; Physical properties and laminar transport characteristics: Industrial and Engineering Chemistry, v. 55, no. 11, p. 18–29.

VanDine, D. F., 1985, Debris flows and debris torrents in the southern Canadian Cordillera: Canadian Geotechnical Journal, v. 22, p. 44–68.

van Rijn, L. C., 1983, Sediment transportation in heavy sediment-laden flows, *in* Proceedings of the Second International Symposium on River Sedimentation, Water Resources and Electrical Power Press, Nanjing, China, p. 482–491.

Van Wazer, J. R., Lyons, J. W., Kim, K. Y., and Colwell, R. E., 1963, Viscosity and flow measurement: New York, Interscience, 405 p.

Varnes, D. J., 1958, Landslide types and processes, *in* Eckel, E. B., ed., Landslides and engineering: Washington, D.C., Highway Research Board Special Report No. 29, p. 20–47.

—— , 1978, Slope movement types and processes, *in* Schuster, R. L., and Krizek, R. J., eds., Landslides analysis and control: Washington, D.C., National Academy of Sciences, Transportation Research Board Special Report 176, p. 11–33.

Voight, B., Janda, R. J., Glicken, H., and Douglass, P. M., 1983, Nature and mechanics of the Mount St. Helens rockslide-avalanche of 18 May 1980: Geotechnique, v. 33, p. 243–273.

—— , 1985, Reply to discussion—Nature and mechanics of the Mount St. Helens rockslide-avalanche of 18 May 1980: Geotechnique, v. 35, p. 362–367.

Wang, M., Zhan, Y., Liu, J., Duan, W., and Wu, W., 1983, An experimental study on turbulence characteristics of flow with hyperconcentrations of sediment, *in* Proceedings of the Second International Symposium on River Sedimentation, Water Resources and Electrical Power Press, Nanjing, China, p. 45–46.

Wilson, C.J.N., and Walker, G.P.L., 1982, Ignimbrite depositional facies; The anatomy of a pyroclastic flow: Journal, Geological Societ of London, v. 139, p. 581–592.

Yang, W., and Zhao, W., 1983, An experimental study of the resistance to flow with hyperconcentration in rough flumes, *in* Proceedings of the Second International Symposium on River Sedimentation, Water Resources and Electrical Power Press, Nanjing, China, p. 54–55.

Manuscript Accepted by the Society December 29, 1986

Geological Society of America
Reviews in Engineering Geology, Volume VII
1987

Comprehensive review of debris flow modeling concepts in Japan

Cheng-lung Chen*
U.S. Geological Survey
Gulf Coast Hydroscience Center
NSTL, Mississippi 39529

ABSTRACT

Japanese concepts of modeling debris flow are thoroughly reviewed in this chapter. Many Japanese models, ranging from highly theoretical non-Newtonian fluid models to the very simple empirical relations of Bingham and Bagnold, are evaluated in terms of accuracy, generality, and practical usefulness, and are compared with a generalized viscoplastic fluid model described herein. Most debris flow formulas and criteria presently used in Japan are closely related to those developed by Takahashi on the basis of Bagnold's "dispersive" pressure concept. Although the generality of Bagnold's model is still at issue, Japanese scientists apparently have accepted Takahashi's debris flow formulas and criteria. For example, Takahashi's velocity profile for (steady) uniform debris flow in wide channels is only valid for grain-intertia regime. Applying Takahaski's solution to modeling other flow regimes than the grain-inertia may thus have to adjust the value of Bagnold's numerical constant in order to better fit the computed velocities to the measured ones. This and many other aspects of debris-flow modeling concepts in Japan are critically examined. An appraisal of the present status of Japanese research in debris flow modeling helps determine the direction of future efforts in debris flow research.

INTRODUCTION

Climate (i.e., rain- or snowmelt-induced) debris flows and mudflows occur most frequently in environments that provide an abundant source of incoherent fine-grained rock debris, steep slopes, sparse vegetation, and a large but intermittent source of water from cloudburst and/or sudden snowmelt. Japan is one such country where geologic, topographic, and hydrometeorologic conditions combine to generate catastrophic debris flows annually. The devastation on mountain basins and alluvial fans by debris flows is enormous. The history of Japan is partly composed of episodes featuring the human struggle against such recurring catastrophic debris flows and other natural disasters. Their continued efforts to cope with debris flow problems have thus moved Japanese scientists into the forefront of debris flow research. This chapter critically reviews Japanese contributions to debris flow research, especially the Japanese concepts of modeling debris flow, thereby addressing major issues of the subject. An appraisal of the present status of Japanese research can help determine the direction of future efforts in debris flow research.

An evaluation of rheological models (or constitutive equations) developed or utilized by Japanese scientists for modeling debris flows and mudflows is presented. Each model, ranging from highly theoretical non-Newtonian fluid models to very simple empirical relations of Bingham (1922) and Bagnold (1954), is compared with a generalized viscoplastic fluid model developed by Chen (1986b). Debris flow equations based on some Japanese models are further evaluated in terms of those based on the generalized vicsoplastic fluid model. Of the rheological models and debris flow equations published in Western journals, those of Takahashi (1978a, 1980a, 1981, 1983) are best known. At present, most of the debris flow modeling concepts and formulas used widely in Japan appear to be closely related to those developed by Takahashi on the basis of Bagnold's (1954) "dispersive" pressure concept.

"Debris flow" may be used as a collective term for a broad spectrum of phenomena observed in the gravity-induced mass movement of debris, but Japanese scientists generally refer to it as

---
*Present address: U.S. Geological Survey, MS 496, 345 Middlefield Road, Menlo Park, California 94025.

a type of heavily loaded sediment flow that carries a large amount of very coarse, noncohesive granular materials, such as sands, gravels, cobbles, and boulders. Generally, Japanese scientists are very conscious of the different usage of terms, such as the distinction between debris flow and mudflow, as classified by Varnes (1978). To account accurately for Japanese concepts of modeling debris flow, therefore, their terminology is closely followed unless stated otherwise.

RHEOLOGICAL MODELS

For modeling debris flows, Japanese scientists have developed or proposed various rheological models, ranging from highly theoretical to very simple semiempirical ones. Models of Kanatani (1979a, b, 1980, 1982), Ogawa (1978), and Ogawa and others (1980) appear to be most theoretical, but use of the Bingham plastic fluid model and a "power-law" fluid model—especially a dilatant fluid model—is quite popular among practicing engineers in Japan. An appraisal of the various Japanese models will be greatly facilitated by a full understanding of the generalized viscoplastic fluid model that is briefly described below.

Generalized Viscoplastic Fluid Model

A viable rheological model of sediment-water mixture, if expressed in terms of the generalized viscoplastic fluid including cohesion (Chen, 1985a, 1986b), should possess both rate-independent and rate-dependent parts as well as two major rheological properties, namely, the normal stress (or Weissenberg) effect and the soil yield criterion. This generalized rheological model for gravity flow in a wide channel consists of the following set of relations:

$$T_{zx} (= T_{xz}) = c \cos \phi + p \sin \phi + \mu_1 (du/dz)^\eta \quad (1)$$

$$T_{zz} (= T_{xx}) = - p + \mu_2 (du/dz)^\eta, \quad (2)$$

or, alternatively, in the differential form:

$$dT_{zx}/dz = (dp/dz) \sin \phi + d [\mu_1 (du/dz)^\eta]/dz \quad (3)$$

$$dT_{zz}/dz = - dp/dz + d [\mu_2 (du/dza)^\eta]/dz, \quad (4)$$

in which T_{zx}, T_{zz} = total shear and normal stresses, respectively; x, z = coordinates in the longitudinal and normal (positive, upward from the bed) directions of flow, respectively; c = cohesion; ϕ = "static" angle of internal friction of colliding sediment particles; p = pressure; μ_1, μ_2 = consistency and "cross-consistency" indices, respectively; u = velocity; and η = flow-behavior index, the value of which may vary from 1 to 2 (or possibly higher when particle concentration is very high) as the flow changes from Bagnold's (1954) macro-viscous to grain-inertia flow state. Note

that the summation of the first two terms on the right-hand side of equation 1 may be referred to as the yield stress, s:

$$s = c \cos \phi + p \sin \phi, \quad (5)$$

which is indeed an extended form of the Mohr-Coulomb yield criterion (Terzaghi, 1943).

The consistency, μ_1, and the cross-consistency, μ_2, in equations 1–4 can be expressed in the following form of Krieger and Dougherty (1959), which was actually deduced from the well-known Einstein (1956) equation for the relative viscosity of rigid uniform spherical particles moving without slip in a medium of equal density at low concentration (Chen, 1986b):

$$\mu_1 = A_1 (1 - KC)^{-B/K} \quad (6)$$

$$\mu_2 = A_2 (1 - KC)^{-B/K}, \quad (7)$$

in which A_1, A_2 = numerical constants; K = factor describing space filling, sedimentation volume, and self-crowding, the reciprocal of which is the maximum concentration, C_m; C = sediment concentration by volume; and B = Einstein's constant, 2.50, which lumps the gross effects of the size, shape, rheological properties, deformability, and orientation of the dispersed particles.

Kanatani's Model

Realizing two distinct flow regimes of the inclined gravity flows (Takahashi, 1937), Kanatani (1979a, b) developed a rheological model for slow flow (i.e., quasi-static or impending flow) of granular materials based on the theory of polar or micropolar continua:

$$T_{zx} = - T_{zz} \tan \phi, \quad (8)$$

in which the sign convention of T_{zz} is opposite to that used in soil mechanics, and $\tan \phi = (3\sqrt{10}/10) \mu$ (where μ = kinetic friction coefficient of interacting particles). Equation 8 is reminiscent of the Mohr-Coulomb yield criterion. Uniform gravity flow is possible only if the angle of inclination, θ, is equal to the static angle of internal friction, ϕ. In other words, if $\theta > \phi$, the flow is accelerated, and if $\theta < \phi$, the flow is decelerated. For slow flow, Kanatani has already taken the rotation of particles into account in his theory as an additional tensor field, and found that the influence of the couple-stress is restricted to the region near the boundary, the thickness of which is a few times the size of the particles. Kanatani's computer simulation of the profiles of the longitudinal velocity and the rotation velocity, using his constitutive equations, has clearly indicated that the interaction of particles at the boundary affects the flow near the boundary.

Kanatani's polar continuum model for slow flow of granular materials was further extended to fast flow in which particle collisions play a more significant role than interparticle friction. The particle fluctuations were regarded as macroscopic "heat," and a thermodynamic analogy was developed. Kanatani (1979a, 1980) assumed "local equilibrium" so as to deduce the "equation of state"; he thereby analyzed the "thermal dilation" of the flow due to the particle collisions, which demonstrates the normal stress effects of granular materials, as observed by Bagnold (1954) and Savage (1979). For fast gravity flow on the inclined plate, Kanatani obtained:

$$T_{zx} = \frac{3\sqrt{15}}{200} C(\rho) (du/dz)^2 \qquad (9)$$

$$T_{zz} = -\frac{\sqrt{6}}{40\mu} \frac{r}{a} C(\rho) (du/dz)^2, \qquad (10)$$

$$C(\rho) = \frac{2\sqrt{6}}{5} T_e \mu \frac{a^3}{r} \frac{\rho_o \rho}{\rho_o - \rho}, \qquad (11)$$

in which T_e = proportionality constant; r = "occupation" radius of the "occupation" volume assigned to one particle; a = radius of the particle; ρ = bulk density; and ρ_o = bulk density of randomly packed spheres. Both T_{zx} and T_{zz} in equations 9 and 10, respectively, are proportional to the square of the shear rate or velocity gradient, as experimentally formulated by Bagnold (1954). For comparison, Bagnold's empirical expressions for the grain normal and shear stress in the grain-inertia region are given in the following.

Bagnold (1954) found from rotating-drum experiments of neutrally buoyant spherical grains that the grain shear stress, T (which is defined to be additional to the shear stress due to momentum transfer within the intergranular or interstitial fluid) and the grain normal stress, P (which is defined to be additional to the normal stress exerted by the intergranular fluid) in the grain-inertia region can be expressed as:

$$T = a_i \rho_s (\lambda d)^2 (du/dz)^2 \sin \phi_d \qquad (12)$$
$$P = a_i \rho_s (\lambda d)^2 (du/dz)^2 \cos \phi_d, \qquad (13)$$

in which a_i = numerical constant; ρ_s = grain density; λ = linear concentration; d = grain diameter; and ϕ_d = "dynamic" angle of internal friction. The linear concentration, λ, can be related geometrically to the volume concentration, C, by:

$$\lambda = [(C_m/C)^{1/3} - 1]^{-1}. \qquad (14)$$

Here the maximum concentration, C_m, as previously defined in connection to equations 6 and 7, denotes the maximum C when all the grains are in static contact (e.g., 0.74 for the closest possible packing of uniform spheres). Bagnold determined $a_i = 0.042$ from the mean experimental values of tan ϕ_d (= 0.32) in the grain-inertia region, which in turn gave $a_i \sin \phi_d = 0.042 \times \sin (17.7°) = 0.0128$ for equation 12 and $a_i \cos \phi_d = 0.042 \times \cos (17.7°) = 0.04$ for equation 13. By virtue of equations 12 and 13, Bagnold further related T to P by:

$$= P \tan \phi_d. \qquad (15)$$

Henceforth, equations 12 and 13 are referred to as Bagnold's dilatant fluid model.

Although Kanatani originally established a relation between T_{zx} and T_{zz} (i.e., equation 8 for slow gravity flow only, it can be shown from equations 9 and 10 that equation 8 can also be valid for fast gravity flow, provided $a/r \rightarrow 1$ and tan $\phi = (3\sqrt{10}/10) \mu$. Because the condition of $a/r \rightarrow 1$ does not seem to be physically attainable for extremely fast flow, it may be more justifiable to express, by virtue of equations 9 and 10:

$$T_{zx} = -T_{zz} \left(\frac{a}{r} \right) \tan \phi, \qquad (16)$$

or, if $(a/r) \tan \phi = \tan \phi_d$ (in which $\phi_d < \phi$ as $a < r$),

$$T_{zx} = -T_{zz} \tan \phi_d. \qquad (17)$$

Note that P in equation 15 and T_{zz} in equation 17 are opposite in sign; therefore, both equations are identical. In fact, this shows that Kanatani's rheological model (equations 9 and 10) for fast flow is equivalent to Bagnold's dilatant fluid model. Consequently, if the generality of Bagnold's model is still at issue (Chen, 1985a), so is Kanatani's model. The inconsistencies in Bagnold's model are covered in more detail later.

It is worth mentioning that the expression of the yield stress, s, derived by Kanatani (1982) based on a plasticity theory for ideal (i.e., isotropic and incompressible) granular materials, as shown in equation 5, is different from that obtained by Drucker and Prager (1952) for dilatable granular materials.

Ogawa's Model

Introducing the quasi-thermal energy as a new variable and using the theory of multitemperature field, Ogawa (1978) and Ogawa and others (1980) formulated the governing equations to describe the motion of granular materials in fully fluidized state. Their constitutive equations of random motion were then obtained by using a simple kinematic model of collision of granular particles. In the case of the local equilibrium of random motion and a simple shearing motion, the constitutive equations so obtained reduce to the following simple relations for the deviatoric stress, τ_{zx}, and the pressure, p:

$$\tau_{zx} \sim b^2 (du/dz)^2 \qquad (18)$$
$$p \sim b^2 (du/dz)^2, \qquad (19)$$

in which b = radius of an imaginary sphere, which is the function of the mass density, ρ, defined as a $(\rho_o/\rho)^{1/3}$. Both Kanatani's model (equations 9 and 10) and Ogawa's model (equations 18 and 19) are expressed in the same functional form as the semiempirical relations of Bagnold (1954), equations 12 and 13. Surprisingly, Ogawa's velocity profile obtained from the equations of momentum and energy for (steady) uniform gravity flow on an inclined plate is shown to be close to that obtained from the differential form of the generalized viscoplastic fluid model, equations 3 and

4. Expressions of velocity profiles for uni-directional uniform gravity flow of granular materials characterizing various rheological models will be given later.

Unlike Kanatani, who took the rotation of particles into consideration in the formulation of his rheological model, Ogawa ignored the rotational motion of particles and the motion of voids. Despite this basic difference in their approaches, both models for gravity flow on an inclined plate have been shown to be in the same form as Bagnold's dilatant fluid model.

Model of Tsubaki and Others

An approach taken by Tsubaki and others (1982, 1983) in the formulation of their rheological model is conceptually similar to that adopted by Bagnold (1954), except that the former is based on the multiple collision of particles whereas the latter is predicated on a relatively simple mode of the binary collision of grains. The total stress exerted on a particle moving in a state of multiple collisions with the surrounding particles was then conveniently divided by Tsubaki and others into the collision stress and the contact stress. The shear stress was shown to depend only on the collision stress, but the normal stress was composed both of the collision stress and the contact stress:

$$T_{zx} = \frac{A_{zx} \, \beta^2 \, k_M \, \rho_s}{d} \frac{(C/C_m)^2}{1 - C/C_m} (du/dz)^2 \qquad (20)$$

$$T_{zz} = -K_p \frac{C}{C_m} \frac{(C - C_s)}{C_s} + \frac{A_{zz} \, \beta^2 \, k_M \, \rho_s}{d} \frac{(C/C_m)^2}{1 - C/C_m} (du/dz)^2, \quad (21)$$

in which A_{zx}, A_{zz} = numerical constants to be determined from experiment (A_{zx}, positive and A_{zz}, negative); β = coefficient associated with the expression of the number of grains per unit volume; k_M = coefficient appearing in the first term of a Taylor's series expansion of the coefficient of restitution, ϵ, around $C = C_m$, i.e., $k_M = 1/(d\epsilon/dC)/C_m$; C_s = concentration at the free surface; K_p = coefficient of the pressure as a function of C, if expanded in a Taylor's series around C_s.

The model of Tsubaki and others (equations 20 and 21) appears to be compatible with the generalized viscoplastic fluid model (equations 1 and 2), provided that the latter ignores the yield stress, s. However, because s varies with c, ϕ, and p, as shown in equation 5, s cannot be zero even for flow of *noncohesive* granular materials (i.e., $c = 0$). Moreover, because μ_1 and μ_2 in equations 1 and 2 are expressed in terms of KC ($= C/C_m$), as shown in equations 6 and 7, which seem compatible with their counterparts, $(C/C_m)^2/(1 - C/C_m)$, in equations 20 and 21, A_1 (positive) and A_2 (negative) in equations 6 and 7 should represent the remaining parameters appearing in equations 20 and 21, respectively. A comparison of equation 21 with equation 2 thus leads to the expected expression of p:

$$p = K_p \frac{C}{C_m} \frac{(C - C_s)}{C_s}, \qquad (22)$$

which is termed as the contact pressure by Tsubaki and others.

Although Tsubaki and others did not consider the cohesion of granules and thus inadvertently ignored the p term from the shear stress expression, equation 20, the model of Tsubaki and others (equations 20 and 21) is expected to perform better than Bagnold's model (equations 12 and 13) thanks to the additional p term in equation 21. Nevertheless, the form of equation 20, which neither contains s in the case of cohesive granular flows nor possesses p sin ϕ in the case of noncohesive granular flows, is incomplete, except for flow at the fully dynamic state. For verification, the theoretical velocity profile of Tsubaki and others will be later compared with that obtained from the generalized viscoplastic fluid model, equations 3 and 4, and also with available experimental data.

It is worth mentioning here that the expression of the so-called contact pressure, equation 22, which is similar to those proposed by other investigators, such as McTigue (1982) and Sayed and Savage (1983). For isothermal flows, p depends only on the bulk density, ρ, or in the case of incompressible granules, the concentration, C. For example, McTigue assumed:

$$p = \alpha \, (C^2 - C_s^2), \qquad (23)$$

in which α = constant, and Sayed and Savage proposed that:

$$p = \alpha \left(\frac{C - C_s}{C_m - C} \right). \qquad (24)$$

In general, the p versus ρ relation can be expressed in the following differential form:

$$dp = \frac{1}{\kappa} \frac{d\rho}{\rho^m}, \qquad (25)$$

in which κ = compressibility of the mixture, and m = exponent. Equation 25 was indeed adopted in the differential form of the generalized viscoplastic fluid model, equations 3 and 4, which were then solved for the velocity profile. Note that equation 25 with varying κ and m values is general enough to cover a wide range of a functional relationship between p and C. For example, equation 25 with $m = -1$ behaves like equation 22 or 23, and that with $m = 2$ behaves like equation 24.

Takahashi's Model

Based on Banold's dilatant fluid model (i.e., equations 12 and 13), Takahashi (1977, 1978a, 1980a, 1981, 1983) has developed viable theories and formulas for modeling debris flows. Therefore, Takahashi's model is essentially identical to Bagnold's, except that the numerical constant, a_i, in equations 12 and 13 is calibrated from data. Bagnold (1966) has found from experiments that the value of a_i remains constant at 0.042 approximately for $\lambda < 14$ (or $C/C_m < 0.813$ from equation 14), but it increases rapidly to 0.24 as λ increases from 14 to 17 (or $C/C_m = 0.813 \rightarrow 0.842$). The increase in a_i value was also discovered by Takahashi (1980a), who calibrated $a_i = 0.35 \sim 0.5$ from his flume experiments.

An explanation on Takahashi's calibrated a_i value, which is different from Bagnold's 0.042, may help reveal the limitation of Bagnold's dilatant model. It can be readily shown that Takahashi's (1978a, 1980a) expression of the velocity profile obtained solely from equation 12 is identical to a simplified version of the general solution obtained from the generalized viscoplastic fluid model (equations 1 and 2) for flow of noncohesive granules ($c = 0$) in the grain-inertia regime ($\eta = 2$), but Bagnold's relation, equation 12, is valid only for flow on the upper limit slope, $\theta = \tan^{-1} [(\bar{\rho}/\rho)(-\mu_1/\mu_2)]$, where $\bar{\rho}/\rho = C/[\rho_w/(\rho_s - \rho_w) + C]$ and $\rho_w =$ mass density of intergranular fluid, i.e., water. In other words, for gravity flow of noncohesive granules ($c = 0$) on an inclined plate with such upper limit slope, it can be proven from equations 1 and 2 that $p = 0$, and thus equation 1 reduces to equation 12. However, in applying Takahashi's solution to modeling a debris flow in regimes other than the grain-inertia ($\eta = 2$), the value of Bagnold's numerical constant may have to be adjusted to better fit the computed velocities to the measured ones.

Daido's Model

Daido started modeling debris flows as early as in 1965 (Yano and Daido, 1965) based both on the viscoelastic theory and the viscoplastic theory. For examples his doctoral thesis (1970), on the "Fundamental Study of Debris Flow," covering both viscoelastic and viscoplastic models, had been one of the most comprehensive debris flow modeling studies in Japan before Takahashi's work. Apparently, Daido was the first to propose the use of a linear viscoelastic (Maxwell or Voight) model in debris flow simulation, but he has not really continued studying such a viscoelastic model since 1970. Probably, if it can be proved that the rheological properties of debris flow vary significantly with time, investigators might revert to the use of a time-dependent viscoelastic model instead of a time-independent viscoplastic model in debris flow modeling.

A continuum-mechanics approach taken by Daido (1979, 1982) to express the total shear stress and the total normal stress in terms of the shear rate and the pressure is somewhat similar to the generalized viscoplastic fluid model, equations 1 and 2. Daido's constitutive equations are:

$$T_{zx} = s + (1 + \lambda)\, \mu_w\, (du/dz) + (1/6)\, K^2\, \rho_s\, \lambda\, d^2\, (du/dz)^2 \tan\phi \qquad (26)$$
$$T_{zz} = -p + (1/6)\, K^2\, \rho_s\, \lambda\, d^2\, (du/dz)^2, \qquad (27)$$

in which s = yield stress, postulated by Daido as:

$$s = c + p \tan\phi. \qquad (28)$$

Other symbols in equations 26 and 27 have already been defined, except that μ_w is the viscosity of intergranular fluid, i.e., water, and K is the numerical constant, different from Bagnold's a_i in equations 12 and 13. Daido further found from experiments that $K = 0.38$ and $\tan\phi = 0.7$ for $C < 0.5$, whereas the values of K and $\tan\phi$ approach those of Bagnold's a_i (= 0.042) and $\tan\phi_d$ (= 0.32), respectively, as C exceeds 0.5.

Despite a close resemblance of Daido's model (equations 26 and 27) to the generalized viscoplastic fluid model (equations 1 and 2), there are some inconsistencies in Daido's model. First, the expression of the yield stress, s, as shown in equation 28, apparently results from the direct application of the Mohr-Coulomb yield criterion for limiting equilibrium (Terzaghi, 1943) on the failure plane (i.e., inclined from the major principal stress with angle, $\pi/4 - \phi/2$):

$$T_{zx} = c - T_{zz} \tan\phi. \qquad (29)$$

In fact, equation 29 constitutes the rate-independent part of the so-called Coulomb-viscous model (Johnson, 1970). If the expression of T_{zz}, as shown in equation 27, is correct, upon substitution of T_{zz} from equation 27, equation 29 would result in the very same expression of equation 26. However, the second term on the right-hand side of equation 26, which describes the effect of intergranular fluid on T_{zx}, is missing. In order to take the effect of intergranular fluid into account, therefore, the "effective" normal stress concept of Terzaghi (1943) should be applied to the expression of T_{zz}. In other words, the "effective" pressure, $\bar{p}$, should be used in place of p in equation 27, thereby expressing:

$$\bar{p} = p - p_w, \qquad (30)$$

in which p_w is the pressure of intergranular fluid (or pore-water pressure), consisting of the transient part and the steady-state part. However, the second term on the right-hand side of equation 26 represents only the transient part of the pore-water pressure. The adequacy of Daido's model (equations 26 and 27) is thus open to question.

Second, unlike equation 5 in which s represents the radius of Mohr's circle:

$$T_{zx}^2 + (T_{zz} + p)^2 = s^2, \qquad (31)$$

s in equation 26 or 28 is merely the radius of Mohr's circle divided by $\cos\phi$ and thus, is greater than that in equation 5. The s expression in equation 28 appears to be inconsistent with the Mohr-Coulomb criterion for limiting equilibrium, equation 29, on the plane where yielding occurs. If none of the velocity gradients vanishes, it can be shown (Cowin, 1974a, b; McTigue, 1979; Sayed and Savage, 1983) that, at limiting equilibrium:

$$T_{xx} = -p - (c \operatorname{ctn}\phi + p) \sin\phi \cos 2\psi \qquad (32)$$
$$T_{zz} = -p + (c \operatorname{ctn}\phi + p) \sin\phi \cos 2\psi \qquad (33)$$
$$T_{zx} = (c \operatorname{ctn}\phi + p) \sin\phi \sin 2\psi, \qquad (34)$$

in which ψ = angle between the major principal stress and the x axis, given by

$$\psi = \frac{\pi}{4} - \frac{\phi}{2}. \qquad (35)$$

Because $\sin 2\psi = \cos\phi$ and $\cos 2\psi = \sin\phi$, equation 34 on substitution of p from equation 33 yields equation 29. Conversely, if there is only one nonzero velocity gradient, du/dz, it can be shown that equations 32–24 reduce to the rate-independent parts of equations 1 and 2.

For modeling debris flows with a great amount of clay, Daido (1976, 1982) also proposed the use of the Bingham plastic fluid model (i.e., equivalent to equation 1 with $\eta = 1$). An effort was then made by Daido to relate the Bingham parameters (i.e., the yield stress and the Bingham viscosity) to their controlling variables such as the floc concentration. Daido has found from experiments that the Bingham parameters are poorly related to the concentration of clay particles. For convenience, Daido split the yield stress into two parts: one represents the cohesion (i.e., the cohesive strength of the network-binding flocs), and the other the structural viscosity stress among flocs (i.e., the internal friction of the network-binding flocs). His empirical formula is:

$$s = a_1 (C_F - C_{Fo})^3 + a_2 C_F^2, \qquad (36)$$

in which a_1, a_2, = empirical constants for the cohesion and the structural viscosity, respectively; C_F = floc concentration by volume, and C_{Fo} = threshold concentration by volume at which the network-binding flocs appear.

Daido's empirical formula for the relative viscosity is:

$$\mu_* = 1 + \frac{3}{1/C_F - 1/C_{Fm}}, \qquad (37)$$

in which μ_* = relative viscosity, defined as μ/μ_w (μ = viscosity of the sediment-water mixture and μ_w = viscosity of water); and C_{Fm} = maximum floc concentration by volume. Surprisingly, this μ_* expressed in terms of C_F/F_{Fm} somewhat resembles those formulated by Chinese scientists (Chen 1986a). For illustration, Daido's (1976) experimental data on μ_* for four samples of clay and a sample of glass beads (size unknown) are plotted against C_F, as shown in Figure 1. Daido determined $C_{Fm} = 0.52$ for equation 37 to pass through these data points. A more theoretically sound expression of μ_* may pose in the form of the Krieger-Dougherty (1959) formula (equation 6 with $A_1 \approx 1$ and $B/K = B C_m = 2.5 \times 0.52 = 1.3$):

$$\mu_* = (1 - C_F/0.52)^{-1.3}, \qquad (38)$$

which is also plotted in Figure 1 for comparison with equation 37. The fact that equation 38 fits Daido's data points better than equation 37 strongly suggests the applicability of the Krieger-Dougherty formulas in debris flow modeling.

Model of Yamaoka and Others

Yamaoka (1981) and his associates (Fujita and others, 1982) at Hokkaido University proposed applying the following generalized Bingham plastic fluid model to modeling debris flows.

$$T_{zx} = s + \mu_1 (du/dz)^\eta, \qquad (39)$$

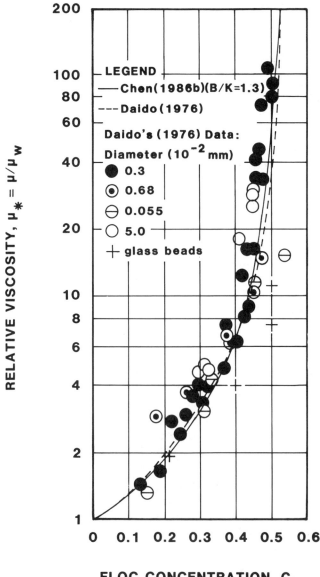

Figure 1. Relation between relative viscosity, μ^*, of clay flocs with respect to water and volume concentration of clay flocs, C_F.

in which the yield stress, s, is assumed to be constant. The major difference between the generalized viscoplastic fluid model (equations 1 and 2) and the generalized Bingham plastic fluid model (equation 39) lies in the fact that the former possesses the necessary elements describing the normal stress effect and the soil yield criteria, whereas the latter does not. This modeling difference is significantly reflected in the different expressions of the velocity profile obtained from both models, as will be shown later.

For flow of Bingham plastic fluids ($\eta = 1$), Yamaoka specifically suggested the use of equation 37 for the expression of the Bingham viscosity, replacing C_F and C_{Fm} by C and C_m, respectively. For fitting experimental data, however, Fujita and others later modified the formula to the form:

$$\mu_* = 1 + \frac{135}{1/C - 1/C_m}, \qquad (40)$$

in which the maximum concentration, C_m, is again assumed to be 0.52, but the numerical constant, 135, is more than an order of magnitude higher than 3 used in equation 37. This may raise a question as to the adaptability of equation 37 or 40 in solving different debris flow problems. In fact, equation 37 or 40 can be arranged into equation 6, which has a more general functional form of C/C_m as shown in equation 38.

Yamaoka and his associates have found from their flume experiments that channel roughness, particle size, and grain concentration all play important roles in the determination of a rheological model for debris flow. They observed from their experimental results that the smaller the roughness, particle size, and concentration, the more likely is the subject flow to behave as a Bingham fluid—otherwise, as a dilatant fluid. Therefore, they proposed from a dimensional analysis the use of the following two parameters in the selection of a rheological model. One parameter is called the roughness Reynolds number, $\mathbf{R}_s$, defined as $u_* \, k_s/\nu_s$ and later redefined as $u_* \, k_s/\nu_w$ (where $u_* = \sqrt{g\,h\sin\theta}$ = friction velocity, g = gravitational acceleration, h = flow depth, θ = channel slope, k_s = roughness size, $\nu_s = \mu_s/\rho_s$ = kinematic viscosity of solid particles, and $\nu_w = \mu_w/\rho_w$ = kinematic viscosity of water). The other parameter characterizing the effects of the particle size, d, and the concentration, C, is denoted by D_*. They expressed $D_* = \sqrt{(\rho_s/\rho_w - 1)\, g\, d^3}\ \lambda/\nu_w$ in such a way that the value of D_* decreases as d and C decrease. Use of $\mathbf{R}_s$ and D_* has thus enabled them to distinguish mainly between Bingham-type and dilatant-type debris flows. Their preliminary analysis of experimental data from available sources had indicated that dilatant-type debris flows occur if $\mathbf{R}_s > 70$ and $D_* > 1,500$, whereas Bingham-type debris flows exist only in the range of $350 < D_* < 800$. They have further found that for $800 < D_* < 1,500$ the flows are transitional from Bingham type to dilatant type, and for $D_* < 350$ the flows become Newtonian (mostly turbulent). A plot of the $\mathbf{R}_s$ versus D relation by Yamaoka and others appears to group data points into such regular patterns, as indicated above. However, unlike Bagnold's (1954) relation between the grain shear-rate number, N, and the grain stress number, G_T or G_p, the $\mathbf{R}_s$ versus D_* relation does not have any theoretical support.

DEBRIS FLOW EQUATIONS

Viable theories and formulas for modeling sediment movement at the various stages of debris flow processes, namely, from initiation to termination, can be developed from the equations of continuity and motion on substitution of a rheological model from one of those reviewed in the previous section. Forms of highly theoretical rheological models, such as Kanatani's (1979a, b, 1980) and Ogawa's (1978, 1980), are usually too complicated

to be useful in practice, although the simplifications of such models are generally possible through some simplifying assumptions. In contrast, Bagnold's (1954) dilatant fluid model has recently gained wide recognition as a viable one in Japan because of its simplicity. As a matter of fact, Takahashi's (1977, 1978a, 1980a) flow equations derived on the basis of Bagnold's concept have been generally accepted and extensively applied to solving debris flow problems. In the following, the most commonly used debris flow equations developed by Japanese scientists, especially Takahashi, are evaluated.

Velocity Profile and Average Velocity

Takahashi's rheological model is exactly identical to Bagnold's dilatant model (equations 12 and 13), as mentioned previously. If the "effective" normal stress concept of Terzaghi (1943) is adopted, P in equation 13 becomes the applied effective normal stress and is expressed as $\bar{\rho}\, g\, (h - z)\cos\theta$, where $\bar{\rho} = \rho - \rho_w = C(\rho_s - \rho_w)$, ρ = bulk density of sediment-water mixture, ρ_s = mass density of solid particles, ρ_w = mass density of intergranular fluid, and C = sediment concentration by volume, as defined before. As usually postulated, T in equation 12 is the applied shear stress due to gravitational force in the direction of flow so that $T = \rho g(h - z)\sin\theta$. A combination of equations 12 and 13 upon substitution of these T and P expressions thus reduces to Bagnold's limiting slope criterion:

$$\tan\theta = \frac{C \tan\phi_d}{\rho_w/(\rho_s - \rho_w) + C}, \qquad (41)$$

which is exactly the debris flow initiation condition proposed by Takahashi (1977, 1978a, 1980a). As a matter of fact, equation 41 corresponds to the lower limit slope obtained from an "effective" stress version of the generalized viscoplastic fluid model, equations 1 and 2. It can be proved from such a model that (steady) uniform debris flow is possible only for channel slope, θ, falling in the range:

$$\tan^{-1}[(\bar{\rho}/\rho)\sin\phi] \leqslant \theta \leqslant \tan^{-1}[(\bar{\rho}/\rho)(-\mu_1/\mu_2)]. \qquad (42)$$

Because $\tan\phi_d = \sin\phi$ for debris flow at the quasi-static state, as theoretically inferred by McTigue (1979), the lower limit of θ in equation 42 is identical to equation 41. Takahashi's velocity profile was simply obtained from equation 12 on substitution of $T = \rho g\,(h - z)\sin\theta$; therefore, his solution corresponds to that obtained from equation 1 with the assumption of $c = 0$, $p = 0$, and $\eta = 2$ (Chen, 1983):

$$u = \frac{2}{3}\left(\frac{\rho\, g\sin\theta}{\mu_1}\right)^{1/2} [h^{3/2} - (h - z)^{3/2}], \qquad (43)$$

in which $\mu_1 = a_i\, \rho_s\, (\lambda\, d)^2 \sin\phi_d$, if expressed in terms of Bagnold's dilatant model (equations 12 and 13). It can be readily shown from an "effective" stress version of equations 1 and 2 that the particular solution, equation 43, for debris flow in the grain-inertia regime ($\eta = 2$) is valid only for the upper limit slope of the θ range specified in equation 42. Takahashi (1980a) performed flume experiments for debris flow and estimated the concentration using the upper limit of equation 42. Takahashi's use of $-\mu_1/\mu_2 = \tan\phi_d = 0.75$ in his computation of the sediment concentration, however, is inconsistent with the assumed $\tan\phi_d = 0.32$ on which equation 43 is based. This may explain why the a_i value calibrated by Takahashi (1980) is higher than Bagnold's 0.042 by nearly an order of magnitude.

The equations of motion for uniform debris flow on an inclined plate formulated from an "effective" stress version of the generalized viscoplastic fluid model are:

$$\rho\,g\,(h-z)\sin\theta = c\cos\theta + \bar{p}\sin\phi + \mu_1\,(du/dz)^\eta \qquad (44)$$
$$-\bar{\rho}\,g\,(h-z)\cos\theta = -\bar{p} + \mu_2\,(du/dz)^\eta, \qquad (45)$$

in which $\bar{p}$ = "effective" dynamic pressure, which at the quasistatic state reduces from equation 45 to $\bar{\rho}\,g\,(h-z)\cos\theta$, as often expressed in soil mechanics.

Solving equations 44 and 45 simultaneously for u yields

$$u = \frac{\eta}{\eta+1}\left(\frac{\rho^* g \sin\theta}{\mu_1}\right)^{1/\eta} z_0^{(\eta+1)/\eta}\left[1 - \left(1 - \frac{z}{z_0}\right)^{(\eta+1)/\eta}\right]$$
$$\text{for } 0 \leqslant z \leqslant z_0 \qquad (46a)$$

$$u = \frac{\eta}{\eta+1}\left(\frac{\rho^* g \sin\theta}{\mu_1}\right)^{1/\eta} z_0^{(\eta+1)/\eta} \text{ for } z_0 \leqslant z \leqslant h, \qquad (46b)$$

in which z_0 = vertical coordinate from the bed at which the shear stress is equal to $s = \rho\,g\,(h-z_0)\sin\theta$, and ρ^* is defined as:

$$\rho^* = \left[\frac{1 - (\bar{\rho}/\rho)\,\text{ctn}\,\theta\sin\phi}{1 + (\mu_2/\mu_1)\sin\phi}\right]\rho = \beta\rho. \qquad (47)$$

For flow of noncohesive granules ($z_0 = h$) in the grain-inertia regime ($\eta = 2$), equation 46 reduces to equation 43 because $\rho^* \to \rho$ as $\phi \to 0$. For flow in other regimes than the grain-inertia, however, Takashi's velocity profile, equation 43, deviates from the "true" solution of the generalized viscoplastic fluid model by a factor, β, which ranges from 0 (for the lower limit slope) to 1 (for the upper limit slope).

The general expression of the average velocity, $\bar{u}$, over the depth of flow, h, can be derived by integrating equation 46 with respect to z over h and then divided by h:

$$\bar{u} = \frac{\eta}{\eta+1}\left(\frac{\rho^* g \sin\theta}{\mu_1}\right)^{1/\eta}\left(\frac{z_0}{h}\right)^{(\eta+1)/\eta}\left[1 - \frac{\eta}{2\eta+1}\left(\frac{z_0}{h}\right)\right]$$
$$h^{(\eta+1)/\eta}, \qquad (48)$$

in which the dimensionless coordinate of the rigid plug, z_0/h, signifies the relative strength of the yield stress, s, against the bed shear, τ_0 ($= \rho\,g\,h\sin\theta$). For flow of noncohesive granules

($z_0/h = 1$) in the grain-inertia regime ($\eta = 2$), equation 48 is simplified to:

$$\bar{u} = \frac{2}{5}\left(\frac{\rho\,g\sin\theta}{\mu_1}\right)^{1/2} h^{3/2}, \qquad (49)$$

which is identical to Takahashi's solution (1978a) again because $\beta \to 1$ as $\phi \to 0$ in equation 47.

The equations of motion for (steady) uniform debris flow with the vertically *varying* concentration can be formulated from the differential form of the generalized viscoplastic fluid model, equations 3 and 4, on substitution of μ_1 and μ_2 from equations 6 and 7, respectively (Chen, 1986b):

$$-\rho\,g\sin\theta = \frac{dp}{dz}\sin\phi + A_1\frac{d}{dz}\left[(1 - KC)^{-B/K}\left(\frac{du}{dz}\right)^\eta\right] \qquad (50)$$

$$\rho\,g\cos\theta = -\frac{dp}{dz} + A_2\frac{d}{dz}\left[(1 - KC)^{-B/K}\left(\frac{du}{dz}\right)^\eta\right]. \qquad (51)$$

Solving equations 50 and 51 with the help of an assumption on the relation between ρ and p (i.e., equation 25) and an approximation involving a Taylor's series expansion of an exponential, logarithmic, or binomial function that describes the concentration distribution, results in p and u profiles. To obtain the general closed-form expressions of p and u profiles for $0 < B/K \leqslant 2.5$ and $\eta > 0$ is unlikely except for some particular values of B/K and η. For the purpose of comparison with the theoretical solutions of Tsubaki and others (1982), possible analytical solutions of u obtained from equations 50 and 51 are simply given in the following. For flow of noncohesive Bingham granular materials ($z_0/h = 1$ and $\eta = 1$),

$$\frac{u}{u_s} = (2 + B/K)\left[1 - \left(\frac{1 + B/K}{2 + B/K}\right)\left(\frac{z}{h}\right)\right]\left(\frac{z}{h}\right)^{1 + B/K}, \qquad (52)$$

in which u_s = velocity at the free surface ($z = h$).

For flow of noncohesive dilatant grains ($z_0/h = 1$ and $\eta = 2$), the analytical solutions of equations 50 and 51 for any value of B/K have not yet been found except for $B/K = 1$ and 2. The solution for $\eta = 2$ and $B/K = 2$ is:

$$\frac{u}{u_s} = 1 - \left[1 + \frac{3}{2}\left(\frac{z}{h}\right)\right]\left[1 - \left(\frac{z}{h}\right)^{3/2}\right], \qquad (53)$$

and that for $\eta = 2$ and $B/K = 1$ is

$$\frac{u}{u_s} = \frac{4}{\pi}\left\{\left(\frac{z}{h} - \frac{1}{2}\right)\sqrt{\left(\frac{z}{h}\right) - \left(\frac{z}{h}\right)^2} + \frac{1}{4}\sin^{-1}\left[2\left(\frac{z}{h}\right) - 1\right] + \frac{\pi}{8}\right\}. \qquad (54)$$

For other values of B/K, of course, one can obtain approximate solutions by integrating the following differential equation, yet to be expressed in a power series expansion.

$$\frac{d(u/\bar{u})}{d(z/h)} = \Lambda\left[\left(\frac{z_0}{h} - \frac{z}{h}\right)\left(\frac{z}{h}\right)^{B/K}\right]^{1/\eta}, \qquad (55)$$

in which Λ = coefficient, defined as:

$$\Lambda = \left[\frac{\beta \, \rho_b \, g \, h \, M^{B/K} \sin \theta}{A_1 \, (1 - \rho_w/\rho_b)^{B/K}} \right]^{1/\eta} \left(\frac{h}{\bar{u}} \right). \quad (56)$$

Here $\rho_b = C_b (\rho_s - \rho_w) + \rho_w$ = bulk density of the mixture on the bed, C_b = concentration on the bed, $M = \kappa \, \alpha \, \rho_b{}^m \, g \, h \, \cos \theta$ = mobility of the dispersed grains in the mixture, and α is defined as:

$$\alpha = \frac{1 + (A_2/A_1) \tan \theta}{1 + (A_2/A_1) \sin \phi}. \quad (57)$$

Tsubaki and others (1982, 1983) formulated the following equations of motion for (steady) uniform debris flow in a wide channel, adopting further the "effective" normal stress concept of Terzaghi (1943):

$$dT_{zx}/dz = - \rho \, g \sin \theta \quad (58)$$
$$dT_{zz}/dz = \bar{\rho} \, g \cos \theta. \quad (59)$$

Equations 58 and 59 on substitution of T_{zx} and T_{zz} from equations 20 and 21 thus constitute the basic working equations of Tsubaki and others for solving the u profile. The dimensionless u profile of Tsubaki and others is expressed in terms of C as:

$$\frac{u}{u_s} = \frac{\int_C^{C_b} F(C) \, dC}{\int_{C_s}^{C_b} F(C) \, dC}, \quad (60)$$

in which C_s = sediment concentration, C, at the free surface and $F(C)$ = a function of C, expressed as:

$$F(C) = \frac{2C - C_s}{C - C_\alpha} \frac{(1 - C/C_b)^{\frac{1}{2}}}{C/C_b} \left\{ (C - C_s) \left[\frac{\rho_s - \rho_w}{\rho_w} (C + 2C_\alpha) + 2 \right] \right.$$
$$\left. + \left(1 + \frac{\rho_s - \rho_w}{\rho_w} C_\alpha \right) (2C_\alpha - C_s) \ln \left(\frac{C - C_\alpha}{C_s - C_\alpha} \right) \right\}^{\frac{1}{2}}, \quad (61)$$

where

$$C_\alpha = \frac{\tan \theta}{[(\rho_s - \rho_w)/\rho_w] (\tan \phi_d - \tan \theta)}. \quad (62)$$

Note that C_α corresponds to the upper limit of θ in equation 42.

For verification, Tsubaki and others (1982, 1983) performed some debris flow experiments in a flume with various θ values and compared the measured u with their theoretical solution. Because five of the six u profiles measured by Tsubaki and others were taken near the snout, it is doubtful that a (steady) uniform debris flow had already developed at the time of measurement. The remaining set of data was taken far upstream from the moving snout; therefore, it is justified to assume that a uniform debris flow had already established when measurements were made. Shown in Figure 2 are profiles of this measured u and the corresponding theoretical u (equation 60). Although the theoretical u of Tsubaki and others does not closely agree with the data points, agreement is better than that based on Bagnold's (1954) assumption of constant C. The best agreement, however, can be achieved

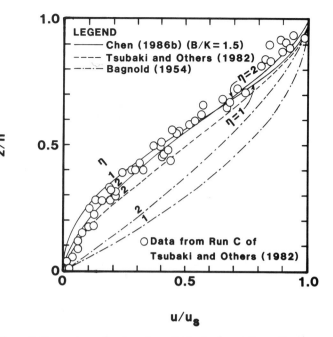

Figure 2. Comparison of various theoretical velocity profiles with experimental data of Tsubaki and others (1982) for (steady) uniform debris flow. Solid profiles representing dimensionless velocity, u/u_s, versus dimensionless vertical coordinate, z/h, are plotted against flow behavior index, η, with given value of parameter, B/K, describing the gross effects of sediment concentration and composition.

by the theoretical solution of equations 50 and 51. The value of C_b measured by Tsubaki and others is approximately 0.6; therefore, $B/K = 2.5 \times 0.6 = 1.5$ is used in the solution of equations 50 and 51. In the case of $\eta = 1$, equation 52 with $B/K = 1.5$ is simplified to:

$$\frac{u}{u_s} = \frac{7}{2} \left(1 - \frac{5}{7} \frac{z}{h} \right) \left(\frac{z}{h} \right)^{5/2}, \quad (63)$$

but for $\eta = 2$, the theoretical u is obtainable only from a power series expansion of equation 55 with $B/K = 1.5$. Both theoretical u profiles for $\eta = 1$ and 2 are also plotted in Figure 2 for comparison. Apparently, the approximate solution of equation 55 with $\eta = 2$ best fits the data points.

In another attempt to verify equation 60, Tsubaki and others used two sets of Takahashi's (1980a) data points, as shown in Figure 3, which are distinguished by different discharges, Q, of overland flow introduced at the head of a flume covered with grains. Because Takahashi's experiments were based on $C_b = 0.7$, it is determined that $B/K = 2.5 \times 0.7 = 1.75$. Therefore, for $\eta = 1$, equation 52 on substitution of $B/K = 1.75$ reduces to:

$$\frac{u}{u_s} = \frac{15}{4} \left(1 - \frac{11}{15} \frac{z}{h} \right) \left(\frac{z}{h} \right)^{11/4}. \quad (64)$$

For $\eta = 2$, however, the theoretical u is again obtainable only from a power series expansion of equation 55 with $B/K = 1.75$.

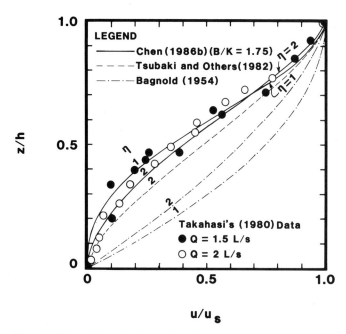

Figure 3. Comparison of various theoretical velocity profiles with experimental data of Takahashi (1980) for (steady) uniform debris flow. Solid profiles representing dimensionless velocity, u/u_s, versus dimensionless vertical coordinate, z/h, are plotted against flow behavior index, η, with given value of parameter, B/K, describing gross effects of sediment concentration and composition. Takahashi's data points are distinguished by different discharges, Q, of overland flow introduced at head of flume.

Both theoretical u profiles for $\eta = 1$ and 2 are thus plotted in Figure 3 for comparison with those of Tsubaki and others (equation 60) and Bagnold. Bagnold's solution in the same dimensionless form can be readily transformed from equation 46 into:

$$\frac{u}{u_s} = 1 - \left(1 - \frac{z}{h} \right)^{(\eta + 1)/\eta}. \qquad (65)$$

Good agreement between Takahashi's data and the Chen's (1986b) theoretical u profiles, especially one for $\eta = 2$, as shown in Figure 3, strongly indicates the need for improvement of the model of Tsubaki and others (equations 20 and 21). The inconsistency of equations 20 and 21 may be attributed to poor agreement between the experimental data and the theoretical solution of Tsubaki and others.

Debris Flow Initiation Criteria

Bagnold's limiting slope criterion, equation 41, is in fact the lower limit slope, equation 42, obtained from an "effective" stress version of the generalized viscoplastic fluid model, equations 44 and 45, as mentioned previously. This criterion is essentially a basic condition for the initiation of debris flow, triggered by overland flow on the grain bed under heavy rainfall, as developed

by Takahashi (1978a, 1981). For comparison, Takahashi's criteria for the occurrence of various types of sediment transport and debris movement are rearranged and given in the following.

Consider a uniform layer of cohesive deposited grains lying on an inclined impervious sill with angle, θ. The thickness of the grain layer is D. It is assumed that at the moment when the overland flow of depth, h_o, appears, the pore spaces among grains are saturated and a parallel seepage flow (i.e., throughflow) without any excessive pore pressure occurs. The shear-stress profile in the deposited-grain layer should pose one of the two cases shown in Figure 4, in which τ is the applied shear stress and τ_L the internal resistance stress:

$$\tau = [C(\rho_s - \rho_w) a + \rho_w (a + h_o)] g \sin \theta \qquad (66)$$
$$\tau_L = c + [C(\rho_s - \rho_w)] g a \cos \theta \tan \phi, \qquad (67)$$

in which a = vertical depth below the grain surface.

Case 1 in Figure 4 occurs under the conditions of $d\tau/da \geqslant d\tau_L/da$, which on substitution of equations 66 and 67 yields:

$$\tan \theta \geqslant \frac{C(\rho_s - \rho_w)}{C(\rho_s - \rho_w) + \rho_w} \tan \phi. \qquad (68)$$

Note that equation 68 with the equal sign is identical to equation 41 because $\phi = \phi_d$ for debris flow at the quasi-static state. Three conditions in Case 1 are visualized, depending on the depth, a_L, where τ and τ_L coincide: (1) for $a_L \leqslant 0$ (i.e., $\tau \geqslant \tau_L$), debris flow without rigid plug occurs; (2) for $0 < a_L < D$, debris flow with rigid plug or land slip may occur; and (3) for $a_L \geqslant D$ (i.e., $\tau \leqslant \tau_L$), no debris flow can be generated. Because Takahashi did not take the cohesion of grains into account, the first term on the right-hand side of equation 67 disappears and only condition 1 noted above is possible. Therefore, if $c = 0$, substituting the expressions of τ and τ_L from equations 66 and 67 into the alternate criterion, $\tau \geqslant \tau_L$, yields at $a = a_L$:

$$\tan \theta \geqslant \frac{C(\rho_s - \rho_w)}{C(\rho_s - \rho_w) + \rho_w (1 + h_o/a_L)} \tan \phi. \qquad (69)$$

Note that equation 69 differs from equation 68 only by the additional term in the denominator on the right-hand side of equation 69, h_o/a_L. This additional term signifies the role that overland flow plays in the landslide and debris flow processes. Equation 69 is formulated in such a way that satisfying $\tau \geqslant \tau_L$ requires $a_L \leqslant a \leqslant D$, but θ is minimum at $a = a_L$ for given h_o. In particular, $\theta = 0$ when $a_L = 0$. If $h_o = 0$ (i.e., in the case that the seepage flow did not reach the grain surface), equations 68 and 69 become identical and a landslide rather than a debris flow is generated (Takahashi, 1978, 1981). In other words, "A landslide would occur before the increment of the stage of seepage flow reaches the surface of the bed. A pile of debris caused by a landslide usually has a smaller gradient than it originally had on the mountain slope, so that it may be moved as debris with the appearance of a surface water flow. The time lag between the occurrence of a landslide and the removal of its deposit by the generation of debris flow would depend on the water supply, and it sometimes

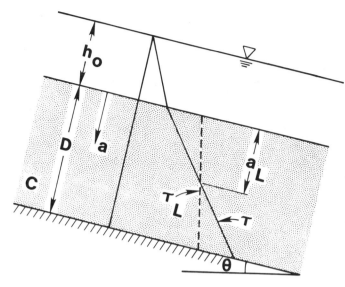

CASE 1: $\quad \dfrac{d\tau}{da} \geq \dfrac{d\tau_L}{da}$

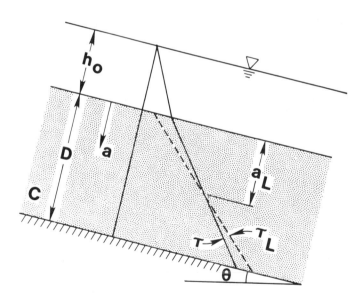

CASE 2: $\quad \dfrac{d\tau}{da} < \dfrac{d\tau_L}{da}$

Figure 4. Diagram describing various stress profiles of applied shear stress, τ, and internal resistance stress, τ_L, in deposited grain layer of thickness, D, and concentration, C, under overland flow of depth, h_o, on inclined impervious sill with angle, θ. Note that "a" is vertical depth below grain surface and "a_L" is corresponding depth where τ and τ_L coincide.

could be so short that one would hardly recognize the transition between the two phenomena" (Takahashi, 1981, p. 64–65).

Case 2 in Figure 4 occurs under the condition of $d\tau/da < d\tau_L/da$, or, equivalently from equations 66 and 67:

$$\tan \theta < \frac{C(\rho_s - \rho_w)}{C(\rho_s - \rho_w) + \rho_w} \tan \phi . \tag{70}$$

Although equation 70 does not meet Bagnold's limiting slope criterion, equation 41, for the full layer of deposited grain, a debris flow may be generated in the partial upper layer ($a \leqslant a_L$) for which $\tau \geqslant \tau_L$ or equation 69 is satisfied. Because θ in equation 69 is minimum at $a = a_L$ and a_L should be greater than or equal to the grain diameter, d, for any grain layer movement, Takahashi (1978a) proposed that:

$$\frac{C(\rho_s - \rho_w)}{C(\rho_s - \rho_w) + \rho_w(1 + h_o/d)} \tan \phi \leqslant \tan \theta <$$
$$\frac{C(\rho_s - \rho_w)}{C(\rho_s - \rho_w) + \rho_w} \tan \phi , \tag{71}$$

for the initiation of "sediment gravity flow" (Takahashi, 1981), which includes both the bed load transportation, resulting from the drag and lift forces of overland flow, and the massive transportation or debris flow, resulting from the dispersive pressure of colliding particles. Therefore, a more restrictive condition for debris flow initiation in Case 2 is $a_L \geqslant k\,h_o$, in which k is a numerical coefficient, determined from experiments to be about 0.7 (Takahashi, 1981). Finally, the corresponding criterion for debris flow initiation in Case 2 is:

$$\frac{C(\rho_s - \rho_w)}{C(\rho_s - \rho_w) + \rho_w(1 + k^{-1})} \tan \phi \leqslant \tan \theta <$$
$$\frac{C(\rho_s - \rho_w)}{C(\rho_s - \rho_w) + \rho_w} \tan \phi . \tag{72}$$

For example, if $C = 0.7$, $\rho_s = 2.6$ g/cm^3, $\rho_w = 1.0$ g/cm^3, $k = 0.75$, and $\tan \phi = 0.8$, as suggested by Takahashi (1978a), from equation 72 $0.259 \leqslant \tan \theta < 0.423$ or $14.5° \leqslant \theta < 22.9°$ is obtained, seemingly in the observed range of gully slopes from which debris flows were generated.

The equilibrium concentration, C_∞, is defined by Takahashi (1978a, 1980a, 1981) as the maximum concentration for debris flow at the quasi-static state:

$$C_\infty = \frac{\rho_w \tan \theta}{(\rho_s - \rho_w)(\tan \phi - \tan \theta)} . \tag{73}$$

Therefore, the initiation criterion posed in the form of equation 68 can be alternately expressed as:

$$C \leqslant C_\infty , \tag{74}$$

and that in the form of equation 69 as:

$$\frac{h_o}{a_L} \geqslant \frac{C}{C_\infty} - 1 . \tag{75}$$

Generally, the debris flow process takes three distinctive stages from the time of occurrence to the time of stoppage: initiation, propagation, and deposition. Bed slope for debris flow decreases gradually from the region of initiation to that of deposition. An analysis of field data on actual events in Japan (Ikeya and Mizuyama, 1982) reveals that bed slopes in the region of initiation are most likely in the range of $\tan \theta \geqslant 1/4$, which agrees with Takahashi's (1981) criterion (equation 72), and bed slopes in the region of propagation and deposition are thus in the range of $\tan \theta \leqslant 1/4$. A transition from debris flow to bed load transport in fact takes place on a slope in the latter range and is specifically termed the "sediment gravity flow" (Takahashi, 1983), to distinguish it from debris flow and bed load transport. The condition for the occurrence of sediment gravity flow developed by Mizuyama (1980, 1981) and Ikeya and Mizuyama (1982) is

$$\frac{h_b}{h_o} \leqslant \frac{C_\infty}{C_b}, \tag{76}$$

in which h_b and C_b are the thickness and the concentration of the bed load transport layer, respectively. Takahashi's (1982, 1983) criterion, which is more general than equation 76, originally comprised the critical tractive force for bed load transport and the shearing stress, but has recently been extended from equation 75 to the following form for the occurrence of sediment gravity flow:

$$\frac{h_o}{d} \geqslant \frac{C}{C_\infty} - 1 + \frac{C_b\, h_b}{C_\infty\, d}, \tag{77a}$$

or expressed in the form of equation 76:

$$\frac{h_b}{h_o} \leqslant \frac{C_\infty}{C_b} + \frac{(C_\infty - C)\, d}{C_b\, h_o}. \tag{77b}$$

An empirical relation for the ratio of sediment to water by volume, q_s/q_w, for sediment gravity flow was also developed by Mizuyama (1980, 1981) and Ikeya and Mizuyama (1982). For $0.05 < \tan \theta < 0.25$, if the tractive force is larger than the critical tractive force, it can be expressed in terms of θ as:

$$\frac{q_s}{q_w} = 5.5\, (\tan \theta)^2. \tag{78}$$

The debris flow initiation criterion for Case 1, equation 69, and that for Case 2, equation 72, so derived are valid only for noncohesive ($c = 0$) granules. Extension of these criteria to the case of a cohesive grain bed has been conducted by Takahashi (1978b, 1980b). Inclusion of c in the derivation of the criteria using equations 66 and 67 necessitates the addition of c ctn $\phi/g\, a_L \cos \theta$ in the numerator on the right-hand side of equation 69 and c ctn $\phi/g\, k\, h_o \cos \theta$ in the numerator on the left-hand side of equation 72. However, such an additional term due to c in the case of equation 72 may violate the inequality shown in equation 72, of course, depending on the magnitudes of c and ϕ. This thus raises a question on the generality of the initiation criteria developed on the basis of $\tau \geqslant \tau_L$ for both cases. Because the criterion, equation 68, developed on the basis of $d\tau/da \geqslant d\tau_L/da$ for Case

1 is identical to the lower limit slope, as specified in equation 42, for quasi-static flow of both cohesive and noncohesive grains, equation 68 may be simply utilized as an initiation criterion for both cases. The role that the cohesion, c, plays in the initiation of debris flows was also studied by Iwamoto and Hirano (1982a), whose criterion includes an additional c term similar to those expressed in the foregoing.

Observing that debris flow and gully erosion often occur right after seepage flow surfaces under heavy rainfall, Iwamoto and Hirano (1982a) developed the following criterion for the occurrence of debris flow based on the kinematic theory of seepage flow and overland flow. This initiation criterion is equivalent to establishing a relation for the location from the upstream end, L, and time, T, required for overland flow to appear on the grain bed under the average rainfall intensity, r:

$$\frac{r}{k} \geqslant \frac{D \tan \theta}{L}, \tag{79}$$

in which k = coefficient of permeability or hydraulic conductivity of the deposited grain layer with thickness D. Their experimental results strongly supported the validity of equation 79.

Adopting Bagnold's limiting slope criterion, equation 41, Sassa (1984b) attempted to account for the initiation mechanism of liquefied landslides and debris flows from field observations and laboratory experiments. He has concluded from direct shear tests in the field that debris flows may be initiated by the liquefaction of the torrent deposit due to the rapid loading of fallen masses from slopes above the torrent bed. He was also able to reproduce a prototype debris flow in the laboratory, using the so-called "ring-shear" type debris flow apparatus, which is similar to, but much larger and more sophisticated than, that developed by Savage and Sayed (1984). After analyzing experimental results, Sassa concluded that the ability of debris flows and liquefied landslides to move on a very gentle slope can be attributed to the floatation of fine particles, and hence the increase in the interstitial fluid density, as readily proved from equation 41, but not to the "flow structure," as suggested by Casagrande (1976).

Sassa's explanation on the mechanism to initiate debris flows and liquefied landslides was entirely based on field observations (Sass, 1984a; Sassa and others, 1980a,b, 1981) and laboratory experiments (1984b). Many field observations suggest that debris flows are triggered more frequently by liquefaction of saturated sediments than the mere addition of sediments into water. For example, on a hillslope of loosely deposited grains where ground water moves locally with a relatively high velocity, the void ratio of the grain layer along the ground-water path increases by underground erosion and infiltration. Sometime thereafter, a loose zone is formed along the path and subsides due to the sudden decrease in the stress when the ground-water table rises. Subsidence then causes rapid loading (undrained shear), which in turn destroys the structure of loosely deposited grains at the saturated state, and the overburden pressure (i.e., the excessive pore pressure) is supported by water. The fallen mass or deposit sitting on water starts to flow like a hovercraft, and thus forms a debris flow. For convenience, a debris flow generated from deposits on a torrent bed is called a torrent-bed-type debris flow and that from hillslopes a slope-type ("valley-off" or "snake-off") debris flow. Note that liquefied landslides are initiated by the same mechanism of slope-type debris flows, but the latter appears to be longer than the former as far as the shape of flow is concerned.

Longitudinal Profile of Snout

The established longitudinal profile of the snout can be theoretically derived by solving the one-dimensional equations of continuity and motion that are based on the assumption of no erosion and deposition under the snout. The snout profile on a "dry" bed (i.e., the depth, h, is zero at the tip of the snout) derived by Takahashi (1980a), using the moving coordinate, ξ ($= x - Ut$, where U is the constant velocity of the moving coordinate system attached to the tip), is:

$$\frac{\tan \theta}{h_\infty} \xi = \frac{h}{h_\infty} + ln \left(1 - \frac{h}{h_\infty} \right), \qquad (80)$$

in which $h_\infty = f \bar{u}_\infty^2 / 8g \sin \theta$ = normal depth of flow at $\xi = -\infty$ (i.e., the asymtotic depth of the steady flow, where $\bar{u}_\infty$ = normal velocity of steady debris flow at $\xi = -\infty$, equal to the constant velocity of the moving coordinate system, U, and f = Darcy-Weisbach resistance coefficient). Takahashi verified equation 80, using experimental data.

In a more general case, if the snout moves on a "wet" bed (i.e., $h = h_o \neq 0$ at $\xi = 0$), the shock condition must be first incorporated in the determination of h_o. Once h_o is determined, the following theoretical snout profile on a wet bed can be similarly derived:

$$\frac{\tan \theta}{h_\infty} \xi = \frac{h}{h_\infty} - \frac{h_o}{h_\infty} + ln \left(\frac{1 - h/h_\infty}{1 - h_o/h_\infty} \right). \qquad (81)$$

Note that equation 80 is only a particular case of equation 81 with $h_o/h_\infty = 0$.

Adopting Prandtl's mixing length theory, Hirano and Iwamoto (1981) and later Iwamoto and Hirano (1982b) have derived the snout profile from the two-dimensional equations of continuity and motion for steady debris flow:

$$\frac{\tan \theta}{h_\infty} \xi = \frac{h}{h_\infty} + \left(1 - \frac{F_\infty^2 A}{\cos \theta} \right) ln \left(1 - \frac{h}{h_\infty} \right), \qquad (82)$$

in which $F_\infty = \bar{u}_\infty / g h_\infty$ = Froude number at $\xi = -\infty$; and $A = \int_0^1 F$ $F'' d(z/h)$, where $F = F(z/h)$ is an unknown function of z/h used in defining the stream function. Because $F_\infty^2 A / \cos \theta$ is of a small order of magnitude (i.e., $F_\infty < 1$, $A = 0.03$, and $\cos \theta \approx 1$) and can be ignored, equation 82 can reduce to equation 80. They have also showed that observed profiles agree with equation 82.

There are other methods for expressing the theoretical profiles of the snout. For example, Brückl and Scheidegger (1973) used Prandtl's solution of plastostatic equations (Hill, 1950, p. 232). One of the two solutions obtained by Brückl and Scheidegger represents the passive Rankine state and the other active

Rankine state. A comparison of observed profiles with both solutions reveals that the existence of an active Rankine state is most probable in nature.

In another method, Johnson (1970) obtained the form of the snout profile for the active Rankine state based on the assumption that the sediment-water mixture is a simple plastic (i.e., $\phi = 0$) and the snout surface is in critical equilibrium (i.e., a principal-stress trajectory):

$$\frac{\rho g}{2c} \xi = ln \left[\cos \left(\frac{\rho g}{2c} z \right) \right]. \qquad (83)$$

Note that equations 80 and 83 are similar, but a direct comparison between them cannot be made because of the difference in the coordinates used in both equations.

Unsteady Debris Flows

For routing debris flows down a narrow valley, the one-dimensional dynamic equations, analogous to those for clear-water flow, can be formulated (Chen, 1985b). The one-dimensional unsteady flow equations for debris flow are identical to those for clear-water flow. The difference between them reflects only in the different values of the flow parameters, such as the momentum (or energy) correction factor and the resistance coefficient. These flow parameters for debris flows in channels with section of arbitrary geometric shape can only be determined empirically. In the most idealized case of no erosion and deposition of sediment in the transport process, the one-dimensional dynamic equations for debris flow in nonprismatic channels can be expressed as:

$$\frac{\partial A}{\partial t} + \frac{\partial (AV)}{\partial x} = 0 \qquad (84)$$

and

$$\frac{\partial (AV)}{\partial t} + \frac{\partial (\beta A V^2)}{\partial x} = g A \sin \theta - g A \frac{\partial h}{\partial x} \cos \theta - g A S_f, \qquad (85)$$

in which A = cross-sectional area of flow; t = time; x = space coordinate in the longitudinal direction of flow; V = average velocity over A; β = momentum correction factor; $h = h (x, t)$ = depth of the flow; and S_f = friction slope, which can be expressed in terms of V and the hydraulic radius, R, using the Darcy-Weisbach equation or the Manning formula. Note that the assumption of $\beta = 1$ seems justified unless there is a rapid change in A, such as at an alluvial fan, where use of the two-dimensional depth-averaged flow equations would be more accurate. The assumption of no erosion and deposition in the sediment transportation process may be justified in the tip region of the snout, but not in the remaining part, where equations 84 and 85 should be modified by adding source and sink terms that describe the erosion and deposition processes of sediment during the flow, respectively. Bagnold's limiting slope criterion, equation 41, may be utilized in the formulation of such source-sink terms.

Takahashi (1978a, 1983) has theoretically analyzed the

processes of growth and deposition of the snout, using Bagnold's limiting slope criterion and the shock equations. The method of solving this problem might be similar to that of solving the dam-break flood wave problem if the shock equations were incorporated with the one-dimensional unsteady debris flow equations (i.e., equations 84 and 85 with source-sink terms) to route the entire body of debris flow through a channel from the time of its initiation to the time of its termination. Details of Takahashi's methods can be found in western journals (Takahashi, 1978a, 1981, 1983), as well as in the Japanese literature (Takahashi, 1977, 1980c, 1982; Takahashi and Yoshida, 1979).

Debris flow may deposit sediment and eventually stop due to rapid or gradual changes in bed slope and channel width. Mizuyama and Uehara (1983) first performed experiments in a concave downward flume and then with an abrupt expansion in channel width to study the deposition process of debris flow. Tsubaki and Hashimoto (1984) also studied the deposition process of debris flows due to an abrupt drop in bed slope, and applied the Lagrange method to computing the time and distance of the stoppage of debris flow from the point where the bed slope is suddenly changed.

Other unsteady debris flow problems investigated by Japanese scientists concern roll waves, the movement of large stones or boulders, and the transformation of landslide into debris flow. For example, Takahashi (1983) has found from laboratory experiments that theoretical results for clear-water roll waves agree with experimental data, except that the momentum correction factor (i.e., 1.25) used in his theoretical approach was equal to that for dilatant fluids with $\eta = 2$. In another example, Takahashi (1980a) attempted to model the process of accumulation of boulders at the front of debris flow, using the equation of motion, and verified his theory by experiments, although a different approach based on "impact force theory" was adopted earlier by Suwa and Okuda (1973). Finally, one of the current issues in debris flow modeling in Japan is to develop a method to predict the critical location where a landslide is transformed into debris flow. Ashida and others (1983) formulated the equations of continuity and momentum for an idealized soil mass sliding on a slope and solved them for the velocity and location of the sliding mass.

Debris Flows around Bends

Behaviors of debris flow around a curved path are very complex in that the streamlines of the flow are not only curvilinear but also interwoven, resulting in spiral currents and cross waves. Furthermore, water and sediment at a certain point in a bend may be separated. Major Japanese efforts have been made to empirically determine the superelevation and the velocity distribution of debris flow in the channel sections in the bend. Mizuyama and Uehara (1981) have found from experiments that a simple formula for superelevation of clear-water flow, such as:

$$\Delta h = \frac{2b}{r_c} \frac{\bar{v}^2}{g},$$
(86)

underestimates the superelevation of debris flow. Here Δh = superelevation, b = width of the channel, r_c = centerline radius of curvature, and $\bar{v}$ = mean velocity in the direction of flow. Although Δh predicted by equation 86 was made twice as high as that predicted by the highly idealized formula:

$$\Delta h = \frac{b}{r_c} \frac{\bar{v}^2}{g},$$
(87)

the superelevation coefficient, K [= $\Delta h/(\bar{v}^2/g)$], has been experimentally found to be as large as $10 \, b/r_c$ for $\theta = 16°$ (Mizuyama and Uehara, 1981; Ikeya and Uehara, 1982). Apparently, the value of K depends on θ, the curvature of the bend, the velocity and concentration distributions of debris flow, and the rheological properties of dispersed grains, among many other factors. The theoretical determination of K values using the generalized viscoplastic fluid model based on the various assumptions of the velocity distribution across the channel width in a bend is possible, but whether it gives a realistic K value remains to be investigated in the future.

The combined effects of the preceding factors on the K value are very difficult to be determined, even by experiments. Further complication of such determination is attributed to the fact that water and sediment may be separated in a bend under a certain condition, as observed by Mizuyama and Uehara (1981). The separation of water and sediment in a curved channel is similar to that observed in the deposition process of debris flow on a concave downward slope, namely, the so-called sediment gravity flow occurring in a transition from debris flow to bed load transport. A critical condition for the occurrence of sediment gravity flow in a bend should be developed in the future.

CONCLUSIONS

Modeling the non-Newtonian behavior of debris flows in Japan relies almost exclusively on Bagnold's (1954) dilatant fluid model. Although the consistency of Bagnold's model is still at issue (Chen, 1985a), Japanese scientists have apparently accepted Takahashi's (1977, 1978a,b, 1980a,b,c, 1981, 1983) debris flow formulas and criteria developed based on Bagnold's "dispersive" pressure concept. Caution should be exercised against the use of Bagnold's model before the inconsistencies are completely resolved.

The principal conclusions drawn from this critical evaluation of Japanese contributions to debris flow modeling are summarized as follows:

1. Many rheological models developed or utilized for modeling debris flows in Japan range from highly theoretical non-Newtonian fluid models to very simple empirical relations of Bingham (1922) and Bagnold (1954). Models of Kanatani (1979a, b, 1980, 1982), Ogawa (1978), Ogawa and others (1980), and Tsubaki and others (1982, 1983) may belong to the former category, whereas models of Takahashi (1977, 1978a, 1980a, 1981), Daido (1979, 1982), and Yamaoka and others (1981) are either identical to Bagnold's model or modified forms

thereof. All the Japanese models have been critically evaluated in terms of a generalized viscoplastic model developed by Chen (1986b). It has been shown that Bagnold's model, which neither possesses rate-independent parts nor soil yield criteria, cannot accurately model debris flows that vary from the quasi-static to dynamic states. Models of Tsubaki and others and Daido appear to be more general than Bagnold's model, but their forms are unfortunately incomplete as far as the expression of the yield stress, s, is concerned.

2. Use of Bagnold's shear-stress versus shear-rate relation (equation 12) alone in the solution of the velocity profile for (steady) uniform debris flow in wide channels, as treated by Takahashi (1980a), resulted in a particular solution that has proved to be valid only for debris flow in the grain-inertia regime ($\eta = 2$ with $\tan \phi_d = 0.32$). Because Takahashi's sediment concentration was estimated from the upper limit of equation 42 with the measured $-\mu_1/\mu_2$ ($= \tan \phi_d$) value equal to 0.75, Bagnold's numerical constant, a_i, in equation 12, calibrated by Takahashi, has been shown to exceed Bagnold's 0.042 by nearly an order of magnitude. Therefore, applying Takahashi's solution to modeling a debris flow in other regimes than the grain-inertia may have to adjust the value of Bagnold's numerical constant to better fit the computed velocities to the measured ones.

3. Good agreement between Chen's (1986b) theoretical velocity profiles and the experimental data of Takahashi (1980a) and Tsubaki and others (1982), as shown in Figures 2 and 3, strongly supports the validity of both the generalized viscoplastic fluid model and the proposed method of solution from the model.

4. Takahashi's (1978a) criterion for the initiation of debris flow (equation 68) is essentially identical to the lower limit slope (equation 42) obtained from an "effective" stress version of the generalized viscoplastic fluid model (equations 44 and 45) for (steady) uniform flow of both cohesive and noncohesive granular materials. Because the role that cohesion plays for various cases considered by Takahashi in the initiation of debris flows is the hardest to determine, the lower limit slope for uniform debris flow may be simply utilized as a general initiation criterion for all the cases.

5. A transition from debris flow to bed load transport (i.e., sediment gravity flow) takes place on a slope where $\tan \theta \leqslant 1/4$. The condition for the occurrence of sediment gravity flow developed by Takahashi (1983) has been shown to be more general than that developed by Mizuyama (1980, 1981) and Ikeya and Mizuyama (1982).

6. The theoretical profile of the snout on a "dry" bed derived by Takahashi (1980) has been shown to be a particular case of the more general expression of the profile on a "wet" bed. Hirano and Iwamoto (1981) also obtained a similar result, as obtained by Takahashi, using Prandtl's mixing length theory.

7. It has been shown that the one-dimensional unsteady debris flow equations including source-sink terms can be incorporated with the shock equations to route a debris flow through a channel from the time of its initiation to the time of its termination. The routing method is perhaps similar to that of solving the dam-break flood wave problem. Takahashi (1977, 1978b, 1980c, 1981, 1982, 1983), however, modeled the growth and deposition of debris flow without resorting to the shock equations.

8. Other unsteady debris flow problems investigated by Japanese scientists concern roll waves (Takahashi, 1983), the movement of large stones or boulders (Suwa and Okuda, 1973; Takahashi, 1980a), and the transformation of landslide into debris flow (Ashida and others, 1983). Much work remains to be done in these areas, especially the development of a generally applicable routing method to deal with two transitions in the debris flow process, namely, from landslide to debris flow and then from debris flow to bed load transport.

9. Determination of the superelevation in a bend is a formidable task, as it is affected by many factors, such as the bed slope, the curvature of bend, the velocity and concentration distributions of debris flow, and the rheological properties of dispersed grains. The value of the superelevation coefficient, K, determined experimentally by Mizuyama and Uehara (1981) and Ikeya and Uehara (1982), can be approximately expressed as 10 b/r_c, depending on the preceding factors. In addition to the K value, a criterion for the initiation of sediment gravity flow in a bend should be investigated in the future.

REFERENCES CITED

Ashida, K., Egashira, S., and Ohtsuki, H., 1983, Dynamic behavior of a soil mass produced by slope failure: Kyoto, Japan, Kyoto University, Disaster Prevention Research Institute Annuals No. 26-B2, p. 315–327 (in Japanese).

Bagnold, R. A., 1954, Experiments on a gravity-free dispersion of large solid spheres in a Newtonian fluid near shear: Proceedings, Royal Society of London, ser. A., v. 225, p. 49–63.

—— , 1966, The shearing and dilation of dry sand and the "singing" mechanism: Proceedings, Royal Society of London, ser. A, v. 295, p. 219–232.

Bingham, E. C., 1922, Fluidity and plasticity: New York, McGraw-Hill, 440 p.

Brückl, E., and Scheidegger, A. E., 1973, Application of the theory of plasticity to slow mud flows: Geotechnique, v. 23, no. 1, p. 101–107.

Casagrande, A., 1976, Liquefaction and cyclic deformation of sands; A critical review: Cambridge, Massachusetts, Harvard University, Harvard Soil Mechanics Series No. 88, 27 p.

Chen, C. L., 1983, On frontier between rheology and mudflow mechanics, *in*

Proceedings of the Hydraulics Division Specialty Conference on Frontiers in Hydraulic Engineering: Cambridge, Massachusetts, American Society of Civil Engineers, p. 113–118.

—— , 1985a, Present status of research in debris flow modeling, *in* Proceedings of the Hydraulics Division Specialty Conference on Hydraulics and Hydrology in the Small Computer Age: Lake Buena Vista, Florida, American Society of Civil Engineers, p. 733–741.

—— , 1985b, Hydraulic concepts in debris flow simulation, *in* Proceedings of the Specialty Conference on Delineation of Landslide, Flash Flood and Debris Flow Hazards in Utah: Logan, Utah State University, p. 236–259.

—— , 1986a, Chinese concepts of modeling hyperconcentrated streamflow and debris flow, *in* Proceedings of the Third International Symposium on River Sedimentation: Jackson, Mississippi, p. 1647–1657.

—— , 1986b, Bingham plastic or Bagnold's dilatant fluid as a rheological model of debris flow?, *in* Proceedings of the Third International Symposium on River

Sedimentation: Jackson, Mississippi, p. 1624–1636.

Cowen, S. C., 1974a, A theory for the flow of granular materials: Powder Technology, v. 9, p. 61–69.

——, 1974b, Constitutive relations that imply a generalized Mohr-Coulomb criterion: Acta Mechanica, v. 20, p. 41–46.

Daido, A., 1970, Fundamental study of debris flow [Ph.D. thesis]: Kyoto, Japan, Kyoto University, 178 p. (in Japanese).

——, 1971, On the occurrence of mud-debris flow: Bulletin of the Disaster Prevention Research Institute, Kyoto University, v. 21, p. 109–135.

——, 1976, Viscosity and yield value of fluid containing clay, *in* Proceedings of the 26th Japan National Congress for Applied Mechanics: Japan National Committee for Theoretical and Applied Mechanics, Science Council of Japan, University of Tokyo Press, p. 461–472.

——, 1979, Flow formula of granular materials, *in* Proceedings of the 16th Natural Disaster Science Symposium: Japan, p. 215–218 (in Japanese).

——, 1982, The mechanism of occurrence of the mud-debris flow and its flow: Kyoto, Japan, Ritsumeikan University, Memoirs of the Research Institute of Science and Engineering, no. 41, p. 105–125.

Drucker, D. C., and Prager, W., 1952, Soil mechanics and plastic analysis or limit design: Quarterly of Applied Mathematics, v. 10, p. 157–165.

Einstein, A., 1956, Investigation on the theory of the Brownian movement: New York, Dover, 119 p.

Fujita, M., Hasegawa, K., Yamaoka, I., and Okayama, K., 1982, Rheological properties of mud flows which consist of fine particles, *in* Proceedings: Hokkaido Branch of the Japanese Socioety of Civil Engineers, v. 38, p. 267–272 (in Japanese).

Hill, R., 1950, Mathematic theory of plasticity: Oxford, Clarendon Press, 356 p.

Hirano, M., and Iwamoto, M., 1981, Experimental study on the grain sorting and the flow characteristics of a bore: Kyushu, Japan, Kyushu University, Memoirs of the Faculty of Engineering, v. 41, no. 3, p. 193–202.

Ikeya, H., and Mizuyama, T., 1982, Flow and deposit properties of debris flow: Public Works Research Institute Report No. 157-2, Ministry of Construction, Government of Japan, 153 p. (in Japanese).

Ikeya, H., and Uehara, S., 1982, Debris flow in S-shaped channel curves: Civil Engineering Journal, Japan, v. 24, no. 12, p. 645–650 (in Japanese).

Iwamoto, M., and Hirano, M., 1982a, A study on the mechanism of the occurrence of debris flow and its flow characteristics: Journal of the Japanese Forestry Society, v. 64, no. 2, p. 48–55.

——, 1982b, Mechanical characteristics of debris flow: Wien, Austria, Mitteilungen Der Forstlichen Bundes-Versuchsanstalt, v. 144, p. 151–161.

Johnson, A. M., 1970, Physical processes in geology: San Francisco, W. H. Freeman, 577 p.

Kanatani, K., 1979a, A micropolar continuum theory for the flow of granular materials: International Journal of Engineering Science, v. 17, p. 419–432.

——, 1979b, A continuum theory for the flow of granular materials: Theoretical and Applied Mechanics, Japan National Committee on Theoretical and Applied Mechanics, v. 27, p. 571–578.

——, 1980, A continuum theory for the flow of granular materials (II): Theoretical and Applied Mechanics, Japan National Committee on Theoretical and Applied Mechanics, v. 28, p. 485–492.

——, 1982, A plasticity theory for the kinematics of ideal granular materials: International Journal of Engineering Science, v. 20, p. 1–13.

Krieger, I. M., and Dougherty, T. J., 1959, A mechanism for non-Newtonian flow in suspensions of rigid spheres: Transactions of the Society of Rheology, v. 3, p. 137–152.

McTigue, D. F., 1979, A nonlinear continuum model for flowing granular materials [Ph.D. thesis]: Stanford, California, Stanford University, 165 p.

——, 1982, A nonlinear constitutive model for granular materials, application to gravity flow: Journal of Applied Mechanics, American Society of Mechanical Engineers, v. 49, p. 291–296.

Mizuyama, T., 1980, Sediment transport rate in the transition region between debris flow and bed load transport: Shin-Sabo, The Erosion Control Engineering Society of Japan, v. 116, p. 1–6 (in Japanese).

——, 1981, An intermediate phenomenon between debris flow and bed load transport, *in* Proceedings of the Erosi on and Sediment Transport in Pacific Rim Steeplands: Christchurch, New Zealand, International Association of Hydrologic Sciences, p. 212–224.

Mizuyama, T., and Uehara, S., 1981, Debris flow in steep slope channel curves: Civil Engineering Journal, Japan, v. 23, no. 5, p. 243–248 (in Japanese).

——, 1983, Experimental study of the depositional process of debris flows: Transactions, Japanese Geomorphological Union, v. 4, no. 1, p. 49–64.

Ogawa, S., 1978, Multitemperature theory of granular materials, *in* Cowin, S. C., and Satake, M., eds., Proceedings of the U.S.-Japan Seminar on Continuum-Mechanical and Statistical Approaches in the Mechanics of Granular Materials: Tokyo, Japan, Gakujutsu Bunken Fukyukai.

Ogawa, S., Umemura, A., and Oshima, N., 1980, On the equations of fully fluidized granular materials: Journal of Applied Mathematics and Physics (ZAMP), v. 31, p. 483–493.

Sassa, K., 1984a, The mechanism to initiate debris flows as undrained shear of loose sediments, *in* Proceedings of the Internationales Symposium INTER-PRAVENT 1984 (International Symposium on Natural Hazard Prevention): Villach, Austria, p. 73–87.

——, 1984b, The mechanism starting liquefied landslides and debris flows, *in* Proceedings of the International Symposium on Landslides: Toronto, Canada, p. 349–354.

Sassa, K., Takei, A., and Kobashi, S., 1980a, Landslides triggered by vertical subsidence, *in* Proceedings of the International Symposium on Landslides: New Delhi, India, Sarita Prakashan, v. 1, p. 49–54.

Sassa, K., Takei, A., and Kobashi, S., 1980b, Consideration of vertical subsidences as a factor influencing slope instability, *in* Proceedings of the International Symposium on Landslides: New Delhi, India, Sarita Prakashan, v. 1, p. 293–296.

——, 1981, The mechanism of liquefied landslides and valley-off type debris flows: Wien, Austria, Mitteilungen Der Forstlichen Bundes-Versuchsanstalt, v. 138, p. 151–162.

Sassa, K., Takei, A., and Marui, H., 1981, Influences of "underground erosion on instability of a crystalline schist slope," *in* Proceedings of the International Symposium on Weak Rock: Soft, Fractured and Weathered Rock, Rotterdam, Netherlands, A. Balkema Co., p. 543–548.

Savage, S. B., 1979, Gravity flow of cohesionless granular materials in chutes and channels: Journal of Fluid Mechanics, v. 92, p. 53–96.

Savage, S. B., and Sayed, M., 1984, Stresses developed by dry cohesionless granular materials sheared in an annular shear cell: Journal of Fluid Mechanics, v. 142, p. 391–430.

Sayed, M., and Savage, S. B., 1983, Rapid gravity flow of cohesionless granular materials down inclined chutes: Journal of Applied Mathematics and Physics (ZAMP), v. 34, p. 84–100.

Suwa, H., and Okuda, S., 1973, Motion of large stone at mudflow front and flow pattern of mudflow: Kyoto Japan, Kyoto University, Disaster Prevention Research Institute Annuals No. 16-B, p. 425–432 (in Japanese).

Takahashi, K., 1937, On the dynamical properties of granular mass: Tokyo, Japan, Japan Meteorological Agency, Geophysical Magazine, v. 11, p. 165–175.

Takahashi, T., 1977, A mechanism of occurrence of mud-debris flow and their characteristics in motion: Kyoto, Japan, Kyoto University, Disaster Prevention Research Institute Annuals No. 20-B2, p. 405–435 (in Japanese).

——, 1978a, Mechanical characteristics of debris flow: Journal of the Hydraulics Division, American Society of Civil Engineers, v. 104, no. HY8, p. 1153–1169.

——, 1978b, The occurrence and flow mechanism of debris flow: Tsuchi to Kiso (Soil and Foundation), v. 26, p. 45–50 (in Japanese).

——, 1980a, Debris flow on prismatic open channel: Journal of the Hydraulics Division, American Society of Civil Engineers, v. 106, no. HY3, p. 381–396.

——, 1980b, Evaluation of the factors relevant to the initiation of debris flow, *in* Proceedings of the International Symposium on Landslides: New Delhi, India, Sarita Prakashan, v. 1, p. 136–140.

——, 1980c, Study on the deposition of debris flows (2); Process of formation of debris fan: Kyoto, Japan, Kyoto University, Disaster Prevention Research

Institute Annuals No. 23-B2, p. 443–456 (in Japanese).

——, 1981, Debris flow, *in* van Dyke, M., Wehauser, J. V., and Lumley, J. L., eds., Annual review of fluid mechanics: Palo Alto, California, Annual Reviews, v. 13, p. 55–77.

——, 1982, Study on the deposition of debris flows (3); Erosion of debris fan: Kyoto, Japan, Kyoto University, Disaster Prevention Research Institute Annuals No. 25-B2, p. 327–348 (in Japanese).

——, 1983, Debris flow and debris flow deposition, *in* Shahinpoor, M., ed., Advances in the mechanics and the flow of granular materials: Clausthal, Germany, Trans Tech Publications, v. 2, p. 699–718.

Takahashi, T., and Yoshida, H., 1979, Study on the deposition of debris flows (1); Deposition due to abrupt change of slope: Kyoto, Japan, Kyoto University, Disaster Prevention Research Institute Annuals No. 22-B2, p. 315–328 (in Japanese).

Terzaghi, K., 1943, Theoretical soil mechanics: New York, John Wiley & Sons, 510 p.

Tsubaki, T., and Hashimoto, H., 1984, Deposition of debris flow due to abrupt change of bed slope, *in* Proceedings of the 28th Hydraulics Symposium, Japan, p. 711–716 (in Japanese).

Tsubaki, T., Hashimoto, H., and Suetsugi, T., 1982, Grain stresses and flow properties of debris flow: Proceedings of the Japanese Society of Civil Engineers, No. 317, p. 79–91 (in Jpanese; a condensed version of the paper in English appeared in the Transaction of the Japanese Society of Civil Engineers, v. 14, p. 413–416).

——, 1983, Interparticle stresses and characteristics of debris flow: Journal of Hydroscience and Hydraulic Engineering, Japanese Society of Civil Engineers, the Committee on Hydraulics, v. 1, no. 2, p. 67–82.

Varnes, D. J., 1978, Slope movement types and processes, *in* Schuster, R. L., and Krizek, R. J., eds., Landslides analysis and control: Washington, D.C., National Academy of Science, Transportation Research Board Special Report 176, p. 11–33.

Yamaoka, I., 1981, Recent research of debris flows in open channels: Hydraulics Engineering Series 81-A-3, Hydraulics Committee, Japanese Society of Civil Engineers, 20 p. (in Japanese).

Yano, K., and Daido, A., 1965, Fundamental study on mud-flow: Kyoto, Japan, Kyoto University, Bulletin of the Disaster Prevention Research Institute, v. 14, p. 69–83.

MANUSCRIPT ACCEPTED BY THE SOCIETY DECEMBER 29, 1986

Geological Society of America
Reviews in Engineering Geology, Volume VII
1987

Mobilization of debris flows from soil slips, San Francisco Bay region, California

Stephen D. Ellen
U.S. Geological Survey
MS 975
345 Middlefield Road
Menlo Park, California 94025

Robert W. Fleming
U.S. Geological Survey
Box 25046, MS 966
Denver Federal Center
Denver, Colorado 80225

ABSTRACT

The thousands of debris flows that mobilized from shallow slides in the San Francisco Bay region during the rainstorm of January 3–5, 1982, left evidence of the range in soil textures susceptible to mobilization and of differences in completeness and speed of mobilization. These differences in mobilization are related to a broad range in the ratio of saturated water content to liquid limit, which we have used as an approximate index of mobilization potential. To understand such differences in mobilization, we have explored the transformation from slide to flow, using relations among inplace void ratio, void ratio needed for flow from the slide scar, and the steady-state line. These relations define two principal means of direct transformation from slide to flow: contractive soil behavior, which commonly results in liquefaction, and dilative soil behavior, which in many cases probably results in partial mobilization of the slide mass. These means of mobilization determine the completeness of mobilization of slides and the time required for mobilization; they also influence the thickness and lumpiness of deposits, as well as the travel distance of debris flows. These relations permit means of mobilization to be predicted in both an approximate and a precise manner through soil testing.

INTRODUCTION

Many debris flows originate from slides (as defined by Varnes, 1978), yet the transformation from slide to flow remains poorly understood. In this chapter, we summarize our findings on the factors that control mobilization of debris flows, particularly the debris flows that occurred during the exceptional rainstorm of January 3–5, 1982, in the San Francisco Bay region. Almost all of these flows developed from slides of the soil mantle. As suggested in Figure 1, individual slides generally transformed into flows directly, rather than through more complex mechanisms of mobilization, such as described by Johnson and Rahn (1970), Morton and Campbell (1974), and Sassa (1984). We call such debris flows "soil slip/debris flows" (after Campbell, 1975). Soil slips that resulted in debris flows generally occurred on slopes of 25° to 40°. Typical soil-slip scars were 5 to 15 m wide and less than 2 m deep; the distance traveled by the resulting debris flows ranged from as little as several tens of meters to more than a kilometer. More complete description of this storm and the thousands of debris flows it triggered may be found in Ellen and Wieczorek (1988).

SOILS INVOLVED

Size analyses of 50 samples representative of soils that

Figure 1. Scars and trails from soil slip/debris flows in Marin County, typical of many generated by 1982 storm in the San Francisco Bay region. Scar near center is about 5 m wide.

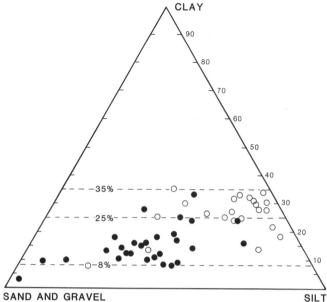

Figure 2. Size analyses of soils that flowed as debris flows during 1982 storm. Clay size is less than 2 μ. Circles represent samples involved in particularly slow-moving debris flows and debris flows from oversteepened areas and from margins of active slow-moving shallow slides. Solid dots represent remainder of debris flows tested, which moved rapidly from hillslopes in long-term equilibrium.

flowed in the storm illustrate the broad range of textures susceptible to soil slip/debris flow (Fig. 2). The content of clay-size particles is of particular interest. The lower limit of clay content is important because sustained flow requires at least a small proportion of clay (Rodine, 1974; Pierson, 1981). The lowest clay content in Figure 2 is 3 percent, and 8 percent clay forms the lower bound for 98 percent of the samples.

Too much clay can inhibit mobilization of soils that must take on water to flow. Clay increases the amount of water needed to reach states capable of flow, provides cohesive strength that impedes remolding, and hinders dilation by reducing permeability. Low rates of dilation require long periods of sustained slide movement for significant amounts of mobilization. Figure 2 suggests that clay content in excess of about 35 percent was sufficient to prohibit mobilization of debris flows during the storm.

The upper limit of clay content that allowed flow is reduced when we consider only fast-moving debris flows originating from hillslopes in long-term equilibrium. This restricted sample, shown by the solid dots in Figure 2, is obtained by excluding debris flows that were anomalously slow-moving (velocities of meters per minute rather than meters per second) and debris flows from cut slopes, from scarps of deep-seated landslides, and from margins of active slow-moving shallow slides, all of which are shown by circles in Figure 2. The upper bound of clay content for 93 percent of this restricted sample is 25 percent.

Soils susceptible to mobilization in this region thus show a

full range in clay content of 3 to 35 percent, a typical range of 8 to 35 percent, and a restricted range (noted above) of 8 to 25 percent. All ranges are so broad that they may not be very useful in themselves for determining susceptibility to soil slip/debris flow.

CONTRASTS IN MOBILIZATION

During the storm, soil slips mobilized into debris flows differently, and recognition of these differences forms a major basis for our inquiry. One prominent difference was the degree of mobilization. Most soil slips mobilized completely, leaving scars empty of failed material (Figs. 1, 3). Other slides mobilized partially, leaving dislocated slide masses as well as scars from which some of the soil had flowed (Fig. 4); debris flows in such cases characteristically issued from the flanks or toes of slides. Many other shallow slides moved during the storm but did not mobilize at all as debris flows (Fig. 5).

Eyewitness reports suggested another significant difference in mobilization—speed. At one site, within a span of several seconds, an observer saw a small waterfall in an intermittent drainage change from white to brown water and then disappear as the hillside collapsed downslope as part of a debris flow. At other sites, rapid flow was preceded by as much as 24 hr of slow slide movement.

Deposits of debris flows differed in a number of respects that

Figure 3. Empty soil-slip scar of debris flow near Nicasio, Marin County.

Figure 4. Partial mobilization of shallow slide, near San Geronimo, Marin County. Shallow slide is about 35 m wide, defined by dark lines at head scarp and toe. Debris flows have mobilized from flank and toe of slide.

may reflect the manner of mobilization. Differences in thickness and lumpiness of deposits particularly caught our attention.

These contrasts raise such questions as, "Why did some slides mobilize and not others? Why did only parts of some slides mobilize? Why did mobilization take longer in some cases than in others?" To answer such questions, we proceed to clarify the relation between slide and flow, and then consider possible means of debris-flow mobilization.

TRANSITION FROM SLIDE TO FLOW

The conditions under which a debris flow can develop from a soil slip may be evaluated using the concept of plug flow, in which flowing debris is modeled as a relatively rigid plug or slab rafted on a zone of laminar flow. Johnson (1970) called the thickness of the plug the critical thickness for flow, because, as a debris flow thins to this point, the plug bottoms out and becomes a deposit. Thus, critical thickness is reflected (at least approximately) in thickness of the lateral deposits or the lobe at the distal end of the flow. For a broad sheet of Bingham material, which is representative of the flow as it leaves the soil-slip scar (Figs. 1, 3), critical thickness (T) measured normal to the slope is given by the relation

$$T = \frac{k_f}{\gamma_f \sin \beta}, \qquad (1)$$

where k_f and γ_f are shear strength and saturated unit weight of the flow, respectively, and β is slope (Johnson, 1970, p. 488, 503). Thus, the thickness of the plug is proportional to the strength of the debris-flow material.

For the process of soil slip/debris flow, there are inherent relations between critical thickness for flow and thickness of the sliding slab. For a sliding slab of soil to transform directly into a debris flow, its critical thickness when remolded must be less than or equal to thickness of the sliding slab; otherwise, the slab must thicken for flow to begin, which is unlikely (Fig. 6). Thus, the theoretical limiting case for flow from the scar is described by equation (1) when T equals slide thickness. In actuality, critical thickness probably must be somewhat less than slide thickness if much of the slab is to be remolded during sliding. As a result, mobilization apparently requires development of slurry strengths low enough that critical thickness is somewhat less than slide thickness.

MEANS OF MOBILIZATION

How can the low slurry strengths required for mobilization be attained? In the discussion that follows, we assume that such strengths generally result from the response of soils to Coulomb failure, rather than from liquefaction induced directly by strong upward seepage (see Iverson and Major, 1986).

Mobility Index

Rodine (1974) and Johnson (1984) approached the low slurry strengths needed for mobilization of debris flows by considering water content, the principal determinant of slurry strength. They devised a mobility index (MI), defined by Johnson (1984) as the ratio of saturated water content of the inplace soil to the water content needed for flow of that soil down the available channel. Water content needed for flow was determined through innovative strength testing and measurement of channel form. Mobilization was considered likely where saturated water content

Figure 5. Hillslope near Tomales Bay, showing soil slip/debris flows generated by 1982 storm, revegetated soil-slip scars from previous storms, and shallow slide that did not mobilize as debris flow (indicated by arrows).

of inplace soil was sufficient for debris flow down the available channel, and less likely where soil must take on additional water in order to flow. Rodine and Johnson found that soils involved in debris flow had an MI >0.85.

Approximate Mobility Index

An approximation of the MI can be obtained by using the Atterberg liquid limit to represent the water content needed for flow. Thus, this approximate mobility index (AMI) is the ratio of saturated water content of inplace or undisturbed soil to its liquid limit. Qualitatively, the liquid limit seems suitable for this use because it is the water content at which soil behavior is marginally fluid under shallow conditions. Quantitatively, the liquid limit represents a shear strength of about 2 kPa (Seed and others, 1964, p. 77), which can be translated to a critical thickness of 20 cm by using equation (1) with typical values for the debris flows under discussion ($\beta = 30°$; saturated unit weight of flow material = 20 kN/m^3). This critical thickness is substantially less than the typical thickness of soil slips induced by the storm (about 1 m), and it lies near the upper end of the typical range of thickness of lateral deposits left by debris flows during the storm. For these reasons, the liquid limit seems well suited to approximate the water content needed for debris flow during the storm.

One drawback of the liquid limit for this purpose is that it is measured on only the fine fraction of the soil (fraction smaller than the no. 40 sieve size—fine sand and smaller). For soils that contain an abundant coarse fraction, the liquid limit is probably significantly larger than the water content needed for flow.

The AMI is plotted in Figure 7 for soils that mobilized as debris flows during the storm (Table 1). Soils that plot above the solid line (case A, AMI > 1) had initial capacity to hold more water than their liquid limit. When remolded, these soils would flow readily because they would have low shear strengths and critical thicknesses well below typical slide thickness.

Soils that plot below the solid line (AMI <1) must have taken on water in order to flow. These soils correspond to low potential for flow according to the MI, yet the plot demonstrates that many such soils flowed during the storm. We subdivide this area of the plot into two zones. For soils in zone B (0.45 <AMI <1), incorporation of water was sufficient for flow, at least in parts of slide masses. Soils in zone C (AMI <0.45) apparently could not incorporate enough water for flow.

The Steady State

The MI approach can be elaborated by considering the initial sliding of a slab of soil. As significant deformation begins at failure, soil in the basal shear zone will approach a critical, or steady, state. Critical state soil mechanics indicates that a saturated soil, if continuously distorted until it flows as a frictional fluid, will come into a well-defined state characterized by a water content and corresponding strength, both of which are related to effective confining stress (Schofield and Wroth, 1968). A similar concept was described by Poulos (1981) as the steady state of deformation.

The transition of soil from an initial void ratio at critical equilibrium just before failure to a steady-state void ratio can be

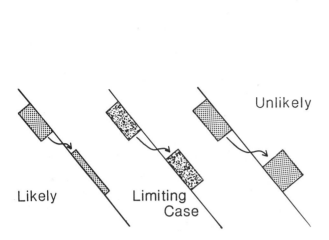

Figure 6. Schematic cross sections of soil slip/debris flows, showing hypothetical relations between slide depth and critical thickness for debris flow. Transformation to flow is likely where critical thickness is less than slide depth, unlikely where slide mass must thicken for flow to begin.

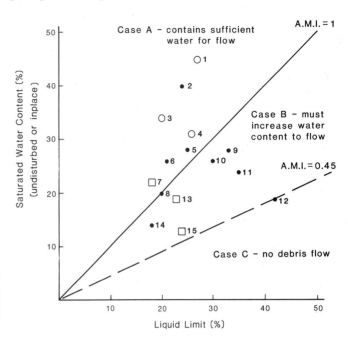

Figure 7. Relation between saturated water content of inplace or undisturbed soil and liquid limit, for soils that mobilized as debris flows during 1982 storm. Numbers identify samples in Table 1. Large symbols represent soils in two-layer soil slip/debris flows at three sites in Marin County; circles, dark surficial soils; squares, tan subsoils.

TABLE 1. GRADATION AND PLASTICITY OF SOILS PLOTTED IN FIGURE 7

No. in Fig. 7	Gravel	Sand	Silt	Clay (<2 μ)	Fines (Silt + Clay)	Plasticity Index	Description
1	2	36	45	17	62	6	Dark top soil at site 2 of Lahr (1982), 0.6 m depth*
2	2	44	–	–	54	4	Dark top soil, 0.5 m depth**
3	0	52	32	16	48	3	Dark top soil at Salmon Creek landslide, 0-0.6 m depth#
4	24	31	33	12	45	1	Dark top soil at site 3 of Lahr (1982), 0.6 m depth *
5	4	44	41	11	52	3	Dark top soil, 0.5 m depth*
6	17	43	30	10	40	–	Tan subsoil, 1.2 m depth*
7	3	47	35	15	50	1	Tan subsoil at site 2 of Lahr (1982), 1.8 m depth*
8	2	48	–	–	50	2	Subsoil, 1.1 m depth**
9	1	58	–	–	41	14	Soil, 1 m depth##
10	4	39	29	28	57	5	Soil, 2.4 m depth##
11	7	53	–	–	40	16	Soil, 3 m depth##
12	10	41	–	–	49	20	Soil, 1 m depth##
13	0	56	32	12	44	4	Tan subsoil at Salmon Creek landslide, 0.9-2.5 m depth#
14	2	55	25	18	43	3	Soil, 2.4 m depth##
15	20	24	48	8	56	2	Tan subsoil at site 3 of Lahr (1982), 1.0 m depth*

Note: Gradations are in percent dry weight.
*Data from Lahr (1982).
**Data from S. L. Reneau and Alan Kropp and Associates.
#Data from R. W. Nichols and M. A. Algus, U.S. Geological Survey.
##Data from J. E. Baldwin II, Howard-Donley and Associates

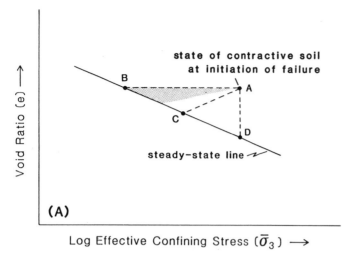

(A)

Log Effective Confining Stress ($\overline{\sigma}_3$) ⟶

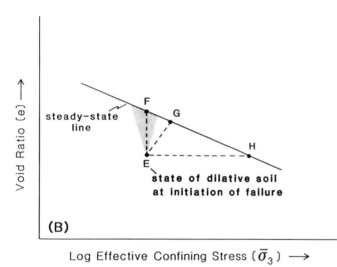

(B)

Log Effective Confining Stress ($\overline{\sigma}_3$) ⟶

Figure 8. "State diagrams" illustrating changes in state during deformation of contractive soil (A), and dilative soil (B). Shading shows state paths likely in rainfall-induced landslides.

described using "state diagrams" (Fig. 8), in which the soil's void ratio (e) is plotted against effective confining stress ($\overline{\sigma}_3$). Loose (contractive) soils (Fig. 8A), which plot above the line that defines steady-state flow conditions, have fabrics that tend to collapse upon shear, generating the potential for liquefaction because pore pressures can thereby increase greatly. For loose soil at an initial state represented by point A in Figure 8A, shear deformation during failure moves the soil state toward the steady-state line. If deformation is undrained, the increased pore pressures result in a horizontal path to point B, at which steady-state flow conditions would be attained. This path is the common result of strongly contractive behavior in soils without high permeability, and so it is emphasized by shading in Figure 8A. Any contraction permitted by drainage during shear reduces e, shifting the state

downward to a point such as C. The unlikely circumstance of drained conditions, in which there is no increase in pore pressure, would permit a vertical path to point D on the steady-state line.

Dense (dilative) soils, in contrast, tend to expand during shear deformation. Such soil must draw water to the dilating zone in order for deformation to continue, and so dilation, and the mobilization that may result, requires time, particularly in soil of low permeability. On the state diagram in Figure 8B, shear deformation shifts the state upward (increases e) from a pre-failure, critical-equilibrium state (point E) that lies below the steady-state line. Drained conditions with no change in effective stress would permit a vertical path to point F. Partially drained and undrained conditions would result in paths toward the right in Figure 8B, such as to points G and H. However, paths that veer far to the right are unlikely in rainfall-induced landslides because movement and the resulting deformation in the basal shear zone are brought about by low effective confining stress. Paths that veer somewhat to the left from point E are possible, for example, where continued rainfall during drained deformation increases pore pressure sufficiently to reduce the effective confining stress below its initial value. In general, however, state paths in dilative soils in basal shear zones of rainfall-induced landslides probably are constrained to a nearly vertical zone, as shown by shading in Figure 8B.

Possible Means

When the steady-state concept is combined with the MI approach, the means of mobilization can be portrayed on state diagrams through relations among three factors: the initial state, the steady-state line, and the minimum void ratio needed for flow from the scar (e_f), which corresponds uniquely to the strength k_f defined by equation (1) when T equals slide thickness. Figure 9 portrays these factors for examples of both contractive and dilative soils, with likely paths of contractive and dilative behavior shown by shading.

To define the position of e_f along the steady-state line in Figure 9, particular hypothetical examples of dilative and contractive soils are plotted. These particular soils are noncohesive, have similar steady-state behavior as represented by the single steady-state line, and similar unit weight; each lies under a slope of inclination β in a potential failure zone at depth h that is at critical equilibrium under slope-parallel seepage with saturation to the ground surface. These soils thus have similar effective confining stress before deformation, in each case resulting from the normal component of buoyant weight of the soil (Fig. 9; see Lambe and Whitman, 1969, p. 354). The position of e_f on this plot can be determined by noting that the driving shear stress at failure of an infinite slab of thickness h, under conditions of slope-parallel seepage with saturation to the ground surface, is equal to the driving shear stress for the limiting case of flow at the same thickness [$T = h$ in equation (1)], namely the downslope component of saturated weight of the soil per unit area (see Lambe and Whitman, 1969, p. 354; Johnson, 1970, p. 488).

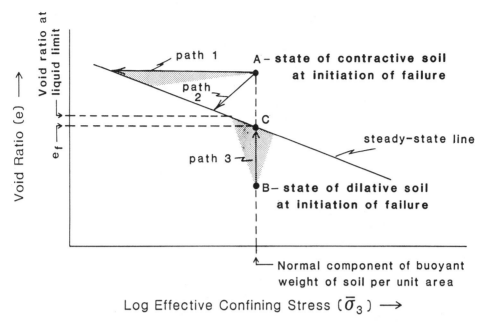

Figure 9. "State diagram" showing contractive and dilative means of mobilization. Shading shows state paths likely in rainfall-induced landslides from initial conditions A and B. Steady-state void ratio greater than e_f is necessary for debris flow from soil-slip scar.

Thus, the frictional strengths mobilized in resistance, and their corresponding effective confining stresses, must also be equal, and the limiting-case steady-state void ratio e_f must correspond to point C in Figure 9.

Mobilization probably requires void ratios somewhat greater than e_f, as mentioned previously, so the void ratio at liquid limit is shown in Figure 9 to approximate the lower limit of void ratios likely to mobilize. The plotted position of liquid limit represents a strength several-fold lower than k_f.

With the basic relations among these factors defined as in Figure 9, just two principal cases of mobilization emerge, the contractive and dilative cases. These results confirm the impressions of many investigators, reported by Costa (1984, p. 270), that liquefaction and dilation constitute the principal processes of debris-flow mobilization.

Contractive Case. For contractive soils, particularly strongly contractive soils, shear deformation at the base of the slide results in paths like path 1 from point A (Fig. 9). Such paths result in steady-state void ratios that are much greater than e_f, and so flow from the scar can occur readily by liquefaction (as defined by Poulos and others, 1985). Mobilization is essentially instantaneous, because strains of only about 1 percent are sufficient to initiate liquefaction (Casagrande, 1976). Mobilization is typically complete because strength is so greatly reduced upon small strain. Deposits that reflect critical thickness are much thinner than the parent scar because slurry strength is much less than k_f; consequently, travel distance may be great because little material tends to be left along the path (Cannon, 1985, 1986).

Deposits are of smooth consistency because excess water was present initially throughout the saturated portion of the soil. This means of mobilization corresponds approximately to case A of Figure 7 (AMI >1).

For soils that are weakly contractive or that have sufficient permeability to permit significant drainage, state paths will intersect the steady-state line lower down (such as path 2 in Fig. 9). Here steady-state void ratio is closer to e_f, resulting in stronger and thicker flows and decreased likelihood of mobilization.

Dilative case. Dilative soils in the basal shear zone start from points such as B, below the steady-state line (Fig. 9). Dilation by basal shear deformation during failure results in paths like path 3, which reach the steady-state line with void ratios near e_f, marginally capable of flow from the scar. Such paths may originate somewhat to the right or left of point B, then follow more or less vertical paths to the steady-state line. Paths to the right of path 3 would occur in cases where failure is triggered by pore pressures lower than those resulting from slope-parallel seepage with saturation to the ground surface. Under the conditions sketched in Figure 9, such paths could not attain mobilization through steady-state deformation in the basal shear zone. Paths to the left of path 3 could occur in cases where failure is triggered by pore pressures greater than those represented by path 3, and such cases may be capable of mobilization by steady-state deformation in the basal shear zone. Regardless of loose or dense soil behavior, initial conditions well to the left of line AB approach the quick conditions ($\bar{\sigma}_3 = 0$) described by Iverson and Major (1986).

In many cases, dilative soils probably cannot mobilize solely

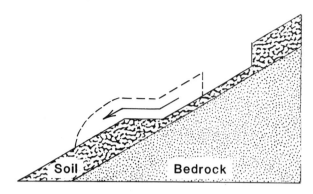

Figure 10. Schematic cross section showing bending distortions in sliding slab as it leaves soil-slip scar.

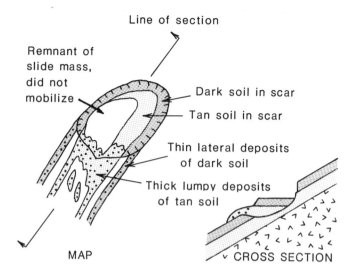

Figure 11. Schematic map and cross section of two-layer soil slip/debris flow.

by steady-state deformation of the basal shear zone; slide movement may not be sustained enough to reach the steady state, and steady-state void ratios, if achieved, may not be quite sufficient for flow. Parts of the sliding mass, however, may be mobilized by local dilations that result from deformation outside of the basal shear zone. Such partial mobilization may occur along flanks of the slide, where shear may be accompanied by extension and by abundant water channeled along pull-away cracks; at the toe of the slide, where dilation may be accompanied by abundant water and oversteepened slopes; and in the body of the slide during bending distortions as it passes from the scar (Fig. 10). Dilation from such sources is reflected in the pattern of flows shown in Figure 4.

Mobilization by dilation is slower than by liquefaction because the water content must increase. Deposits that reflect critical thickness are thinner than scar depth, but they are typically thicker with respect to scar depth than deposits mobilized by liquefaction; consequently, travel distance is generally less. Deposits are lumpy because water content has increased in some parts of the mass more than others, as when milk is added to oatmeal. Dilative mobilization is documented by Fleming and others (1987). This means of mobilization corresponds approximately to case B in Figure 7.

The foregoing analysis of means of mobilization has focused largely on behavior in the basal shear zone. Mobilization of a slide mass is also facilitated by other deformations incurred as it moves from the scar, some of which are illustrated in Figure 10. The results of these deformations are influenced by soil state in the general manner discussed above. In homogeneous soil, deformation in the body of the slide mimics that in the basal shear zone, resulting in the features described above for each case. Where soil is heterogeneous at a site, means of mobilization and the resulting features may be mixed.

MOBILIZATION DURING THE STORM

Although we lack the steady-state test data needed to con-

firm the specific means of mobilization that occurred in the storm, the wide range in AMI (Fig. 7) indicates that mobilization occurred by both contractive and dilative means. Debris flows that eyewitnesses observed to follow from slow sliding probably occurred in dilative soils, whereas apparently instantaneous debris flows probably resulted from liquefaction of contractive soils. Empty scars (as in Figs. 1, 3) probably resulted from contractive behavior, although complete mobilization may be possible also in dilative soils under favorable effective-stress conditions. The partial mobilization in Figure 4 is typical of dilative behavior. Non-mobilized slides like the one in Figure 5 probably occurred in dilative soils, possibly where movement toward the steady state was not sustained.

TWO-LAYER SOIL SLIP/DEBRIS FLOWS

Contrasts in mobilization were particularly intriguing in cases in which two debris flows issued from a single scar (Fig. 11). At each of the several sites where we recognized this phenomenon, one flow developed from dark surficial soil and one from underlying tan colluvial soil; a zone of clay enrichment separated these two soils. Field relations indicate that the dark surficial soil flowed first, leaving thin lateral deposits that were relatively smooth textured except for lumps of sod; then the underlying tan soil mobilized, leaving thicker lumpy deposits (Fig. 12). The single scar suggests that both flows began mobilization at the same instant from a sliding failure that extended down into the tan colluvial soil; otherwise the precise superposition of scars observed at several sites would be fortuitous.

The behavior of two-layer soil slip/debris flows is clarified through test results for three sites (Fig. 7, Table 1). At all three

Figure 12. Deposits from two-layer soil slip/debris flow, Marin County. Dark surficial soil forms thin deposit of relatively smooth consistency near auger; underlying tan colluvial soil forms thicker lumpy deposits at bottom center of view.

sites, dark surficial soil had an AMI >1, suggesting contractive behavior. The underlying tan soil at two sites had an AMI <1, suggesting dilative behavior; at the third site, where relation of scar to deposits was less well defined, the AMI of tan soil was slightly greater than 1, and so this soil would appear to be slightly contractive. These results are consistent with the observed relations between rapidly mobilized, thin, smooth deposits derived from the dark soil, and more slowly mobilized, thicker, lumpy deposits derived from the tan soil.

Some features of the deposits at these sites may have been influenced by other factors. Water held by the grass before passage of the flows probably was incorporated into the flows and contributed to thinning and smoothing of the first flow episode at each site. The geometry of the landslide failure surface probably also affected the results. Because rotational slides tend to stabilize themselves by movement, they are less likely than slab slides to mobilize completely, particularly for soils that must dilate to flow. Partial mobilization at these sites may have resulted in part because sliding in the tan soil involved considerable rotation.

PREDICTING MOBILIZATION

At sites subject to shallow slope failure, clay content serves as a crude first cut at predicting susceptibility to debris flow, but the broad range in texture of susceptible soils makes this measure of limited use (Fig. 2).

The ratio of saturated water content to liquid limit, the AMI (Fig. 7), distinguishes in approximate manner soils capable of rapid mobilization by liquefaction from soils that must dilate in order to flow. This index also provides an empirical limit for soils susceptible to soil slip/debris flow (the boundary between cases B and C in Fig. 7), and the simplicity of this index encourages additional testing that can define this boundary more precisely. At sites where failure is likely, the AMI may provide a simple and inexpensive means for estimating the likelihood of debris flow and predicting the nature of its initiation.

A more precise site-specific method of prediction uses the liquefaction evaluation procedures of Poulos and others (1985). For critical soils at sites of potential failure, these procedures permit determination of the initial state and the steady-state line, and thus the soil's contractive or dilative behavior, the magnitude of divergence from steady-state conditions, and the steady-state strengths that can be expected—most of the factors critical to mobilization. Testing required by the steady-state method may be complicated by coarse particles in the soil and by the low confining stresses that characterize shallow landslides.

CONCLUSIONS

The January 1982 storm in the San Francisco Bay region left evidence of differences in the mobilization of debris flows from soil slips. Analysis suggests that rapid and complete mobilization that produced thin deposits resulted from liquefaction of contractive soils. Mobilization that was slow and partial, or slide movement that did not produce debris flow, probably resulted from dilative soil behavior.

Susceptibility to mobilization can be evaluated using several approaches. First, clay content of soils that flowed in the 1982 storm defines approximate and broad limits for susceptible soils in the region. Second, the ratio of saturated water content to liquid limit, an approximation of the mobility index of Rodine (1974) and Johnson (1984), serves as a convenient approximate test to distinguish contractive from dilative mobilization and to determine the limit of soils susceptible to mobilization. The third approach uses the liquefaction evaluation procedures of Poulos and others (1985) to more precisely delineate the means of mobilization.

The potential for slides to mobilize as debris flows, and the means of this mobilization, are critical to thorough evaluation of landslide hazard. The methods discussed here help in predicting (1) the potential for mobilization, whether a debris flow is likely from a given slide or potential slide; (2) completeness of mobilization, the proportion of a slide or potential slide that may be expected to transform into a debris flow; (3) speed of mobilization, the lag time between initial failure and flow; (4) velocity and thickness of flow from the scar, based on likely strength of slurry; and (5) travel distance of debris flows.

ACKNOWLEDGMENTS

We acknowledge the contribution of Homa J. Lee, whose clarification of the relation between e_f and the steady-state parameters assisted fundamentally in the theoretical development.

REFERENCES CITED

Campbell, R. H., 1975, Soil slips, debris flows, and rainstorms in the Santa Monica Mountains and vicinity, southern California: U.S. Geological Survey Professional Paper 851, 51 p.

Cannon, S. H., 1985, The lag rate and the travel-distance potential of debris flows (M.S. thesis): University of Colorado at Boulder, 141 p.

—— , 1986, The lag rate and the travel-distance potential of debris flows: Geological Society of America Abstracts with Programs, v. 18, no. 2, p. 93.

Casagrande, A., 1976, Liquefaction and cyclic deformation of sands, a critical review: Harvard University, Soil Mechanics Series, no. 88, 27 p.

Costa, J. E., 1984, Physical geomorphology of debris flows, *in* Costa, J. E., and Fleisher, P. J., eds., Developments and applications of geomorphology: Berlin, Springer-Verlag, p. 268–317.

Ellen, S. D., and Wieczorek, G. F., eds., 1988, Landslides, floods, and marine effects of the storm of January 3-5, 1982, in the San Francisco Bay region, California: U.S. Geological Survey Professional Paper 1434 (in press).

Fleming, R. W., Ellen, S. D., and Algus, M. A., 1987, Transformation of dilative and contractive landslide debris into debris flows, an example from Marin County, California, *in* Johnson, A. M., ed., Memorial volume dedicated to R. H. Jahns: Amsterdam, Elsevier (in press).

Iverson, R. M., and Major, J. J., 1986, Groundwater seepage vectors and the potential for hillslope failure and debris flow mobilization: Water Resources Research, v. 22, no. 11, p. 1543–1548.

Johnson, A. M., 1970, Physical processes in geology: San Francisco, Freeman, Cooper and Company, 577 p.

Johnson, A. M., and Rahn, P. H., 1970, Mobilization of debris flows, *in* Macar, Paul, ed., New contributions to slope evolution: Zeitschrift für Geomorphologie, suppl. 9, p. 168–186.

Johnson, A. M., with contributions by Rodine, J. D., 1984, Debris flow, *in* Brunsden, D., and Prior, D. B., eds., Slope instability: New York, John Wiley & Sons, p. 257–361.

Lahr, P. C., 1982, A study of debris flows and investigation of debris flow theories (B. S. report): San Luis Obispo, California Polytechnic State University, 64 p.

Lambe, T. W., and Whitman, R. V., 1969, Soil mechanics: New York, John Wiley & Sons, 553 p.

Morton, D. M., and Campbell, R. H., 1974, Spring mudflows at Wrightwood, southern California: Quarterly Journal of Engineering Geology, v. 7, no. 4, p. 377–384.

Pierson, T. C., 1981, Dominant particle support mechanisms in debris flows at Mt. Thomas, New Zealand, and implications for flow mobility: Sedimentology, v. 28, no. 1, p. 49–60.

Poulos, S. J., 1981, The steady state of deformation: American Society of Civil Engineers Proceedings, Geotechnical Engineering Division Journal, v. 107, no. GT5, p. 553–562.

Poulos, S. J., Castro, G., and France, J. W., 1985, Liquefaction evaluation procedure: Journal of Geotechnical Engineering, v. 11, no. 6, p. 772–791.

Rodine, J. D., 1974, Analysis of the mobilization of debris flows (Ph.D. thesis): Stanford, California, Stanford University, 226 p.

Sassa, K., 1984, The mechanism starting liquefied landslides and debris flows, *in* Proceedings, International Symposium on Landslides, 4th, Toronto: Ontario, Canadian Geotechnical Society, v. 2, p. 349–354.

Schofield, A. N., and Wroth, C. P., 1968, Critical state soil mechanics: London, McGraw-Hill, 310 p.

Seed, H. B., Woodward, R. S., and Lundgren, R., 1964, Fundamental aspects of the Atterberg limits: American Society of Civil Engineers Proceedings, Soil Mechanics and Foundations Division Journal, v. 90, no. SM6, p. 75–105.

Varnes, D. J., 1978, Slope movement types and processes, *in* Schuster, R. L., and Krizek, R. J., eds., Landslides; Analysis and control: Washington, D.C., National Academy of Sciences, National Research Council, Transportation Research Board Special Report 176, p. 11–33.

MANUSCRIPT ACCEPTED BY THE SOCIETY DECEMBER 29, 1986

Geological Society of America
Reviews in Engineering Geology, Volume VII
1987

The mechanics of large rock avalanches

H. Jay Melosh
Lunar and Planetary Laboratory and
Geosciences Department
University of Arizona
Tucson, Arizona 85721

ABSTRACT

Very large rock avalanches, involving more than about 10^6 m^3 of rock debris, exhibit anomalously low coefficients of friction. Consequently they travel much farther than conventional slope-stability criteria predict. Such long-runout landslides (*sturzstrom*) include the catastrophic Elm (1881), Frank (1903), and Sherman Glacier (1964) events. Attempts to explain this behavior have considered water or air lubrication, local steam generation, or even the formation of melt layers within the rock debris. Discovery of deposits of such landslides on Mars and the moon, however, appears to rule out the fundamental involvement of volatiles or atmospheric gases in the flow mechanism.

It appears that large, high-frequency pressure fluctuations due to irregularities in the flow of the debris may locally relieve overburden stresses in the rock mass and allow rapid pseudoviscous flow of even dry rock debris. If the avalanche volume is large enough, the rate of production of this vibrational (acoustic) energy exceeds its loss rate, and sustained motion is possible. Small-scale laboratory experiments have verified theoretical predictions of the rheology of such acoustically fluidized debris. This rheology is consistent with the rate and pattern of observed large rock avalanches. Although much work remains to be done, acoustic fluidization is the most plausible explanation of the fluidity of large, dry debris avalanches.

INTRODUCTION

Small landslides and debris flows are familiar surficial processes. The mechanics of such mass movements are generally well understood in terms of the balance between gravity and material strength or inertia and friction. However, there is a class of very large landslides, or, technically, rock avalanches, that do not obey normal rules relating the total vertical drop to the distance of forward horizontal travel. These avalanches travel extraordinarily far for their vertical fall and are even capable of climbing slopes and topping ridges in their paths. They move as if the coefficient of friction that usually regulates rock avalanches is temporarily reduced by an order of magnitude or more.

The first written observation of the fluidity of large rock avalanches occurred in September, 1881, when the Swiss village of Elm was nearly obliterated by an enormous rockfall that came from a slate quarry upslope of the village. In the aftermath of this disaster, geologist Albert Heim (see Hsu, 1978) noted that 10^7 m^3 of apparently dry debris had flowed down an average slope of only 17° at a speed of about 45 m/sec. Heim emphasized that the

debris *flowed* down the slope, although more recent investigations have suggested that the motion of such avalanches is more similar to sliding than flowing. A very similar rock avalanche in 1903 wiped out the town of Frank, in Alberta, Canada (McConnell and Brock, 1904). The debris mass at Frank traveled 4 km horizontally after an initial 1,000-m fall down the steep slope of Turtle Mountain, then rose 130 m upslope on the opposite side of the valley.

Since their initial recognition by Heim, highly fluidized rock avalanches (long-runout landslides, or *sturzstrom*) have been widely recognized in nearly all mountainous areas on earth. Until recently, the largest known terrestrial avalanche was the Siadmarreh landslip in Iran (Harrison and Falcon, 1937), with a volume estimated at 2×10^{10} m^3 and a runout of 15 km. Recent investigations, however, have revealed a somewhat larger prehistoric debris avalanche at the foot of Mt. Shasta, California, in which 2.6×10^{10} m^3 of debris traveled 43 km from its source (Crandell and others, 1984). A smaller ancient avalanche (1.5×10^{10} m^3), also associated with a volcano, has been reported in Chile (Francis and others, 1985).

The cause of the fluidity of these avalanches is still unclear. In a very detailed study of the prehistoric Blackhawk slide, Shreve (1968), was impressed by the preservation of the source area's stratigraphy far out in the slide lobe. The same three units occurring in the source area (the Furnace Limestone; a green, chloritized gneiss; and the Old Woman Sandstone) can be found outcropping near the edge of the slide, fractured and greatly attenuated, but still distinct. Shreve concluded that the Blackhawk must have slid, not flowed, to its present location 9.5 km from its probable source, and that the slide simply thinned as it spread out. He proposed that the slide moved by trapping a pocket of air beneath it during its initial fall, then rode the compressed air layer "hovercraft"-style down the gently sloping fan surface away from the mountain front. This mode of motion permits the slide to travel as a coherent body and avoids internal shearing that might mix the various stratigraphic horizons.

Shreve's mechanism is no longer widely accepted, partly because of the difficulty of trapping a pocket of air beneath the slide, even where a "launching ramp" is available. This is partly because the permeabilities required to trap the air are implausibly low for nearly all observed slides (Erismann, 1979), and, perhaps most significantly, because very similar rock avalanche deposits have been seen on Mars (Lucchitta, 1978, 1979), where the atmospheric pressure is only 0.1 percent that of earth, and on the moon (Howard, 1973), where neither air nor water is present. Several examples are shown in Figure 1. This is not to say that air blasts are not a part of large terrestrial rock avalanches; Heim (1882) amassed considerable evidence that air blasts are locally important. However, such blasts are an inevitable accompaniment of large masses of solid debris that move rapidly and displace the air. It seems likely that the presence of air or water in the moving debris will facilitate fluidization and enhance its mobility. Nevertheless, the occurrence of fluidized lunar rock avalanches indicates that neither air nor water is *required* to cause fluidization. This observation places severe constraints on any mechanism proposed to account for the mobility of large masses of rock debris.

Note that the major problem in understanding these rock avalanches is not their initiation: the event that triggered long-runout avalanches, when it can be determined, is always one of the many recognized situations that start conventional avalanches or landslides (see, for example, Varnes, 1978). Thus, the Sherman rockfall (Shreve, 1966; McSaveney, 1978) was initiated by the 1964 Good Friday earthquake in Alaska and the Elm and Frank slides were caused by workers undermining steep slopes. The Shasta and Chilean avalanches may have been initiated by volcanic eruptions, just as the avalanches accompanying the May 18, 1980, eruption of Mt. St. Helens began. Interestingly, there are few records of large rock avalanches initiated by heavy rainfall.

A nascent long-runout event appears to start as an ordinary, although large, landslide. The falling debris first travels down a steep slope, picking up speed over an initial fall of several hundred to 1,000 m (see the excellent descriptions of earthquake-triggered rockslides by Eisbacher, 1979). Only after this initial stage does the behavior of the debris become remarkable. Sufficiently large volumes of rock debris may then travel great distances from the foot of the initial steep slope. There is a general correlation between the volume of the debris mass (or, nearly equivalently, the potential energy lost in the fall) and the distance the debris travels.

Figure 2 illustrates this correlation for a number of large terrestrial and a few extraterrestrial rock avalanches. In this figure the "coefficient of friction," that is, the ratio between the total vertical drop, H (rim of scarp to tip of avalanche deposit), and the distance traveled, L, is plotted versus the estimated volume of the deposit. The points in the figure show a great deal of scatter that is accounted for by varying conditions of flow (some flows are tightly confined in valleys, others spread out freely, and still others are halted by an upslope run), material, and other special conditions. (For example, the Sherman rock avalanche slid across an ice surface for much of its flow, and the volcanic examples may have had an initial velocity boost from expanding gases.)

A coefficient of friction near 0.5 is normal for small avalanches and rockfalls. However, if the volume of debris exceeds about 10^6 m^3, the coefficient declines, dropping to less than 0.1 in the largest events. This size- or scale-dependence must be explained by any successful theory of the fluidization mechanism. Unfortunately, since only very large avalanches exhibit low coefficients of friction, the phenomenon is both difficult to observe and to instrument scientifically. Theories of their movement mechanisms involve a certain amount of guesswork.

PROPOSED MECHANISMS

The air lubrication hypothesis of Shreve (1968) has already been discussed. A number of other mechanisms have been proposed to account for the mobility of large rock avalanches. The following discussion is not exhaustive; it considers some of the most plausible alternatives prior to a discussion of the mechanism I favor.

Goguel (1978) suggested that frictional heating in large landslides might vaporize small amounts of included water and that the resulting steam could fluidize the debris mass. Although this mechanism might explain why only large slides become fluidized, it cannot account for lunar landslides where no water at all is present. Like Shreve's, Goguel's mechanism also requires an implausibly low permeability of the moving debris to confine the lubricating fluid.

In his study of the Koefels landslide and its included glassy layers, Erismann (1979) proposed that frictional heat might even melt rock debris near the sole of the slide. The slide would then glide on a thin layer of melt, thus attaining a high mobility. This mechanism has some difficulty explaining slides in predominantly carbonate rock, such as the Swiss Flims slide, since carbonates do not melt. However, Erismann suggested that the CO_2 produced by thermal dissociation of the carbonate also fluidizes these slides.

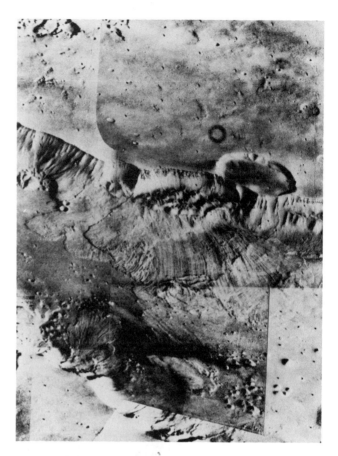

Figure 1. Large rock avalanche deposits on three planets. Left top photo (K642-108 by A. Post) is of Sherman landslide that flowed 5 km across glacier after 1964 Alaskan earthquake. Top right photo (Viking Orbiter mosaic 14A27-32) depicts rock avalanche on Mars that traveled 60 km across floor of Valles Marineris. Left bottom photo (AS17-2608) shows lunar landslide that slid 80 km from farside crater Tsilokovsky.

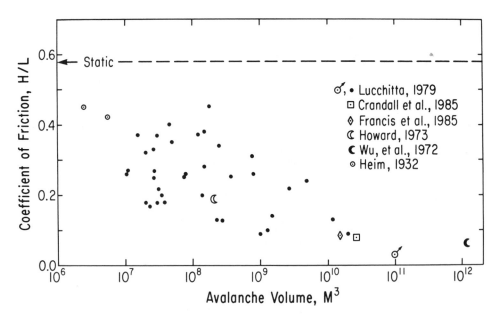

Figure 2. Coefficient of friction, *H/L,* plotted versus avalanche volume for many terrestrial rock avalanches, Martian avalanche (Fig. 1, center), and two lunar rockslides. Extraterrestrial points fit easily within scatter of terrestrial data, indicating probable similarity of mechanism.

This mechanism suffers from the common problem of all proposals involving vapor—that the flowing slide debris must have an uncommonly low permeability. Although there is little doubt that friction can produce small amounts of melt in large landslides (it is found in both the Koefels slide and in a large landslide in central Nepal: Heuberger and others, 1984), it is not found in other large slides, such as the Blackhawk. In the Blackhawk slide, the lowermost breccia unit is well exposed, but no glass layers or fragments are reported, nor is glass found in the clastic dikes that apparently originate in the basal zone and cut through the slide mass (Johnson, 1978). These dikes are particularly significant, as they sometimes incorporate material from the alluvial fan surface over which the Blackhawk landslide slid.

Another class of theories begins with Bagnold's (1956) theory of the flow of cohesionless grains in fluids (e.g., McSaveney, 1978). In these theories the rocks in a moving debris avalanche are likened to the molecules in a gas. It is supposed that the weight of the debris in the slide is supported by numerous impacts of rock fragments with each other throughout the slide. Shearing takes place within this fluidized region and the avalanche moves rapidly downhill. Hsu (1975) suggested that fine dust in the slide might additionally play the role of a fluid, surrounding and partially supporting the larger rock fragments. Although Bagnold's "dispersive grain stresses" do exist and can be verified experimentally (Bagnold, 1954), it is unclear that this phenomenon can actually lower the coefficient of friction in large rock avalanches. Experiments on rapid dry grain flows (Savage, 1979; Hui and Haff, 1986) show the development of expanded layers were dispersive flow may occur, but the sliding always takes place near

the angle of repose of the granular material, not well below it. Bagnold himself (1954) recognized that dispersive stresses could lower the coefficient of friction by a factor of two at most. This is supported by Savage's (1983) and Hanes and Inman's (1985) experiments on rapid granular flow. These experiments demonstrated that the internal friction in a rapidly flowing granular aggregate is actually *higher* than static friction.

The reason that Bagnold grain flow has difficulty explaining the fluidity of large dry rock avalanches is that rock fragments, unlike molecules in a gas, dissipate energy when they collide. This dissipation is so rapid that the gravitational potential energy gained as the avalanche falls is inadequate to keep the rock fragments moving fast enough to support the slide (see Melosh, 1983).

On the positive side, Bagnold grain flow can operate independent of the presence of gases or liquids. However, it does not explain the size dependence of the coefficient of friction, its small observed value, nor the tendency of large rock avalanches to slide, not flow.

ACOUSTIC FLUIDIZATION

Acoustic fluidization of large rock avalanches is a recently proposed process (Melosh, 1979). This possible explanation of the mobility of large rock avalanches is similar to Bagnold grain flow because it supposes that the weight of the rock mass is supported by random motions within the debris. It differs because the random movement is not that of individual rock fragments, but of groups of fragments organized into elastic waves. Since

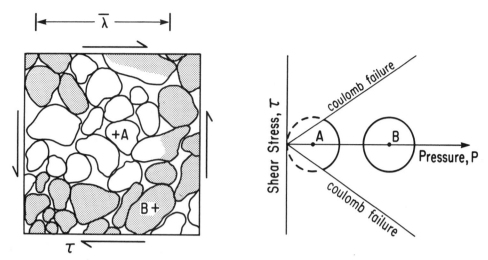

Figure 3. Basis of acoustic fluidization mechanism. Left panel schematically illustrates region near base of flowing rockslide; shear stress, τ, acts across this volume that contains many fragments of rock debris. Acoustic wave (elastic wave transmitted through contacts of one rock with another) of mean wavelength, λ, passes through debris. Rock fragments in compression are shaded, and fragments in extension are light. Wavelength is larger than size of an individual fragment. Right panel is Mohr diagram of stresses in rock mass on which are superposed Coulomb failure lines. Stress at point B in rock mass is well within failure envelope. At point A, stresses intersect failure envelope and sliding takes place, allowing plastic strain to accumulate. This failure is dynamic; stresses change rapidly with time as compressions and rarefactions shift through rock mass, eventually allowing entire mass to slide.

rock fragments seldom lose contact with one another, this process dissipates energy at a far lower rate than grain flow.

A strong acoustic field fluidizes rock debris not by altering the Coulomb friction law that normally relates shear stress at failure to overburden stress, but by relieving the overburden. The pressure in a small volume of the debris (a region smaller than the acoustic wavelength but larger than a rock fragment) fluctuates between much less than the static overburden pressure and much more. Its average, however, must equal the static overburden. During the times when the pressure is low, the rock debris in a limited region can slide under a shear stress much lower than possible with the static overburden (Fig. 3). The frequent occurrence of failure events of this type results in a creep-like motion of the rock debris in response to small shear stresses. During the times when the pressure in some region is larger than average, the rock debris there simply does not slide. Instead, it accumulates elastic strain from the general motion of the entire rock mass that will be released in the next failure event. A portion of the elastic energy liberated by this failure contributes to the acoustic field and thus continues the process of flow.

Figure 4 schematically illustrates the difference between a debris mass at rest, a mass that is acoustically fluidized, and one undergoing dispersive grain flow. It is clear from this figure that acoustic fluidization and Bagnold dispersive grain flow are closely related. As the acoustic field becomes stronger, individual grains spend less of their time moving together as parts of an elastic wave and more time colliding as individual rocks. Dispersive

grain flow is thus the high-energy end member of acoustically fluidized debris. Acoustic fluidization is similar to the liquid state of matter in which flow may occur in response to very small shear stresses, even though the fluid's constituent particles seldom lose contact with one another. A rapidly flowing debris mass is more likely to flow in the low-energy "liquid" regime than the high-energy "vapor" regime because energy dissipation is so intense that the higher energy levels may never be attained.

Acoustic fluidization was originally proposed to account for the collapse of impact craters on the moon and elsewhere in the solar system (Melosh, 1979). Gravity-driven crater slumping is observed in large craters (greater than a 15-km diameter on the moon) in spite of their relatively shallow average internal slopes of only 20°, less than the angle of repose of rock debris. McKinnon (1978) showed that the observed deep-seated collapse implies internal coefficients of friction smaller than 0.03 (2° angle of internal friction), similar to those observed in large rock avalanches.

In crater collapse it is believed that the shock wave that excavates the crater leaves a strong random acoustic field of scattered wave energy behind in the debris surrounding the newly formed crater. This acoustic field has been directly observed in explosion cratering tests (Gaffney and Melosh, 1982). The acoustic energy fluidizes the surrounding debris, as predicted by theory (Melosh, 1979) and observed experimentally (Goetz and Melosh, 1980), allowing the crater to collapse if it is large enough to retain the acoustic energy for longer than its gravity collapse time. This

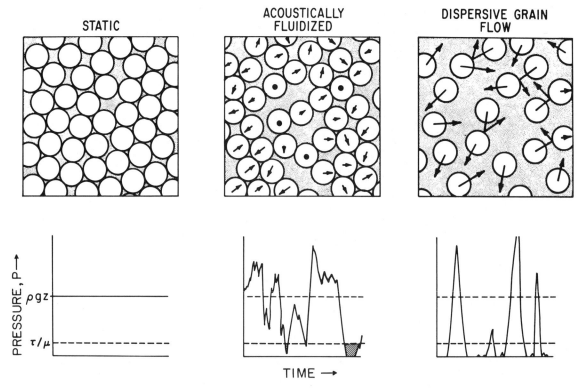

Figure 4. Schematic illustration of relation between static rock mass, acoustic fluidization, and Bagnold dispersive grain flow. Pressure in static rock mass is constant with time; overburden is supported by elastic deformation of rock fragments. Dashed line in this frame is pressure at which sliding may begin, τ/μ, where μ is coefficient of friction. In acoustically fluidized debris, rocks seldom lose contact, but pressure fluctuates about mean overburden value, occasionally becoming low enough for sliding to occur (shaded area on pressure-time plot below). Rock fragments undergoing dispersive grain flow are seldom in contact and their impacts produce large, rare, excursions in pressure. Adapted from Melosh (1983).

scenario is in good agreement with the extraterrestrial crater observations (Melosh and Gaffney, 1983).

Large rock avalanches may acquire large amounts of random acoustic energy during their initial fall down a steep slope. Movement of the rock debris over an irregular surface causes internal jostling that propagates as elastic waves. As in crater collapse, this acoustic energy may fluidize the rock debris and allow continued, rapid flow. Because pressure is transmitted by elastic waves, not rock collisions, far less energy is dissipated than by Bagnold dispersive grain flow. Nevertheless, the acoustic energy is dissipated, and it must be regenerated for flow to continue over long distances.

The ultimate sources of energy in the moving debris are the kinetic energy from the initial fall and the gravitational potential energy acquired during subsequent downslope motion. Some of this energy is converted into acoustic energy as the rock mass moves. The acoustic energy then facilitates the motion, regenerating itself in the process. Acoustic energy is lost in one of two ways: either it is absorbed internally and converted to heat, or it

leaks out the bottom (and, less importantly, the top and sides) of the debris mass. This latter loss process is particularly important in small slides, in which the surface-to-volume ratio is high. This may account for the lack of fluidization in small rock avalanches: the acoustic field simply cannot build up to the point where it causes great mobility. Larger avalanches lose a proportionately smaller amount of acoustic energy by leakage, and are therefore limited only by internal dissipation.

The observed tendency of large rock avalanches to slide without much internal deformation is explained by the power-law rheology induced by acoustic fluidization. Figure 5 illustrates some of the experimental results of Goetz (1981) on a normalized plot of the theoretical flow law from Melosh and Gaffney (1983). The experimental data define a relationship in which the strain rate is proportional to the stress to the eighth power. As is well known from glaciology (e.g., Paterson, 1969, ch. 6), power-law flows concentrate shear near the base of the moving mass. With a power of eight, one-half the total shear is concentrated in the lower 7.4 percent of the moving debris. The geologic appearance of the avalanche deposit thus suggests sliding on a thin basal zone, not penetrative flow.

This basal zone is very active, in contrast to the overlying debris mass. Strain rates are high in this layer, and nearly all the shear is concentrated here. This is where most acoustic energy is generated and its energy density is highest. Scattering of acoustic energy is intense. Small amounts of the underlying ground surface may be incorporated here and mixed with the laterally transported rock debris.

CONCLUSIONS

Acoustic fluidization is the most plausible explanation for large, highly mobile rock avalanches. Its actual operation in these events, however, has yet to be proved. Large rock avalanches are so rare and difficult to predict that we do not yet have detailed instrumental observations of any during their runout. Arguments about the mechanism must center around the theoretical possibilities and the study of the deposits. Unfortunately, all of the proposed mechanisms involve processes that take place only during flow or sliding and then dissipate, leaving little or no direct evidence of their existence.

Perhaps the easiest hypothesis to prove (or disprove) is that of melt lubrication, since the glass layer should still be present at the base of the avalanche deposit, possibly accessible to drilling. However, glass is seldom reported in the geologic investigation of large landslides, and its occurrence in the Koefels and central Nepalese slides may be exceptional.

Other hypotheses that involve transient air or vapor fluidization are more difficult to test, as are Bagnold dispersive grain flow and its variants. All of these proposals, however, fail (or seem to fail) to explain all the observed facts. Air lubrication founders on the observation of Martian and lunar fluidized rock avalanches, and vapor fluidization cannot operate on the moon. Grain flow mechanisms are the most attractive explanations in light of these extraterrestrial avalanches, but neither theoretical study nor laboratory observation of small-scale grain flows supports a large reduction in the coefficient of friction, nor do they suggest how large rock avalanches can behave differently from small-scale flows.

Acoustic fluidization seems uniquely capable of explaining the facts. The high power-law rheology of acoustically fluidized debris accounts for the frequent observation that large rock avalanches slide, preserving gross stratigraphic relations in the debris mass. It accounts naturally for the scale-dependence of large avalanches, since acoustic energy is lost too easily from small volumes of debris due to their large surface-to-volume ratio. Acoustic waves are transmitted from one rock fragment to another elastically and need no gas or liquid medium to carry them. Acoustic fluidization is thus capable of operating in a complete vacuum, although the presence of a fluid probably enhances the flow.

Figure 6 illustrates schematically how acoustic energy might build up during the initial collapse of a steep slope, producing a

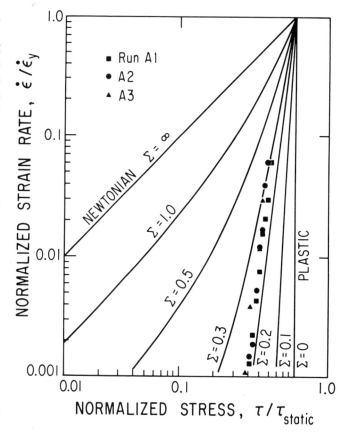

Figure 5. Experimental results versus theoretical predictions of relation between stress, τ, and strain rate, $\dot{\epsilon}$, in acoustically fluidized sand. Acoustically fluidized flow is highly non-Newtonian. $\dot{\epsilon}_y$ is strain rate at stress equal to static yield stress τ_{static}. Σ is ratio between mean pressure fluctuation and overburden. After Melosh and Gaffney (1983).

fluidized debris mass that is capable of traveling down low slopes and even running uphill. Acoustic energy generated in the zone of high shear strain near the base of the moving mass more than balances the acoustic energy losses as the flow spreads out. Eventually the flow becomes so thin that a favorable balance can no longer be maintained and the motion comes to a halt.

In spite of these similarities to the characteristics of observed large rock avalanches, however, neither acoustic fluidization nor any other proposed mechanism for explaining the low coefficient of friction in large rock avalanches is proved. The ultimate test of our theories may await the detailed instrumental study of an actual large rock avalanche. The different hypotheses may at least suggest what kinds of instruments could be most useful. The major difficulty in such an enterprise is predicting the occurrence of an avalanche. However, as the population in mountainous areas rises, the possibility of a reliable prediction increases. The Swiss prediction of the 1973 ice avalanche from the Weisshorn is a prototype of this kind of activity.

Progress on acoustic fluidization can also be made in the

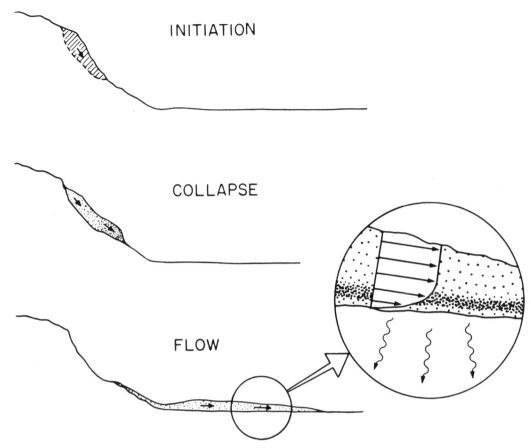

Figure 6. Schematic illustration of events in large rock avalanche on hypothesis of acoustic fluidization. After initiation, rock debris moves down steep slope, increasing its acoustic energy content. If this energy becomes large enough, rock mass may fluidize and continue to flow down low slopes. Inset illustrates velocity profile expected for highly non-Newtonian flow. Stipple density represents acoustic energy density as largest in basal layer where it is generated. Wavy arrows denote loss of acoustic energy to substrate. After Melosh (1983).

laboratory. The details of the flow law of acoustically fluidized debris must still be worked out. More importantly, the energetics of this process are still largely unknown experimentally. Although theory predicts that energy losses are lower than for dispersive grain flow, this is not yet experimentally verified. Study of scattering and absorption of acoustic energy in granular debris may indicate how likely the acoustic field is to regenerate itself during flow and allow estimates of how large a debris mass must be before it fluidizes under various conditions of fluid saturation, grain size, and initial velocity. These results may also aid in predicting the reach of large rock avalanches, once fluidization is established.

The fluidization of large rock avalanches is interesting both from the purely scientific point of view and for the practical reason that human lives and structures may be threatened by debris masses that travel much farther than expected. This fluidization is clearly a geologic fact that affects the surfaces of all terrestrial planets. Understanding the nature of this process promises to be a challenging but fruitful undertaking.

ACKNOWLEDGMENT

Research on the mechanics of impact crater collapse and large rock avalanches has been funded by the Planetary Geology and Geophysics program of the National Aeronautics and Space Administration, grant NASW-428.

REFERENCES CITED

Bagnold, R. A., 1954, Experiments on a gravity-free dispersion of large solid spheres in a Newtonian fluid under shear: Proceedings of the Royal Society of London, A, v. 225, p. 49–63.
—— , 1956, The flow of cohesionless grains in fluids: Philosophical Transactions of the Royal Society of London, A, v. 249, p. 235–297.
Crandell, D. R., Miller, C. D., Glicken, H. X., Christiansen, R. L., and Newhall, G. G., 1984, Catastrophic debris avalanche from ancestral Mount Shasta Volcano, California: Geology, v. 12, p. 143–146.
Eisbacher, G. H., 1979, Cliff collapse and rock avalanches (sturzstroms) in the MacKenzie Mountains, Northwestern Canada: Canadian Geotechnical Journal, v. 16, p. 309–334.

Erismann, T. H., 1979, Mechanisms of large landslides: Rock Mechanics, v. 12, p. 15–46.

Francis, P. W., Gardeweg, M., Ramirez, C. F., and Rothery, D. A., 1985, Catastrophic debris avalanche deposit of Socompa volcano, northern Chile: Geology, v. 13, p. 600–603.

Gaffney, E. S., and Melosh, H. J., 1982, Noise and target strength degradation accompanying shallow-buried explosions: Journal of Geophysical Research, v. 87, p. 1871–1879.

Goetz, P. C., 1981, Systematics of the acoustic fluidization mechanism and its application to catastrophic landslides [M.S. thesis]: State University of New York at Stony Brook, 81 p.

Goetz, P., and Melosh, H. J., 1980, Experimental observation of acoustic fluidization in sand: EOS Transactions of the American Geophysical Union, v. 61, p. 373.

Goguel, J., 1978, Scale-dependent rockslide mechanisms, with emphasis on the role of pore fluid vaporization, *in* Voight, B., eds., Rockslides and avalanches, v. 1; Natural phenomena: Amsterdam, Elsevier, p. 693–705.

Hanes, D. M., and Inman, D. L., 1985, Observations of rapidly flowing granular-fluid materials: Journal of Fluid Mechanics, v. 150, p. 357–380.

Harrison, J. V., and Falcon, N. L., 1937, The Siadmarreh landslip, southern Iran: Geographical Journal, v. 89, p. 42–47.

Heim, A., 1882, Der Bergsturz von Elm: Zeitschrift der Deutschen geologischen gesellschaft, v. 34, p. 74–115.

—— , 1932, Bergsturz und Menschleben: Zurich, Fretz and Wasmuth, 218 p.

Heuberger, H., Masch, L. Preuss, E., and Schrocker, A., 1984, Quaternary landslides and rock fusion in central Nepal and in the Tyrolean Alps: Mountain Research and Development, v. 4, p. 345–362.

Howard, K. A., 1973, Avalanche mode of motion; Implications from lunar examples: Science, v. 180, p. 1052–1055.

Hsu, K. J., 1975, Catastrophic debris streams (sturzstroms) generated by rockfalls: Geological Society of America Bulletin, v. 86, p. 129–140.

—— , 1978, Albert Heim; Observations on landslides and relevance to modern interpretations, *in* Voight, B., ed., Rockslides and avalanches, v. 1; Natural phenomena: Amsterdam, Elsevier, p. 71–93.

Hui, K., and Haff, P. K., 1986, Kinetic grain flow in a vertical channel: International Journal of Multiphase Flow, v. 12, p. 289–298.

Johnson, B., 1978, Blackhawk Landslide, California, *in* Voight, B., ed., Rockslides and avalanches, v. 1; Natural phenomena: Amsterdam, Elsevier, p. 481–504.

Lucchitta, B. K., 1978, A large landslide on Mars: Geological Society of America Bulletin, v. 89, p. 1601–1609.

—— , 1979, Landslides in Valles Marineris, Mars: Journal of Geophysical Research, v. 84, p. 8097–8113.

McConnell, R. G., and Brock, R. W., 1904, The great landslide at Frank, Alberta: Canadian Department of the Interior Annual Report 1902–1903, pt. 8, Report of the Superintendent of Mines, Appendix, 17 p.

McKinnon, W. B., 1978, An investigation into the role of plastic failure in crater modification; Proceedings of the Lunar and Planetary Science Conference, 9th: Geochimica et Cosmochimica Acta, suppl. 10, p. 3965–3973.

McSaveney, M. J., 1978, Sherman Glacier rock avalanche, Alaska, U.S.A., *in* Voight, B., ed., Rockslides and avalanches, v. 1; Natural Phenomena: Amsterdam, Elsevier, p. 197–258.

Melosh, H. J., 1979, Acoustic fluidization; A new geologic process?: Journal of Geophysical Research, v. 84, p. 7513–7520.

—— , 1983, Acoustic fluidization: American Scientist, v. 71, p. 158–165.

Melosh, H. J., and Gaffney, E. S., 1983, Acoustic fluidization and the scale dependence of impact crater morphology: Journal of Geophysical Research, v. 88, suppl. A, p. 830–834.

Paterson, W.S.B., 1969, The physics of glaciers: New York, Pergamon Press, 250 p.

Savage, S. B., 1979, Gravity flow of cohesionless granular materials in chutes and channels: Journal of Fluid Mechanics, v. 92, p. 53–96.

—— , 1983, Granular flows at high strain rates, *in* Theory of dispersed multiphase flow: New York, Academic Press, p. 339–358.

Shreve, R. L., 1966, Sherman landslide, Alaska: Science, v. 154, p. 1639–1643.

—— , 1968, The Blackhawk landslide: Geological Society of America Special Paper 108, 47 p.

Varnes, D. J., 1978, Slope movement types and processes, *in* Schuster, R. L., and Krizek, R. J., eds., Landslides; Analysis and control: Washington, D.C., Transportation Research Board, Natural Research Council, National Academy of Science Special Report 176.

Wu, S.S.C., Photogrammetry of Apollo 15 photography: Apollo 15 Preliminary science report, NASA SP-289, p. 25–43.

MANUSCRIPT ACCEPTED BY THE SOCIETY DECEMBER 29, 1986

Printed in U.S.A.

Geological Society of America
Reviews in Engineering Geology, Volume VII
1987

The importance of lahar initiation processes

*Lee H. Fairchild**
Department of Geological Sciences
University of Washington
Seattle, Washington 98195

ABSTRACT

There were two lahars that reached the Toutle River during the eruption of Mount St. Helens, Washington, on May 18, 1980. The North Fork lahar was much larger than the South Fork lahar, had a much more rectangular hydrograph shape, and was much more destructive. Hydrographs (graphs of discharge versus time) constructed for both lahars demonstrate that differences between the lahars existed as close to the lahar sources as measurements were made, indicating that differences in processes that initiated the lahars must have been responsible for observed disparities between the lahars.

The South Fork lahar was apparently generated when a laterally directed pyroclastic cloud triggered slab snow avalanches, and then rapidly incorporated and melted the snow. The North Fork lahar was generated from a small portion of avalanche debris in which ice was comminuted to an abnormally small size. This ice melted rapidly and saturated the host avalanche debris, which then liquefied during a long harmonic tremor event.

The North Fork lahar differed greatly from the South Fork lahar because of significant dissimilarities between the pyroclastic cloud and harmonic tremor sequence that were directly responsible for the characteristics of each lahar. Because differences in lahar characteristics were ultimately responsible for the contrast in destructiveness, I have concluded that the process of initiation is an extremely important factor controlling downchannel destruction. The importance of initiation must be accounted for in the quantitative analysis of lahar hazard.

INTRODUCTION

My studies of lahars at Mount St. Helens, Washington, have established that lahar characteristics and destructive potential—and how these change as the lahar moves downvalley—strongly depend on the process of lahar initiation. Important characteristics that were influenced by initiation include water content, sediment-size distribution, and properties represented by hydrographs, comprising lahar duration, volume, peak discharge (and indirectly the peak stage), and hydrograph shape.

The importance of initiation was recognized when significant differences were identified between two lahars that flowed down the Toutle River on May 18, 1980, and linked to dissimilarities in the initiation of the lahars. Hydrographs reconstructed for each lahar demonstrate that the lahars were very different (as

was the destructiveness of each). These dissimilarities were identified in the hydrographs closest to the areas of initiation of each lahar, suggesting that initiation processes were responsible for the observed disparity between the lahars. Detailed studies documented aspects of the initiation process that were responsible for the contrast in lahar characteristics and destructiveness.

By recognizing the importance of initiation processes, it is now understood that volcanic hazards, and the impact of lahars on engineering structures downvalley, cannot be accurately evaluated without an adequate understanding of the processes that generate lahars. Until now, initiation processes have not received the attention they deserve (Fairchild, 1987, in press).

In this paper, evidence demonstrating the importance of initiation is reviewed, and an explanation of how initiation processes were responsible for the observed dissimilarities between the lahars is postulated. The differences in destructive potential and

---

*Present address: Exxon Production Research Company, P.O. Box 2189, Houston, Texas 77252-2189.

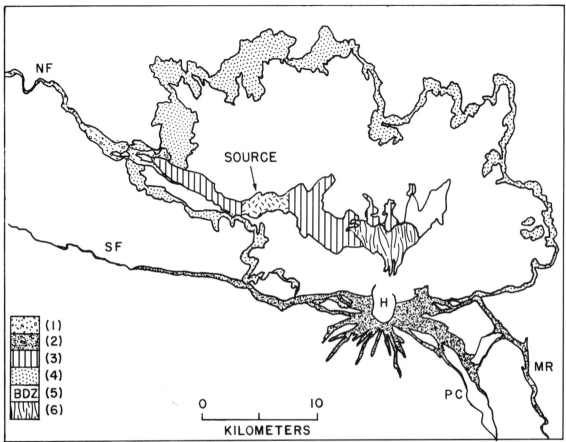

Figure 1. Generalized map of products of May 18, 1980, eruption of Mount St. Helens, Washington. Key to diagram: (1) indicates area inundated by the North Fork lahar, (2), area inundated by early lahars (including South Fork lahar), (3), debris deposited by the avalanches, (4), zone singed by the lateral blast, (5), blow-down and blast zone of the lateral blast, (6), deposits from pumiceous pyroclastic flows. NF indicates North Fork Toutle River; SF, South Fork Toutle River; H, amphitheater of Mount St. Helens; PC, Pine Creek; MC, Muddy River. Adapted from Lipman and Mullineaux (1981).

hydrograph characteristics are emphasized. Fairchild (1985) discussed in detail the differences in the sediment deposited by lahars. This chapter represents an overview rather than an exhaustive review of either the reconstructed hydrographs or initiation processes, which are both discussed by Fairchild (1985).

The two lahars that flowed down the Toutle River were part of a complex sequence of events during the eruption on May 18, 1980. The eruption began at approximately 0832 PDT, when a large earthquake triggered a series of landslides, which deposited unconsolidated volcanic debris 25 to 150 m thick in the upper 22 km of the North Fork Toutle River (Fig. 1). The landslides were accompanied by a laterally directed pyroclastic cloud which traveled rapidly in a 180° arc centered to the north, and damaged 525 km^2 of forested, mountainous terrain. At approximately 0834 PDT, the cloud overtopped the summit of Mount St. Helens and flowed down the west and east flanks of the volcano. At this time, lahars were generated in the Pine Creek, Muddy River, and South Fork Toutle River drainages (Fig. 1).

After the initial earthquake and laterally directed eruption, seismicity returned to background levels, and the volcano settled into a steady, energetic, vertical eruption phase that continued until approximately 1140 PDT. During this time little or no juvenile magma was erupted, nor were any new lahars or pyroclastic events observed. At approximately 1140 PDT, juvenile magma was first erupted. It was accompanied by harmonic tremors generated by the upward movement of magma. The harmonic tremors and eruption of juvenile magma continued until approximately 1730 PDT, when the energy of the eruption declined sharply, and seismicity returned to background levels. Pumiceous pyroclastic flows collapsing from the eruptive column were observed during most of the time that juvenile magma was erupted. Most of them flowed northward out of the ampitheater as far as 5 km from Mount St. Helens (Fig. 1), but some small flows also traveled down the west, south, and east flanks of the volcano. Some of these flows generated very small lahars, but none was large enough to be of great consequence.

The North Fork Toutle River lahar was unique because it did not begin to move downvalley until approximately 1310 PDT, more than 4.5 hr after the eruption started. It was an extremely long and large lahar that lasted until approximately 2120 PDT at its source. The South Fork lahar, which was generated in the early minutes of the eruption, and the North Fork lahar are the subjects of this paper.

DIFFERENCES IN LAHAR CHARACTERISTICS AND DESTRUCTIVENESS

Characteristics of Constructed Hydrographs

Hydrographs (using the term here to refer to a graph of discharge vs. time, for mud rather than water), which provide a convenient means of describing the lahars, can be constructed at locations where four of the following five variables can be determined: (1) peak discharge (Q_{pk}), (2) lahar volume, and the times of lahar (3) arrival, (4) peak, and (5) termination (Fig. 2).

Superelevations of the lahar surface as the lahar flowed around channel bends were reconstructed from surveys of channel bends and the mudlines preserved on channel walls. These surveys provided the information required to compute the cross-sectionally averaged velocity of the lahar at peak flow (Smith and McLean, 1984; Fairchild, 1985),

$$U = [(R(\Delta h)g)/\omega]^{0.5}, \qquad (1)$$

where R is the channel radius at the channel centerline, Δh is the mudline superelevation, ω is the channel width, and g is gravitational acceleration. The peak discharges needed to reconstruct hydrographs were computed from the product of these average velocities and surveyed cross-sectional areas of the lahar.

Times of arrival, peak, and termination of the lahar were reconstructed at hydrograph locations primarily from eye-witness observations compiled by Cummans (1981a,b). At most locations, all of the necessary times were not available, so that flow volume had to be calculated independently to provide enough information for hydrograph construction. Measurements of the volume of all debris deposited and eroded by each lahar allowed computation of the net change of lahar volume for any specified reach. Once lahar volume was established at one location, the deposit volume data were used to determine lahar volume at any other location.

Because the hydrographs were reconstructed from limited observations rather than from continuous gauge records, they are simple approximations of the hydrographs that would have been measured during the flow. No inferences have been made about hydrograph shape, so that the hydrographs have been constructed with linear limbs connecting known points on the hydrograph. Hydrographs reconstructed for both lahars are shown in Figure 3.

The South Fork lahar started within a few minutes of the beginning of the eruption, and reached the first hydrograph location 4 km downvalley approximately 5 min later. There the peak

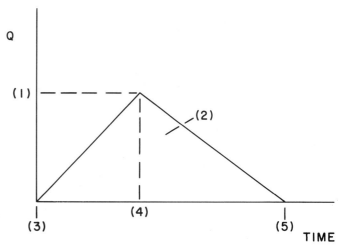

Figure 2. Simple hydrograph showing (1) magnitude of peak discharge, (2) volume of lahar equals area under hydrograph ($V = Qdt$), (3) time of arrival, (4) time of peak discharge, and (5) time of termination of lahar.

discharge of the lahar was 68,000 m³/sec, its volume was 13 million m³, but its duration was only approximately 6.5 min. When the lahar reached the confluence (44 km), about 108 min after the eruption began, its volume was approximately 8 million m³, the peak discharge, 3,800 m³/sec, and the duration, about 72 min. By the time the lahar reached the mouth of the Toutle at the Cowlitz River, its duration had increased to 90 min, and it had an estimated peak discharge of 2,900 m³/sec.

If the North Fork lahar hydrographs in Figure 3 are compared with hydrographs for the South Fork lahar, it is clear that the North Fork lahar was a much larger, longer event that started much later. At 4.5 km from its source, the lahar lasted approximately 480 min; discharge was maintained near its peak value of 7,200 m³/sec for about 2.5 hr. The calculated lahar volume was 140 million m³, more than 10 times larger than the South Fork lahar. The lahar reached the confluence, 38 km from its source, at 1748 PDT. At the confluence, its duration had increased significantly to 590 min, and its volume had decreased to 130 million m³ as a result of deposition. Peak discharge had decreased to 6,600 m³/sec. At the mouth of the Toutle River, 59 km downchannel, lahar volume had decreased to approximately 120 million m³, and peak discharge had diminished to 6,050 m³/sec, while flow duration had increased to 11 hr.

The constructed hydrographs clearly document great differences between the two lahars; the North Fork lahar was much larger and longer, and its peak discharge was maintained for a long time. The hydrographs also demonstrate that these differences characterized the lahars from their inception. For this reason, differences in the processes of lahar initiation must be responsible for observed dissimilarities between the lahars.

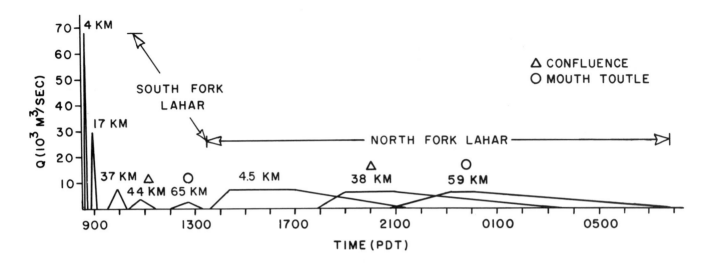

Figure 3. Hydrographs constructed for both lahars using method described in text. Distances above each hydrograph indicate distance of that hydrograph location from source of lahar. Triangle and circle identify hydrograph locations passed by both lahars.

Differences in Destruction by the Lahars

The South Fork lahar did very little damage. It damaged part of a log storage area, rendered a small number of houses unusable (primarily by partially burying them with deposits), and knocked out one large, decrepit railroad bridge.

Conversely, damage by the North Fork lahar was extensive. Two large log and equipment storage facilities were completely inundated and destroyed. Six large bridges and three smaller bridges were destroyed. More than 100 houses were destroyed either by being floated off their foundations and transported or by being partially buried in their original position by laharic deposits. Sedimentation by the North Fork lahar also substantially filled the channels of the Cowlitz and Columbia Rivers, significantly increasing the probability of overbank flooding on the Cowlitz River and temporarily closing Columbia River shipping channels. Sediment had to be dredged from both rivers to alleviate these problems at a cost of more than $200 million.

The North Fork lahar was much more destructive than the South Fork lahar because it maintained high peak discharges, and thereby high peak stage, in areas where damage could be done (Fig. 3). Peak discharge of the South Fork lahar decreased rapidly downchannel so that damage was done only to property closest to Mount St. Helens, between 40 and 44 km, where discharge was between approximately 7,000 and 3,800 m^3/sec. The North Fork lahar, however, maintained peak discharge between 7,000 and 6,000 m^3/sec along the entire Toutle River, reaching peak stages sufficient to do tremendous damage along most channel reaches.

The rapid downchannel decrease in peak discharge of the South Fork lahar is in part a result of deposition by the lahar. Lahar volume was reduced approximately 37 percent by deposition along the South Fork (Fairchild and Wigmosta, 1983; Fairchild, 1985). But the large downchannel increase in flow duration indicates that attenuation of the wave in response to temporary channel storage contributed significantly to the documented decrease in Q_{pk}. Similarly, both deposition and attenuation modified the form of the North Fork lahar hydrograph. The North Fork lahar deposited approximately 18 million m^3 of debris along the Toutle River, by itself more than the original volume of the South Fork lahar (Fairchild, 1985). But because of the extremely large initial volume of the North Fork lahar, this constituted only 11 percent of the original volume, a much smaller proportion than that deposited by the South Fork lahar. The increase in duration of the North Fork lahar of nearly 200 min indicates that the hydrograph was attenuated by temporary channel storage during downchannel translation. However, the long, 2.5-hr initial duration of discharge at peak level kept attenuation from significantly reducing peak discharge (Fig. 3). Rather, the primary effect was to shorten the duration of flow at peak from 2.5 hr to 1 hr; the magnitude of peak discharge decreased only 15 percent in response to both deposition and attenuation.

Thus, the peak discharge of the South Fork lahar decreased rapidly because attenuation and deposition rapidly modified the short, sharp-peaked hydrograph. The North Fork lahar, on the other hand, was able to maintain peak discharges sufficiently high to do extensive damage because of its extremely large volume and the long duration of its peak discharge, which inhibited the effects of deposition and attenuation. These critical characteristics are present in the initial hydrograph for each lahar (Fig. 3). It is these differences in the characteristics of the initial hydrographs of the two lahars that are directly responsible for the great disparity both in the magnitude of downchannel change of the lahars and in their destructiveness. Therefore, the processes of initiation were responsible for differences in the downchannel changes of the lahars and ultimately controlled the potential for destruction.

INITIATION OF THE SOUTH FORK LAHAR

Observational Evidence of Initiation Process

The South Fork lahar apparently evolved from the laterally directed pyroclastic cloud. The lahar was observed 5 km from the base of Mount St. Helens within a few minutes of the initial earthquake (Cummans, 1981a,b). Photographs taken of Mount St. Helens from the south show that the laterally directed pyroclastic cloud overtopped the summit of Mount St. Helens and entered the South Fork drainage at 0834:51 PDT (S. Malone, University of Washington, personal communication). By 0834:00 PDT its front reached the canyons that drain into the South Fork at the base of Mount St. Helens. A lahar evolving from the pyroclastic cloud would have reached the observation point (5 km from Mount St. Helens) at the time it was observed. Similar close correlations were demonstrated on Pine Creek and Muddy River (Pierson, 1983).

The pyroclastic cloud apparently evolved into lahars by rapidly melting snow. The cloud triggered lahars on the flanks of Mount St. Helens, which were mantled by a thick spring snowpack, but did not trigger lahars in mountains to the north, which were intermittently covered by a thinner snowpack. The temperature of the blast cloud, which was estimated to be approximately 300°C (Davis and Graeber, 1980), was hot enough to vaporize and melt snow. Survey data of Brugman and Post (1981) showed that the cloud removed enough snow from Shoestring, Nelson, and Ape Glaciers to account for the water in lahars that flowed down the southeast slope of Mount St. Helens. They inferred that similar removal of snow contributed water to the South Fork lahar.

State of Stress and Strength in Snow

Estimates of snowpack strength indicate that slab avalanches could have been triggered if relatively small shear stresses had been applied to the snowpack surface by the pyroclastic cloud. Slab avalanches would have served to mobilize and disrupt the snowpack, thereby facilitating rapid incorporation and melting of snow by the cloud.

To a first approximation, Perla and LaChapelle (1970) modeled the failure of a snowpack and release of slab avalanches by evaluating the factor of safety at an assumed or reconstructed basal failure surface. Their analysis considered only the forces required to separate the slab along the basal sliding surface, and

neglected separation at the crown and flanks. That this approximation appears to predict the conditions required for avalanche failure with reasonable accuracy is thought to indicate that these additional forces are negligible (Perla, 1977a). Thus, it is important to determine the difference between shear stress and strength in the snowpack in order to evaluate the magnitude of additional shear stresses required to destabilize the snowpack.

In the absence of weak layers, snow density and strength increase downward, and a relatively strong correlation between them can be used to estimate the strength of uniformly densified snow (Perla, 1977a; Ballard and Feldt, 1966). Layers of new snow may have a density of between 30 and 300 kg/m^3. After new snow is attached to the pack, it densifies under its own weight in response to thermodynamic processes. According to Perla (1977b), densities greater than 500 kg/m^3 are rare in seasonal snowpacks in response to overburden loads alone.

E. R. LaChappelle (personal communication, 1984) has observed that snow density at significant depth in Cascade snowpacks rarely exceeds 500 to 550 kg/m^3. This is apparently because a change in process from densification to melting, compression, vapor exchange, and other processes is needed to increase density further. A density of 600 kg/m^3 requires the formation of firn, and generally is not observed except in late-summer snow. Snow exceeding 500 kg/m^3 is typically that which fell early in the season, and therefore has undergone densification for a long period, and lies near the base of the snowpack.

LaChapelle and others (e.g., Perla, 1977a,b; Mellor, 1977) emphasized that failure generally occurs at weak boundaries between layers in the snowpack. According to LaChappelle, many weak layers with strength significantly lower than densified snow are likely in late winter and spring Cascade snowpacks; strengths calculated for uniform densified snow provide an upper limit of snowpack strength.

If a representative density profile is constructed for uniformly densified snow, a shear stress profile (arising from the weight of the snowpack) can be computed directly from it, and a strength profile can be constructed from the strong correlation between snow strength and density demonstrated by Perla (1977a, Fig. 3). Perla (1977b, Fig. 11) published a section for the upper 1 m of a snowpack that is typical of a large number of measured sections. This is adopted to represent the upper 1 m of the snowpack. But late winter and spring snowpacks on Mount St. Helens typically vary in thickness from 4 to 9 m, so that the profile must be extrapolated below 1 m. On the basis of the evidence presented above, density probably increases downward to a maximum of 500 kg/m^3. To construct this profile, I have conservatively assumed that density linearly increases to 500 kg/m^3 and then remains constant, and have assumed as a conservative case that there are no weak layers. The resulting density profile is shown in Figure 4 from which a shear stress profile was constructed for a slope of 20°, which represents slopes of interest on Mount St. Helens, and a profile of strength was constructed from the data of Perla (1977a, Fig. 3).

The additional surface stress required from a pyroclastic

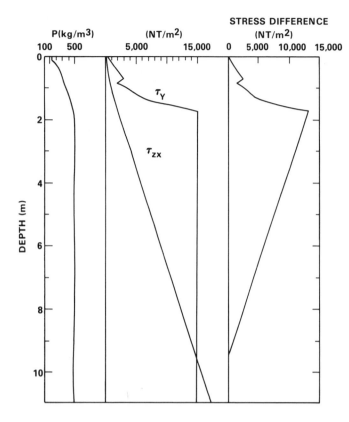

Figure 4. Profiles of density, shear stress, strength, and stress difference (strength - shear stress) for profile through snowpack inferred to be typical of those at Mount St. Helens.

cloud to destabilize the snowpack is the difference between strength and shear stress. The profile predicts stability if the snowpack is less than 9.5 m thick, which is consistent with the observed stability of the snowpack under all but wet late summer conditions. An applied shear stress as small as 2,000 NT/m² is sufficient to cause slab failure of the upper 0.5 to 1.5 m. Most spring snowpacks at the elevation of the flanks of Mount St. Helens are 4 to 9 m thick; the stress required to destabilize an entire homogeneous snowpack decreases from 9,000 to 1,000 NT/m² as snowpack depth increases in this range. Since weak layers are typically present in the snowpack, stresses significantly lower than these for a uniform profile of densified snow may be sufficient to trigger thick slab avalanches.

Hypothesis for Initiation Process

The observations described above suggest that the laterally directed pyroclastic cloud initiated the South Fork lahar by somehow melting snow. Specifically, I propose that because small stresses were required to destabilize the snowpack on St. Helens, the pyroclastic cloud could have applied a shear stress to the snowpack that was large enough to trigger thick slab avalanches. Slab avalanches would have broken the snowpack into

relatively small pieces that could have been incorporated and rapidly melted by the hot cloud, which could then evolve into a lahar as the addition of melted water increased its water content.

To test the reasonableness of this proposal, the shear stress that the laterally directed pyroclastic cloud could have applied to the snowpack can be estimated. The laterally directed pyroclastic cloud should have differed little from pyroclastic clouds that are initiated by the collapse of vertical eruption columns. These start as homogeneous, highly inflated, turbulent suspensions of pyroclasts; the model of Sparks and Wilson (1976) predicts their initial concentration to be between 0.005 and 0.03 by volume. Turbulent suspension theory argues that random turbulent fluctuations in such a suspension provide an upward transport of sediment that is opposed by settling in response to gravitational acceleration (Gillette and others, 1974; Shreffler, 1975). According to diffusion theory, these forces balance for each grain size in suspension. There is also a critical diameter that defines the largest size that can be suspended. In a pyroclastic cloud, larger sediment settles out of suspension into a basal zone. In this way, the homogeneous cloud should evolve into an equilibrium stratified cloud with a basal layer overlain by a suspension layer. The basal layer is analogous to the zone of bedload transport in the cases of fluvial transport or entrained aerosols (although the process of sediment transport in the basal layer of pyroclastic clouds is unknown) in the respect that it comprises sediment too coarse to be maintained in suspension. Fairchild (1985) used simple turbulent suspension theory to estimate that the concentration of the basal zone should be between 0.05 and 0.20 by volume. In the overlying suspension layer, the concentration of sediment decreases upward (as is characteristic of turbulent suspensions), with the coarsest sediment decreasing the most.

The concentration of sediment at the base of the cloud is important to the initiation of lahars for two reasons. First, the primary sources of the heat needed to melt snow are pyroclasts, and they are concentrated at the base of the cloud where snow would be mixed: this favors rapid melting. Second, coarse sediment bounces and digs into the snow surface, creating form drag that couples the cloud to the snow and transmits a shear stress to the snowpack.

If these interactions between bouncing sediment and the snow surface provide enough form drag to maintain approximately steady, uniform flow, then the shear stress applied to the snowpack is:

$$\tau = \rho <c> g \, H \sin\theta \qquad (2)$$

where ρ is the average density of pyroclasts in the cloud, $<c>$ is the average concentration of the cloud, H is the cloud thickness, g is gravitational acceleration, and θ is the slope of the volcano. The computations below assume steady, uniform flow, and use this equation to compute shear stress. As long as the cloud maintains constant velocity or decelerates, the shear stress applied to the snowpack will be at least as large as the prediction based on this steady, uniform flow equation. There are not enough measurements of pyroclastic cloud velocities to confirm that flow is steady and uniform, although the assumption is plausible because one would expect the course clasts at the base of the cloud to greatly impede acceleration.

The laterally directed pyroclastic cloud comprised lithic debris with an average density of approximately 2,600 kg/m^3. Cloud height, which was measured from photographs of the cloud as it flowed down the South Fork drainage, was 500 m. The average slope was 20°. The stratification of the cloud described above should not have altered its average concentration unless sediment was lost from the cloud. The only processes by which sediment could have been removed from the cloud are deposition of sediment onto the snow pack, or the upward rise of sediment by thermally bouyant convection. Thermally bouyant convection is not visible in photographs of the cloud, and a negligible amount of sediment was deposited by the cloud on the slopes of Mount St. Helens. Therefore, the vertically averaged concentration of the cloud should have been maintained in the range of 0.005 to 0.03 predicted for an initial homogeneous cloud by Sparks and Wilson (1976). Using these values, the shear stress applied to the snowpack should have been between 64,000 and 380,000 NT/m^2, or 7 to 40 times larger than the shear stress necessary to trigger slab avalanches along a failure surface at the base of the thick, late spring snowpack. The simplifying assumptions used in these computations introduce considerable error, but because the predicted shear stresses are an order of magnitude larger than necessary, it is reasonable to propose that the laterally directed cloud applied shear stresses large enough to destabilize the snowpack.

Fairchild (1985) used standard thermodynamic relationships to demonstrate that enough snow was probably available in the late May snowpack on Mount St. Helens to provide the water required by the lahar. First the volume of snow that would be subliminated as the cloud was cooled from its initial temperature of 300° to 100°C was computed. Then the snow melted as the cloud cooled from 100°C to its final temperature between 10° and 30°C (corresponding to an initial lahar water content between 0.37 and 0.31 by volume, which rheological and sedimentological evidence suggests were the limits for the possible initial water content) was computed. The combined volume of snow needed was compared to snowpack records to demonstrate that much more snow should have been available in the drainage than was needed to generate the South Fork lahar.

CONCLUSIONS

Observations suggest that the South Fork lahar evolved from the laterally directed pyroclastic cloud. Computations suggest that the lahar formed after the cloud triggered deep slab avalanches and rapidly mixed and melted the snow. The assumption that snow can be mixed and melted rapidly enough remains untested, but the computations summarized above indicate that the pyroclastic cloud could have applied a shear stress large

enough to trigger deep slab avalanches, and that there was sufficient snow for the cloud to evolve to a lahar.

INITIATION OF THE NORTH FORK LAHAR

Observational Evidence of Initiation Process

Fairchild (1985) compiled evidence that shows that the North Fork lahar originated in a small portion of the avalanche debris ("source," Fig. 1). He also concluded that: (1) only a small volume of mud could have been generated upvalley from the source, (2) the heads of gullies incised in the avalanche debris by the lahar are at the downvalley edge of the source, (3) the lower avalanche was free of mud when the front of the lahar was observed 4 km downvalley from the source, and (4) side-looking airborne radar images show the lahar starting at the source.

Because the lahar was generated from only a small portion of the avalanche debris, the source must have characteristics uniquely suited to the initiation of a lahar. The avalanche debris surrounding the source is characterized by blocks of soft, unconsolidated, hydrothermally altered volcanic lava and breccia, meters to tens of meters in diameter, and pits that were once occupied by equally large blocks of ice that have since melted (Fig. 5a). The lahar source is distinctive because the same volcanic debris occurs in contorted, deformed fragments with dimensions on the order of centimeters (Fig. 5b). The modal diameter of the fragments is approximately 10 to 25 cm. Ice melt-out pits are conspicuously absent in the source, indicating that the ice blocks were approximately the same size as the volcanic blocks. Fairchild (1985, p. 353) speculated that both lithic and ice blocks may have been comminuted during avalanche transport. Reduction in the size of ice blocks increases the rate of melting, and facilitates the rapid melting of ice necessary to generate the North Fork lahar in less than 5 hr.

The timing of the lahar compares closely with the timing of seismicity. The hydrograph constructed for the lahar 4.5 km below the source is plotted in Figure 6, along with two other times of significance. The time at which mud was first observed ponding on the surface of avalanche deposits by Harry Glicken (U.S. Geological Survey, personal communication, 1981) was approximately 1230 PDT [Time (1)]. It must be emphasized that mud may have accumulated on the deposit surface earlier, but Glicken was the first observer to penetrate sufficiently close to Mount St. Helens to make an observation. It was not until 1310 PDT (Time 2 in Fig. 6), that a recognizable front was observed moving downchannel by the Army Air National Guard. This front reached the hydrograph location at 1325 PDT.

Superimposed on the same plot is an "envelope of seismicity" recorded on the South Fork Toutle River at approximately the same distance from the vent of Mount St. Helens as the source (S. C. Malone, University of Washington, personal communication, 1981). The envelope defines the relative levels of seismic accelerations because absolute values cannot be computed for a saturated record of harmonic tremors; for this reason no absolute

a   b

Figure 5. a, View of avalanche surface underlain by debris typical of that surrounding the source. Large
mounds on surface (for example, light-colored mound slightly right of center) are underlain by large
blocks that are internally undisrupted. b, View of contorted lithic fragments typical of source area.

scale is provided on the vertical axis. The magnitude 5+ earthquake that triggered the eruption, and shaking accompanying
landsliding, produced the sharp spike in the record at 0832. The
next 3 hr, however, were characterized by only minor seismic
activity related to phreatic clearing of the vent. Then the upward
movement of juvenile magma triggered a long succession of harmonic tremors that began at approximately 1140 PDT, built to a
peak at 1535 PDT, and abruptly terminated at approximately
1730 PDT. Figure 6 clearly shows that the timing of the lahar
hydrograph and observations of the lahar correspond very closely
with the timing of seismicity. Mud was first observed on the
avalanche surface within 50 min of the onset of seismicity. The
beginning of peak discharge and the period it was maintained
correlate well with the timing of most intense seismicity. The
termination of seismicity closely matches the beginning of a decline in discharge. Close correlation of the timing and intensity of
seismicity with the timing and intensity of lahar discharge
strongly suggests that liquefaction in response to seismic loading
was involved in the generation of the North Fork lahar.

Hypothesis for Initiation Process

The evidence presented above documents that the North
Fork lahar was generated from a relatively small portion of the
avalanche where ice was evidently abnormally small; it also suggests the following testable hypothesis: melted ice and hydrothermal water saturated the source debris, and subsequent
harmonic tremors were sufficiently strong and continued long
enough to liquefy this debris and generate the North Fork lahar.
To verify this hypothesis, it must be shown that enough ice and
heat was available in the source area to provide the water necessary for the lahar, that the ice could have melted in the time
available, and that the debris in the source area would have
liquefied.

The volume of ice required to account for the water in the
North Fork lahar can be computed if the water content of the
lahar is known. The concentration of sediment of the lahar at
peak stage was reconstructed from matrix-supported laharic deposits to be 0.65 by volume (Fairchild, 1985). Samples taken by
the U.S. Geological Survey from near the lahar surface (R. Dien-
hart, personal communication) measured concentrations near
0.50 during rising lahar stage, and videophotography suggests
that concentrations were comparable during falling lahar stage.
For an average lahar sediment concentration between these
values, the volume of water in the lahar would have been be-
tween 4.6×10^7 and 6.5×10^7 m^3. There are two possible sources
for this water. Hydrothermal water preserved in the avalanche
debris could have contributed between 1.0×10^7 and 1.4×10^7
m^3. The only other source is water from melted ice; between 3.6
$\times 10^7$ and 6.1×10^7 m^3 ice would be required to provide the
remaining volume of water needed by the lahar. The volume
of ice removed from the volcano by landslides was 1.2×10^8 m^3
(Fairchild, 1985; based on the data of Brugman and Post, 1981),
much greater than the volume needed by the lahar. Unfortunately, it cannot be directly confirmed that the required ice was in
the source because it is not known how this ice was distributed in
the avalanche debris, and hence the volume of ice in the source
cannot be directly computed. For this reason, the above calculations only indicate that enough ice was removed by landslides to
provide the water needed by the lahar if the ice was properly
distributed, and that sources other than ice alone apparently
could not have provided enough water.

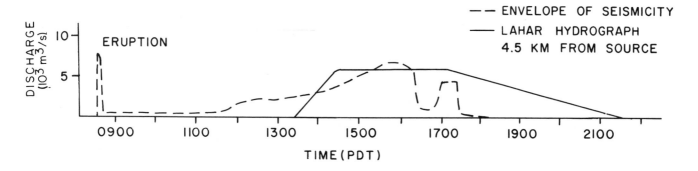

Figure 6. Comparison of lahar hydrograph 4.5 km from source with timing of seismicity.

Using measurements made by the U.S. Geological Survey (Voight and others, 1981), I interpreted the initial avalanche debris temperature in the source area to be approximately 95°C. The initial lahar temperature was approximately 40°C. The heat released by the undersaturated avalanche debris in the source as it cooled over this temperature range was sufficient to melt 1.1×10^8 m^3 of ice (Fairchild, 1985, Table 3.2). Thus, there was more than enough heat to melt the ice needed by the lahar, and it now must be shown that the ice could have melted quickly enough to generate the lahar by 1300 PDT.

The question is whether the ice melted before the end of seismic shaking. The melting system comprised blocks of ice of various sizes scattered randomly in undersaturated avalanche debris at 95°C. Each block drew heat from a spherical shell of avalanche debris that would have expanded with time; shells for adjacent blocks of ice may have intersected, especially in the case of large ice blocks after long time periods. Measurements of the temperature of the North Fork lahar indicate that once water was generated by melting, it was heated to approximately 40°C.

The melting rate of a single ice block drawing heat from a spherical shell can be evaluated mathematically. I chose to model heat flow to an individual block using a one-dimensional heat-flow model solved with finite difference methods. Because the one-dimensional model does not account for the convergence of heat as it flows toward the center of the sphere, the model underestimated the rate of melting, but this error proved to be unimportant (see below). A one-dimensional, finite difference solution was chosen rather than an analytical solution for spherical heat flow because it allowed us to better approximate conditions at the boundary of the shell from which heat was drawn to the ice block. The heat capacity and conductivity of the debris were estimated from measurements reported in the literature for similar debris (Fairchild, 1985).

It was inferred from the size of lithic fragments that the median diameter of ice blocks in the source was probably 10 to 25 cm, and from the absence of ice pits, that very few blocks were as large as 1 m in diameter (since these would leave visible ice pits if melted near the surface). The melting model indicates that ice blocks smaller than 60 cm in diameter should have melted completely by the beginning of seismicity (1140 PDT), while a 1-m block would have been at least 75 percent melted. By the end of seismicity, blocks smaller than 1 m should have melted completely. Since model assumptions were made so that, if anything, the melting rate was more rapid than the model predicts, the results indicate that ice blocks in the source should have melted rapidly enough to provide the water needed by the lahar.

The melting rates of ice blocks with diameters of 25 and 50 m, which typified the range of block diameters in the debris surrounding the source, were also computed. The model predicts that blocks of this size would still not have completely melted 1 mo after the eruption, which is consistent with observations of large ice blocks in avalanche debris near Coldwater basin in June 1980. Furthermore, only 8 to 25 percent of the volume of ice in these large blocks would have melted before the end of seismicity. If the ice in the source area had been this size, a much smaller volume of meltwater would have been generated, and it is much less likely that enough ice would have melted to provide the water required by the lahar. This result is consistent with the absence of major lahar sources elsewhere in the avalanche debris. Without comminution of ice, the North Fork lahar probably would not have occurred.

The final question is whether the avalanche debris would have liquefied when shaken by the harmonic tremor event. The avalanche debris was sufficiently poorly sorted that it was probably poorly drained, and values of void ratio measured in the debris are in the range of void ratios of materials with high liquefaction potential (Seed and others, 1975). Hence, the debris could have been susceptible to liquefaction.

Seed and others (1975) and Seed and Idriss (1971) have developed empirical methods to evaluate the liquefaction potential of soils or unconsolidated debris from soil and seismic parameters. This approach is attractive because in this case neither debris physical properties or seismic history can be accurately determined. The minimum input necessary for the method includes relative density of the avalanche debris (D_r), the magnitude of seismic acceleration, and the cyclic frequency. None of these variables can be determined accurately. The best available value for relative density is 0.5, which is the mean of four values measured by Voight and others (1983). S. C. Malone and S. W. Smith (University of Washington, personal communication, 1981) estimate that the magnitude of seismic acceleration at the lahar source area was between 0.01 and 0.1 g. They estimate that the average cyclic frequency was between 2.5 and 5 cycles/sec.

Because of the inaccuracy of input values, various combinations of variables were tested to determine the range of values of each variable for which liquefaction could occur. Because liquefaction potential is much less sensitive to variation in cyclic frequency than to relative density or seismic acceleration, cyclic frequency was assumed to be constant at 2.5 cycles/sec. The lowest value estimated by Malone and Smith was used to ensure that the results would tend to underestimate liquefaction potential. The empirical data of seed and others indicate that liquefaction would not have occurred if the relative density of avalanche deposits exceeded 0.70, and that liquefaction could not have occurred rapidly enough unless relative density was less than 0.60. For values of D_r less than 0.60, liquefaction of the upper 10 m of debris would have occurred if seismic acceleration exceeded approximately 0.03 g. Furthermore, liquefaction would have occurred before the first observation of mud on the avalanche surface as long as seismic acceleration exceeded 0.03 g before 1200 to 1230 PDT, depending on the relative density of the debris.

The results indicate, therefore, that liquefaction of the upper 10 m of debris could have occurred before the first observation of mud on the avalanche surface if D_r was less than approximately 0.60, and if seismic acceleration exceeded 0.03 g before 1200 to 1230 PDT. The available estimates of seismic acceleration and relative density suggest that these criteria were probably satisfied. It is important to emphasize that since the input data are not well known, the results do not prove that liquefaction occurred. However, when model results are considered along with the indirect evidence supporting liquefaction provided by the relative timing of seismicity and the lahar hydrograph at 4.5 km, it is reasonable to expect that at least the upper 10 m of material in the source liquefied.

Conclusions

The tests presented above show that it is reasonable to conclude that enough ice was available, that it melted sufficiently rapidly, and that the resulting debris-water section could have liquefied to produce a lahar. In combination with observed evidence, the tests provide substantial evidence to support the hypothesized initiation model. In summary, the model states that the lahar started from a source zone of comminuted debris and ice. Ice melted rapidly, adding a large volume of water to the debris section. Seismicity caused liquefaction of the wet debris, generating the North Fork lahar.

The initiation model explains very well all of the empirical observations. The geometry of the initial hydrograph is a product of the characteristics of the seismic event that directly generated the lahar, and the late initiation of the lahar coincides with the similarly late beginning of harmonic tremor activity. Results of the melting rate model confirm that the lahar was generated only in a very restricted source area because only there were ice blocks small enough to melt sufficiently rapidly. Had ice blocks in the source area been large, as they were elsewhere in the avalanche deposits, there would not have been enough water generated for a large lahar. Finally, avalanche deposit morphology and structure are consistent with the initiation model. Gullies end at the boundary of the source area because liquefied debris could not have maintained the steep sides characteristic of the gullies. Large mounds and pits are absent in the source area both because of the originally small size of material and because of subsequent liquefaction.

CAUSES OF THE DIFFERENCES IN LAHAR CHARACTERISTICS AND DESTRUCTION

The characteristics of the South Fork lahar changed dramatically downchannel, and the lahar did relatively little damage because it was initially brief and sharp-peaked. This, in turn, can be attributed to the fact that the laterally directed pyroclastic cloud, from which the lahar evolved, was initially brief and intense. Kieffer (1981) estimated that the lateral eruption lasted only 20 sec at its vent. The cloud apparently attenuated from this duration until it evolved into a lahar, and then continued to attenuate as a lahar.

In contrast, the long total duration, long duration of steadily maintained peak discharge, large volume, and hence great destructiveness of the North Fork lahar can be directly correlated to the characteristics of the harmonic tremor event. The sensitivity of lahar characteristics can be appreciated if one imagines what kind of lahar would have been generated if, for instance, the harmonic tremors had stopped at 1300 PDT. If any lahar would have been generated, presumably, it would have been extremely small and unlikely to have been very destructive.

Hence, the contrasts between the characteristics of the laterally directed pyroclastic cloud and the harmonic tremor event, which are both integral aspects of the initiation processes, explain the contrasts between the two lahars.

DISCUSSION

The importance of initiation to the destructiveness of the Toutle River lahars clearly demonstrates that analyses of initiation process must be an essential element in the assessment of lahar hazard. Accordingly, we have employed a three-step procedure for the quantitative analysis of lahar hazard. It includes (1) developing a physical model of the initiation process that is designed to predict an initial hydrograph, (2) a mathematical routing of this hydrograph to predict the downchannel characteristics of the lahar, and (3) a definition of hazard based on the characteristics predicted by the routing model (Dunne and Fairchild, 1984a,b; Fairchild, 1987). My experience in routing hydrographs downchannel indicates that the form of the initial hydrograph has at least as great an effect on the predicted downchannel characteristics of the hydrograph as the parameters used to simulate the contribution of channel geometry to attenuation.

Fairchild (1985) showed that changes in the sediment size distribution and concentration in the Toutle River lahars depended on the proportion of the initial flow volume that was deposited. Hence, the sediment composition of the South Fork lahar changed much more than the North Fork lahar because it deposited a much higher proportion of the sediment originally in the lahar. Fairchild (1985) also demonstrated that lahar rheological properties are very sensitive to sediment size distribution and concentration. Accurate rheological information is necessary if the stresses imposed by lahars on buildings, bridges, or other structures is to be properly assessed. These results emphasize the importance of understanding initiation processes, in this case to accurately predict initial lahar composition, so that both the initial rheological properties of the lahar and changes in properties as the lahar moves downchannel can be adequately evaluated.

ACKNOWLEDGMENTS

The work on which this publication is based was supported in part by funds provided by the Washington State Department of Fisheries, Office of Water Research and Technology (Project No. 14-34-0001-1411) through the Washington Water Research Center, the U.S. Geological Survey, Sigma Xi, and the University of Washington Graduate School and Department of Geological Sciences. I express my deep appreciation to Thomas Dunne, who supervised this research at the University of Washington.

REFERENCES CITED

Ballard, G.E.H., and Feldt, E. D., 1966, A theoretical consideration of the strength of snow: Journal of Glaciology, v. 6, p. 159–170.

Brugman, M. M., and Post, A., 1981, Effects of volcanism on the glaciers of Mount St. Helens, Washington: U.S. Geological Survey Circular 850-D, 11 p.

Cummans, J., 1981a, Mudflows resulting from the May 18, 1980, eruption of Mount St. Helens, Washington: U.S. Geological Survey Circular 850-B, 16 p.

—— , 1981b, Chronology of mudflows on the South Fork and North Fork Toutle River following the May 18 eruption, *in* Lipman, P. W., and Mullineaux, D. R., eds., The 1980 eruption of Mount St. Helens, Washington: U.S. Geological Survey Professional Paper 1250, p. 479–486.

Davis, M. J., and Graeber, E. J., 1980, Temperature estimates of the May 18 eruption of Mount St. Helens made from observations of material response [abs.]: EOS Transactions of the American Geophysical Union, v. 61, p. 1136.

Dunne, T., and Fairchild, L. H., 1984, Estimation of flood sedimentation hazards around Mt. St. Helens, (1): Shin-Sabo, v. 37, no. 1, p. 13–22.

Dunne, T., and Fairchild, L. H., 1984, Estimation of flood and sedimentation hazards around Mt. St. Helens, (2): Shin-Sabo, v. 37, no. 1, p. 13–22.

Fairchild, L. H., 1985, Lahars at Mount St. Helens [Ph.D. thesis]: Seattle, University of Washington, 374 p.

—— , 1987, Quantitative analysis of lahar hazard, *in* Keller, S.A.H., ed., Mount St. Helens, five years after: Cheney, Eastern Washington University Press (in press).

Fairchild, L. H., and Wigmosta, M., 1983, Dynamic and volumetric characteristics of the 18 May 1980 lahars on the Toutle River, Washington: Technical Memorandum of Public Works Research Institute (Japan), Proceedings of the Symposium on Erosion Control in Volcanic Areas, p. 131–154.

Gillette, D. A., Blifford, I. H., and Fryrear, D. W., 1974, The influence of wind velocity on the size distribution of aerosols generated by the wind erosion of soils: Journal of Geophysical Research, v. 79, p. 4068–4075.

Kieffer, S. W., 1981, Fluid dynamics of the May 18 blast at Mount St. Helens, *in* Lipman, P. W., and Mullineaux, D. R., eds., The 1980 eruptions of Mount St. Helens, Washington: U.S. Geological Survey Professional Paper 1250, p. 379–400.

Mellor, M., 1977, Dynamics of snow avalanches, *in* Voight, B., ed., Rockslides and avalanches, v. 1; Natural Phenomena: Amsterdam, Elsevier, p. 753–792.

Perla, R. I., 1977a, Slab avalanche measurements: Canadian Geotechnical Journal, v. 14, p. 206–213.

—— , 1977b, Failure on snow slopes, *in* Voight, B., ed., Rockslides and avalanches, v. 1; Natural Phenomena: Amsterdam, Elsevier, p. 731–752.

Perla, R. I., and LaChapelle, E. R., 1970, A theory of snow slab failure: Journal of Geophysical Research, v. 75, p. 7619–7627.

Pierson, T. C., 1983, Flow behavior of two major lahars triggered by the May 18, 1980, eruption of Mount St. Helens, Washington: Technical Memorandum of Public Works Research Institute (Japan), Proceedings of the Symposium on Erosion Control in Volcanic Areas, p. 99–130.

Seed, H. B., and Idriss, I. M., 1971, Simplified procedure for evaluating soil liquefaction potential: Proceedings of the American Society of Civil Engineers, Journal of the Soil Mechanics and Foundations Division, v. 97, no. SM9, p. 1249–1273.

Seed, H. B., Martin, P. P., and Lysmer, J., 1975, The generation and dissipation of pore water pressures during soil liquefaction: University of California at Berkeley, Earthquake Engineering Research Center Report #EERC 75-26, 33 p.

Shreffler, J. H., 1975, Numerical experimentation with particles having non-zero terminal velocity in the atmospheric surface layer: Boundary-layer Meteorology, v. 9, p. 191–204.

Smith, J. D., and McLean, S. R., 1984, A model for flow in meandering streams: Water Resources Research, v. 20, p. 1301–1315.

Sparks, R.S.J., and Wilson, L., 1976, A model for the formation of ignimbrite by gravitational column collapse: Journal of the Geological Society of London, v. 132, p. 441–451.

Voight, B., Glicken, H., Janda, R. J., and Douglass, P. M., 1981, Catastrophic rockslide avalanche of May 18, *in* Lipman, P. W., and Mullineax, D. R., eds., The 1980 eruptions of Mount St. Helens, Washington: U.S. Geological Survey Professional Paper 1250, p. 347–378.

Voight, B., Glicken, H., and Douglass, P. M., 1983, Nature and mechanics of the Mount St. Helens rockslide-avalanche of 18 May 1980: Geotechnique, v. 33, p. 243–273.

Geological Society of America
Reviews in Engineering Geology, Volume VII
1987

Meteorological antecedents to debris flow in southwestern British Columbia; Some case studies

Michael Church
Department of Geography
University of British Columbia
Vancouver, British Columbia V6T 1W5
Canada

Michael J. Miles
M. Miles and Associates, Ltd.
502 Craigflower Road
Victoria, British Columbia V9A 2V8
Canada

ABSTRACT

Development within the mountains of coastal British Columbia has recently increased the exposure of people and facilities to debris flows. Attempts to specify weather conditions under which debris flows are apt to occur—such as threshold precipitation—appear not to work because of the highly contingent nature of the flows. Debris must exist in unstable position in or near the channel, and conditions prior to the flow may strongly condition the necessary trigger to mobilize it.

Events have been observed in the following circumstances: locally concentrated rainfall with high antecedent moisture and no snowmelt (the "classical case"); uniformly distributed, moderate rainfall with snowmelt; low intensity rainfall and heavy snowmelt; and heavy rainfall onto deeply frozen, but thawing, ground. A weather-based warning threshold for the British Columbia coast would be fairly complex. At present, such a system would include the substantial probability of issuing nuisance predictions of nonoccurring events.

There is an indication that the incidence of debris flows has increased since 1980. Reasons why this might be so are investigated. Aside from the occurrence of four very wet years since then, no clear meteorologic correlation can be made.

INTRODUCTION

Debris flow is a relatively common phenomenon in coastal British Columbia. Glacially oversteepened slopes, sometimes more than 1,000 m high, shallow regoliths comprised of till or colluvium, and seasonally heavy, often intense, rainfall combine to create this situation. In recent years, extension of communication lines and settlement onto mountain slopes has increased the frequency of damaging events. Consequently, an interest has developed in forecasting their occurrence.

Debris flows in steep, headward channels of the Coast and Cascade Mountains in southwestern British Columbia entrain mixtures of boulders, gravel, and sand, with very little silt or clay. Organic matter, including humic soil, mulch, and plant parts up to large tree trunks, may contribute little to more than half the volume of solid matter in the flow. The flows may move at greater than 10 m^3 sec^{-1} (Hungr and others, 1984), and events containing up to 22,000 m^3 of debris have been surveyed (Nasmith and Mercer, 1979). Substantially larger flows are known (see Clague and others, 1985). These fast-moving flows are known regionally as debris "torrents," following Swanston and Swanson (1976; see also Van Dine, 1985). The term has no

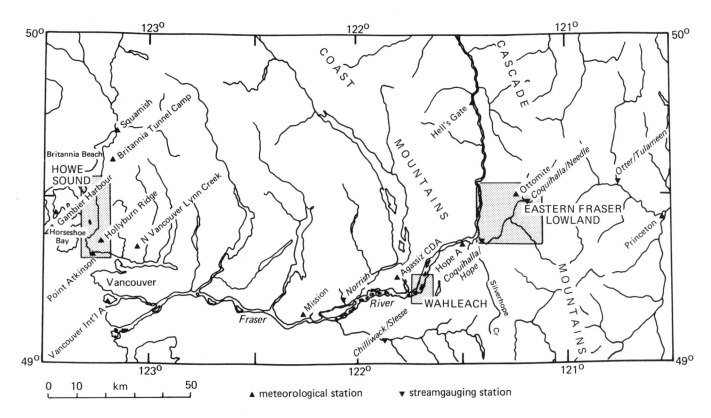

Figure 1. Map of southwestern British Columbia, showing the study areas and principal hydrometeorologic and hydrologic observing stations cited in text.

specific mechanical connotations, although it is applied only to rapid debris flows in noncohesive material confined in steep channels. Such flows present an especially dangerous hazard, since no practical warning is possible when a flow is underway.

Furthermore, the complex and largely contingent nature of trigger mechanisms for debris flow makes forecasting an impractical proposition so far as individual sites are concerned. It is possible to identify sites prone to debris flow, and to study the regional aspects of their recurrence. This is sufficient for hazard avoidance planning, for maintenance planning along communication routes, and for studies of the effects of land use on debris flow occurrence.

This chapter examines the meteorological conditions surrounding several episodes of debris flow in southwestern British Columbia that have occurred since 1980. The review confirms that there is no unequivocal threshold for their initiation, or, at least, none that is practically measurable. An interesting aspect of the recent history of events in this region is the appearance of increasing frequency. The trend is examined in light of climate and other possible reasons for it.

ANALYSIS OF HISTORIC EVENTS

Eastern Fraser Lowland

Fraser Lowland is a broad valley running east from the sea

for about 100 km to the vicinity of Agassiz (Fig. 1). There it narrows to a valley about 3 km wide, and turns to run northeast toward Hope between the 2,000-m peaks of the southernmost Coast Mountains and the Cascade Ranges to the south and east. In this region, orographic lift strongly enhances storm convergence of air, and extreme precipitation may result. Several sites in the area experience recurrent debris flow.

Fraser and Coquihalla Valleys: Christmas 1980. December 1980, was unusually wet in the eastern Fraser valley. At Hope Airport, the total precipitation for December was 441 mm, 152 percent of the long-term average. Of this, 185 mm fell on December 25-27. During the preceding 3 days, 35 to 60 mm of precipitation occurred in the region, mainly as snow. At high elevations, a deep snowpack existed.

The Christmas storm was the culmination of a series of cyclonic disturbances that moved into the area from the southwest after December 20, replacing a high-pressure ridge that had become established about December 17. Freezing level records from two upper air stations in southern British Columbia illustrate the weather pattern very well (Fig. 2) and emphasize the possibility for snowmelt during the storm. The worst day of the storm was December 26, when debris torrents blocked both major highways north and east from Hope, and the Coqhihalla Valley road. Additional events occurred in the mountains: Miles and Kellerhals (1981) described deposits in Coquihalla Valley,

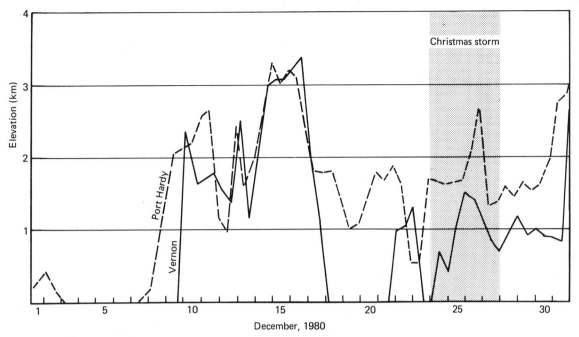

Figure 2. Freezing levels at Port Hardy (marine location: northern Vancouver Island at 50°41′N, 127°22′W) and Vernon (interior location, east of Coast and Cascade mountains at 50°14′N, 119°17′W) during December 1980.

TABLE 1. EVENT RETURN PERIODS (T)* FOR THE MAJOR STORMS OF 1980 AND 1984 IN EASTERN FRASER LOWLAND

Station	Elevation Drainage Area	Length of Record (yr)	Christmas 1980				New Year 1984			
			24-hr	T (yr)	2-day‡	T	24-hr	T	3-day‡‡	T
Precipitation										
Mission	56 m	28	92.0 mm	15	105.6	4.9	–		–	
Agassiz CDA	15	87	78.0	5	97.0	2.2	112.8	55	162.2	7.8
Hope A**	38	39	82.3	3.1	127.4	4	136.5	61	205.6	17
Hell's Gate	114	33	73	na	na		47.5	1.4	87.1	na
Princeton A	696	41	9.0	1.0	12.6	–	13.8	1.2	21.0	na
Streamflow										
08MH088 Norrish Creek	117 km²	22	166 m³s⁻¹	7.0			–			
08MH103 Chilliwack River above Slesse Creek	645	22	262	18			278	23		
08MF003 Coquihalla River near Hope	741	36	490	25			520 est.			
08MF062 Coquihalla River below Needle Creek	85.5	19	46	38			33.5	11		
08NL023 Otter Creek at Tulameen	673	37	29.1	2.0			8.4	1.0		

*Precipitation return period based on the Gumbel distribution; streamflow based on three-parameter lognormal distribution, for annual extreme value sequences. Streamflow sequences include the 1980 and 1984 events.
**Station moved in 1973; record not homogeneous.
‡December 25-26.
‡‡January 2-4.

and torrents are known to have occurred in the valley of Silver-hope Creek. In Fraser Canyon near Yale, both Highway No. 1 and the Canadian Pacific Railway line were cut. Flood damage was widespread, extending from Squamish to Princeton (Fig. 1).

Table 1 compares estimated return periods for 24-hr precipitation and daily runoff in the region on the peak day. Return periods for precipitation declined steadily eastward, and, in the

study area, were generally within the range of 3 to 5 yr. Records from several stations within Coquihalla Valley that have much shorter histories indicated similar return periods and confirm that 24-hr precipitation on December 26 was surprisingly uniform at 70 to 80 mm (hence, the decline in return period into the mountains). Short-term precipitation was not unusual either (cf. Fig. 3B). In comparison, return periods of daily mean streamflows on

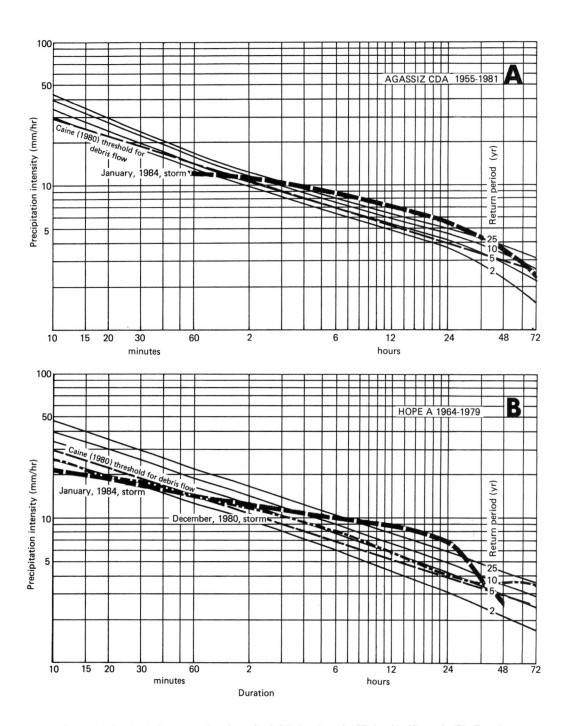

Figure 3. Magnitude-frequency-duration of rainfall for Agassiz CDA (A); Hope A (B). Based on Atmospheric Environment Service analyses to 24 hr, thereafter on compilation from British Columbia Ministry of the Environment (Gumbel's extreme value distribution).

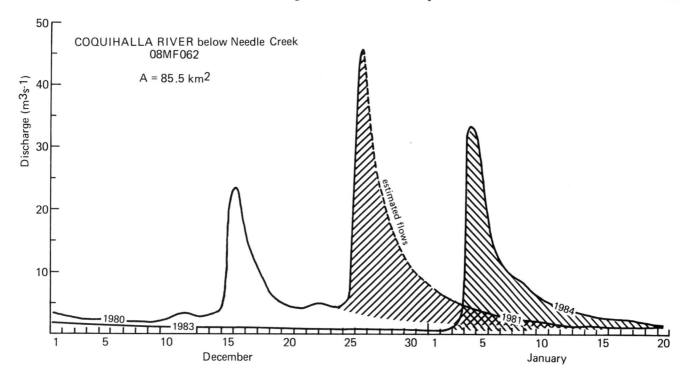

Figure 4. Hydrographs of Coquihalla River below Needle Creek for December and January 1980 and 1984. Storm event runoff is indicated by line pattern. From Water Survey of Canada records.

December 26 were in the range of 20 to 40 yr. Instantaneous peak flows generally were somewhat less extreme (except on Chilliwack River, where the 387-m^3 sec^{-1} peak flow has an indicated 25-yr return period). The flows became more extreme eastward into the Cascade Mountains.

The regional discrepancy between the two sets of records may derive from any of the following circumstances: (1) unmeasured, locally intense precipitation around the monntain peaks; (2) high base flows derived from the generally wet month; (3) snowmelt contribution to the storm runoff. The coherent pattern of increasingly extreme flows eastward into the mountains, running exactly counter to the trend of precipitation return period, provides circumstantial evidence for the importance of snowmelt at high elevation. A snowpillow at 1,440-m elevation within Coquihalla Valley (Ottomite Station) recorded 21 mm of water loss on December 25-27. Nonetheless, to raise the return period for *water input* to a near 25-yr precipitation figure (i.e., to correspond more nearly with the return period of the runoff), it appears, using the Hope Record as an example, that about 50 mm of additional water would be required. Figure 4 reveals about 4 m^3 sec^{-1} base flow on Coquihalla River below Needle Creek, that is, about 4 mm of runoff per day. Either substantial additional snowmelt effects occurred or major, unmeasured precipitation occurred locally. The former seems more likely. We continue this discussion after the next example.

Coquihalla Valley: New Year 1984. Air temperatures in late December 1983 were unusually cold, and freezing levels in southwestern British Columbia generally were at less than 150 m.a.s.l. Little precipitation occurred in this period, so the ground was deeply frozen and many streams were frozen or had very low residual base flow. The high-pressure ridge responsible for this situation began to break down on January 1 as a major storm reached the north coast of British Columbia. This multifront storm moved southeast, drawing in a strong southwesterly flow and sending freezing levels up to 2,500 or 3,000 m. There was substantial precipitation on January 2, 3, and 4, culminating in very heavy rain in the early morning hours of January 4. Severe flooding and debris torrents occurred over a substantial area in the Coquihalla and Nicolum valleys east of Hope. The Trans-Canada Highway was closed west of Hope, and many debris torrents occurred in the mountains east of Mission.

Return periods for precipitation and streamflow at long-term stations are given in Table 1. They reveal that runoff varied regionally in accordance with precipitation extremity, although no streamflow approached the exceptional rainfall return periods recorded at Agassiz CDA and Hope A. This is not surprising, since the substantial areal integration present in the runoff records may not reflect locally extreme precipitation.

Figure 5 illustrates how local the extreme precipitation was in this storm. Short duration records at Agassiz CDA and Hope

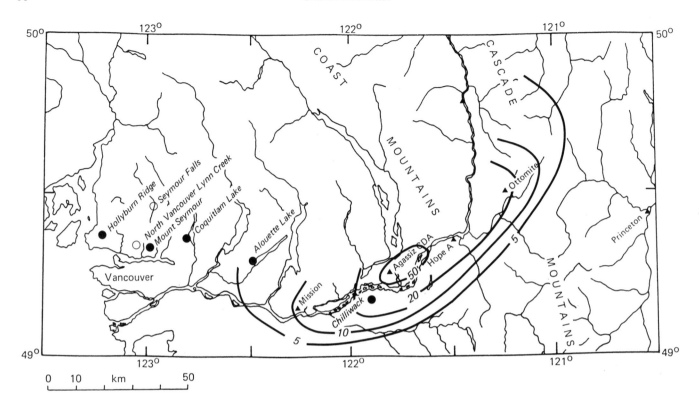

Figure 5. Return period map for the maximum 24-hr rain; January 3-4, 1984, eastern Fraser Lowland (contours are values of time in years). Stations named in italics pertain to analysis of storm trends reported in text (last section). Open circles indicate the two stations that have short records and thus are not among stations analyzed.

A are even more extreme (Fig. 3). Although the very short durations were not exceptional, the 6- to 12-hr precipitation intensity early on January 4 exceeded the 100-yr return period (T) at Hope A. At Agassiz CDA, the 6-hr intensity has T = 211 yr; at 12 hrs, T = 140 yrs.

The runoff records reveal a further point of interest: the minimum flow for 1984 on Chilliwack River was recorded on January 1 at 9.9 m^3 sec^{-1} (the flow is lake-controlled), and the Coquihalla below Needle Creek recorded less than 1.0 m^3 sec^{-1} (Fig. 4). In effect, there was nearly no baseflow regionally. The January 1984, storm runoff was the result of intense rainfall, in which frozen ground probably increased the storm runoff beyond usual proportions. The snowmelt contribution was very limited.

A comparison of runoff from the 1980 and 1984 storms throws further light on the origin of the 1980 runoff. Ottomite Station is near the Coquihalla/Needle Creek stream gauge. Table 2 gives storm statistics based on these stations. The two storms yield remarkably similar runoff ratios despite the quite different antecedent conditions. In view of the modest snowmelt contribution at Ottomite, it appears as if the pattern of storm precipitation (relatively more precipitation early in the 1980 storm) and possibly an initial delay in runoff while the water established passageways through the snowpack may have contributed to the

relatively extreme flood flow in 1980. Snowpack depth and drainage network transmission of water would influence the final outcome significantly.

Wahleach: July 11-12, 1983. A summer storm on these dates, following a prolonged wet spell, generated debris flows onto the Trans-Canada Highway near Agassiz. The regional synoptic situation featured a near-stationary frontal zone over central British Columbia, with the development of a weak low-pressure center over the coast during July 11 to 13. On July 12, westerly to southwesterly flows occurred onshore. This is a relatively common summer situation and often does not give rise to heavy precipitation. However, the forced lift of air over the mountains can trigger free convection aloft and produce very intense rain locally. This evidently is what occurred at Wahleach late on July 11 or early on July 12.

Table 3 reports July 11 precipitation at stations near Wahleach. The heaviest precipitation was at the stations nearest the mountains on both sides of the valley (Mission, Agassiz, Rosedale). The return period at Agassiz was just under 9 yr. However, one of the lower totals for the area was recorded at Foley Creek, a station within the mountains about 18 km south of Wahleach.

Eighteen debris torrents occurred, all within 10 km of each other. They are mapped and described by Evans and Lister

TABLE 2. STATISTICS FOR STUDY STORMS, UPPER COQUIHALLA VALLEY

	December 1980	January 1984
Dates	24-27	1-4
Ottomite		
Precipitation (P)	218 mm	175
Snowmelt (M)	21 mm	*
Coquihalla River below Needle Creek		
Storm runoff volume	$12.1 \times 10^6 m^3$	9.4×10^6
Storm runoff depth (R)	142 mm	110
Instantaneous peak flow	$65.3\ m^3 sec^{-1}$	47.7
R/(P + M)	0.59	0.63

*Unknown, but small.

TABLE 3. 24-HR PRECIPITATION NEAR WAHLEACH ON JULY 11, 1983

Station	Elevation (m)	Length of Record (yr)	24-hr Precipitation (mm)	Return Period (yr)
Abbotsford A	60	40	59.2	2.4
Mission 2nd Ave.	47	28	80.6	6.5
Mission Westminster Abbey	221	22	87.4	7.1
Chilliwack Westview	6	na	77.0	na
Chilliwack Gibson R	12	23	34.7	1.0
Chilliwack	6	35	69.0	na
Foley Creek	457	18	50.8	na
Rosedale	11	17	83.5	na
Agassiz CDA	15	87	85.4	8.8
Hope A	38	39	47.0	1.1

(1984). Their close spatial distribution on the mountain ridge at Wahleach is further circumstantial evidence for locally intense rain not picked up by the rain gauge network.

Howe Sound

Howe Sound (Fig. 1) is a fjord typical of the Pacific Coast Ranges of mainland British Columbia. On the east shore, the land rises from sea level to elevations between 1,500 and 2,000 m within 3 km. This remarkably steep mountain wall and the confined nature of the inlet are important mesoscale factors that influence the climate within Howe Sound. A strong orographic effect occurs on the mountains and toward the head of the fjord, as can be seen by comparing the climate at Point Atkinson—a sea-level station with unrestricted fetch—with that at Hollyburn Ridge and at Squamish (Figs. 6 and 7). Recurrent episodes of debris flow in the steep channels on the east shore have become a serious threat to communication lines and settlement in recent years. Three events are reviewed here.

M Creek: October 28, 1981. This marked the first occurrence of debris flow in the region in 9 yr. After October 24, a sequence of Pacific storms moved onshore, first a weak, double-centered low that dissipated over the coast, then a major cyclonic storm that formed in the southern Gulf of Alaska on October 27. Warm-front rain on October 27 from that storm produced the M Creek debris torrent and minor debris movements on two other creeks. Late on October 28, its occluded front moved inland and a new storm approached the coast. On October 30 and 31 this storm delivered far heavier rain to the region without setting off new debris torrents in Howe Sound, although local flooding occurred. Debris torrents were triggered in the mountains east of Howe Sound.

Table 4 gives the 24-hr precipitation and return period for these late October storms for several stations (Fig. 1). The "max-

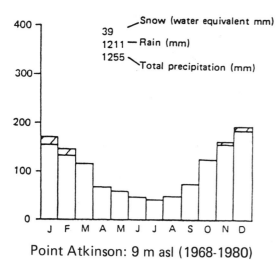

Point Atkinson: 9 m asl (1968-1980)

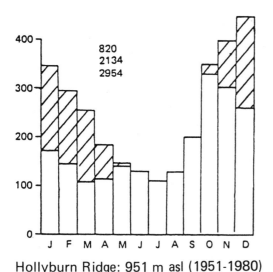

Hollyburn Ridge: 951 m asl (1951-1980)

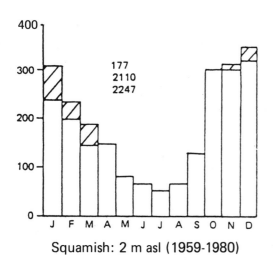

Squamish: 2 m asl (1959-1980)

Figure 6. Mean climate for three Howe Sound stations. Cross hatching indicates water equivalent of snowfall; data are mean annual totals. See Figure 1 for station locations.

imum day" precipitation for the month occurred on October 30 or 31 at all stations: the rain occurred overnight and the difference in date is an artifact of variations in the reporting-day period at the climatologic stations listed. The 2-day precipitation at Hollyburn Ridge for October 26-27 was 81.8 mm; on October 30-31, it was 210.6 mm. The return periods for these 2-day totals are less than 1 yr, and 5.1 yr.

The debris torrent occurred in the early hours of October 28. After it destroyed a highway trestle, nine persons were killed when they drove their cars into the gap on the dark highway. The torrent evidently was triggered by a small rock and debris slide into the channel near the 1,000-m level. Near the 800-m level, however, a major retrogressive rock slide had charged the channel heavily with rock debris over some years, and the log crib of an abandoned logging road bridge formed a substantial barrier to debris movement. Disturbance of this situation—whether by temporary damming of water or by debris surcharge is not known—triggered a major debris flow that cleared out the rockbound gully to its base near sea level. About 20,000 m³ of debris were involved (Thurber Consultants, 1983).

Alberta Creek: February 11, 1983. On February 8-10, 1983, an intense Pacific cyclonic storm approached the British Columbia coast from the west-southwest, drawing a strong southwesterly airflow onto the coast. There was substantial precipitation in the region ahead of the low-pressure center, falling as snow at high elevations. Hollyburn Ridge reported a 46.4-mm water equivalent of snow on February 8 and 9, when the local freezing level was at about 400 m. Precipitation was heaviest on February 10 (see Table 4) when the freezing level rose abruptly to near 2,000 m, so that significant snowmelt occurred. Precipitation intensity was not unusual: it was greatest on February 10, at about T = 2.0 yr for 24-hrs at the stations nearest the debris flows (Table 4).

Debris flows occurred on three creeks within 3.5 km of each other. The large debris flow (more than 12,000 m³) on Alberta Creek severed all bridges except the railway overpass right at the bottom, smashed four houses, and took two lives. Some details may be inferred of the trigger mechanism for this flow (Church, 1985). In the early hours of February 11 a saturated snow avalanche appears to have occurred in the very steep, rockbound upper gully of the creek. Launched over a 6-m waterfall, it set in motion abundant earth and rock debris in the channel below. An abortive debris flow had occurred in this channel the previous December. While this event clearly depended on the weather, unusually intense precipitation was not a necessary part of it.

Charles Creek: November 15, 1983. The storm during which this event occurred (Fig. 8) was as close a synoptic analogue of that of February 11, 1983, as one could expect to find, but the antecedent conditions were different. This occasion occurred during a spell of very active cyclogenesis in the North Pacific Ocean and Gulf of Alaska. There was measurable precipitation in the region on every one of the first 19 days of the month, and the monthly total precipitation was between 190 and 240 percent of average at regional stations. Late on November 12

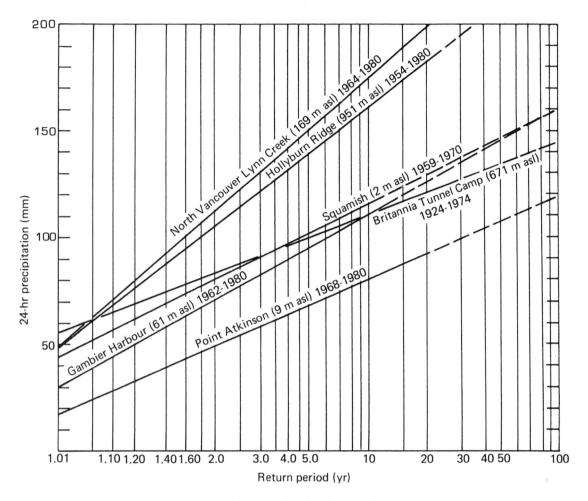

Figure 7. Magnitude and frequency of 24-hr precipitation for Howe Sound stations. See Figure 1 for station locations.

TABLE 4. 24-HR EVENT RETURN PERIODS FOR TORRENT-PRODUCING STORMS IN 1981 AND 1983 IN HOWE SOUND

Station	Elevation (m)	Length of Record (yr)	October 1981				February 1983			November 1983		
			27th	T (yr)	Max Day	T	10th	T	3-day**	15th	T	3-day#
Point Atkinson	9	16	1.4 mm	<1.0	28.8	1.10	32.4	1.18	6.66	4.62	1.82	107.6
Hollyburn Ridge	951	30	43.8	1.005	138.6	5.0	105.0	2.04	151.4##	129.2	3.85	270.2
North Vancouver Lynn Creek	191	20	37.1	1.001	148.7	5.0	50.0	1.01	110.0	87.3	1.32	216.4
Gambier Harbour	61	22	49.0	1.18	-		67.4	1.79	121.2	59.2	1.47	164.0
Squamish STP*	2	25	45.2	<1.0	122.8	15.4	57.0	1.11	110.0	88.0	2.78	161.4
Vancouver International Airport	5	49	11.6	<1.0	57.2	3	13.6	<1.0	37.8	29.9	<1.0	77.3

*Squamish FMC (elevation 1.5 m) in February 1983.
**February 8-10.
#November 13-15.
##Includes substantial snow.

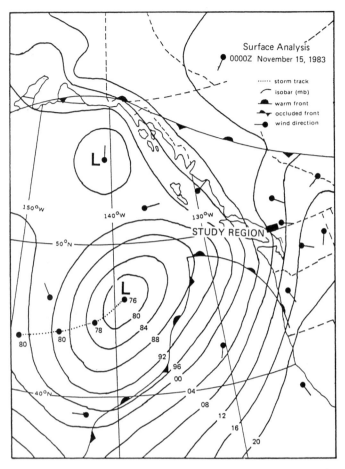

Figure 8. Synoptic surface chart, OOOOZ, November 15, 1983 (1600 PST, November 14). Storm track and 3-hrly previous positions of low-pressure center are indicated.

a double low-pressure center moved onto the British Columbia coast and persisted in the region through November 13. By the 14th, it had moved eastward to Alberta as the very deep storm (shown in Fig. 8) moved in. During the 15th, the storm moved up the coast toward the Queen Charlotte Islands.

The precipitation yielded by this storm sequence was much greater than that yielded by the February storm (Table 4). At Hollyburn Ridge, the return period was near 4 yr for November 15 precipitation, and about 12 yr for the 3-day total (compare 2 yr and much less than 2 yr in February).

Freezing level remained high throughout the November storm and no snow was involved. The Hollyburn Ridge station is only 3.5 km from the starting zone of the Charles Creek torrent; the significantly higher return period for this station on November 15 is symptomatic of locally intense rain. Debris flows occurred in three creeks within 2.5 km of each other.

In Charles Creek, rocky material derived from rapidly weathering quartz diorite cliffs above 500 m in elevation, where the creek follows a fracture zone, is the chief source of debris. The source is prolific and the creek is rapidly recharged. There have been six events here in 16 yr. This site probably represents the nearest approach to a purely meteorologically controlled torrent in the region.

SOME LESSONS

The foregoing cases illustrate some important characteristics of debris flow occurrence in southwestern British Columbia. Events are associated with notable but not exceptional storms. Of the two winter storms in the eastern Fraser Lowland that were studied, the first exhibited return periods for all durations on the order of 5 yr or less: the other locally was a 50+ year event over 24 hours. In Howe Sound, no 1-day precipitation total approached 5-yr intensity, although the 3-day magnitude of the November 15, 1983, storm exceeded a 10-yr return period.

Two things need be said in further explanation of this outcome. First, it is apparent from the spatial pattern of debris torrent occurrence in some of the cases (Wahleach; July 1983; Howe Sound), and from eyewitness reports, that locally intense, short-period precipitation, not necessarily observed in the rain gauge network, may trigger events. Such locally intense precipitation in this region is generated by convection cells of order 1 to 5 km in diameter, that are embedded within larger storms (see Houze, 1981, for a useful review of the microstructure of frontal precipitation). Impingement of the air stream on steep mountain slopes enhances this process by rapid forced lifting, so that warm air may be brought to the level of free convection. The exposure of the mountain walls in both Howe Sound and at Wahleach and the mesoscale topographic steering of low level airflow encourage this process. This does not always happen: the precipitation in the Christmas 1980 event appears to have been rather uniformly distributed.

Second, water in the surface environment may influence events significantly. We have discussed the probable influence of snowmelt and the snowpack on the Christmas 1980 storm to produce surface runoff that was substantially more exceptional than the precipitation. The unusually wet month and 3 days preceding the November 15, 1983, Charles Creek flow represents the more usual antecedent conditions for debris flows. Mountain slope soils are thoroughly wetted and the long storm produces high pore-water pressures and high runoff to set off debris slides, streambank collapse, or mass movements in the channel, all possible trigger mechanisms for a debris torrent.

In comparison, the October 1981 M-Creek event appears to be unusual. The preceding period was not unusually wet and total precipitation remained modest. A minor event on the neighboring creek suggests the possibility for intense rain to have occurred locally. Nonetheless, a much larger storm followed the event and produced no further activity in Howe Sound. Table 5 gives the daily precipitation at Hollyburn Ridge immediately preceding all dated events in Howe Sound since 1958. (For early morning events, the previous daily total was selected: these results are

TABLE 5. RECORDED EVENTS IN HOWE SOUND SINCE 1958

	Disbrow	Unnamed 1	Sclufield	Montizambert	Strip	Charles	Turpin	Newman	Lone Tree	Rundle	Harvey	Alberta	Magnesia	M Creek	Loggers	Deeks	Brunswick Point	Bertram	Kallahne	Unnamed 7	Unnamed 8	Furry	Unnamed 9	Daisy	Thistle	Britannia	24-hr Precipitation* Hollyburn Ridge (mm)	Prior 7-day Precipitation* (mm)
	SOUTH								CREEK									NORTH										
Fall, 1960													O															
Early 1960s																		O					O					
Oct. 12, 1962**													●														24	132
Dec. 22, 1963																									O		125	146
Sept. 18, 1969			●	●					O																		59	90
?, 1972														O														
Nov. 3, 1972						●																					52	81
Nov. 7, 1972						●																					46	195
Dec. 15, 1972									O																		56‡	36
May 23, 1973									O																		71	28
1976/77																				O								
Sept. 9, 1978									O																		30	64
Dec., 1979	O																											
Oct. 28, 1981												●	●				●										44	41
Oct. 31, 1981																			O								72	227
Dec. 4, 1981			●	●				O																			18‡	58
Oct. 6, 1982			●	O																							27	76
Dec. 3, 1982											●																82	147
Feb. 11, 1983				●	●						●																80‡	175
Nov. 15, 1983					●	●	●												O								130	207
Oct. 8, 1984									O																		31	136
Dec. 14, 1984		●																									26‡	154

*Indicative only; amounts vary greatly locally.
**Huricane Freda.
‡Plus significant snowmelt.

O Flood
● Debris torrent

climate-day values, *not necessarily* the maximum 24-hr precipitation, which may be spread between two reporting days.) For 10 debris torrent occasions (excluding the most recent, which appears to have been largely a snowmelt phenomenon), the mean recorded precipitation is 58.7 ± 36.6 mm SD (standard deviation). On this result, the M-Creek event appears not unusual after all.

These results fall well below Caine's (1980) criterion of a 100-mm rainfall in 24 hr as the minimum precipitation required to initiate slope failures and debris flows. That figure surely is only an index, for much greater rainfall intensities would occur within the period than the 4.2-mm/hr average that would lead to this total. Nonetheless, the variance of antecedent precipitation is also very high in Howe Sound and snow plays a variable role. We conclude that no useful criterion for predicting debris torrent occurrence can be based on routinely realizable meteorological records.

Additional important conditions for a debris torrent to occur have to do with debris availability and stability in or near channels. Debris torrents may be initiated by a number of mechanisms, notably the concentration of slope runoff in a steep channel, or the sliding or slumping of debris from headwater side slopes. The occurrence of slides depends on the character of candidate slide planes (hence, soil layering); soil strength as influenced by material, weathering, and moisture (hence, antecedent precipitation history and local slope drainage pattern); restraining factors such as slope base support (hence recent history of stream bank erosion) and vegetation (hence fire, disease, or logging history); and disturbance (road building, logging operations, or windthrow of trees). Some of these conditions are regionally consistent (depending on soil materials and weathering); some depend mainly on slope geometry (hence remain constant at a site); some are entirely casual in occurrence.

The occurrence of a significant volume of debris in the channel remains an important condition. Hence, the recent history of "normal" sediment transport by the stream, bank collapse, or forest debris yield is significant. The particular history of sediment movement in the channel—especially the development of debris jams that retain sediment and interrupt its downstream progress—may affect the probability for a debris torrent to occur. Finally, the time since the last torrent in the channel and the history of that event will influence the likelihood for a new event to occur at any given time.

For the reasons noted above, no reliable means of *predicting* the occurrence of debris torrent events is likely to be developed. However, experienced observers may detect where one or several contributory conditions occur, and hence may designate areas prone to experience debris torrents (see VanDine, 1985; Jackson and others, this volume). This capability, which is diagnostic but not predictive, has important management implications, since it means that sites may be identified where there is a continuing danger, although no useful prediction can be made about the timing or magnitude of a particular event.

However, it may become possible to provide generalized

forecasts of the potential occurrence of debris flows in torrent-prone areas based on incoming storm characteristics. This could provide a life-saving warning to travelers, and could help to rationalize a highway patrol effort. Insofar as residing in or continuing one's activities in hazardous zones is concerned, though, such forecasts could easily generate a "cry wolf" syndrome. Given the difficulty of prediction, properly conservative forecasts would include sufficient nonevents to promote heedlessness. Avoidance through zoning, or structural protection, are the only prudent measures for land use within the hazard zone.

REGIONAL PATTERN OF DEBRIS FLOW OCCURRENCE

Some additional interesting lessons may be learned from a study of regional frequency of recurrence and distribution of debris flow. A systematic record is available of those events large enough to have disrupted traffic along one or both of the highway and railway (both completed in 1958) on the east shore of Howe Sound. The record is summarized in Table 5 and Figure 9. It includes 35 "natural" events in 15 of the 26 creeks between Britannia Beach and Horseshoe Bay; just over half of the recorded events were debris torrents. Twelve people have lost their lives, 9 of them in the M-Creek debris torrent of October 28, 1981. Since 1956, debris flows have destroyed 17 structures (bridges, houses, culverts) and blocked or damaged 24 more: flooding has destroyed seven structures and damaged five more (Thurber Consultants, 1983, updated to December 1986).

Seasonally, events are nearly entirely restricted to the autumn months when intense polar front activity, generated by the strong air mass contrasts that develop at that time of year, characteristically produces the most severe storms of the year in southwestern British Columbia. All three February events occurred in 1983, during the storm described above.

Chronologically, there have been two periods of activity, the lesser in 1969 and 1972, the greater since 1981. There appear to be two possible reasons for this: (1) once activity is initiated in a gully, repeated debris flows may occur until sediment-contributing landslides or channel storage zones heal and restabilize; (2) climatic trends yield periods of increased numbers or severity of storms, which increase the likelihood for debris flows. The former possibility is supported by the fact that two channels have yielded 10 of the 19 debris flow events, and four channels account for 14 of the 19; the latter possibility is discussed in the last section of this chapter.

There is also a remarkable spatial concentration of activity. All but one of the debris flows in the 30-km study reach have occurred in the southern 17 km, between Horseshoe Bay and M Creek. (The exception was a very small event involving principally brush and logs.) Source region geology does not vary significantly between the two sectors. The southern (active) sector, however, presents the highest, least broken stretch of the east shore mountain wall. Moreover, southwesterly storm winds move relatively unimpeded onto this shore across the wide,

southern portion of the sound so that forced lift and orographic enhancement of precipitation may be great. North of Brunswick Point, the trajectory of low-level airflows unimpeded by substantial topography before landfall on the east shore of Howe Sound must turn to lie less than 45° off the bearing of that shore, when the lifting effectiveness of the mountain wall must be substantially reduced. This is seen graphically in the comparison (Fig. 7) of frequency-magnitude estimates of 24-hr precipitation for sets of stations in or near the two sectors: in the southern sector, Hollyburn Ridge and North Vancouver Lynn Creek have magnitudes about double those of Point Atkinson (sea level) for all return periods. In the northern sector, there is little difference among Gambier Harbour (sea level: midsound): Squamish (sea level: head of sound) and Britannia Tunnel Camp (mountain station).

We conclude from this analysis, and also from the frequent recurrence of debris flows in the topographically constricted eastern Fraser Lowland, that the interaction of local topography and mesoscale wind fields exercises important influence over the location of channels persistently prone to debris flow.

CLIMATE SPELLS AND EPISODES OF DEBRIS FLOW

In the broader regional context of this study, there apparently has been a relatively large number of floods and debris torrents in recent years. A compilation by VanDine (1985) shows an apparent increase in frequency of debris torrents in the post-1960 period. Reasons for this may be: increased land disturbance, resulting here primarily from logging activity; climate trends; and increased reporting as the result of extension of human activities into more hazardous areas of the mountains, and a consequent increase of interest in the phenomenon. We cannot entirely resolve the role of these factors, but we can present some analyses that bear on the question. We proceed from local to regional considerations.

Figure 9B illustrates the chronology of events in Howe Sound in comparison with annual extreme 24-hr precipitation (in every case, rainfall or rain on snow) at Hollyburn Ridge. Most of the torrents were initiated in unlogged terrain, so land use does not appear to be a dominant factor in these major events. Only a slight correlation exists between annual extreme 24-hr precipitation and debris torrent occurrence. In fact, none of the extreme storms set off debris flows. Although the sequence of extremes is grouped, there is no obvious trend in it; the sequence of debris flows is much more highly grouped.

Since we already know that no strict precipitation threshold characterizes the onset of debris flow activity, it is perhaps appropriate to seek a more generalized measure of storm severity. Sporns (1962) presented a regional index of severe storm occurrence in the lower Fraser Valley as the number of days in a year in which precipitation exceeded 100 mm (4 in.) at one or more observing stations. The measure is imperfect: an intense convectional storm over one station counts equally with a regional severe storm; heavy precipitation from one storm may affect stations at opposite ends of the region on 2 days, thus doubling

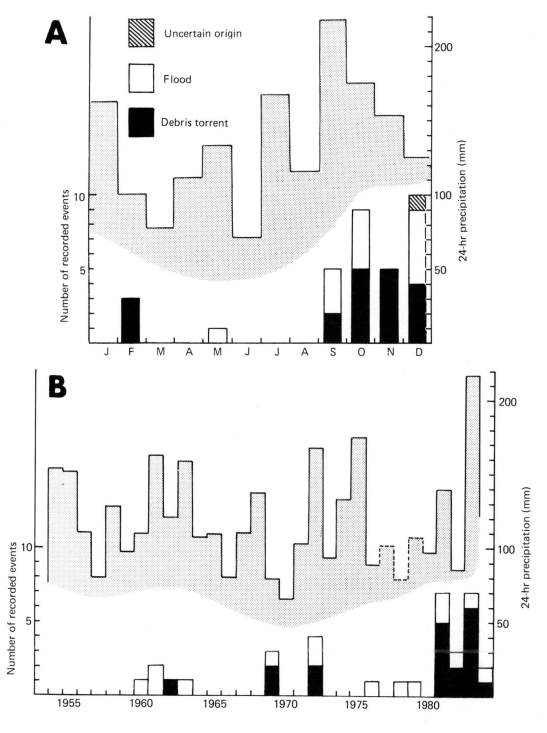

Figure 9. Type and frequency of events in Howe Sound: seasonal, with Hollyburn Ridge monthly extreme 24-hr precipitation superimposed (A); chronologic, with Hollyburn Ridge annual extreme 24-hr precipitation (B). Dashed lines indicate gaps in record within year.

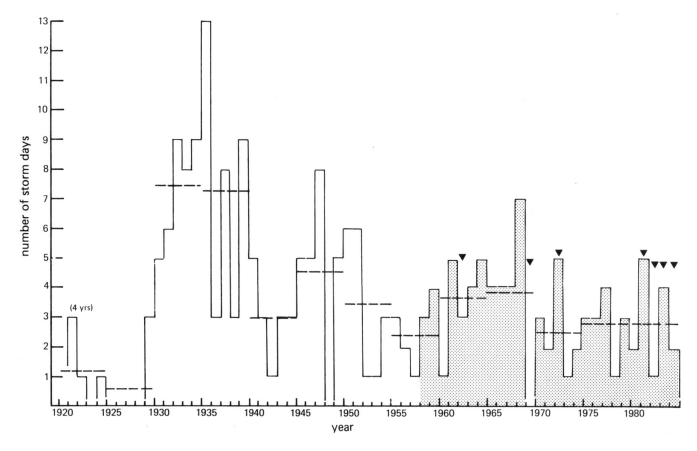

Figure 10. Number of days in each year, 1921 to present, in which storm precipitation has exceeded 100 mm in a day at one station or more in lower Fraser Valley. Dashed lines indicate 5-yr means (not overlapped); stipple, period of Howe Sound event record (Fig. 9B); triangles, years in that record with debris torrents. See text for further discussion.

the count. More seriously, the number of stations scrutinized by Sporns within the study area—which is approximately the map area of Figures 1 and 5—increased from 8 to 50 between 1921 and 1961, so that the probability to observe locally severe events increased sharply in later years. Nonetheless we have adopted his measure as a tool for initial analysis and updated his record through 1984 using only his 50 stations.

In this exercise, two interesting factors came to light: that the record is virtually that of a single station (Coquitlam Lake) that nearly always receives the greatest precipitation in the region; and that a small group of mountain stations on the edge of the Coast Range, located in Figure 5, always contribute the greatest precipitation. The first factor suggests that the record is relatively consistent: the second confirms the importance of the augmented lift mechanism to produce extreme precipitation. In our extension of the record, we noted that almost no isolated summer showers produced enumerable events, that very few successive-day double counts occurred (6 of 72 records in 1962–1984), and that only seven events occurred outside the October-March winter period. The results are displayed in Figure 10.

Despite the increased number of stations scrutinized, there is a substantial decline in severe storm days since a remarkable peak in the early 1930s. Since 1950, a minor peak in activity in the early 1960s does not correspond with the apparent pattern of debris flow activity. The 1980s are not exceptional for regional storm severity.

Finally we consider the possibility of climate change increasing total precipitation, soil moisture levels, runoff, and hence slope instability. For this analysis we return to consideration of individual station records. We selected two stations with reliable long-term records: Agassiz CDA (from 1890) and Vancouver International Airport (from 1938) and examined the sequence of cumulative departures from the mean,

$$S_j = \sum_{i=1}^{j} (x_i - \bar{x}); j = 1, n \text{ yr,}$$

for total annual precipitation and annual maximum 24-hr precipitation. The technique and some statistical tests are described by Buishand (1982). The records are illustrated in Figure 11. So long as S_j becomes more negative, values below the long term mean in the original record are indicated: when S_j becomes more positive, values above the long-term mean occur.

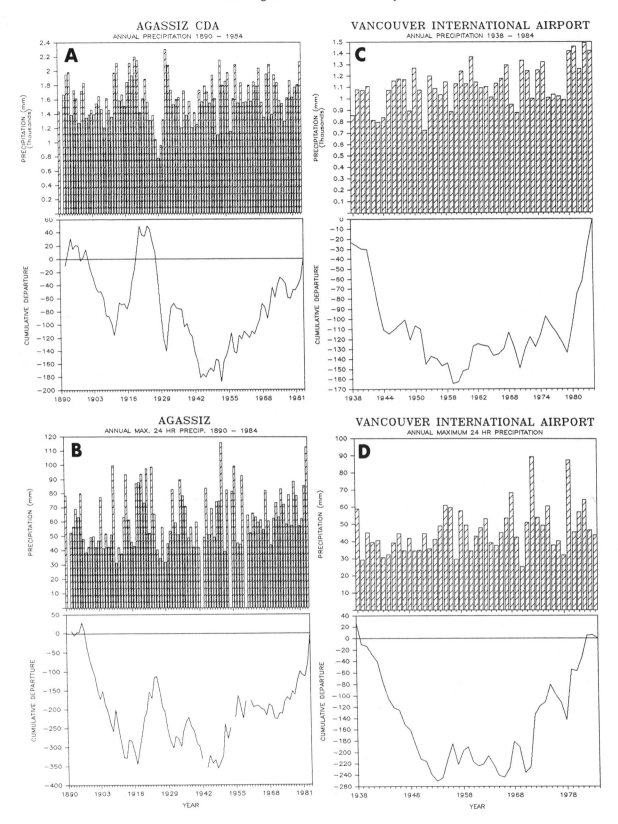

Figure 11. Annual precipitation and sum of cumulative departures (*S*) for Agassiz CDA: annual precipitation (A); Agassiz CDA: annual maximum 24-hr precipitation (B); Vancouver Airport: annual precipitation (C); Vancouver International Airport: annual maximum 24-hr precipitation (D). Note that scales vary between plots.

All the records reveal substantial runs of above- and below-average conditions, with a major period of below-average conditions from the 1930s until about 1950, and relatively wet conditions since. At Agassiz CDA, the average annual precipitation in the period 1925–1952 was 1,497 mm. For 1953–1983 it was 1,719 mm, a 15 percent increase over 1925–1952. Average annual maximum 24-hr precipitation for the same periods changed from 57 mm to 69 mm, a 21 percent rise. At Vancouver, the least probable departure occurs in 1957, with similar changes between the two periods of record. The 5-yr period 1980–1984 includes the four wettest years of record at Vancouver.

Statistical tests on the apparent nonstationarities in the records are inconclusive with, on the whole, marginally greater than 10 percent probability that the records are random except for the annual total precipitation sequence at Vancouver, for which there is less than a 5 percent chance. The trend of increasing precipitation is visually evident in this example (Fig. 11C). Adjustment of the sequence standard deviations to account for the apparent nonstationarity does not alter the outcome (G. Barrett, personal communication, 1985).

There remains the question of the physical significance of the changes that have occurred. The remarkably wet period at Vancouver since 1980 is the best correlate that we have found with the increased tempo of debris flow activity in adjacent Howe Sound, but it is not helpful for prediction. This issue is important, impinging as it does upon the adequacy of historical data to provide design criteria for highways and bridge and culvert openings, and to indicate the safety of sites near steep channels.

It should be clear from our study that the circumstances that trigger debris flows are complex, involving contingent conditions on the ground as well as a hydrometeorological "trigger." We conclude that traditional hydrometeorological indices based on routine meteorological measurements are unlikely to provide consistent indications of the likelihood for debris flow to occur.

CONCLUSIONS

Debris flow events in southwestern British Columbia are associated with storms of low return period. On the evidence of data from meteorologic stations, Caine's (1980) threshold criterion for debris flow occurrence does not apply. We lack the continuous records of precipitation near failure sites to determine whether events can be related to the time of highest precipitation intensity within storms, as has been observed by Japanese investigators, but the wide range of antecedent circumstances suggests that no simple meteorologic correlation exists.

Events have been observed in the following circumstances:

(1) locally concentrated rainfall, high antecedent moisture, no snowmelt (see Wahleach, July 1983; Howe Sound, November 1983); (2) widespread, moderate rainfall and snowmelt (see Coquihalla, December 1980; Howe Sound, February 1983); (3) heavy rainfall onto thawing ground with little snowmelt (see Coquihalla, January 1984); (4) apparently unremarkable rain, rain on snow, or snowmelt (see Howe Sound, October 1981, and other entries in Table 5). So far as processes are concerned, the last category should be viewed with considerable skepticism. Events rarely occur close to a rain gauge and very local downpours may occur in the mountains. From the perspective of prediction with available data, however, the category is present and troublesome.

As a result of this variety, a weather-based forecast system or warning threshold for the British Columbia coast would involve relatively complex procedures to take into account precipitation intensity and duration; antecedent conditions including soil moisture, snowpack occurrence, and frozen ground; snowmelt (hence temperatures); and the spatial distribution of all these conditions. Such a procedure is unlikely to be developed soon.

To considerable degree, mesoscale wind fields and their interaction with topography determine the areas most prone to experience debris flows. Geology does not provide a significant constraint, since many failures occur in the nearly ubiquitous Quaternary overburden. Soil stability on slopes and in channels is a factor that would make prediction of events very difficult except, perhaps, at a site such as Charles Creek with a prolific source of debris.

In these circumstances, then, only very generalized forecasts of the likelihood for debris flows to be experienced in the region seem possible for the foreseeable future. This may provide useful warnings for travelers and public safety officials, and for maintenance crews. On exposed sites, land use restriction or structural defenses are the only reasonable safeguards.

ACKNOWLEDGMENTS

The meterologic synoptic summaries herein draw substantially on the informal reports of D. G. Schaefer, formerly Scientific Services Officer at the Atmospheric Environment Service, Pacific Regional Center, Vancouver. Hydrometerological analyses were carried out partly under contracts with Kellerhals Engineering Services, Thurber Consultants, and the British Columbia Ministry of Transportation and Highways. Gary Barrett contributed statistical results on climate stability. Oldrich Hungr provided a very helpful review of the paper.

REFERENCES CITED

Buishand, T. A., 1982, Some methods for testing the homogeneity of rainfall records: Journal of Hydrology, v. 58, p. 11–27.

Caine, N., 1980, The rainfall intensity-duration control of shallow landslides and debris flows: Geografiska Annaler, v. 62A, p. 23–27.

Church, M., 1985, Debris torrents and natural hazards of steep mountain channels; East shore of Howe Sound: *in* Jackson, L. E., Church, M., Clague, J. J., and Eisbacher, G. M., Slope hazards in the southern Coast Mountains of British Columbia: Geological Society of America Cordilleran Section Annual Meeting, Vancouver, British Columbia, May 6-10, Field Trip 4, Guidebook, p. 4.2–4.22.

Clague, J. J., Evans, S. G., and Blown, I., 1985, A debris flow triggered by the breaking of a moraine-dammed lake, Klattasine Creek, British Columbia: Canadian Journal of Earth Sciences, v. 22, p. 1492–1502.

Evans, S. G., and Lister, D. R., 1984, The geomorphic effects of the July 1983 rainstorms in the southern Cordillera and their impact on transportation facilities: Geological Survey of Canada Paper 84-1B, p. 223–235.

Houze, R. A., 1981, Structures of atmospheric precipitation systems; A global survey: Radio Science, v. 16, p. 671–689.

Hungr, O., Morgan, G. C., and Kellerhals, R., 1984, Quantitative analysis of debris torrent hazards for design of remedial measures: Canadian Geotechnical Journal, v. 21, p. 663–677.

Miles, M. J., and Kellerhals, R., 1981, Some engineering aspects of debris torrents: Canadian Society of Civil Engineering, 5th Canadian Hydrotechnical Conference, Fredericton, New Brunswick, Proceedings, p. 395–420.

Nasmith, H. W., and Mercer, A. G., 1979, Design of dykes to protect against earthflows at Port Alice, British Columbia: Canadian Geotechnical Journal, v. 16, p. 748–757.

Sporns, U., 1962, Occurrence of severe storms in the lower Fraser Valley, B.C.: Canada Department of Transport, Meteorological Branch Circular 3631, TEC 404, 11 p.

Swanston, D. N., and Swanson, F. J., 1976, Timber harvesting, mass erosion, and steepland forest geomorphology in the Pacific Northwest, *in* Coates, D. R., ed., Geomorphology and engineering: Stroudsberg, Pennsylvania, Dowden, Hutchinson and Ross, p. 199–221.

VanDine, D. F., 1985, Debris flows and debris torrents in the southern Canadian Cordillera: Canadian Geotechnical Journal, v. 22, p. 44–68.

Thurber Consultants, 1983, Debris torrent and flooding hazards, Highway 99, Howe Sound: Report to British Columbia, Ministry of Transportation and Highways, 24 p. plus appendices.

Manuscript Accepted by the Society December 29, 1986

Geological Society of America
Reviews in Engineering Geology, Volume VII
1987

Rainfall thresholds for triggering a debris avalanching event in the southern Appalachian Mountains

D. G. Neary
Southeastern Forest Experiment Station
School of Forest Resources and Conservation
University of Florida
Gainesville, Florida 32611

L. W. Swift, Jr.
Coweeta Hydrologic Laboratory
Otto, North Carolina 28763

ABSTRACT

In early November 1977, a storm system that formed in the Gulf of Mexico moved northeastward into the Appalachian Mountains. It produced intense (as much as 102 mm/hr) and heavy (200–300 mm) rainfall that set off debris avalanching in steep terrain of the Pisgah National Forest, North Carolina. Antecedent rainfall during September and October was 177 percent of normal and the wettest on record for these 2 months. The storm began on 2 November, and rainfall was relatively continuous and even (20–50 mm/day) for the next 3 days. The long-duration rainfall was capped by intense convective downpours the night of 5–6 November when debris avalanching occurred. Peak intensities measured at 15 gauges near Asheville, North Carolina, ranged from 21 to 102 mm/hr, with nearly half exceeding 75 mm/hr. Return intervals for peak intensity rainfall in the range of 75 to 102 mm/hr are 50 to 200+ yr. Total storm rainfall for these gauges ranged from 35 to 250 mm, with peak 24-hr rainfalls of 30 to 180 mm. Rainfall intensities for 1-, 3-, 6-, 12-, and 24-hr periods at a gauge near one avalanching site were 69, 137, 159, 164, and 180 mm, respectively.

Development of the storm was monitored by *GOES* infrared satellite imagery in real time, and flash flood warnings were issued. Debris avalanching and high stormflow produced peak stream flows with return periods ranging from 20 to 100+ yr. The largest debris avalanches occurred on steep slopes (70% +), started at high elevations (900–1,100 m) in shallow residual soils (less than 1 m deep), had tracks commonly greater than 700 m, and carried a volume of material averaging 2,500 m^3 per avalanche.

INTRODUCTION

A number of recent studies have improved understanding of the climatic and geomorphic processes that trigger debris avalanches. These studies have investigated the physical properties of failed slopes, the effects of slope angle and pore water pressure, the mechanism of debris avalanche movement, and the properties of the resulting deposits (Fisher, 1971; Hutchinson and Bhandari, 1971; Scott, 1972; Williams and Guy, 1973; Swanston, 1974;

Campbell, 1975; Hollingsworth and Kovacs, 1981; Istok and Harward, 1983). Failures usually begin with sufficient rainfall to bring the entire soil mantle to field capacity. Then rainfall with an intensity exceeding percolation and interflow rates saturates the soil above some slowly permeable stratum. As the piezometric head in this stratum increases, the frictional component of the shear forces holding the soil on-slope decreases. This, combined

81

with decreased cohesion due to water displacing air in soil interstices, reduces the shear resistance force enough to produce slope failure. Conditions that aggravate this process include a thin soil mantle, steep slopes, concentrated drainage, shallow-rooted vegetation, and high clay content in the soil mantle. Prior and current land use, such as roads, logging, farming, and construction, can aggravate slope instability (Megahan and Kidd, 1972; Greswell and others, 1979; Swanston, 1979; Swanson and others, 1981).

Eschner and Patric (1982), in their report on known cases of debris avalanching in forested regions of the eastern United States, noted some common characteristics of these slope failures. Within forests of this region, debris avalanches occur irrespective of vegetative cover. In contrast, logging aggravates slope failures in Pacific coast mountains (O'Loughlin, 1974; Swanson and others, 1981). Scott (1972) mentioned clear-cutting in his study of 1,700 debris avalanches in the Appalachian Mountains, but did not report evidence that clear-cutting was a major factor contributing to eastern debris avalanching.

The storm events triggering debris avalanching in the East appear to have a threshold of 125 mm in 24 hr and occur from May through November (Fig. 1; after Eschner and Patric, 1982). These are the months when high-intensity, convection, and cyclonic storms are most abundant in the East. Eschner and Patric (1982) estimated a general return period of 100 yr for storms producing debris avalanching. However, few studies of historic debris avalanching episodes in the eastern United States have had sufficient data to analyze in detail the rainfall conditions that trigger slope failure.

We have elaborated a November 1977 debris avalanching event in western North Carolina, also reported by Eschner and Patric (1982). Some of the information on this event, particularly the characteristics of the storm that triggered the slope failures, is among the most complete for an event of this type. This chapter describes the antecedent moisture conditions, storm development, and rainfall intensities and amounts that contributed to the most recent episode of slope failure in the southern Appalachian Mountains.

CLIMATOLOGICAL BACKGROUND

The southern Appalachian region has one of the highest annual rainfalls east of the Cascade Mountains of Oregon and Washington. This wet climate and its effects on the hydrology of forest watersheds has been studied for 50 yr at the U.S. Department of Agriculture (USDA) Forest Service's Coweeta Hydrologic Laboratory (Swift and others, 1987). Mean annual rainfall of the southern Appalachian Mountains ranges from 1,000 to 2,700 mm, but can reach 3,800 mm in wet years. Snowfall usually accounts for less than 5 percent of total precipitation.

The characteristics of the November 1977 storm contrast markedly with typical duration, size, and intensity characteristics for the southern Appalachian storms. In general, the majority of storms in this region last less than 6 hr, and only 5 percent exceed 24 hr (Fig. 2a). Thus, the storm described here is unique in that its

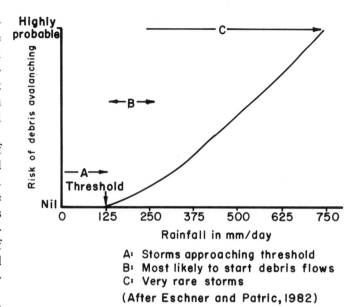

A: Storms approaching threshold
B: Most likely to start debris flows
C: Very rare storms
(After Eschner and Patric, 1982)

Figure 1. Risk of debris avalanching in southern Appalachian Mountains: A indicates storms approaching threshold of 125 mm/day; B indicates storms most likely to start debris avalanches and flows with rainfall of 125 to 250 mm/day; C indicates very rare storms, definitely producing debris avalanches, with rainfall of more than 250 mm/day (after Eschner and Patric, 1982).

duration was 96 to 120 hr. Of the 133 storms that, on the average, occur yearly in the southern Appalachians, only 6 percent exceed 50 mm (Fig. 2b), although they account for 34 percent of the annual precipitation (Fig. 2c). Most of the storm periods have low-intensity rainfall because rates surpass 10 mm/hr only 4 percent of the time (Fig. 2d). Rain in excess of 10 mm/hr produces 31 percent of the average total annual precipitation, whereas only 5 percent of the precipitation comes from rainfall greater than 50 mm/hr. The storm of November 1977 had peak intensities double the latter rate.

Antecedent conditions prior to the 1977 debris avalanche storm were conducive to slope failure conditions. Rainfall in western North Carolina during September and October was 177 percent of normal. Including November, this was the wettest fall period on record (Tennessee Valley Authority, 1977). Debris avalanches were triggered by one intense storm that comprised 70 to 80 percent of November 1977 precipitation on soils that had two previous months of record-high moisture inputs.

METEOROLOGICAL SITUATION

The storm of 3–7 November 1977 was produced by a low-pressure system that pulled moist air from the Gulf of Mexico. Precipitation accompanied a slow-moving cold front on 2–3 November. A low-pressure center reformed on 4 November over the Florida Gulf Coast along the then-stationary cold front. It moved

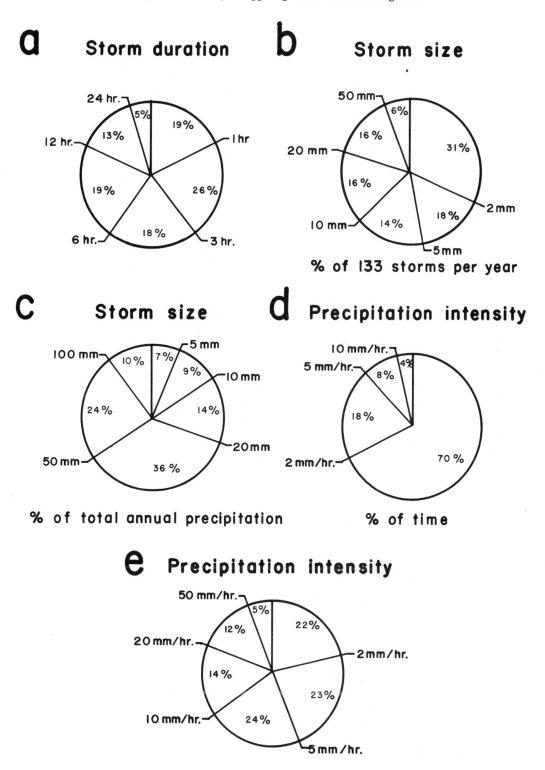

Figure 2. Long-term rainfall patterns at recording gauge 6, Coweeta Hydrologic Laboratory, Otto, North Carolina, based on 40-yr record. A, storm duration; b, storm size as percentage of average of 133 storms/yr; c, storm size as percentage of total annual precipitation; d, precipitation intensity as percentage of time; e, precipitation intensity as percentage of total precipitation.

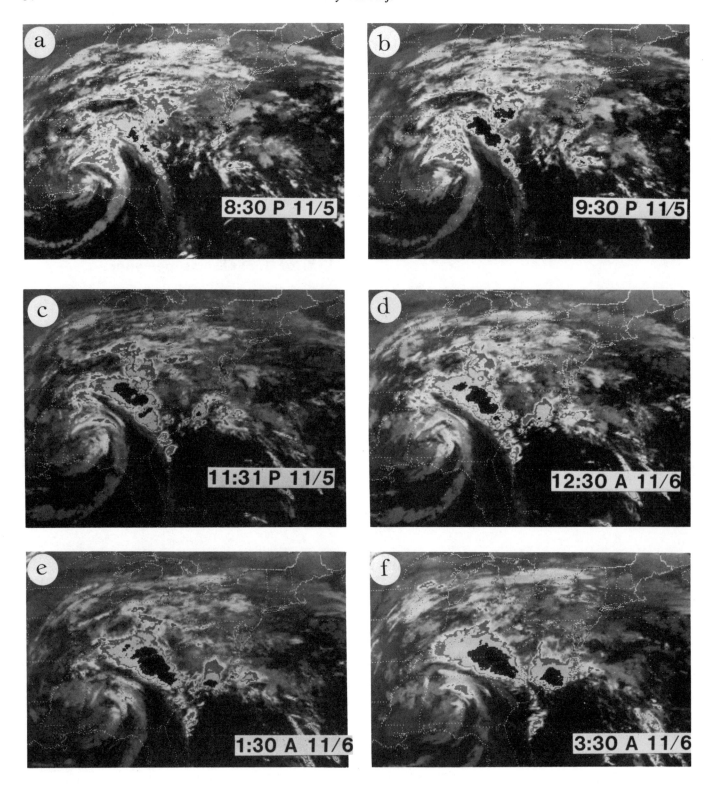

Figure 3. *GOES* infrared satellite imagery of southeastern United States during night of 5-6 November 1977. A, 8:30 p.m. EST; b, 9:30 p.m. EST; c, 11:31 p.m. EST; d, 12:30 p.m. EST; e, 1:30 a.m. EST; f, 3:30 a.m. EST (highest convective cells in black).

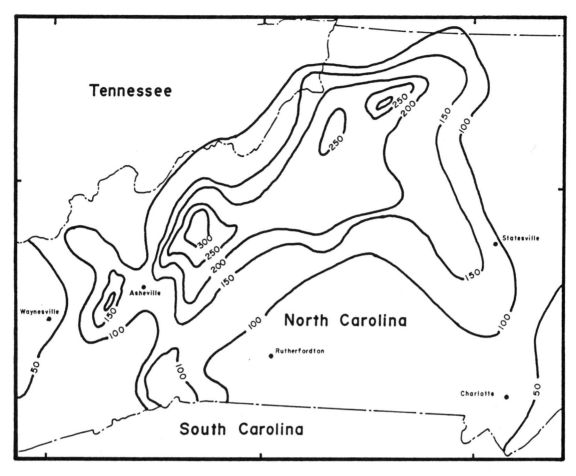

Figure 4. Map of Asheville-Statesville, North Carolina, area showing precipitation (in millimeters) that caused flood of November 1977. [Map adapted from National Weather Service (Stewart and others, 1978).]

slightly westward on 5 November and then tracked north-northeast over Georgia, Tennessee, and Kentucky on 6–7 November. Rainfall began in western North Carolina in the early morning of 2 November. Precipitation was generally continual and even (20 to 50 mm/day) from 2–5 November, by which time cumulating rainfall generally exceeded 60 mm.

The long-duration rainfall before 5 November was capped by intense downpours that initiated the debris avalanching. The heavy rainfall on the night of 5–6 November was produced by convective activity in association with orographic lifting over the southern Appalachian Mountains. Development of the convective cells was simultaneously observed in near real time on *GOES* infrared satellite imagery. Forecasts of flash flooding were issued for the area involved using a (then) newly developed forecasting procedure (Scofield and Oliver, 1977; Heidelberger, 1977).

Intensive convective cells formed within the storm cloud around 2030 EST (8:30 p.m.) on 5 November (dark patches in Fig. 3a). These cells centered over western North Carolina, intensified, and grew in area coverage by 2130 EST (Fig. 3b). The

convective cells moved slightly to the northeast by 2331 (Fig. 3c) and intensified further by 0030 EST (12:30 a.m.) on 6 November (Fig. 3d). Later satellite images showed increased area coverage at 0130 EST and continued drift to the northeast (Fig. 3e). By 0330 EST, the main convective cells were still over western North Carolina but were beginning a gradual dissipation as another cell intensified farther east over the Atlantic coastline.

The general isohyetal map prepared by the National Weather Service (National Oceanographic and Atmospheric Administration, 1977) for this storm shows the distribution pattern of the rainfall (Fig. 4). Four isohyetal peaks ranging from 200 to 320 mm occurred in a southwest-northeast line along the Appalachian Mountains. The largest peak occurred in the Mt. Mitchell area. This discussion focuses on the most southwestern of the isohyetal peaks, specifically, the vicinity of Hominy Creek and Bent Creek watersheds, southwest of Asheville (Fig. 5). On these watersheds, exceptionally complete rainfall and debris avalanching data were collected. Both streams originate in the Pisgah National Forest and flow into the French Broad River. They are

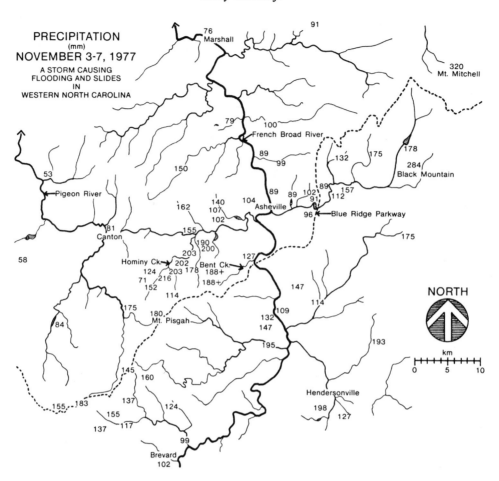

Figure 5. Total precipitation (in millimeters) in vicinity of Asheville, North Carolina, for 3-7 November 1977 storm.

separated by a forested ridgeline which exceeds 1,100 m in elevation.

Total precipitation in the Asheville, North Carolina, area during the 3–7 November 1977 storm ranged from 53 to 320 mm (Fig. 5). Rainfall in the Hominy Creek drainage was generally in the range of 190 to 216 mm, based on a survey of unofficial gauges and exposed containers made immediately after the storm (NOAA, 1977). Across the ridge to the east in the Bent Creek basin, two USDA Forest Service gauges overtopped at 188 mm sometime during the storm. Both of these basins had previously received total storm rainfalls in excess of 200 mm without occurrence of debris avalanching. However, antecedent moisture conditions predisposed the slopes to failure with sufficient rainfall loading (TVA, 1977). The unique feature of the November 1977 storm was the particularly intense burst of rainfall that culminated an otherwise normal, long-duration event. This is precisely the type of situation that Campbell (1975) described as providing the climatic conditions for slope failure.

The U.S. Geological Survey estimated return intervals for peak flows of streams in the storm area to range from 25 to more than 100 yr (Fig. 6) (U.S. Geological Survey, 1977; Stewart and others, 1978). A record flood occurred on Hominy Creek northwest of Bent Creek (Fig. 5). The stream gauge at Candler was destroyed, but high-water marks established the crest at 7.37 m, nearly 2 m above the previous record set in 1940 (TVA, 1977). Although the flow on ungauged Bent Creek is unknown, the Highway 191 bridge across the creek was washed out.

An indication of the storm sequence over the Bent Creek and Hominy Creek basins can be illustrated from the Tennessee Valley Authority recording rain gauges near Mt. Pisgah, Cedar Mountain, Roan High Knob, and Little Switzerland. Figure 7a shows that 120 mm of rain had fallen at Mt. Pisgah during the 90 hr prior to the intense rainfall the night of 5–6 November. Then, during a 6-hr period, an additional 55 mm of rain fell. Peak rainfall intensities calculated from Tennessee Valley Authority gauges around Asheville showed a range from 21 to 102 mm/hr (Table 1). At the Mt. Pisgah gauge, peak intensity was only 21 mm/hr despite its high total storm rainfall (180 mm) and high

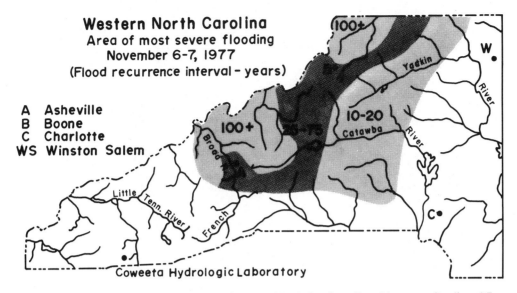

Figure 6. Flooding return period in areas of western North Carolina affected by severe flooding, 6-7 November 1977.

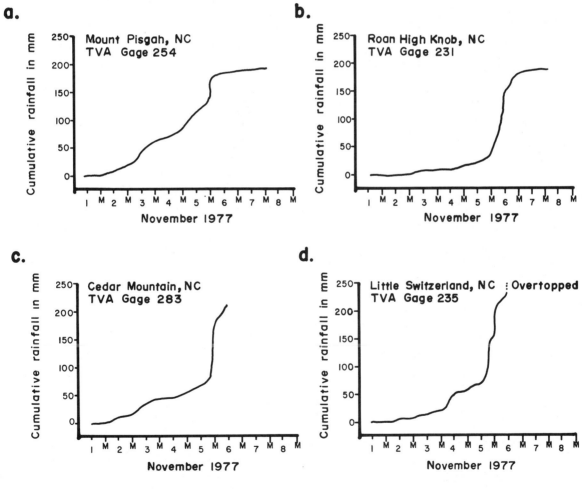

Figure 7. Recording rain gauge analog traces from Tennessee Valley Authority. Recording rain gauges 1-8 November 1977: a, Mt. Pisgah TVA gauge 254; b, Roan High Knob TVA gauge 231; c, Cedar Mountain TVA gauge 283; d, Little Switzerland TVA gauge 235.

TABLE 1. PRECIPITATION AMOUNT AND INTENSITY FOR 3-7 NOVEMBER 1977 STORM
AT SEVERAL TENNESSEE VALLEY AUTHORITY GAUGES NEAR ASHEVILLE, NORTH CAROLINA

Gauge Site*	Elevation (m)	Storm Amount (mm)	Peak Intensity (mm)	
			1 hr	24 hr
1. Cataloochee Ranch	1463	53	15	34
2. Waynesville Watershed	789	53	22	41
3. Parker Branch	658	79	25	77
4. Sassafras Mountain	1048	>87	91	71
5. Laurel Mountain	1244	125	34	51
6. Gloucester Gap	951	145	76	70
7. Coxcombe Mountain	1274	154	24	67
8. Haywood Gap	1646	155	86	80
9. Roan High Knob	1865	173	38	140
10. North Fork	756	>178	46	176
11. Mount Pisgah	1573	180	21	87
12. Blueridge P.O.	689	193	91	144
13. Mills River	610	195	69	180
14. Cedar Mountain	823	202	96	141
15. Little Switzerland	1085	250	102	>163

*All gauge charts show intense rain between 2000 and 2400 EST on 5 November 1977.

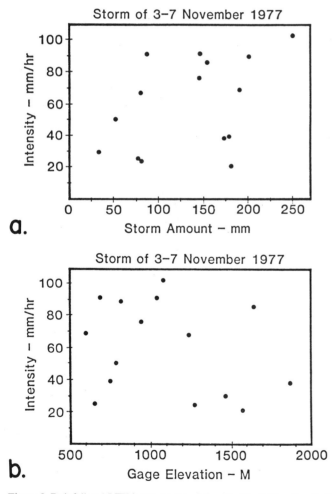

Figure 8. Rainfall at 15 TVA gauges near Asheville, North Carolina, 3–7 November 1977. a, Total storm rainfall in relation to peak hourly intensity. b, Peak hourly intensity in relation to gauge elevation.

elevation (1,573 m). At Roan High Knob (Fig. 7b), the total rainfall (173 mm) was similar to that at Mt. Pisgah, but most of it came during the night of 5–6 November. Consequently, the peak hourly intensity at Roan High Knob was 181 percent higher and the 24-hr peak intensity was 60 percent greater than at Mt. Pisgah (Table 1). At Cedar Mountain (Fig. 7c), the peak 24-hr intensity was similar to that at Roan High Knob, but the peak 1-hr intensity of 96 mm/hr was 4.5 times that at Mt. Pisgah (Table 1).

The rain gauge at Little Switzerland (Fig. 7d) had the highest 1-hr intensity (102 mm/hr) and second highest 24-hr intensity (163+ mm). The Little Switzerland gauge was overtopped toward the end of the storm so the actual peak 24-hr intensity is unknown. It could have been 10 to 20 mm higher, or in the range of the Mills River gauge, which had the highest measured 24-hr rainfall intensity of the sites listed in Table 1. Some of the gauges listed in Table 1 are outside the area shown in Figure 5. Thus, peak hourly intensities varied considerably from point to point, and intensities high enough to initiate slope failures can only be inferred. Storm totals in the Bent and Hominy Creek areas were similar to the four highest totals in Table 1 (Blue Ridge P.O., Mills River, Cedar Mountain, and Little Switzerland). If rainfall intensities were also similar, then intensities of 90 to 100 mm/hr probably set off the debris avalanching. At Mills River, 13 km southeast of Bent Creek, the rainfall intensities during the night of 5–6 November were 69, 137, 159, 164, and 180 mm for periods of 1, 3, 6, 12, and 24 hr, respectively.

The peak hourly intensities, given in Table 1, were weakly related to storm total rainfall (Fig. 8a) and were not related to altitude (Fig. 8b). Gauges entirely within the French Broad River Basin had total storm rainfalls of less than 81 mm and 173 to 180 mm and had maximum intensities less than 60 mm/hr. Gauges with middle (81 to 155 mm) and upper total rainfall ranges (greater than 191 mm) recorded the most intense rainfall. These

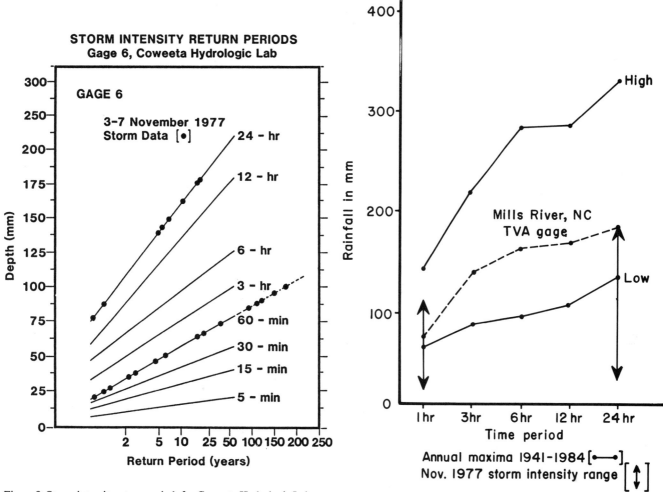

Figure 9. Storm intensity return periods for Coweeta Hydrologic Laboratory gauge 6 with storm data from 3-7 November 1977 storm (dots).

Figure 10. Tennessee River Basin rainfall intensity range with annual maxima for 1-, 3-, 6-, 12-, and 24-hr intensities, 1941-1984, and November 1977 rainfall intensities for Mills River TVA gauge. High and low ranges represent highest and lowest annual maximum rainfall intensities for indicated time periods and length of record.

gauges were all located along the ridges that form the southeastern boundary of the French Broad River watershed. This ridgeline is the divide for the Mississippi and Atlantic continental watersheds and also the main topographic structure for producing orographic lifting of air masses coming from the south.

Forty percent of the peak hourly rainfall intensities listed in Table 1 exceeded 75 mm/hr. Based on long-term data from the Coweeta Hydrologic Laboratory located 96 km southwest of Asheville, rainfalls greater than 75 mm/hr have return periods in excess of 50 yr (Fig. 9). Peak intensities greater than 86 mm/hr in Table 1 (Sassafras Mountain, Blue Ridge P.O., Haywood Gap, and Cedar Mountain) compare to return periods of 100 to 150 yr. The peak hourly intensity at Little Switzerland (102 mm/hr) may have been a 175 to 200-yr event. However, none of the 24-hr rainfalls were exceptional, with 24-hr precipita-

tion less than 150 mm, approximating a 1- to 10-yr return period. The remainder (155 to 180 mm in 24 hr) were 10- to 25-yr return period rainfalls. Thus, the exceptional characteristic of this November 1977 storm was the high 1-hr peak intensities. Total storm and 24-hr rainfalls were not unusual for the area.

Indeed, in comparison to the historical range of rainfall intensities for the entire Tennessee Valley network, the maximum intensities at Mills River for the November 1977 storm fall in the middle to low range (Fig. 10). Although much higher intensity rainfalls have occurred within the Tennessee River Basin, the combination of very wet antecedent conditions on steep slopes with high-intensity, short-duration rainfalls created conditions especially favorable for slope failures in the southern Appalachians. Recorded intensities at several sites exceeded the 125 mm in 24-hr threshold suggested by Eschner and Patric (1982).

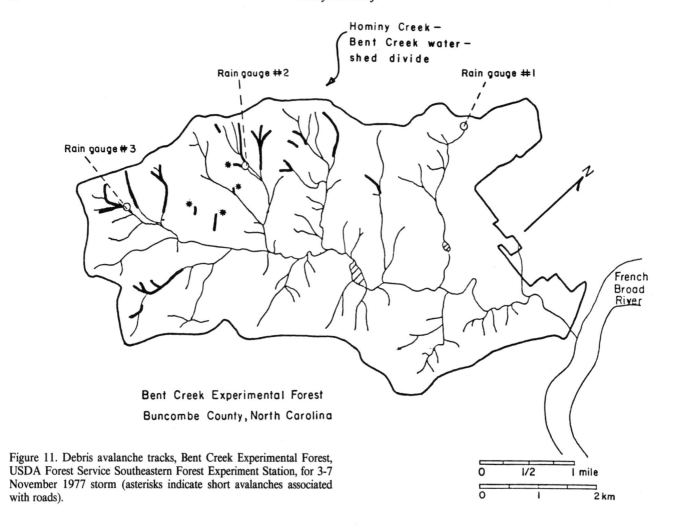

Figure 11. Debris avalanche tracks, Bent Creek Experimental Forest, USDA Forest Service Southeastern Forest Experiment Station, for 3-7 November 1977 storm (asterisks indicate short avalanches associated with roads).

DEBRIS AVALANCHING

The most extensive debris avalanching triggered by the 3–7 November 1977 storm occurred near Hominy Creek and Mt. Mitchell. However, the best information on the debris avalanching came from Bent Creek where a survey was conducted after the storm (Fig. 11). This basin is an experimental forest managed by the USDA Forest Service, Southeastern Forest Experiment Station.

Except for one debris avalanche, all the major slope failures occurred along the ridge between Bent and Hominy Creek. Seven major avalanches were identified. A large number of smaller slope failures occurred, some of these associated with roads (asterisks in Fig. 11). Most of the avalanches originated on undisturbed forest slopes. The heads of the seven largest slope failures were located between elevations of 945 and 1,100 m on slopes of 70 percent and greater (Table 2). Four of these debris avalanches had multiple scarps. Exact runout lengths were difficult to establish because debris avalanche material merged into existing stream bottom colluvium, alluvium, and other debris. Most of the easily identifiable debris avalanche tracks were estimated to be from 655 to more than 810 m long.

Some of the avalanches entrained a considerable amount of woody material. Most of this debris was deposited on lower gradient slopes, old debris fans, or terraces formed by roads. Measurements of debris avalanche volumes were not conducted at Bent Creek. A report by the National Forest in North Carolina indicated that 24 major debris avalanches occurred on federal land in the Bent Creek basin and the Beaverdam drainage of Hominy Creek (USDA Forest Service, 1979). These avalanches covered a total area of 12 ha. If an average failure depth of 0.5 m in the source area is assumed (based on visual and photographic review of most avalanches), then a conservative estimate of the average volume per debris avalanche was about 2,500 m^3. This value is in the middle of the range of slope failure volumes reported by Swanson and others (1981). Deep scouring

TABLE 2. CHARACTERISTICS OF SEVEN MAJOR DEBRIS AVALANCHES, BENT CREEK EXPERIMENTAL FOREST, BUNCOMBE COUNTY, NORTH CAROLINA, STORM 3-7 NOVEMBER 1977

| Debris Avalanche | Debris Avalanche Head | | | Runout Length (m) | Aspect |
	Elevation (m)	Slope (%)	Character		
1	1055	80	Multiple	1235+*	N
2	1035	80	Multiple	700+	NE
3	1100	120	Single	655+	SE
4	990	80	Multiple	810+	SE
5	1035	60	Single	700+	SE
6	975	60	Multiple	700+	SE
7	945	80	Single	760	SE

*Minimum track length; actual length is impossible to determine because of track coincidence with major stream channels.

of some stream channels suggests that even larger amounts of material were moved. More details on the debris avalanching can be obtained from Neary and others (1986).

CONCLUSIONS

This study examines the conditions that produced an episode of debris avalanching in forests of the southern Appalachian Mountains. All the classical conditions of antecedent moisture (177 percent above normal), heavy rainfall (more than 125 mm over 3 days), intense downpours (as much as 102 mm/hr), steep slopes (35 to 80 percent), and shallow soils (depth to bedrock less than 2 m) were present. Although slope stability is not recognized as a general problem in mountainous areas of the East, debris avalanching is a major contributor to long-term erosion rates and influences formation of some of the more productive forest soils. Long-return periods of 100 to more than 200 yr for these destruc-

tive events obscure the perception of their importance as an erosional process. Peak hourly rainfall intensities of 90 to 100 mm/hr approached the suggested 24-hr threshold for initiating debris avalanches in mountainous regions of the humid East. These high hourly intensities were the key to triggering slope failure in well-drained and highly permeable forest soils of the southern Appalachians.

ACKNOWLEDGMENTS

We acknowledge assistance of the staff of the National Oceanographic and Atmospheric Administration. Particular thanks are due Grant Goodge of the National Climatic Center and to the staff of the USDA Forest Service National Forests in North Carolina for assistance in assembling information and illustrations.

REFERENCES CITED

Campbell, R. H., 1975, Soil slips, debris flows, and rainstorms in the Santa Monica Mountains and vicinity, southern California: U.S. Geological Survey Professional Paper 851, 51 p.

Eschner, A. R., and Patric, J. H., 1982, Debris avalanches in eastern upland forests: Journal of Forestry, v. 80, 343–347.

Fisher, R. V., 1971, Features of coarse-grained, high concentrations fluids and their deposits: Journal of Sedimentary Petrology, v. 41, p. 916–927.

Greswell, S., Heller, D., and Swanston, D. N., 1979, Mass movement response to forest management in the central Oregon Coast Range: U.S. Department of Agriculture Forest Service General Technical Report PNW-84, Pacific Northwest Forest and Range Experiment Station, Portland, Oregon, 26 p.

Heidelberger, E. D., 1977, Value of GOES data in recent floods: Eastern Region Technical Attachment No. 77-24, National Weather Service, Department of Commerce, Washington, D.C., 4 p.

Hollingsworth, R., and Kovacs, G. S., 1981, Soil slumps and debris flows; Prediction and protection: Bulletin of the Association of Engineering Geologists, v. 18, p. 17–28.

Hutchinson, J. N., and Bhandari, R. K., 1971, Undrained loading; A fundamental mechanism of mudflows and other mass movements: Geotechnique, v. 21, p. 353–358.

Istok, J. O., and Harward, M. E., 1983, Clay mineralogy in relation to landscape instability in the Coast Range of Oregon: Soil Science Society of America Journal, v. 46, p. 1326–1331.

Megahan, W. F., and Kidd, W. J., 1972, Effect of logging and logging roads on erosion and sediment deposition from steep terrain: Journal of Forestry, v. 70, p. 136–141.

Neary, D. G., Swift, L. W., Jr., Manning, D., and Burns, R. G., 1986, Debris avalanching in the Southern Appalachians; An influence on forest soil formation: Soil Science Society of American Journal, v. 50, p. 465–471.

National Oceanographic and Atmospheric Administration (NOAA), 1977, Climatological data, November 1977, North Carolina: Asheville, North Carolina, NOAA Environmental Data Service, National Climatic Center, 19 p.

O'Loughlin, C. L., 1974, The effect of timber removal on the stability of forest soils: Journal of Hydrology, v. 13, p. 121–134.

Scofield, R. A., and Oliver, W. J., 1977, A scheme for estimating convective rainfall from satellite imagery: Washington, D.C., National Oceanographic and Atmospheric Administration Technical Memorandum, National Environmental Satellite Service, v. 86, 41 p.

Scott, R. C., 1972, The geomorphic significance of debris avalanching in the Appalachian Blue Ridge Mountains [Ph.D. thesis]: Athens, University of Georgia, 124 p.

Stewart, J. M., Heath, R. C., and Morris, J. N., 1978, Floods in western North Carolina, November 1977: Chapel Hill, Water Resources Research Institute, University of North Carolina at Chapel Hill, 24 p.

Swanson, F. J., Swanson, M. M., and Woods, C., 1981, Analysis of debris-avalanche erosion in steep forest lands, *in* Davies, T.R.H., and Pearce, A. J., eds., Erosion and sediment transport in Pacific Rim Steeplands: Christchurch, New Zealand, International Association Hydrological Sciences Publication no. 132, p. 67–94.

Swanston, D. N., 1974, Slope stability problems associated with timber harvesting in mountainous regions of the western United States: U.S. Department of Agriculture Forest Service General Technical Report PNW-21, Portland, Oregon, 14 p.

——, 1979, Effect of geology on soil mass movement activity in the Pacific Northwest, *in* Forest soils and land use, Proceedings, 5th North American Forest Soils Conference: Fort Collins, Colorado State University, p. 89–116.

Swift, L. W., Jr., Cunningham, G. B., and Douglass, J. E., 1987, Climatology and hydrology at Coweeta, *in* Swank, W. T., and Crossley, D. A., eds., Forest hydrology and ecology at Coweeta: Berlin, Springer-Verlag (in press).

Tennessee Valley Authority (TVA), 1977, Precipitation in the Tennessee River Basin—November 1977: Knoxville, TVA, Division of Water Management, 10 p.

U.S. Department of Agriculture Forest Service, Southern Region, 1979, Final report on emergency flood repair: Asheville, North Carolina, National Forests in North Carolina, 12 p. (unpublished).

U.S. Geological Survey, 1977, Water resource conditions in North Carolina—November 1977: U.S. Geological Survey Water Resources Division and North Carolina Department of Natural Resources and Community Development, Raleigh, North Carolina, 2 p.

Williams, G. P., and Guy, H. P., 1973, Erosional and depositional aspects of Hurricane Camille in Virginia, 1969: U.S. Geological Survey Professional Paper 804, 80 p.

MANUSCRIPT ACCEPTED BY THE SOCIETY DECEMBER 29, 1986

Geological Society of America
Reviews in Engineering Geology, Volume VII
1987

Effect of rainfall intensity and duration on debris flows in central Santa Cruz Mountains, California

Gerald F. Wieczorek
U.S. Geological Survey
MS 998
345 Middlefield Road
Menlo Park, California 94025

ABSTRACT

Rainfall intensity and duration of storms has been shown to influence the triggering of debris flows. After examining storm records of the San Francisco Bay region, documenting when debris flows occurred, and measuring piezometric levels in shallow hillside soils, continuous high-intensity rainfall was found to play a key role in building pore-water pressures that trigger debris flows.

Debris flows in 10 storms between 1975 and 1984 in a 10-km^2 area near La Honda, California, were examined, and their rainfall records compared to the records of other storms to determine the antecedent conditions and the levels of continuous, high-intensity rainfall necessary for triggering debris flows. No flows were triggered before 28 cm of rainfall had accumulated each season, which suggests that prestorm soil-moisture conditions are important. After this sufficient antecedent rainfall, a threshold of rainfall duration and intensity—which accounted for triggering at least one debris flow per storm within the study area—was identified. The number of debris flows increased in storms with intensity and duration characteristics significantly above this threshold.

By studying where debris flows initiated in storms of different intensity and duration, debris flow susceptibility was found to depend on soil thickness and hillside concavity and steepness. Moderate intensity storms of long duration triggered complex soil slump/debris flows in thick soils on concave slopes below large drainage areas, whereas high-intensity storms of short duration caused complex soil slide/debris flows in thinner soils without respect to size of drainage area. From these observations, an empirical model based on geology, hydrology, and topography is proposed to account for the triggering of debris flows at selective sites by storms with different combinations of intensity and duration once the antecedent and intensity-duration thresholds are exceeded.

INTRODUCTION

The importance of antecedent rainfall prior to storms triggering debris flows has been identified in many places, including Southern California (Campbell, 1975), New Zealand (Eyles, 1979), and Alaska (Sidle and Swanston, 1982). The significant period of antecedent rainfall, however, may vary from days to months, depending on local site conditions, particularly soil permeability and thickness. In the case of high-permeability soils such as those of Hong Kong (Brand and others, 1984), the period of necessary antecedent rainfall may be extremely short or the amount of necessary antecedent rainfall may be supplied by the early part of a storm.

Although the association between high-intensity rainfall and debris flows has been documented in Japan (Fukuoka, 1980), New Zealand (Selby, 1976), and Brazil (Jones, 1973), as well as in many other places worldwide, the significance of the duration of continuous high-intensity rainfall in triggering debris flows has not been thoroughly examined. Geologic, climatologic, hydrologic, and topographic factors have been identified that contribute to debris flow susceptibility (Campbell, 1975; Ellen and others, 1982; Reneau and others, 1984; Smith, 1987), but the combined effect of these factors with storm intensity and duration on triggering debris flows has not been adequately examined.

In Southern California, Campbell (1975) correlated known times of observed debris flows with specific rates of high-intensity rainfall, and postulated that high-intensity rainfall caused the build-up of high positive pore-water pressures that in turn triggered debris flows. Since then, Wu and Swanston (1980), Sidle and Swanston (1982), and Nielsen (1984) have measured high positive pore-water pressures during high-intensity rainfall associated with the nearby triggering of debris flows.

Several studies have examined thresholds of storm intensity and duration with respect to triggering debris flows. Caine (1980), using published worldwide data based principally on average storm intensity, developed an equation relating intensity and duration of storms that had triggered debris flows. Within the San Francisco Bay region, Cannon and Ellen (1985) identified a threshold for abundant debris flows based on hourly intensities and storm duration. They documented times of debris flows during the January 3–5, 1982, storm and found a strong correlation with periods of continuous high-intensity rainfall during the storm exceeding the threshold.

Several investigators have noted geologic, hydrologic, or topographic factors favorable for locations of debris flow initiation; however, no correlation between these factors and storm intensity and duration has been proposed to account for sites where debris flows initiate. Campbell (1975), as well as others, have generally identified slopes ranging in steepness from 26° to 45° mantled with soil as most likely sites for debris flow initiation. Reneau and others (1984) identified colluvium-filled bedrock hollows as being particularly susceptible to initiating debris flows because of ground-water flow convergence. During numerous storms, investigators have noted a propensity for debris flows initiating in first-order drainages or on hillsides with concave topography suggestive of colluvial hollows (for example, Hack and Goodlet, 1960). However, debris flows have also been noted, albeit less frequently, on planar to slightly convex hillsides (Smith, 1987; Moser and Hohensinn, 1983; and Tsukamoto and others, 1982). Sassa (1984) identified three typical situations, dependent on surface topography, bedrock profile, and the presence of loose soil, where debris flows are likely to initiate because of the convergence of ground-water flow.

I examined debris flow scars in a selected area and noted soil properties and thickness, as well as hillside steepness, profile, and concavity. Continuous rainfall data were used to characterize the intensity and duration of storms that triggered debris flows. Based on comparisons of the intensity and duration of storms that triggered debris flows, I have postulated an empirical model to account for the triggering of debris flows in selected areas by storms with different intensity and duration.

SETTING

The central Santa Cruz Mountains of Northern California consist mainly of Tertiary sedimentary rocks with some in-

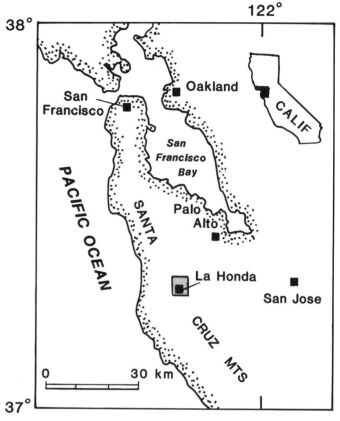

Figure 1. Location of study area near La Honda, in central Santa Cruz Mountains of the San Francisco Bay region, California.

terspersed volcanic rocks (Brabb and Pampeyan, 1983). The mountains rise gradually from the sea coast to heights as much as 1,000 m some 10 to 15 km inland. The mountains have never been glaciated and a thick cover of soil and vegetation mantles most of the area. The area has a mild Mediterranean climate, with the majority (about 85 percent) of the annual precipitation falling as rainfall from November through March (Rantz, 1971) during the cool winter and spring seasons.

STUDY AREA

A 10-km^2 area northwest of the town of La Honda, California (Fig. 1), was chosen for study: the slope movement processes observed there are believed to be representative of those in most of the central Santa Cruz Mountains. The study area ranges in elevation from 60 to 360 m; it contains both gently sloping areas in which grasses, chaparral, and oaks predominate, and steep canyons in which a variety of conifers and redwoods are concentrated. The area receives, on the average, 76 cm/yr of seasonal rainfall (Rantz, 1971), measured between July 1 and June 30.

Bedrock geology (Brabb, 1980) consists of three Tertiary units: (1) the Tahana Member of the Purisima Formation (Miocene and Pliocene); (2) the Mindego Basalt and related volcanic rocks (Oligocene and/or Miocene); and (3) the Lambert Shale and San Lorenzo Formation, undivided (Eocene, Oligocene, and Miocene). The Tahana Member of the Purisima Formation consists principally of very fine grained sandstone and siltstone. The Mindego Basalt consists of basaltic volcanic rocks, including flow breccia, pillow lava, and lithic tuff. The Lambert Shale and San Lorenzo Formation contain mudstone, siltstone, and shale. Soils developed on all three bedrock units are inorganic clays, silts, or clayey silts of medium to high plasticity, with a clay-size fraction composed predominantly of smectites (Wieczorek, 1982).

METHODOLOGY

Between 1975 and 1984 I inventoried slope failures in the study area and measured rainfall using continuously recording gauges, hourly recording gauges, and bucket gauges during major storms. To determine the storm characteristics required for triggering debris flows, meteorologic data were collected for those storms that triggered debris flows, and these data were compared with similar data on other storms. Several measures of prestorm and storm rainfall were compared.

During this period 10 storms triggered a total of 110 debris flows; the majority (74) occurred during the January 3-5, 1982, storm. Examination of rainfall records for 22 major storms revealed two general conditions necessary for storms to initiate debris flows: antecedent rainfall at the time of the storm had to exceed a minimum threshold, and the duration of rainfall had to exceed certain levels of intensity for specified duration.

Antecedent Rainfall

Antecedent rainfall is important for establishing soil-moisture conditions conducive to rapid infiltration and build-up of high pore-water pressures during subsequent major storms. Prior to the development of positive pore-water pressures, the infiltration of rainfall reduces intergranular capillary tension (alternately referred to as soil suction or negative pore-water pressure) in unsaturated or partly saturated soils. The reduction of capillary tension and the increase of positive pore-water pressure reduces soil strength and has been linked with triggering debris flows in many parts of the world.

In the generally low-permeability clay, silt, and clayey-silt soils of the study area, antecedent rainfall is important over a period from probably as short as 7 days to perhaps 2 months. Antecedent seasonal rainfall of at least 28 cm was observed before subsequent storms triggered debris flows, as noted by comparing antecedent rainfall for storms in groups 1 and 2 in Table 1. The rainy season generally starts in October or November, so the required antecedent rainfall is not generally reached until December or January.

Closer examination of antecedent rainfall records revealed that rainfall values during the preceding 7- to 30-day period accounted for about 80 percent of the antecedent seasonal value

and that 7- to 30-day antecedent values for debris flow–triggering storms were about twice those of storms that did not trigger debris flows.

Continuous Intense Rainfall

During this study, a new measure, intensity-duration (ID), which defines the duration (in hours) that rainfall intensity (in centimeters per hour) exceeds a particular value was developed to characterize continuous periods of intense rainfall. For example, an $ID_{0.50} = 3$ hr signifies that an intensity of at least 0.50 cm/hr lasted 3 hr. This measure permits a precise determination of the effect of the time distribution of rainfall in the triggering of debris flows.

By comparing values of intensity-duration for the different storms in groups 1 and 3 (Table 1), a minimum value or threshold intensity-duration was identified for storms that triggered at least one debris flow within the study area. A plot of duration for different levels of intensity for storms in groups 1 and 3 of Table 1 shows a threshold that separates storms that triggered debris flows from storms that did not (Fig. 2A). Each storm is represented by a family of circles, each value corresponding to a duration of each particular intensity. The two empty circles which lie to the left of the threshold are minimum values, and the error of measurement associated with these spans the threshold and confirms the trend.

At low intensity of approximately 0.25 cm/hr, the threshold in Figure 2A is not particularly well constrained. Physically, the independence of duration and intensity on triggering debris flows in this low-intensity range may correspond to the ability of soils on steep slopes to drain under low rates of rainfall infiltration without appreciable build-up of pore-water pressure. The data are not sufficiently accurate to extend the threshold for high intensities with duration less than 1 hr. High-intensity rainfall of this short duration may not be as significant for triggering debris flows in the cohesive, low-permeability soils of this area, as in other areas of more highly permeable cohesionless soils where pore pressures can rapidly respond to high-intensity rainfall (Sidle and Swanston, 1982).

The threshold is best defined within the range of intensities from 0.5 to 1.0 cm/hr. If the threshold is considered as asymptotic at its extremes, then for debris flows to be triggered, the relation between continuous rainfall duration and intensity can be expressed by the equation:

$$D = 0.90/(I-0.17),$$

where D = continuous duration of rainfall (in hours) equal to or exceeding intensity I (in centimeters per hour) (Raymond Wilson, written communication, November 1985).

The effect of antecedent rainfall is illustrated in Figure 2B, in which duration and intensity for storms with less than 28-cm antecedent rainfall (group 2 in Table 1) are plotted. The triangles (representing storms in group 2 in Table 1) are distributed on both sides of the indicated threshold line. Significantly higher

TABLE 1. STORM-RAINFALL CHARACTERISTICS RELATED TO DEBRIS FLOWS
IN LA HONDA STUDY AREA, 1975-1983

Storm (no.)	Date	Prestorm Seasonal Rainfall (cm)	Total Storm Rainfall (cm)	Maximum 1 hr (cm)	$ID_{0.25}$ (hr)	$ID_{0.5}$ (hr)	$ID_{0.65}$ (hr)	$ID_{0.75}$ (hr)	$ID_{1.02}$ (hr)	Debris Flows
Group 1										
1	1/13-14/78*	38.8	7.0	0.81	4**	3**	2**	2**	0**	3
2	2/13/79*	28.2	5.6	1.02	9	3	1.5	1	1	1
3	2/18/80*	49.2	4.6	1.02	7	3	2.5	2	1	1
4	12/29/81	39.6	5.7	0.81	6.7	6.3	5.5	2.4	0	5
5	1/3-5/82	48.0	15.3	1.07	19.2	16.5	13.8	4.3	1.7	74
6	12/20-22/82	35.1	10.4	1.09	3.8	3.3	3.2	2.8	1.3	2
7	1/22-23/83	49.5	9.8	1.42	6.4	3.1	2.2	2.1	1.3	8
8	1/26/83	60.1	7.7	2.44	6.1	5.0	4.8	4.5	2.0	13
9	2/25-3/2/83	87.3	15.5	1.09	3.5	3.1	2.3	2.1	1.2	1
10	3/12-13/83*	105.9	5.6	1.02	6	5	3.5	3	1	2
Group 2										
11	3/15-16/77	26.4	5.2	0.64	8.7	3.1	1.0	0	0	0
12	1/7-11/79	9.0	10.4	1.52	5.5	2.0	1.6	1.6	1.6	0
13	1/14-15/79	19.7	6.9	1.40	5.5	3.4	1.6	1.6	1.3	0
14	12/23-24/79*	23.1	12.7	2.03	10	4	3	3	2	0
15	1/26-29/81	16.5	12.3	1.09	5.2	3.5	2.5	1.2	1.0	0
16	11/18/82	16.8	8.1	1.02	9.3	7.4	5.5	5.3	1.0	0
17	11/27-30/82	25.6	8.2	1.27	4.9	2.4	2.3	2.1	1.4	0
Group 3										
18	3/12-13/81	37.6	6.0	1.19	7.9	2.2	2.0	1.7	1.0	0
19	2/13-17/82	72.3	12.8	0.89	8.1	2.7	1.5	1.0	0	0
20	3/28-4/3/82	94.9	14.0	0.89	7.0	2.4	1.7	1.5	0	0
21	4/10-11/82	109.7	6.0	0.69	3.8	1.7	1.2	0	0	0
22	2/5-8/83	70.8	10.1	0.89	2.4	1.7	1.6	1.2	0	0

Note: Group 1 includes storms that triggered debris flows; Group 2, storms without sufficient antecedent rainfall to trigger debris flows; Group 3, storms without sufficient intensity and duration to trigger debris flows.

*Data for storm numbers 1, 2, 3, 10, and 14 are from hourly recording rain gauges, and therefore ID values are not reported to same precision as values for other storms.

**Intensity-duration values for storm number 1 averaged from National Oceanic and Atmospheric Administration continuously recording rain gauges at Berkeley and San Francisco Airport for similar total rainfall measured at La Honda.

intensities and longer durations, above the threshold in some of these storms, confirms strong influence of antecedent rainfall on triggering debris flows within the range of storm intensity and duration observed.

This threshold is notably less than that identified for abundant debris flows in the San Francisco Bay region (Cannon and Ellen, 1985) and less than that proposed by Caine (1980) for debris flows reported worldwide. However, because the threshold for the study area is based on storms that caused as few as one debris flow in the 10-km^2 study area, this difference is not too surprising. A comparison among these various thresholds plus two major storms in the study area in terms of values of average intensity for 2- and 3-hr duration are presented in Table 2.

Storms that caused more than one debris flow per square kilometer area (Table 1, storms 5 and 8) had higher values of intensity-duration that are more nearly comparable with the threshold for worldwide data and approach the threshold for abundant debris flows in the San Francisco Bay region. Within the study area, the number of debris flows generally increased with increasing values of intensity-duration above the threshold shown in Figure 2A.

Debris Flow Initiation Sites

After debris flows occurred, I examined the source areas where the slope movements started. The debris flows were actually complex types of movement, involving either a rotational or translational soil slide that subsequently mobilized into a debris flow (terminology of slope movement according to Varnes, 1978). In the source area where sliding started, I noted the shape and dimensions of the slide and the geometry of the basal shear surface (if exposed) or the orientation of the displaced surface material relative to the original ground surface to detect rotation.

In exposures of the main scarp, lateral flanks, or basal shear surface, I documented geologic conditions such as composition and profile of soil-bedrock materials, paying particular attention to presence of impermeable layers and zones of contrasting strength. Soil samples from scarp and flanks, representing original

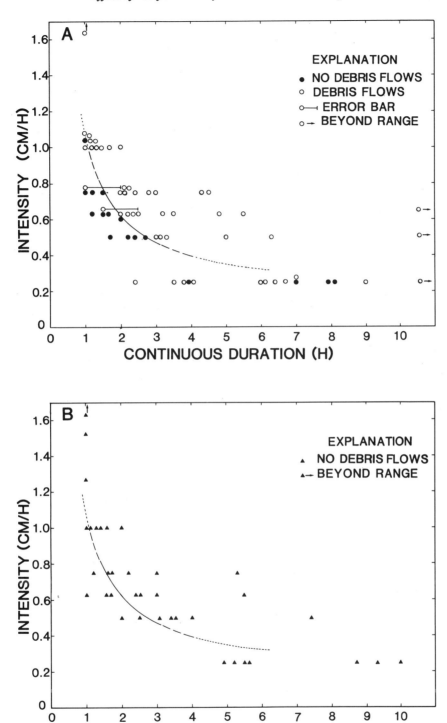

Figure 2. Relations among rainfall intensity-duration from records of 22 storms in La Honda area from data in Table 1. A, Values from storms that occurred after seasonal antecedent rainfall threshold of 28 cm. Solid line represents intensity-duration threshold that delineates storm-rainfall conditions that resulted in debris flows; line is dashed and dotted where threshold is less certain. B, Values from storms that occurred before seasonal antecedent rainfall threshold of 28 cm had been achieved. For comparison, threshold line from (*A*) is shown.

　　　　　　　　　　　　　　　　　　G. F. Wieczorek

TABLE 2. COMPARISON OF SELECTED STORMS IN LA HONDA AREA
AND VARIOUS THRESHOLDS FOR TRIGGERING DEBRIS FLOWS

	2-hr Duration Intensity (cm/hr)	3-hr Duration Intensity (cm/hr)
Threshold-La Honda area	0.63	0.48
Storm 1/3-5/82, La Honda area	0.98	0.87
Storm 1/26/83, La Honda area	1.02	0.90
Threshold-worldwide data*	1.13	0.97
Threshold-San Francisco Bay region**	1.79	1.67

*From Caine (1980).
**From Cannon and Ellen (1985).

slide material, and soil samples from the basal shear surface were tested to determine geotechnical index properties. At one location, seismic-refraction geophysical testing was used in conjuction with augering to examine subsurface conditions.

Hillside morphology near source areas was inspected to ascertain if convergence of ground-water flow from adjacent slopes influenced the development of critical pore pressures near slides. Hillside shape, both along a vertical profile and along a horizontal planar cross section, was noted in the field and on contour maps at a scale of 1:4,800. These maps were used to determine whether the source area was located on planar, convex, or concave slopes. In measuring profiles, the relative hillside position of the slide was noted to ascertain whether the slide occurred in a segment near the crest, midsection, or bottom of a slope.

RESULTS

Three categories of debris flows were observed based on type of initial slope movement, depth of movement, profile of materials involved, steepness of slope, and hillside topography: deep slumps in thick soil, shallow slumps and slides in soil, and very shallow slides in soil over bedrock surfaces. Table 3 shows the distribution of each category of failure associated with each particular storm.

Deep Slumps

Deep slumps, ranging from 1 to 3 m in maximum depth, occurred at middle to low positions on concave slopes. Despite their low relative position on hillsides, these failures were not associated with gully erosion or undercutting by streams. Slopes where failures initiated were relatively gentle, ranging from 20° to 28°. In terms of the ratio of maximum depth to length of initial failure (D/L), measurements on two slumps of 0.16 and 0.18 agree with an average value of 0.17 (Moser and Hohensinn, 1983) from a large sample of partly rotational slides in Alpine regions that led to debris flows.

A profile exposed in the main scarp of a deep slump typi-

cally showed at least 1 m of uniform black, organic-rich, loose clayey-silt soil sometimes overlying a matrix of tan, stiff, silty soil with interspersed hard rock fragments. Weathered bedrock was only rarely exposed beneath these soils. At one such site, a downslope seismic refraction profile detected a soil-colluvial wedge, several meters thick, with weathered bedrock boundaries beneath.

The concave topography and the thick accumulation of soils suggest that these sites may be colluvium-filled bedrock hollows where soils accumulate only to be periodically flushed out as debris flows (Dietrich and Dunne, 1978). If the majority of such sites are emptied in a major storm and if the accumulation of colluvium is slow—taking decades or even longer (Dietrich and others, 1986)—a quantitative analysis of debris flow recurrence is complicated, because future storms will not have the same opportunity to trigger as many failures. This factor was not considered significant in the field area, because following the January 3–5, 1982, storm that caused the majority of failures in the area over the period of observation many sites failed subsequently in 1983 (Table 1).

The concave topography and the location of ground failures at middle to low positions of concave slopes suggest that convergence of throughflow from site slopes may be responsible for initiating slumps at these sites. After major storms, the water table was quite close to the surface at these positions. In some instances artesian pressures were measured, suggesting that ground-water convergence from upslope may result in springs at such locations. Such extremely high pore-water pressures indicated by springs and artesian conditions reduce effective soil strength and help account for initiation of sliding on these relatively flat slopes.

Shallow Slumps and Slides

Shallow slumps and slides within soil occurred on slopes of intermediate steepness ranging from 24° to 40°. They occurred predominantly at middle to upper positions of planar to slightly concave hillsides in uniform, black, loose, clayey-silt soils. Several of these shallow failures, between 0.3 to 1.0 m in depth, had D/L

TABLE 3. DISTRIBUTION OF DEBRIS FLOWS (IN PERCENT)
ACCORDING TO CHARACTERISTICS OF INITIAL SLOPE MOVEMENT

Storm	Date	Total Debris Flows	Slope Movement			
			Deep Slump	Shallow Slump	Shallow Slide	Shallow Slide over Bedrock
1	1/13-14/78	3	67	0	0	33
2	2/13/79	1	100	0	0	0
3	2/18/80	1	0	0	100	0
4	12/29/81	5	0	0	80	20
5	1/3-5/82	74*	14	23	43	20
6	12/20-23/82	2	0	50	50	0
7	1/22-23/83	8	13	87	0	0
8	1/26/83	13	0	23	15	62
9	2/25-3/2/83	1	0	0	100	0
10	3/12-13/83	2	0	50	50	0

*Only 30 of these 74 were field-checked for this characterization; remainder identified from aerial photographs, but not characterized.

ratios ranging from 0.08 to 0.23, indicating a range of values from planar to rotational geometrics. They frequently occurred at or near sites of previous instability, either on oversteepened scarps of massive, deeper seated landslides or adjacent to scars of previous debris flows. Their location is thus significantly influenced by oversteepening or modifications in local hillside geometry.

These failures showed little preference for hillside location conducive to ground-water flow convergence. Because of generally steeper slopes for these failures, the pore-water pressure on the slip surface need not be as great for failure of deep slumps on flatter slopes. Ground-water levels were still relatively high, as indicated by water seeping from the main scarp after failure and by levels measured in a few nearby wells within hours after major storms, but did not reach excessive levels achieved beneath concave slopes. Subsequent to storms such levels dropped rapidly within hours due to greater drainage of short steep slopes and relatively small upslope drainage areas.

Very Shallow Slides Over Bedrock

Very shallow slides of soil over planar bedrock surfaces, between 0.2 and 0.5 m deep, occurred on steep slopes ranging from 26° to 47°. The extremely planar geometry of several of these features is indicated by low D/L values, ranging from 0.03 to 0.07, comparable to those cited by Moser and Hohensinn (1983) for planar slides. These slides occurred on planar and even slightly convex middle and upper portions of hillsides.

A marked contrast in consistency was noted between the upper loosely cemented soil and the lower, weathered, well-cemented, harder bedrock. Such a contrast establishes a permeability barrier, ideal for the rapid build-up of pore-water pressures during intense rainfall (Campbell, 1975). No ground-water level measurements were available near such sites; however, because

no seepage was observed from scars following major storms, dissipation of pore pressures is probably very rapid. These slides were neither associated with topographic locations of ground-water flow convergence nor with sites of previous instability, but showed preference for locations where bedrock could serve as a shallow permeability barrier and infiltration of rainwater above the drainage capacity of the soil rapidly raised the pore-water pressure.

Storm Intensity and Duration

The frequency and distribution of these three categories of ground failures was related to the intensity and duration characteristics of individual storms. Although in most instances several types of ground failures occurred in a given storm, deep slumps in soils usually occurred only for long duration, moderate intensity storms (Table 1; storms 1, 2, 5); whereas, very shallow slides of soil over bedrock occurred for short-duration, high-intensity storms (Table 1; storms 4 and 8). Shallow slumps and slides occurred during both types of storms and in the other storms whose characteristics fell in the intermediate range of these two extremes.

The February 13, 1979, storm (Table 1, storm 2) is the best example of a storm of long duration and moderate intensity that triggered a deep slump in thick soil. The maximum hourly intensity was a moderate 1.0 cm/hr; however, the storm maintained an intensity of at least 0.25 cm/hr for 9 consecutive hr. With the exception of the January 3–5, 1982, storm, this duration of moderate intensity continuous rainfall was unequalled by any other storm (Table 1).

This slump started on a slope of only 20° at a low position below an extremely concave drainage (see Fig. 3). Because of this concave topography, ground water would discharge and pore

Figure 3. Debris flow from February 13, 1979, storm that originated as deep slump in soil below concave hillside. Width of main scarp (arrow) is approximately 11 m across. Average slope near slump is 20°. From scarp, debris flow traveled approximately 60 m.

pressures would be exceptionally high where this slump initiated during rainfall of long duration and moderate intensity.

The January 26, 1983, storm (Table 1, storm 8) best illustrates a short-duration, high-intensity storm that predominantly triggered shallow soil slides over bedrock (Table 3). The main burst of the storm lasted only 4 hr, during which 6.35 cm of rain fell; toward the end of the burst, a maximum hourly intensity of 2.44 cm/hr was achieved. This high intensity far exceeded that measured in any storm in this area during the period of observation (Table 1).

In this storm debris flows started on steep, planar slopes ranging from 32° to 43°, where ground-water flow convergence from adjacent hillsides was minimal. In the empty scar from where the soil mobilized (Fig. 4), no seepage from underlying bedrock was observed, so these failures resulted from rainfall having an intensity exceeding percolation and from interflow rates that saturated the soil and developed high pore-water pressures in the thin soil over less permeable bedrock.

The January 3–5, 1982, storm (Table 1, storm 5) was exceptional, because both abundant deep slumps and shallow slides over bedrock occurred (Table 3). The maximum hourly intensity—1.07 cm/hr after 16 consecutive hr of moderate-intensity rainfall—was only moderately high but probably sufficient to build high pore-water pressures that triggered the very shallow soil slides over bedrock surfaces. Likewise, the long total duration (19.2 hr) of moderate intensity rainfall (equal to or

exceeding 0.25 cm/hr) was probably sufficient to build high pore pressures in deep soils that started deep slumps.

DISCUSSION

A preliminary model is proposed to account for the types of initial ground failures where debris flows occurred in this area during storms with different combinations of intensity and duration. The model qualitatively relates the rates of infiltration of rainfall to storage, drainage, and pore-water pressure with respect to different geologic and topographic hillside conditions. The model considers only a few basic factors that were observed or measured and relies on several assumptions. The following factors act as independent variables influencing pore-water pressure: relative depth of soil, position on a hillside profile, hillside shape, and storm intensity and duration. Increases in pore-water pressure are assumed to have been the principal triggering mechanism of debris flows.

Soils were assumed uniform with respect to strength and drainage characteristics with depth because soils from the several different geologic units are similar in grain size, plasticity, and mineralogy (Wieczorek, 1982). A relatively impermeable stratum, such as weathered bedrock, was assumed to exist beneath the soil. This impermeable stratum is necessary for the build-up of temporary pore-water pressures in a manner similar to that proposed by Campbell (1975). In situations in which the bedrock

Figure 4. Debris flow from January 26, 1983, storm that originated as a translational slide of soil across planar bedrock surface. A, Scar of soil slide is approximately 4 m wide, 8 m long, and from 23 to 40 cm deep on uniform slope of between 35° and 38° of steepness. B, Debris-flow path from scar; margins indicated by dashed lines. In foreground of view, flow was approximately 70 cm deep.

surface was exposed at the base of debris flow scars, the marked contrast in strength and permeability was noticeable. However, in deeper soils in which bedrock was not directly observed, the impermeable stratum influencing pore-water pressure exists at some undetermined shallow depth.

Several additional assumptions have been made for this model: (1) flow and development of pore pressure occurred in a fully saturated soil, without separately accounting for the partly saturated zone; (2) there was no significant inflow or outflow from bedrock; (3) because of low amounts of runoff observed in intermittent streams during storms, infiltration was the dominant hillside process; and (4) gully erosion caused by surface runoff or undercutting of slopes by streams had minimal effect on triggering debris flows.

The model to depict the hillside conditions where the ground failures led to debris flows can be represented by three geologic settings and flow conditions within soil-block elements. In the first case (Fig. 5A), a shallow bedrock surface exists beneath a thin soil on a planar slope at the middle to upper part of a very steep hillside. Permeability of soil (K_s) greatly exceeds that of bedrock (K_{BD}), resulting in a shallow permeability barrier. Low-intensity rainfall infiltrates and drains (Q_{OUT}) rapidly through the thin soil because of the steep slope, without appreciable build-up of pore pressure. There is little ground-water convergence because of the planar upslope topography; through- and side-flow contributions (Q_{TF} and Q_{SF}) to an element are minimal, and direct infiltration (Q_{INF}) supplies most of the ground water. Because soil elements of this type are quite thin ($D = 0.2$ to 0.5 m) and moisture storage is small, direct infiltration of high-intensity rainfall for relatively short duration is sufficient for saturation. As subsequent high-intensity rainfall infiltrates more rapidly than the soil can drain, the soil builds a perched ground-water table that can reach critical values of pore pressure and cause failure.

An example at the other end of the spectrum is a thick soil ($D = 1$ to 3 m) on a middle to low position below a concave hillside (Fig. 5B). In this situation thick soils require more water than thin soils for saturation before downslope drainage begins. Bedrock or another low-permeability barrier perches ground water during the later stages of and/or following long-duration storms. Contributions of base flow (Q_{BF}) may be into or out of this soil-block element; small flow contributions from bedrock have even been measured in some situations (Hayes, 1985), although they are not judged significant for this model. In the element, through- and side-flow contributions (Q_{TF} and Q_{SF}) from upslope concave hillsides converge and may greatly exceed direct infiltration (Q_{INF}). When infiltration, through-flow and side-flow contributions (Q_{INF}, Q_{TF}, Q_{SF}) combine to exceed outflow and base flow (Q_{OUT} and Q_{BF}), a perched ground-water table is formed and pore pressures develop.

Because of the greater soil thickness and longer flow paths down the hillsides for side-flow and through-flow, greater time is required to maximize flow and the pore-water pressure response. This response time depends on the size of the drainage and the location within the drainage. The longer the flow paths are, the longer is the time necessary for pore pressure to maximize.

Because of the maximizing effect of flow convergence from through- and side-flow contributions, rainfall intensity and direct infiltration need not be as great to generate similar values of pore pressure as for planar slopes (Reneau and others, 1984). However, with lower intensity rainfall, storms of long duration are necessary to develop critical levels of pore pressures at such locations.

An intermediate condition to these first two cases is represented in Figure 5C. In this case, shallow soil slumps and slides occurred on steep planar and slightly concave slopes without any particular preferred hillside location with respect to ground-water convergence. The intermediate range of depth ($D = 0.3$ to 1.0 m) and the planar to slightly concave location suggest that direct infiltration, as well as some minor contribution from through-flow and side-flow, combine to generate high pore-water pressures. These ground failures occurred in storms without exceptionally high values of duration and intensity, such as storms 3, 4, 6, 9, and 10 (Table 1). Because they frequently occurred at oversteepened locations or at locations modified by previous slope failures, their stability was initially marginal and easily upset by storms having an intermediate range of intensity and duration.

CONCLUSIONS

Antecedent rainfall and duration of continuous moderate- to high-intensity rainfall are important factors determining *whether* debris flows will occur. Rainfall intensity and duration, are also significant in determining *where* debris flows initiate; however, other factors including slope steepness, hillside topography, soil thickness, and the presence of an impermeable barrier are important as well. Storms of long duration and moderate intensity can cause debris flows that initiate as slumps in thick soils on moderate slopes beneath concave hillsides where ground-water flow converges. Storms of short duration and high-intensity can trigger

Figure 5. Typical sites of debris-flow initiation and soil-block elements to represent permeability and flow conditions. Sites have original average ground-surface slope of angle, θ; maximum depth of slide, D; maximum length, L. Original slope indicated by dashed line; soil, by dotted pattern; bedrock, by slanted pattern. Key abbreviations for flow, Q, and permeability K for the soil-block elements; Q_{INF} = infiltration, Q_{TF} = throughflow into element from upslope, Q_{SF} = sideflow, Q_{BF} = base flow, Q_{OUT} = outflow, K_{BD} = permeability of bedrock, K_S = permeability of soil. A, Very shallow soil slide over planar bedrock surface, commonly on planar to convex middle to upper portion of hillside. B, Deep soil slump at middle to low position on concave hillside, influenced by ground-water flow convergence from upslope drainage. Rotational movement of slump over basal slide surface indicated by arrows. C, Shallow soil slump or slide at middle to upper portion of planar to slightly concave hillside. Location is influenced by oversteepening or modifications in local hillside geometry.

A   Very Shallow Soil Slide Over Bedrock

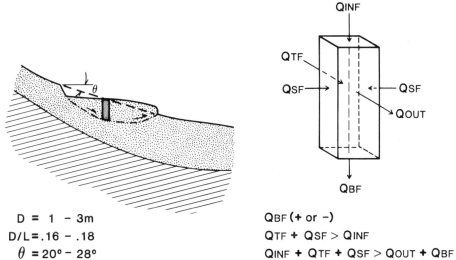

D = 0.2 – 0.5
D/L = .03 – .07
θ = 26° – 47°

$K_S > K_{BD}$
$Q_{BF} \approx 0$
$Q_{INF} \gg Q_{TF} > Q_{SF}$
$Q_{INF} + Q_{TF} + Q_{SF} > Q_{OUT}$

DOWNSLOPE
DIRECTION

B   Deep Soil Slump

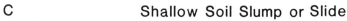

D = 1 – 3m
D/L = .16 – .18
θ = 20° – 28°

Q_{BF} (+ or −)
$Q_{TF} + Q_{SF} > Q_{INF}$
$Q_{INF} + Q_{TF} + Q_{SF} > Q_{OUT} + Q_{BF}$

C   Shallow Soil Slump or Slide

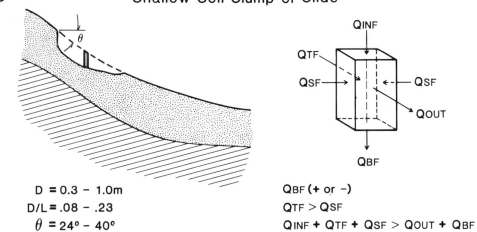

D = 0.3 – 1.0m
D/L = .08 – .23
θ = 24° – 40°

Q_{BF} (+ or −)
$Q_{TF} > Q_{SF}$
$Q_{INF} + Q_{TF} + Q_{SF} > Q_{OUT} + Q_{BF}$

debris flows on steep planar hillsides where shallow bedrock surfaces beneath a thin soil mantle serve as an effective permeability barrier for rapid infiltration and build-up of high pore-water pressures. These observations fit a qualitative model that links geology, hydrology, and topography with storm intensity and duration.

REFERENCES CITED

Brabb, E. E., 1980, Preliminary geologic map of the La Honda and San Gregorio quadrangles, San Mateo County, California: U.S. Geological Survey Open-File Report 80-245, scale 1:24,000.

Brabb, E. E., and Pampeyan, E. H., 1983, Geologic map of San Mateo County, California: U.S. Geological Survey Miscellaneous Investigations Map I-1257A, scale 1:62,500.

Brand, E. W., Premchitt, J., and Phillipson, H. B., 1984, Relationship between rainfall and landslides in Hong Kong, in Proceedings, IV International Symposium on Landslides, Toronto: Toronto, Canadian Geotechnical Society, v. 1, p. 377–384.

Caine, N., 1980, The rainfall intensity-duration control of shallow landslides and debris flows: Geografiska Annaler, v. 62, s. A, nos. 1-2, p. 23–27.

Campbell, R. H., 1975, Soil slips, debris flows, and rainstorms in the Santa Monica Mountains and vicinity, southern California: U.S. Geological Survey Professional Paper 851, 51 p.

Cannon, S. H., and Ellen, S., 1985, Rainfall conditions for abundant debris avalanches in the San Francisco Bay region, California: California Geology, v. 38, no. 12, p. 267–272.

Dietrich, W. E., and Dunne, T., 1978, Sediment budget for a small catchment in mountainous terrain: Zeitschrift für Geomorphologie, suppl. v. 29, p. 191–206.

Dietrich, W. E., Wilson, C. J., and Reneau, S. L., 1986, Hollows, colluvium, and landslides in soil-mantled landscapes, in Abrahams, A., ed., Hillslope Processes, Sixteenth Annual Geomorphology Symposium, Binghampton, September 1985: Winchester, Massachusetts, Allen and Unwin, Ltd., p. 361–388.

Ellen, S., Peterson, D. M., and Reid, G. O., 1982, Map showing areas susceptible to different hazards from shallow landsliding, Marin County and adjacent parts of Sonoma County, California: U.S. Geological Survey Miscellaneous Field Studies Map MF-1406, 8 p., scale 1:62,500.

Eyles, R. J., 1979, Slip-triggering rainfalls in Wellington City, New Zealand: New Zealand Journal of Science, v. 22, no. 2, p. 117–122.

Fukuoka, M., 1980, Landslides associated with rainfall: Geotechnical Engineering, v. 11, p. 1–29.

Hack, J. T., and Goodlet, J. C., 1960, Geomorphology and forest ecology of a mountain region in the central Appalachians: U.S. Geological Survey Professional Paper 347, 64 p.

Hayes, J. P., 1985, Pore pressure development and shallow groundwater flow in a colluvium-filled bedrock hollow (M.S. thesis): University of California at Santa Cruz, 92 p.

Jones, F. O., 1973, Landslides of Rio de Janeiro and the Serra das Araras Escarpment, Brazil: U.S. Geological Survey Professional Paper 697, 42 p.

Moser, M., and Hohensinn, F., 1983, Geotechnical aspects of soil slips in Alpine regions: Engineering Geology, v. 19, p. 185–211.

Nielsen, H. P., 1984, Geology, rainfall, and groundwater associated with several debris flows in Santa Cruz County, California (M.S. thesis): University of California at Santa Cruz, 104 p.

Rantz, S. E., 1971, Mean annual precipitation and precipitation depth-duration frequency data for the San Francisco Bay region: U.S. Geological Survey Open-File Report, 23 p.

Reneau, S. L., Dietrich, W. E., Wilson, C. J., and Rogers, J. D., 1984, Colluvial deposits and associated landslides in the northern San Francisco Bay area, California, USA, in Proceedings, IV International Symposium on Landslides, Toronto: Toronto, Canadian Geotechnical Society, p. 425–430.

Sassa, K., 1984, The mechanism starting liquefied landslides and debris flows, in Proceedings, IV International Symposium on Landslides, Toronto: Toronto, Canadian Geotechnical Society, p. 349–354.

Selby, M. J., 1976, Slope erosion due to extreme rainfall; A case study from New Zealand: Geografiska Annaler, v. 58A, p. 131–138.

Sidle, R. C., and Swanston, D. N., 1982, Analysis of a small debris slide in coastal Alaska: Canadian Geotechnical Journal, v. 19, no. 2, p. 167–174.

Smith, T. C., 1987, A method for mapping relative susceptibility to debris avalanches with an example from San Mateo County, California: Sacramento, California Division of Mines and Geology Special Publication (in press).

Tsukamoto, Y., Ohta, T., and Noguchi, H., 1982, Hydrological and geomorphological studies of debris slides on forested hillsides in Japan: International Association of Hydrological Sciences Publication No. 137, p. 89–98.

Varnes, D. J., 1978, Slope movement types and processes, in Schuster, R. L., and Krizek, R. S., eds., Landslides; Analysis and control: Washington, D.C., National Academy of Sciences, Transportation Research Board, Special Report 176, p. 12–33.

Wieczorek, G. F., 1982, Map showing recently active and dormant landslides near La Honda, central Santa Cruz Mountains, California: U.S. Geological Survey Miscellaneous Field Studies Map MF-1422, 1:4800.

Wu, T. H., and Swanston, D. N., 1980, Risk of landslides in shallow soils and its relation to clear cutting in southeastern Alaska: Forest Science, v. 26, no. 3, p. 495–510.

MANUSCRIPT ACCEPTED BY THE SOCIETY DECEMBER 29, 1986

Geological Society of America
Reviews in Engineering Geology, Volume VII
1987

The effects of fire on the generation of debris flows in southern California

Wade G. Wells II
Pacific Southwest Forest and Range Experiment Station
Forest Service, U.S. Department of Agriculture
4955 Canyon Crest Drive
Riverside, California 92507

ABSTRACT

Debris flows following fire are a common, but poorly understood, problem in southern California. Research to date suggests that they result from greatly accelerated rates of surface erosion by both wet and dry processes during the days and weeks following a fire. Significant amounts of hillslope debris are delivered to stream channels during the fire by a process called dry ravel. An important feature of postfire erosion is the rapid development of extensive rill networks on hillslopes. These rill networks are linked to a layer of water-repellent soil that forms a few millimeters below the ground surface during the fire. These rill networks result from numerous, tiny debris flows that occur on the hillslopes during the early storms. The rill networks form rapidly, often in a matter of minutes, and provide an efficient means for transporting surface runoff to stream channels. This helps explain why postfire debris flows often occur during very small storms and after short periods of rainfall.

INTRODUCTION

Every year southern California faces the unusual problem of debris flows from freshly burned watersheds. This problem arises from a unique combination of factors involving the region's vegetation, physical setting, and climate. First, the native vegetation, California chaparral and its associated ecosystems, is subject to periodic fires. As a given site can potentially burn every 10 to 40 years (Hanes, 1977), fires can be expected to occur somewhere in southern California almost every year. Second, the area is one of high tectonic activity where steep, chaparral-covered mountain slopes are drained by steep, short, bedrock-controlled channels. Finally, because of California's Mediterranean climate, the peak fire season occurs immediately before the winter rainy season. Thus, it is not unusual for the early rains to fall on barren, freshly burned slopes.

Postfire debris flows occur most commonly on smaller watersheds. They are unusual in that they can occur in response to rather small storms and do not require a particularly long period of antecedent rainfall. They occur during the earliest postfire storms and tend to diminish in frequency as the rainy season progresses. This suggests that the debris flows are a typical re-

sponse of the unique conditions of the postfire environment to the early storms.

BACKGROUND

A review of available literature reveals that the relationship between fires and floods was recognized at least by 1930 and possibly as much as 10 years earlier. Eaton (1935) was the first to recognize that these floods were actually debris flows. He discussed the flooding from burned watersheds that occurred on January 1, 1934, in the towns of Montrose and La Crescenta near Los Angeles, California, and characterized these floods as a series of debris flows.

From Eaton's descriptions and from the published discussions accompanying his paper, it is evident that this phenomenon was recognized and understood by workers from the Los Angeles area, but not by those unfamiliar with the area and its flooding problems. Three discussions that supported and elaborated on his findings were by engineers from the area (Baker, 1935; Blaney, 1935; Pickett, 1935). Most other discussions either disputed his findings or focused on other aspects of his paper. Two foresters, Kotok and Kraebel (1935), who were closely associated with the then-recently established San Dimas Experimental Forest in Los Angeles County, were also familiar with the area and understood its flooding problems. They agreed with Eaton's views but did not call the flooding a series of debris flows. Rather, they described it as "the sequence of fire and flood." This was soon shortened to "fire-flood sequence," and because of the active research at San Dimas for the next 30 years, it became the most common term in local usage.

It seems that Eaton may have been ahead of his time, or that debris flows, as a distinct phenomenon, were not widely recognized in the 1930s, because Eaton is rarely cited in subsequent articles on postfire flooding. In their later paper on the La Crescenta floods, Troxell and Peterson (1937) cited Eaton's work but treated the floods as alluvial flows of water-borne debris and not as actual debris flows. Their descriptions of the flows accurately reflect what we know today about the actual behavior of debris flows, but they did not identify them as debris flows. Their extensive discussion of the mechanics of flow and sediment transport clearly shows that they thought they were dealing with alluvial flows and with sediment that moved as suspended and bed load in these flows. However, they also described "walls of water" 8 to 10 ft high and flows whose surface was "greatly raised in the center of the cross section." This last description (Troxell and Peterson, 1937) generally agrees with more recent descriptions of debris flows.

After 1937, most of the work on postfire flooding in southern California was done by USDA Forest Service researchers at the San Dimas Experimental Forest. This research was guided by the philosophical concepts of soil conservation and focused on accelerated erosion after fire and on increased peak flows. A report by the Division of Forest Influences Research staff (1951) described dramatic increases in erosion on study plots following a fire in November 1938. The San Dimas Experimental Forest Staff (1954) also published an eyewitness account of what was certainly a debris flow that occurred during January 1954 in an area that burned in November 1953. The debris flow occurred during darkness and was again described as a debris-laden flood and not as a debris flow.

Scott (1971) described the debris flows of January 1969 in Glendora, California, and, while noting that most of the mountain slopes above Glendora had burned in the summer of 1968, he did not make a strong connection between the fires and the debris flows. Rather, he cited the extremely large storms of that period as the principal cause of the flows. Later work by Wells (1982) suggested that large flows are more strongly linked to fires than to even the largest storms. The problem of postfire debris flows is not confined to southern California. Brown (1972) reported high peak flows and sedimentation rates from freshly burned watersheds in Australia. From his account, it seems clear that these were also debris flows.

By the early 1940s, the connection between recent fires and flooding was clearly recognized. Rowe and others (1949, 1954)

did an extensive study of the effects of fires on peak flows and annual sediment production. This was a regional study that covered virtually all of coastal southern California from San Luis Obispo to the Mexican border. As a result of this study they compiled a series of tables showing expected future peak flows and sediment production from burned watersheds in their study area. Unfortunately, this study was never published, although the methodology used in compiling the tables is described in Section 22 of the *Handbook of Hydrology* (Chow, 1964). Even though the study deals extensively with fires and flooding, there is every indication that the authors did not consider the flows to be debris flows or anything other than ordinary floods.

RECENT DEBRIS FLOW STUDIES

Work by Davis (1977) again suggests that many postfire flows are debris flows. He analyzed the records of 12 large reservoirs in the Los Angeles area and estimated the bulking ratios of sediment in their flows. He concluded that bulking ratios tended to remain nearly constant over a wide range of flow rates (two orders of magnitude) in a given drainage. High flows tended to carry the same proportion of sediment as low flows, and each drainage had a characteristic bulking ratio. Davis noted that postfire flows were an important exception to this trend. In the watersheds he studied, Davis found that bulking ratios ranged from about 0.005 to 0.025 (0.5 to 2.5 percent sediment by volume) for normal flows. For postfire flows, he found bulking ratios of 0.4 to 0.6 (40 to 60 percent by volume)!

A connection between fires and debris flows was again demonstrated in 1978 when a debris flow was observed and photographed in a recently burned watershed near Los Angeles, California (Wells, 1981). Carter Canyon, a small (31 ha) drainage in the San Gabriel Mountains above Sierra Madre, California, was burned by the Mountain Trail Fire on October 23, 1978. On November 11, 1978, a debris flow containing 500 to 700 m^3 of sediment was observed in Carter Canyon during a small (38 mm) storm. The flow occurred during a brief burst of heavy rainfall near the end of the storm and came down a channel in which there had been no previous flow. As it emerged from the canyon and entered a debris basin, the snout of the flow was about 2 m high and could have been described as a "wall of water." Figure 1 shows the actual debris flow a few seconds after it entered the debris basin. During the winter of 1978–79, Carter Canyon was monitored, and at least two subsequent flows were identified from bank and channel deposits, although they were not actually observed. During that year, Carter Canyon produced 3,100 m^3 of debris, most of it as debris flows.

During the fall and winter of 1984–85, an experiment to investigate the effects of burning on small watersheds was done at the San Dimas Experimental Forest about 32 km northeast of Los Angeles, California. Four watersheds ranging in size from 15 to 30 ha were prescribe-burned on October 29 and 30. Studies of debris movement both on hillslopes and in channels were among several conducted in conjunction with the fires. Observations and

Figure 1. Carter Canyon debris flow. Flow has just entered debris basin from canyon on left. Lasting about 4 min, flow delivered 500 to 700 m^3 of sediment.

TABLE 1. TALLY OF DEBRIS FLOW OCCURRENCES DURING THE FIRST 12 STORMS
FOLLOWING BURNING OF 4 EXPERIMENTAL WATERSHEDS IN 1984

Storm No.		Rainfall Total* (mm)	Peak 15-min Intensity* (mm/hr)	Debris Flows**
1	November 8	32	15	4
2	November 13	26	17	2
3	November 16	29	22	2
4	November 21	18	12	2
5	November 24	24	9	–
6	November 28	5	–	–
7	December 3	7	–	–
8	December 8	13	9	–
9	December 11	11	8	–
10	December 17	59	21	–
11	December 20	91	31	4
12	December 27	64	10	–

*Average of 3 gauges within or just outside the study area.
**Numbers are the number of watersheds whose channels showed fresh debris flow deposits, not an actual count of debris flows. In addition to the four study basins, a small burned watershed (area, ~2 ha) not part of the study, also produced at least three debris flows.

preliminary data from the burned areas confirmed that debris flows occur during the early storms and contribute significantly to total sediment production from a burned site. Also observed was a period of very active downslope sediment movement and channel filling by the dry, unconsolidated flow of surface material, the process locally called dry ravel. The rapid formation and elaboration of extensive rill networks on the burned slopes was also observed during the early storms.

Preliminary observations of debris flow occurrence are presented in Table 1, a simple tally of debris flow deposits found at the mouths of each of the four watersheds after major storms. The tally was made by counting the number of basins in which debris flows occurred and did not indicate the number of actual flows per storm. If new deposits were found after a storm they were counted as one debris flow, although it is possible that more than one flow had actually occurred. Data regarding the actual number of flows as well as their magnitudes and volumes are still being analyzed. Bulking in these flows ranged from 30 to 60 percent by weight. Assuming a specific gravity of 2.65 for the solids in these flows, this indicates 11 to 23 percent by volume (Frank H. Weirich, personal communication, 1985).

Data in Table 1 support the idea that large debris movements are concentrated in the earliest storms following a fire. They also suggest that peak storm intensity is more strongly associated with debris flow production than is actual storm size. Storms 1 through 4 produced debris flows large enough to be recognized from their deposits, and no such flows occurred again until storm 11, almost a month later. Storm 11 was the largest and also had the highest 15-minute intensity of any storm that winter. The fact that storms 10 and 12 produced no recognizable debris flows may indicate a depletion of sediment available for mobilization, but much more rigorous analysis is needed to confirm this.

Further analysis may also indicate that more than one debris flow occurred during some of the early storms but were not recognized from their deposits. After storm 11 no new debris flow deposits were observed. The hillslope studies revealed that extremely large amounts of sediment moved down hillslopes as dry ravel during and immediately after the fire. Slope movement rates during the fire were greater by two orders of magnitude than those before the fire. During the early storms, slope movement rates were even higher, exceeding the prefire rates by almost three orders of magnitude (W. G. Wells, unpublished data). During the early storms, extensive rill networks formed; this probably was the principal source of the high sediment production recorded. The rill networks observed for the remainder of the rainy season were found to be somewhat ephemeral. Typically, a rill network formed during each storm and disappeared during the interval between storms. The number and density of rills in a network tended to vary with storm size and intensity; that is, the larger and more intense storms tended to produce denser networks with more individual rills. Midway through the rainy season, the rill networks stopped forming. A storm on January 7–8, 1985, was the last one that produced a distinct rill network. Not surprisingly, it was also the last one to produce a significant amount of sediment movement.

DEBRIS FLOW PROPAGATION

Evidence gathered to date suggests that debris flows are caused by the combined effects of two erosion processes that are greatly accelerated by fire. The first of these is dry ravel, the dry, unconsolidated flow of small particles downslope under gravity. This process, fairly common in the steep mountains of southern California, shows a marked increase in activity during and immediately after fire. The second process is the rapid development of extensive rill networks on the burned slopes during the early storms.

Dry ravel is common in most steep terrain. It is a mass failure process like landslides, but the volume of sediment moved

Figure 2. Dry ravel, West Fork, San Dimas Canyon, San Dimas Experimental Forest. Photo, taken about 10 min after fire had burned the area, shows actual flow of particles taking place (arrow). Width of flow at arrow is 2 to 3 cm.

in a single dry ravel event is extremely small. The frequency with which individual events occur is high, and, as a result, large deposits can build up in a matter of hours or days. It is very common in the Transverse Ranges, where high weathering rates provide an abundance of sand and fine gravel, and steep slopes provide an environment for frequent and rapid downslope movements of the weathered material. The rate of occurrence for these individual movements is greatly accelerated by fire.

Figure 3. Dry ravel cone; a typical dry ravel deposit. Back pack on center of deposit indicates scale. After severe fires such deposits are commonly large enough to fill stream channels and even block roads.

Figure 4. Stream channel filled with dry ravel deposits. Photo taken 2 days after fire.

Examples of dry ravel and its effects are shown in Figures 2 through 4. Figure 2 shows actual raveling in progress. The photograph was taken shortly after a fire had passed over the area and the site had begun to cool down. The chief effect of dry ravel is to deliver large amounts of debris to dry stream channels where it is available for mobilization when flow occurs. Because of the extremely high rate of dry ravel activity after fire, smaller channels may be completely filled within hours or days. Figure 3 shows a small channel filled with raveled sediment. Figure 4 shows a cone of raveled sediment in a somewhat larger channel. Such dry ravel cones are a common sight at the foot of recently burned slopes.

Rill formation and the development of rill networks is the second major erosion process contributing to the formation of debris flows. It is a source of both sediment and water for these flows and is a more complex process than dry ravel. It is catalyzed a layer of water-repellent soil that forms a few millimeters below the soil surface during fire. DeBano (1980) provided an

excellent review of water-repellent soils, including a discussion of their formation and extent of occurrence. On a typical burned slope, the surface soil is loosely compacted and easily wettable. A few millimeters below the surface, however, is a layer of soil that is virtually waterproof. This water-repellent layer is created when organic molecules, formed by the burning of the litter on the surface, are driven down into the soil where they coat individual soil particles a few millimeters below. This organic coating creates a layer of soil that resists penetration by water and forms a barrier to percolation into the regolith (DeBano, 1980).

The extensive rill networks seen on burned slopes after early storms can be formed by a process that involves this water-repellent layer (Wells, 1981, Fig. 5). On a typical burned slope, the upper soil layers consist of a wettable surface layer underlain by a water-repellent layer (Fig. 5A). Rain falling on the slope infiltrates the surface layer and percolates downward until it encounters the water-repellent layer where it is confined and begins

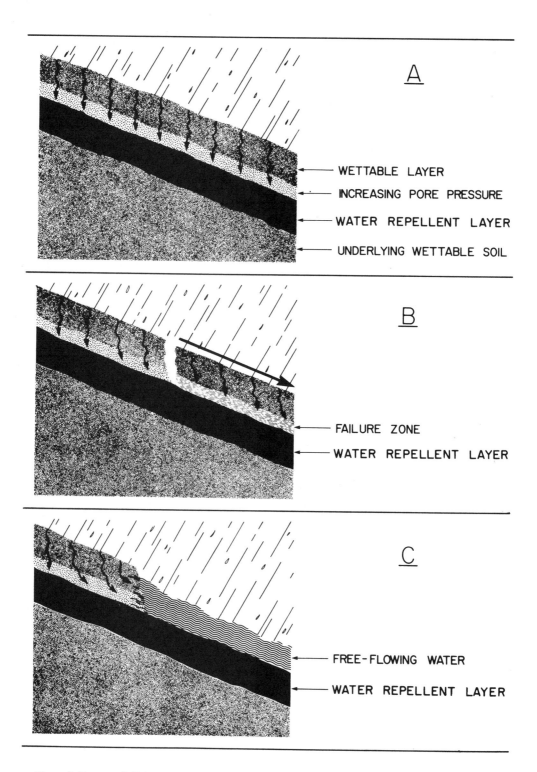

Figure 5. Process of rill formation over water-repellent soil layer. A, Water enters soil and encounters water-repellent layer; pores fill and pore pressures build up. B, Soil liquifies above water-repellent layer, causing small onslope failure that slides downslope, creating small onslope debris flow. C, Rill formed by small debris flow fills with water that then moves rapidly downslope.

Figure 6. Onslope debris flow (5 to 8 cm wide) forming rill (arrow). Location, West Fork, San Dimas Canyon.

to accumulate in the pore spaces between soil particles. As the rain continues, the pores fill with water and begin to exert positive pressure on the soil particles near the boundary between the two layers. As a result of this pore pressure, the soil near the boundary liquifies, causing a small slope failure (Fig. 5B). This failure quickly becomes a small onslope debris flow, which excavates a rill in the wet soil overlying the water-repellent layer. Water on the surface and in the soil adjacent to the rill, flows into the newly formed rill and downslope as shown in Figure 5C.

This rill formation process was observed during the prescribed burn study described earlier, giving qualitative confirmation to the above hypothesis. In this study, an array of sprinklers was placed on a burned slope to provide simulated rainfall. The sprinklers were turned on, and the result was recorded using videotape, movies, and still photography. Rainfall application rates were hard to control and ranged from 12 to 55 mm/hr. The first debris flows were observed as early as 3 min after the sprinklers were turned on. Although precise velocity measurements were not made, these flows were estimated to be moving about 0.3 m/sec. One of these flows is illustrated in Figure 6. The snouts of the flows were heavily bulked, but sediment concentration decreased rapidly in the trailing flow.

Behind them, the flows left distinct rills often with clearly exposed water-repellent beds. Figure 7 shows clear water flowing over one of the water-repellent rill beds. The flows soon joined together or entered preexisting rills rapidly forming a dendritic drainage network.

The rapid formation of this drainage network may explain

the rapid response of burned watersheds to small storms. Consider a small catchment of a few square meters near a drainage divide like the one shown in Figure 8A. This small catchment has three permanent, first-order drainage channels that join to form a second-order channel at its lower end. Under unburned conditions, any runoff entering these channels must travel a rather long distance as overland flow through the litter layer—a journey requiring considerable time. During this time, a significant part of the flow can be expected to infiltrate the soil and never appear as runoff. If this area is burned, however, water cannot infiltrate, and several small onslope debris flows start to form (Fig. 8B). These flows rapidly join together to create an elaborate network of rills (Fig. 8C). With this network in place, runoff water travels only a short distance before it enters a rill, where it is then rapidly transported to the main channel. From the sprinkler experiment described above, it seems clear that this entire network can form in a matter of minutes under fairly mild rainfall conditions. Figure 9 shows a typical burned slope with such a rill network established on it.

With a rill network in place and a channel heavily charged with sediment, the stage is set for a debris flow as soon as there is sufficient water. Recent observations indicate that the rill-forming debris flows probably stop when they reach the main channel, where they add still more debris to that previously deposited. These channel deposits are remobilized when sufficient water is delivered to the channel by the rill network, and a debris flow results. Normally, only a part of the channel deposits is mobilized in any given debris flow, and as additional water enters the chan-

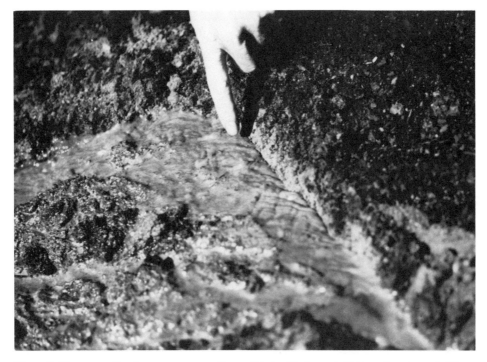

Figure 7. Clear water flowing over water-repellent soil in freshly formed rill. Same location as in Figure 6. Flow is from left to right. Hand is upslope from flow; width at hand, 10 to 12 cm.

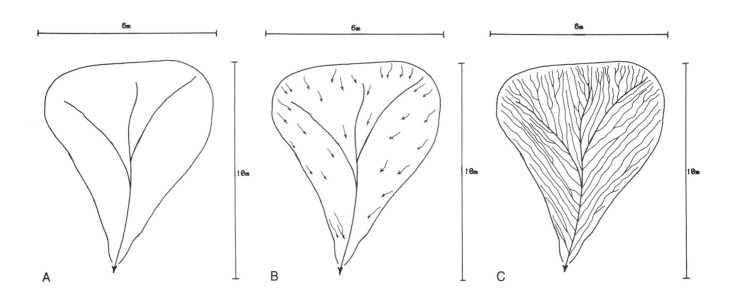

Figure 8. Process of rill network developed by many debris flows on burned area. A, Small catchment near a drainage divide with three first-order channels joining to form second-order channel. Approximate dimensions are shown. B, Debris flows forming on burned slopes move downslope and begin joining together to form networks. C, Fully developed rill network. Original second-order drainage channel has been raised to fifth order by newly formed rills.

Figure 9. Aerial view of rill network developed on burned slope. Location, Santa Monica, Mountains. Width of slope, ca. 50 m at bottom of photo; longest rills (to bottom of photo), ca. 40 m.

nel, additional deposits are mobilized. This results in a series of flows instead of just one single debris flow. Although single flows have been observed, series of flows seem to be more common.

DEBRIS FLOWS FROM LARGE WATERSHEDS

Until now, this discussion has concentrated on small (less than 100 ha) watersheds, where postfire debris flows are most common. The typical debris flow from such watersheds is also small, usually only a few hundred cubic meters in volume. Large watersheds also produce postfire debris flows, although they occur less often and their behavior is more conventional. They occur only during heavier storms and usually require a period of antecedent precipitation. While rare, debris flows occurring under these conditions are extremely large and have caused major disasters in populated areas. The size and behavior of these very large flows result from the size and geometry of the watershed, not from any change in the processes involved. When a very large storm strikes a large, burned watershed, the stage is set for a disaster. An example of this was the debris flow that destroyed the town of Hidden Springs, California, in 1978. This debris flow demonstrated the combined effects of a severe storm on a large, severely burned watershed.

The Hidden Springs debris flow came from the Middle Fork of Mill Creek in northern Los Angeles County. This 12-km^2 watershed was burned by the Middle Fire during the summer of 1977. The chaparral in this watershed was 99 years old and extremely flammable when the fire occurred. This, combined with the extremely hot and dry weather of 1977, caused an unusually severe fire that consumed virtually all vegetation on the slopes and in the stream channels. On February 9, 1978, a large storm struck the watershed, and during the next 24 hr delivered 250 mm of rain to an area that had already received 450 mm.

At about 2 a.m. on the morning of February 10, 1978, a large debris flow came down the Middle Fork, inundating the town of Hidden Springs which is located on the banks of Mill Creek about 1 km below its junction with the Middle Fork. When the flow reached the town, its depth was estimated at 5 to 6 m and its peak flow rate at more than 255 m^3/sec. Total sediment delivered was 300,000 m^3. This single debris flow completely destroyed Hidden Springs and killed 12 people (Davis, 1978).

SUMMARY

Postfire debris flows present an interesting example of a unique set of interrelated geomorphic processes. The principal processes are dry ravel and the formation of rill networks. They are surface processes whose rate of action are greatly accelerated by fires. The rill networks develop rapidly and deliver runoff water to the stream channels where large amounts of debris, delivered by both processes, are stored. The result is a rapid mobilization of channel deposits into a debris flow. Such debris flows occur in response to unusually small amounts of rainfall, and in small watersheds they are rather common. Large events such as the Hidden Springs debris flow are rare, but they point out the potential danger present when a major storm and a severe fire, two extreme but seemingly unrelated events, combine.

REFERENCES CITED

Baker, D. M., 1935, Discussion *of* "Flood and erosion control problems and their solutions": American Society of Civil Engineers Transactions, v. 101, p. 1356–1359.

Blaney, H. F., 1935, Discussion *of* "Flood and erosion control problems and their solutions": American Society of Civil Engineers Transactions, v. 101, p. 1337–1340.

Brown, J.A.H., 1972, Hydrologic effects of a brushfire in a catchment in southeastern New South Wales: Journal of Hydrology, v. 15, p. 77–96.

Chow, V. T., 1964, Handbook of applied hydrology: New York, McGraw-Hill, 1,450 p.

Davis, J. D., 1977, Southern California reservoir sedimentation, fall meeting and exhibits: San Francisco, American Society of Civil Engineers (preprint).

—— , 1978, Storm damage report Hidden Springs area of Big Tujunga Canyon: Los Angeles County, Department of Public Works, Memorandum, File No. 2-20.62. March 27, 1978, 11 p.

DeBano, L. F., 1980, Water repellant soils; A state-of-the-art: Berkeley, California, Pacific Southwest Forest and Range Experiment Station, General Technical Report PSW-46, USDA Forest Service, 21 p.

Division of Forest Influences Research Staff, 1951, Some aspects of watershed management in southern California: Berkeley, California, Pacific Southwest Forest and Range Experiment Station, USDA Forest Service, Miscellaneous Paper No. 1, 29 p.

Eaton, E. C., 1935, Flood and erosion control problems and their solution: American Society of Civil Engineers Transactions, v. 101, p. 1302–1330.

Hanes, T. L., 1977, Chaparral, *in* Barbour, M. G., and Major, J., eds., Terrestrial vegetation of California: New York, John Wiley & Sons, p. 417–470.

Kotok, E. I., and Kraebel, C. J., 1935, Discussion *of* "Flood and erosion control problems and their solution": American Society of Civil Engineers Transac-

tions, v. 101, p. 1350–1355.

Pickett, A. G., 1935, Discussion *of* "Flood and erosion control problems and their solution": American Society of Civil Engineers Transactions, v. 101, p. 1331–1333.

Rowe, P. B., Countryman, C. M., and Storey, H. C., 1949, Probable peak discharges and erosion rates from southern California watersheds as influenced by fire: Berkeley, California, Pacific Southwest Forest and Range Experiment Station, USDA Forest Service, (unpublished manuscript), on file at USDA Forest Service, Forest Fire Laboratory, 4955 Canyon Crest Drive, Riverside, CA 92507).

Rowe, P. B., Countryman, C. M., and Storey, H. C., 1954, Hydrologic analysis used to determine effects of fire on peak discharge and erosion rates in southern California watersheds: Berkeley, California, Pacific Southwest Forest and Range Experiment Station, USDA Forest Service, (unpublished manuscript, on file at USDA Forest Service, Forest Fire Laboratory, 4955 Canyon Crest Drive, Riverside, CA 92507).

San Dimas Experimental Forest Staff, 1954, Fire-flood sequences on the San Dimas Experimental Forest: Berkeley, California, Pacific Southwest Forest and Range Experiment Station, USDA Forest Service, Technical Paper 6, 29 p.

Scott, K. M., 1971, Origin and sedimentology of 1969 debris flows near Glendora, California: U.S. Geological Survey Professional Paper 750-C, p. C242–C247.

Troxell, H. C., and Peterson, J. Q., 1937, Flood in La Canada Valley, California, January 1, 1934: U.S. Geological Survey Water-Supply Paper 796-C, p. 53–98.

Wells, W. G., II., 1981, Some effects of brushfires on erosion processes in coastal southern California, *in* Erosion and sediment transport in Pacific-rim steeplands, Proceedings of the Christchurch symposium, Christchurch, New Zealand, January 25-31, 1981: International Association of Hydrological Sciences Publication 132, p. 305–342.

—— , 1982, The storms of 1978 and 1980 and their effect on sediment movement in the eastern San Gabriel front, *in* Proceedings, Storms, floods, and debris flows in southern California and Arizona 1978 and 1980, Pasadena, CA, September 1980: Washington, D.C., National Academy Press, Report No. CSS-CND-019, p. 229–242.

MANUSCRIPT ACCEPTED BY THE SOCIETY DECEMBER 29, 1986

Geological Society of America
Reviews in Engineering Geology, Volume VII
1987

Identification of debris flow hazard on alluvial fans in the Canadian Rocky Mountains

Lionel E. Jackson, Jr.
Geological Survey of Canada
Terrain Sciences Division
100 West Pender Street
Vancouver, British Columbia V6B 1R8
Canada

R. A. Kostaschuk
Department of Geography
University of Guelph
Guelph, Ontario N1G 2W1
Canada

G. M. MacDonald
Department of Geography
McMaster University
Hamilton, Ontario L8S 4K1
Canada

ABSTRACT

This chapter presents a method by which morphometric criteria can be used to obtain a rapid first-approximation of potential debris flow hazard on alluvial fans in the Canadian Rocky Mountain Front Ranges. Geomorphic and sedimentologic evidence indicates that many fans are affected by debris flow processes. Such fans generally are steeper than 4° and have small, steep first- or second-order drainage basins with Melton's ruggedness number (R) more than 0.25 to 0.3. Fans not prone to debris flows are dominated by fluvial processes and have gentler slopes in less rugged third-order or higher drainage basins. This morphometric approach should have wide applicability for continuously graded basins in unglacierized regions.

INTRODUCTION

Bottomland sites are comparatively rare in the Canadian Rocky Mountains. Most of the land surface is ridge or slope. Roads, powerlines, and settlements must, out of necessity, be sited along valley margins. This siting frequently places these works in the path of episodic, highly destructive geomorphic processes such as debris flows, snow and rock avalanches, and flash floods. Until recently (VanDine, 1985), debris flow has been little appreciated or understood by civil engineers and planners involved in the siting of public and private works in this region. Debris flows are now recognized as unique and severe natural hazards that require distinct remedial measures (VanDine, 1985).

Sites at greatest risk to inundation by debris flows are those located on alluvial fan landforms (any terrestrial, clastic fan-like deposit) partly or dominantly built by debris flow sedimentation. However, not all fans contain a significant component of debris flow deposits. Our studies of fans in the Canadian Rocky Mountains indicate a continuum of fan landforms from those of purely fluvial origin to mixed debris flow–fluvial to those of predominantly mixed debris flow–avalanche genesis (Jackson, 1987; Kostaschuk and others, 1987).

This continuum of landforms dictates that the first step in evaluating debris flow hazard is the discrimination of debris flow–component fans from purely fluvial ones. This chapter details attempts at making rapid discrimination between the two fan types through morphometric analysis of fan and basin parameters. A method by which debris flow–prone fans can be identified by map and airphoto analysis eliminates unnecessary field study of fluvial fans and permits more time to be devoted to the evaluation of past debris flow frequency and volume on fans.

SETTING

The Rocky Mountain Front and Main ranges (Bally and others, 1966) consist of thrust-faulted Late Precambrian to Mesozoic carbonates and clastics. The major structural elements and mountain ranges strike northwest-southeast (Fig. 1). Elevations range between 1,450 and 3,500 m above sea level, and relief locally may exceed 1,000 m. The climate of the area is continental, modified by high elevation and topography. Valley floors are usually blanketed by Pleistocene drift and postglacial sediments. The Rocky Mountains were intensely glaciated by ice cap and valley glaciers during the late Wisconsinan glaciation. Glaciers retreated to their modern extent by 10 ka (Luckman and Osborn, 1979).

STUDY AREAS

Fans and their drainage basins were chosen for study in three areas in which the physiography and geology is representative of most of the Rocky Mountain Front Ranges. Each of the three areas is described below. Topographic maps of the areas are presented in Figure 2, and fan locations are plotted on these diagrams.

Bow Valley Area

This area includes the segment of the Front Ranges traversed by the Bow Valley from the mountain front to the margin of the Main Ranges near the confluence of Johnston Creek with the Bow River (Fig. 2a). The area is typical of extremely rugged glaciated areas of the Rocky Mountain Front Ranges that are not presently glacierized beyond the scattered occurrence of small cirque or niche glaciers. Adjacent drainages usually are separated by knife-edge divides and horn peaks. Cirques are present on most peaks; relief often exceeds 1,500 m over a distance of a few kilometers. Mountain slopes are often marked by avalanche tracks and talus cones. The southwest-dipping imbricated thrust sheets of the Front Ranges are topographically expressed as northwest-trending mountain ranges and intervening valleys. Mountain summits are Paleozoic carbonates whereas lower slopes and valleys are predominantly underlain by Mesozoic clastics. This structure has imparted an asymmetry to drainage patterns between adjoining mountain ranges. Northeast-facing slopes are scarp slopes. Basins draining these slopes are small in area and steep. In contrast, southwest-facing slopes are dip slopes. Basins developed on them are larger in area and less steep.

Kananaskis Valley–Spray Lakes Reservoir Area

This area (Fig. 2b) is located immediately south of the Bow Valley area. It includes a part of the Front Ranges comparable to the Bow Valley area in most respects.

As with the Bow Valley area, the Kananaskis–Spray Lakes Reservoir area was intensely glaciated during the last glaciation, and landforms of alpine glaciation abound. Only scattered cirque and niche glaciers are currently present in the area.

Crowsnest Pass Area

This area (Fig. 2c) is less rugged than the two study areas to the north. Although it was glaciated during the late Wisconsinan, it was not a center of ice accumulation, with the exception of local cirque glaciers. Relief in this area rarely exceeds 760 m, and slopes are vegetated and predominantly forested. Bedrock is almost entirely Mesozoic clastics. Avalanche tracks are restricted to the steepest slopes.

METHODOLOGY

Fan Classification

Fans were classified as having a debris flow component on the basis of the following field geomorphic and/or sedimentologic criteria: (1) exposures of debris flow diamictons characterized by weak stratification, poor sorting and matrix-supported angular clasts (Nilsen, 1982; Bull, 1972; Kostaschuk and others, 1987) (Fig. 3); (2) the presence of debris flow levees or debris flow lobes on fan surfaces (Costa, 1984) (Fig. 4); and (3) the presence of oversized (>1 m) lone boulders on the fan surface (Costa, 1984) (Fig. 5).

Fans were classified as being entirely fluvial if they lacked criteria 2 and 3, and all exposures revealed "fluvial" sediments characterized by obvious stratification, moderate sorting, and rounded clasts that support the deposit (Nilsen, 1982; Kostaschuk and others, 1987). Forty-two fans in the study areas had sufficient exposures and/or surficial features to allow us to assign them to exclusively fluvial or debris flow component classifications.

Morphometric Methods

Once fan genesis was determined, four morphometric parameters were obtained for each fan and its drainage basin through field measurements and measurements obtained from topographic maps at a scale of 1:50,000:

Fan area. The total contemporary planimetric area of each fan

Fan slope. The average slope of the fan surface between its apex and its contemporary toe along its bisector

Drainage basin. The total planimetric area for each drainage basin

Drainage basin height. The difference in elevation be-

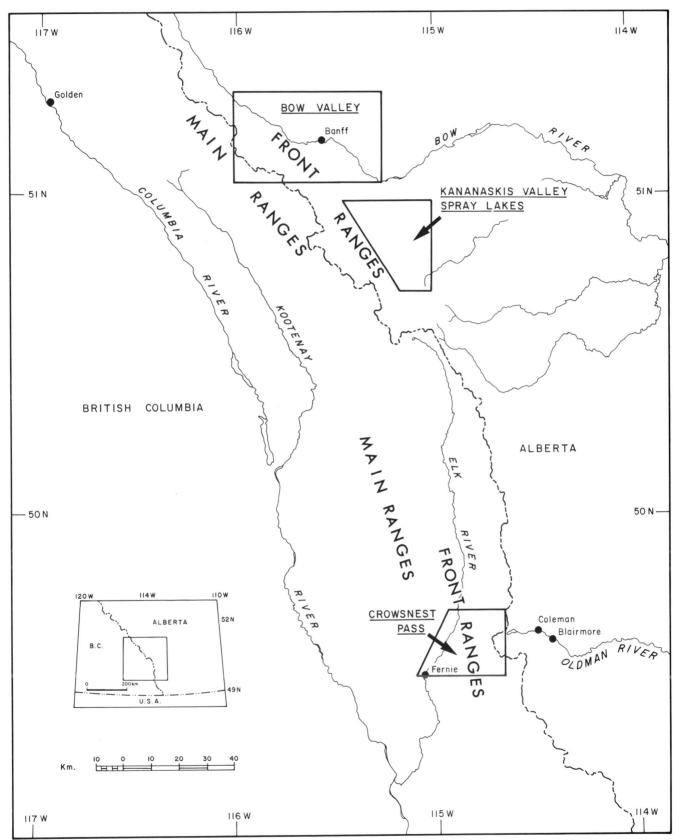

Figure 1. Geography of Canadian Rocky Mountains in southwestern Alberta and southeastern British Columbia and locations of three areas studied in Front Ranges.

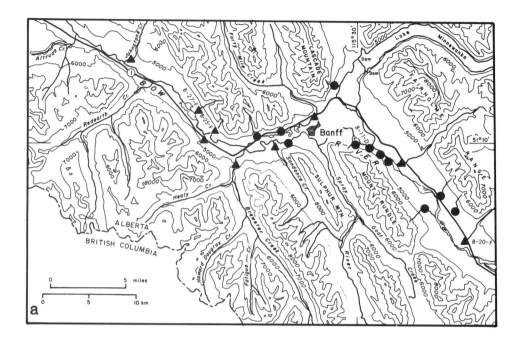

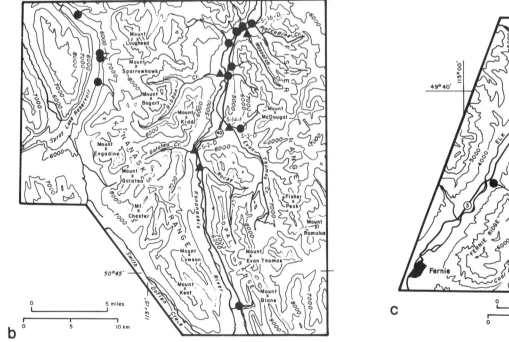

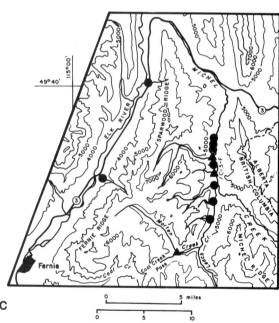

Figure 2. Topographic maps. a, Bow Valley; b, Kananaskis Valley/Spray Lakes Reservoir; c, Crowsnest Pass study areas. Contours are in feet. Fans identified by solid circles are debris flow component; solid triangles identify entirely fluvial fans. Fans identified by designation number are discussed in text.

tween the highest point in the drainage basin and the elevation of the fan apex.

These parameters were chosen because previous studies (e.g., Melton, 1965; Bull, 1964) have shown that they form tight correlation sets and hence may form a basis for inference from map-measurable properties to fan type.

RESULTS

We tried a number of statistical analyses of the measured fan and drainage basin morphometric parameters and found fan area to be of little value because of erosion of fans by trunk rivers. Comparisons of fan slope with drainage basin area and height were consistently the best for discriminating fluvial from debris flow–component fans (Kostaschuk and others, 1987). This relationship followed from a general dichotomy between basins producing debris flow and entirely fluvial fans. Debris flow-producing basins tend to be small, steep first- and second-order basins with steep fans. In contrast, fluvial basins are usually larger and less steep, with third-order or greater streams and gently sloping fans (Fig. 6).

Basin area (A_b) and basin height (H_b) were combined as a measure of basin ruggedness according to Melton's (1965) equation:

$$R = H_b A_b^{-0.5}.$$

A plot of fan slope versus Melton's ruggedness number (R) for all fans from the three study areas is shown in Figure 7. It is apparent that the fluvial and debris flow populations form two nearly distinct groups. In order to quantify this discrimination, we employed a separate variance approximation of the standard one-tailed pooled variance t-test (Nie and others, 1975) to test the distinctiveness of fan slopes and R values for debris flow versus fluvial fans. The assumptions are made that the fan populations are normally distributed and that we have a random sample of these populations. As might be expected, the results suggest that fan slopes and R values are significantly different between the two types of fans.

Eight of the 11 fluvial fans have slopes of less than 2.5° and drainage basins with R values of less than 0.3. Conversely, debris flow–component fans dominantly have slopes of more than 4° and basins with R values of more than 0.25 to 0.3. A transition area lies between these values.

DISCUSSION

The R versus fan slope plot (Fig. 7) discriminates in most cases between fluvial fans and fans having a debris flow–component. However, details of the stratigraphy of fans falling in the transition area in Figure 7 indicate that the discrimination of contemporary sedimentary environments is even more complete than it appears. Fans S-2-D and S-16-D (Fig. 2) are relict fans. They are incised from apex to toe by their fan streams. The

Figure 3. Debris flow diamicton, Bow Valley. Note matrix support and angular nature of clasts. D refers to debris flow; scale bar = 15 cm.

Kananaskis River began to degrade its bed by at least 6,600 yr B.P. (Jackson and others, 1982). Thus, debris flow deposition on these fans must predate the mid-Holocene. The lack of organic detritus within and below the debris flow horizons in these paraglacial fans suggests that they occurred during deglaciation or early postglacial time. The debris flows that reached fans S-2-D and S-16-D likely were very large events associated with deglaciation. Their greater depths, volumes, and velocities apparently gave them mobilities greater than those of debris flows that presently occur in the basin. Fan S-2-D is especially noteworthy in this respect. Much of the fan appears to be the remnant of a single large flow similar to the glacially induced debris flow described by Osborn and Luckman (1981). In any event, the antecedent conditions that resulted in these flows no longer exist in their basins.

Fans C-5-F B-25-F and B-27-F (Fig. 2) are fluvial fans

Figure 4. a, Fresh debris flow lobe, Bow Valley (back pack indicates scale). b, Vegetated debris flow lobe, Kananaskis Valley. Rod divisions = 1 ft.

Figure 5. Large lone boulder on fan, Kananaskis Valley. Isolated boulders are indicative of past debris flows.

plotting within what otherwise would be exclusively the debris flow–component field of values. Fan C-5-F was classified as fluvial on the basis of a lack of levees, debris flow lobes, or large lone boulders on its surface, and one good exposure of a massive, poorly sorted coarse gravel that was intermediate in sediment character between a clearly fluvial deposit and a debris flow diamicton. Thus, this fan should be considered suspect. Likewise, fans B-25-F and B-27-F showed no surficial evidence of debris flow activity, and their limited natural exposures revealed only coarse, stratified sediments. However, their steepness suggests that debris flow deposits are present in the fans but are unexposed. Furthermore, nearby basins with comparable R values have produced debris flows. Taking fan slope and R values together, the conservative interpretation would be to assume a debris flow hazard on these fans. Consequently, the line in Figure 7 separates fans that are fluvial or relict debris flow–component fans from those that are demonstrably active debris flow–component fans or fans of basins of sufficient ruggedness to produce debris flows capable of reaching their fans.

The good discrimination between fans with a current debris flow hazard and those that are presently fluvial using the R versus fan slope plot is anticipated by past studies of debris flow rheology. Hooke (1967) found that slopes of fans built by alternating debris flow and fluvial sedimentation range between 4° and 8° in model studies. He regarded these slopes as being average for fans with a large content of cobbles and boulders. A slope of 3° to 4° appears to mark a threshold between the debris flow activity and

no debris flow activity on almost all fans studied. Both the dilatant fluid (Takahashi, 1981) and the plastico-fluid (Johnson, 1970; Hampton, 1975; Rodine and Johnson, 1976) models of debris flow recognize a minimum channel slope, hence shear stress, required to maintain flow when other factors such as moisture and clay content are optimum (Owens, 1973; Rodine and Johnson, 1976).

Fan channel slope is directly proportional to basin ruggedness (Ryder 1971; Kostaschuk and others, 1987). It appears that, within the three areas studied, drainage basins above a threshold R have valley and channel slopes greater than required for debris flow to initiate and reach fan apices. R values of 0.25 to 0.3 in the areas studied represents the range of this threshold value. Although debris flows still occur in fluvial basins with smaller R values, these flows are contained within the basin and are reworked into fluvial sediment. An example is fan S-3-D, which is situated at the mouth of a tributary to Evan-Thomas Creek (Fig. 2). Fan S-14-F was built by Evans-Thomas Creek. No debris flows have advanced beyond S-3-D (slope 5°) and S-14-F is entirely fluvial.

These results demonstrate that the R versus fan slope plot can provide a rapid means of assessing debris flow hazards on alluvial fans in the Front Ranges. In initial (map and airphoto) reconnaissance, R is accessible but fan slope may not be. Figure 7 indicates that, in such cases, R alone can be used to evaluate the hazard. A conservative discrimination occurs at an R of 0.25, which misclassified very few fluvial fans.

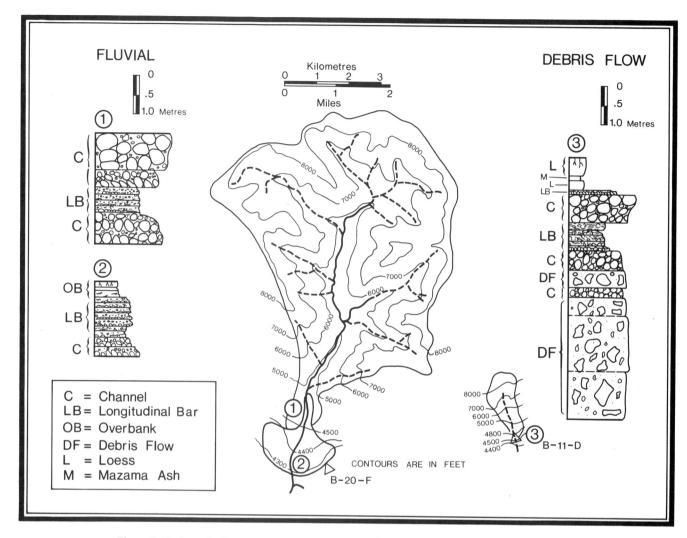

Figure 6. Drainage basin topography and fan stratigraphy for fluvial fan B-20-F and debris flow fan B-11-D, Bow Valley study area (see Fig. 2a). Sediments of fluvial origin include moderately sorted, weakly imbricated cobbles associated with deposition in channels (C); well-sorted, strongly imbricated gravels of lower longitudinal bar (LB) origin; and laminated medium to fine sand of overbank (OB) origin. Debris flow deposits (DF) consist of weakly stratified, matrix-supported angular clasts. Mantles of massive windblown loess (L) may cap fans. Mazama ash (6,600 BP) serves as useful stratigraphic marker. Small, rugged basins produce small steep fans dominated by debris flows. These fans may be periodically reworked by fluvial action. Larger, less rugged basins result in large, gently sloping fluvial fans not prone to debris flow deposition.

LIMITATIONS TO MORPHOMETRIC IDENTIFICATION OF DEBRIS FLOW HAZARD

The use of fan-basin morphometry to initially identify debris flow hazard should have wide applicability throughout the Rocky Mountain Front Ranges and geologically similar provinces. However, an attempt to extend the technique to the Rocky Mountain Main Ranges has served to identify two significant variables that can invalidate this approach: stepped valley profiles and the presence of extensive glaciers. Unlike the Front Ranges, Main

Range thrust sheets are nearly horizontal. These are composed of alternating thick carbonate and clastic units. The imposition of glacial erosion on this structure and stratigraphy has resulted in a markedly stepped profile in many basins of this province. Stepped basins in the Main Ranges are as rugged as the continuously graded basins in the Front Ranges. However, the low gradient-steps may trap debris, which is then reworked into fluvial sediments. Consequently Main Ranges Basins with Melton values greater than 0.25 to 0.3 do not necessarily have a fan with a debris flow hazard.

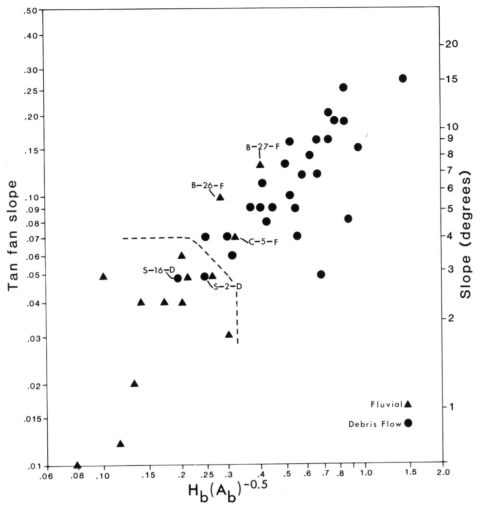

Figure 7. Plot of tangent of fan slope versus Melton's ruggedness number ($H_b A_b^{-0.5}$) for 42 fans from three study areas. H_b is basin height measured from fan apex to basin high point, and A_b is basin area above fan apex. B refers to Bow Valley; S, Kananaskis Valley/Spray Lakes Reservoir; C, Crowsnest Pass. Broken line separates fans presently having and presently lacking debris flow hazard.

Glaciers introduce many variables to debris flow occurrence that are largely unrelated or indirectly related to basin morphometry. For example, moraine-dammed lakes may drain catastrophically generating debris flows that can reach distant fluvial fans (Clague and others, 1985). In the Canadian Rocky Mountains, the magnitude of the Little Ice Age advances of the past few hundred years were unprecedented during the past 8,000 yr (Luckman and Osborn, 1979). They have left numerous ice-cored moraines and moraine- and glacier-dammed lakes. Consequently, the morphometry and stratigraphy of fans of glacierized basins that represent the past 8,000 yr may not accurately reflect hazards to be experienced during the next 50 yr. A morphometric approach to evaluating debris flow hazard on the fans in glacierized basins is inadequate by itself. Furthermore, any morphometric method must be regarded as complementing, rather than substituting for, airphoto analysis of debris flow–generating factors within drainage basins of all types.

CONCLUSIONS

The following conclusions can be drawn from this study. 1. Fan slope and drainage basin ruggedness (R), or ruggedness alone, can be used to discriminate between fluvial fans and those that have a debris flow hazard. 2. Debris flows are likely to reach fan apices where fan slopes exceed 4° and R values exceed 0.25 to 0.3. 3. Consideration of debris flow models suggests that this morphometric approach to discrimination of fans with a debris flow hazard should have wide applicability for continuously graded basins in unglacierized regions.

ACKNOWLEDGMENTS

We thank Dr. J. J. Clague and Dr. M. A. Church for reviewing the paper and greatly contributing to its improvement.

REFERENCES CITED

Bally, A. W., Gordy, P. L., and Stewart, G. A., 1966, Orogenic evolution of southern Canadian Rocky Mountains: Canadian Petroleum Geology Bulletin, v. 14, p. 337–381.

Bull, W. B., 1964, Alluvial fans and near surface subsidence in western Fresno County, California: U.S. Geological Survey Professional Paper 437A, p. A1–A71.

—— , 1972, Recognition of alluvial fan deposits in the stratigraphic record *in* Rigby, J. K., and Hamblin, W. K., eds., Recognition of ancient sedimentary environments: Society of Economic Paleontologists and Mineralogists Special Publication 16, p. 63–83.

Clague, J. J., Evans, S. G., and Blown, I. G., 1985, A debris flow triggered by the breaching of a moraine dammed lake, Klattasine Creek, B.C.: Canadian Journal of Earth Sciences, v. 22, p. 1492–1502.

Costa, J. E., 1984, Physical geomorphology of debris flows, *in* Costa, J. E., and Fleisher, P. J., eds., Developments and applications of geomorphology: Berlin, Spring-Verlag, p. 268–317.

Hampton, M., 1975, Competence of fine grain debris flows: Journal of Sedimentary Petrology, v. 42, p. 834–844.

Hooke, R. LeB., 1967, Processes on arid-region alluvial fans: Journal of Geology, v. 75, p. 438–460.

Jackson, L. E., Jr., 1987, Debris flow hazard in the Rocky Mountains: Geological Survey of Canada (in press).

Jackson, L. E., Jr., MacDonald, G. M., and Wilson, M. C., 1982, Paraglacial origins for river terrace sediments in Bow Valley, Alberta, Canada: Canadian Journal of Earth Sciences, v. 19, p. 2219–2231.

Johnson, A. M., 1970, Physical processes in geology: San Francisco, Freeman, Cooper and Company, 577 p.

Kostaschuk, R. A., MacDonald, G. M., and Putman, P., 1987, The morphometry and sedimentology of alluvial fans near Banff, Alberta: Earth Surface Processes and Landforms (in press).

Luckman, B. H., and Osborn, G. D., 1979, Holocene glacier fluctuations in the middle Canadian Rocky Mountains: Quaternary Research, v. 11, p. 52–77.

Melton, M. A., 1965, The geomorphic and paleoclimatic significance of alluvial deposits in southern Arizona: Journal of Geology, v. 73, p. 1–38.

Nie, N. H., Hull, C. N., Jenkins, J. G., Steinbrenner, K., and Brent, D. H., 1975, Statistical package for the social sciences, 2nd ed.: New York, McGraw-Hill, 676 p.

Nilsen, T. H., 1982, Alluvial fan deposits, *in* Scholle, P. A., and Spearing, D., eds., Sandstone depositional environments: Tulsa, American Association of Petroleum Geologists Memoir 31, p. 49–114.

Osborn, G., and Luckman, B. H., 1981, The origin of an unusual diamicton in Banff National Park, Alberta, Canada: Zeitschrift für Geomorphologie N.S., v. 25, no. 3, p. 290–299.

Owens, I. F., 1973, Alpine mudflows in the Nigel Pass area, Canadian Rocky Mountains [Ph.D. thesis]: Toronto, Department of Geography, University of Toronto, 218 p.

Rodine, J. S., and Johnson, A. M., 1976, The ability of debris, heavily freighted with coarse clastic material, to flow on gentle slopes: Sedimentology, v. 23, p. 213–234.

Ryder, J. M., 1971, Some aspects of the morphometry of paraglacial alluvial fans in south central British Columbia: Canadian Journal of Earth Sciences, v. 8, p. 1252–1264.

Takahashi, T., 1981, Debris flow: Annual review of fluid mechanics, v. 13, p. 57–77.

VanDine, D. F., 1985, Debris flows and debris torrents in the southern Canadian Cordillera, Canadian Geotechnical Journal, v. 22, p. 44–68.

MANUSCRIPT ACCEPTED BY THE SOCIETY DECEMBER 29, 1986

Geological Society of America
Reviews in Engineering Geology, Volume VII
1987

Debris slide and debris flow historical events in the Appalachians south of the glacial border

G. Michael Clark
Department of Geological Sciences
University of Tennessee
Knoxville, Tennessee 37996-1410

ABSTRACT

The central and southern Appalachian region experiences intense rainfall events that trigger episodes of debris slides and debris flows. High rainfalls may be preceded by wet periods, normal conditions, or droughts, and still result in rapid mass movements. Most slides and flows occur in existing hillslope depressions and move downslope. The bedrock-soil contact is the most common movement interface, although slippage and flowage are also common in deep soils. Lithologic, structural, soil, vegetative, and land-use influences on mass movements are identifiable in some areas, yet not apparent in others.

Better data on precipitation thresholds, movement mechanisms, and slide and flow precursors are urgently needed. Accelerating tourism growth rates and development of mountainous areas are accompanied by greater losses of human property and life caused by slope failures. The dangers of rapid debris slides and flows threaten increasing numbers of people in developing areas.

INTRODUCTION

This initial regional survey lies mainly within that part of the Appalachian Highlands mapped as having high landslide potential (U.S. Geological Survey, 1982, p. 5). Data used in this chapter are from 51 selected sites where unequivocal evidence of multiple debris slide and flow movement exists. Additional sites will be added to the inventory as they are identified and field-checked. Excluded from the inventory are individual isolated failures (for example, Sitterly, 1979, p. 49) and subsidiary events with followed movements of other origins (see Davies and others, 1972, p. 23–24). With two exceptions (Table 1, Events 43, 51) listed sites have centralized areas of widespread mass movements involving terrains that are usually relatively undisturbed by human modification. Typically these core areas are surrounded by zones with smaller mass movements, often spatially associated with human activities such as forest clearing, building, and road construction. Widespread events that have numerous landslides are reported in this study for several reasons. The problem of event detection is a primary consideration. Steeply sloping and heavily forested mountainous terrains are typical of areas commonly affected by debris slide–debris flow events. It is usual for occurrences to be reported only if human activity is affected, or if

the resultant landslide chutes and associated flood activity are highly visible. Another reason why multiple landslide events have been selected for initial publication is because of their destructive effects on human activity, as briefly illustrated at the end of this paper. A file of individual slide-flow events is being maintained (G. M. Clark, unpublished data), but the information is based mainly on personal communications and aerial photographs. The dating of individual landslides with these types of information is often tenuous or impossible. The aggregate geomorphic effects of small debris slide–debris flow events are problematic, and may be very important. Until the advent of regional level detection and reporting capabilities, however, study of this problem seems difficult. Unclassified high-resolution satellite imagery may be a highly promising tool, especially if the times between imaging repetition are short.

To minimize local effects of geology, pedology, forest ecology, weather, and climate on data, information is being collected regionally as major intense precipitation events and resultant mass movement sites are identified from sources. To date, these include written historical accounts, published and unpublished scientific and technical reports, airborne photographic and non-

photographic remote-sensing media, and oral transmissions including rare eyewitness accounts.

In addition, site-specific studies shed light on causative and
localizing factors, triggering and propagating mechanisms, areas
and volumes of involved materials, postevent soil and vegetative
adjustments, and monitoring and predicting instrumentation
strategies. The works of Bogucki (1970, 1976), Koch (1974), and
Schneider (1973) exemplify this approach. Supplementary research in progress focuses on identified geotechnical, instrumentation, prediction, dating, and precipitation model problems. As
this study is an initial attempt to bring together formerly isolated
reports of debris slide and debris flow activity in the region, I
consider the results, interpretations, and conclusions herein as
tentative. I solicit further information on listed events, and reports
on unlisted events, so that a more accurate picture of debris
slide–debris flow occurrences can be developed in the future.

REGIONAL GEOLOGIC SETTING

As of November 1985, identified and selected sites (Fig. 1)
are in the Blue Ridge, Ridge and Valley (including Middle Ridge
and Valley section and Southern Valley and Ridge section), and
Appalachian Plateaus provinces of the Appalachian Highlands
major geomorphic division (after Thornbury, 1965). Although
much of the site clustering is believed to be natural, there are
artifactual contributions that affect the data. These include, but
are not limited to, the proximity of events to loci of early reporting media (primarily newspapers), the presence of interested governmental agencies within certain sectors of the region, the
availability of appropriate remote-sensing imagery, and investiga-
tor closeness to many susceptible sites that experience intense
precipitation events.

Slightly more than three-fifths of identified sites are in Blue
Ridge terranes. All but the well-known Nelson County, Virginia,
site (Table 1, site 36) are in the southern section of this province.
Here are complex ridge and ravine landscapes developed on
highly deformed igneous, metaigneous, and metasedimentary
rock units. Upland and hillslope soils typically vary from less than
1 m to several meters in thickness. Soils underlying the colluvial
and alluvial hollows, footslopes, toeslopes, and valleys generally
are thicker. Very deep soils are known in certain topographic
environments.

Appalachian Plateau localities account for more than one-
fifth of the reported events. These sites are underlain predominantly by Paleozoic clastic sedimentary rock units of Mississip-
pian and Pennsylvanian age. In most areas, bedrock is almost
horizontal to very gently dipping. Joints, however, are typically
steeply dipping. In Kentucky, Virginia, and West Virginia, much
valley development is well advanced and many terrains are
highly dissected. This is not so in all Pennsylvania sites identified
to date, where hollow development may or may not localize mass
movements. Plateau colluvial soils on affected hillslopes typically
range from a fraction of a meter to several meters in thickness.

Less than a fifth of cataloged events are in the Valley and

Ridge section of the southern Appalachians and the Ridge and
Valley section of the central Appalachians. These specific localities are underlain by Paleozoic sedimentary rock sequences,
primarily sandstones, siltstones, and shales. The rock units are
moderately to highly deformed by folding and faulting. Upland
and hillslope soils vary greatly in thickness, and affected hillslope
soils commonly range from less than 1 m to several meters in
depth.

REPORTED STORM EVENTS

Introduction

There are 51 occurrences that have been isolated for study
(Table 1). Their concentration in southern Blue Ridge localities is
remarkable, even considering the caveats of artifactual contribution already noted. A second and much lesser concentration is in
southwestern Virginia and southern West Virginia (Fig. 1), where
seven events are recognized. Additional data are needed before
objective cluster limits can be drawn. Both of these subregions,
however, are characterized by drainage basins with relatively
steep side slopes, hollows, and channelways. Perhaps coinciden-
tally, Frederick and others (1977, p. 17) showed two maxima of
precipitation intensities near each of these event clusters. Both the
2-yr and 100-yr 60-min precipitation-frequency values center
around the areas. A third apparent site concentration (Fig. 1, sites
6, 8, 9, 17, 41, and 47) in the southern Blue Ridge is northeast of
the main grouping and is topographically separated from it by the
Asheville-Hendersonville basin. Here are many areas of relatively
high elevation, relief, and steep slopes including the Black Mountains with Mount Mitchell, and the high Blue Ridge frontal escarpment areas. Probable strong interactions between topography
and meteorology in all of the above areas will require additional
study (U.S. Department of Commerce, 1969; World Meteorological Organization, 1969).

Historic Rainfall Events

Of reported storms, 16 lack either definitive descriptions of
storm type, or are under further investigation. Of the remaining
35 events, 24 are cloudbursts or thunderstorms, 6 involve frontal
and associated anticyclone storm systems, and 5—including two
localities affected by Hurricane Camille—are hurricanes. From
reports (Table 1), frontal and associated anticyclone systems and
hurricanes appear to have the most widespread regional effects.
Of these, hurricanes historically have taken the greatest toll in
both property damage and human lives.

Storm types are well reflected in the seasonality of events.
The majority of catastrophic rainfalls—37—were in June, July,
and August. To date, no events have been reported for December, January, or February. Perhaps, except for very unsea-
sonal conditions, air columns during the winter months cannot
hold the requisite moisture volumes, and the intensity-duration
thresholds for existing ground conditions may be possible only

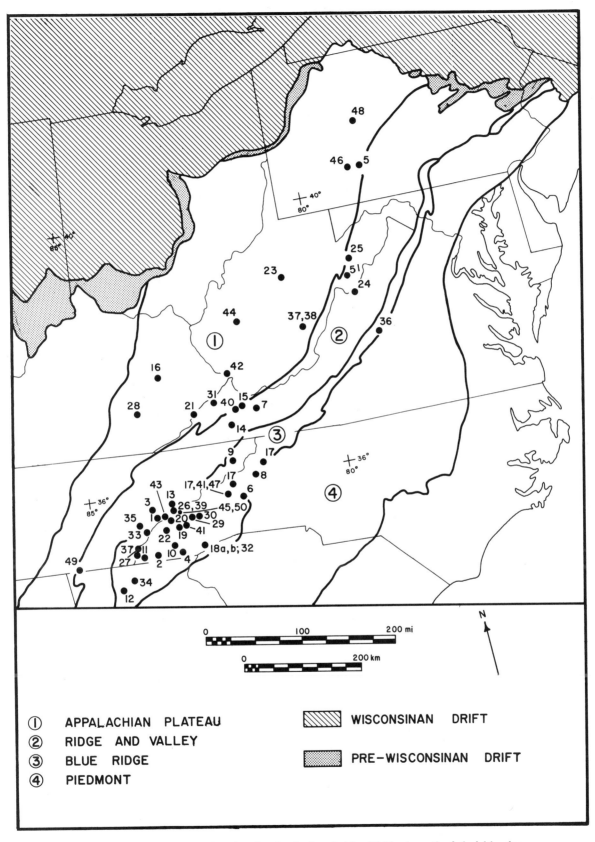

Figure 1. Index map showing selected major sites in Appalachian Highlands south of glacial border, excluding Ohio. Site numbers given in Table 1.

TABLE 1. SELECTED MAJOR DEBRIS SLIDE/DEBRIS FLOW EVENTS IN THE APPALACHIAN HIGHLANDS
SOUTH OF THE GLACIAL BORDER

Location No. (Fig. 1)	Date as Given	Type of Storm as Reported	Geomorphic Province	Area Name as Listed	Information Source
1	27 July 1844	"Waterspouts"	Blue Ridge	Chilhowee Mountain TN	Newspaper account: Knoxville (TN) Register (19 March 1845)
2	7 July 1847	"Waterspouts"	Blue Ridge	Fires Mountain NC	Clingman (1877)
3	March 1875	"Waterspouts"	Blue Ridge	Nine Mile Creek TN	Newspaper account: The Press and Messenger (Knoxville, TN, 10 March 1875)
			Blue Ridge	Ellijoy Creek, TN	
			Valley and Ridge	Bays Mountain, TN	
4	15 June 1876	"Waterspouts"	Blue Ridge	Tessentee Creek, NC	Clingman (1877)
5	30–31 May 1889	"Waterspouts"	Plateau	Johnstown Flood, PA	McCullough (1968, O'Connor (1957)
6	May 1901	"Freshet"	Blue Ridge	Marion, NC	Holmes (1917), Myers (1902)
7	23(?) June 1901	Cloudburst	Valley and Ridge	Tazewell, VA	Newspaper account: Atlanta Constitution (26 June 1901); Myers (1902)
8	15–16 July 1916	Hurricane	Blue Ridge	Blobe, NC	Holmes (1917)
9	13 June 1924	Thunderstorm	Blue Ridge	Carter County, TN	Unpublished Tennessee Valley Authority report (TVA HD-976); King (1924)
10	30 July 1928	"Waterspout"	Blue Ridge	Burningtown, NC	Unpublished Tennessee Valley Authority report (TVA HD-976)
11	7 April 1938	"Waterspout"	Blue Ridge	Fain Mountain, NC	Unpublished Tennessee Valley Authority report (TVA HD 976)
12	7 April 1938	–	Blue Ridge	Talona Creek Valley, GA	Unpublished Tennessee Valley Authority report (TVA Precipitation TN River Basin, April 1938)
13	4–5 August 1938	Cloudburst	Blue Ridge	Greenbriar, TN Web Mountain, TN	Moneymaker (1939), Koch (1974)
14	25 May 1939	–	Valley and Ridge	Brumley Mountain, VA	Unpublished Tennessee Valley Authority report (TVA HD-976)
15	9 June 1939	–	Valley and Ridge	Richlands, VA	Unpublished Tennessee Valley Authority report (TVA HD-976)
16	4–5 July 1939	Thunderstorms	Plateau	Frozen Creek KY	Schrader (1945)
17	13–14 August 1940	Hurricane	Blue Ridge	Mount Mitchell, NC; Elk Creek, NC; Deep Gap, NC	Tennessee Valley Authority (1940); U.S. Geological Survey (1949)
18	29–30 August 1940	Thunderstorm	Blue Ridge	West Fork, Pigeon River, NC	Tennessee Valley Authority (1940); U.S. Geological Survey (1949)
				East and Tuckasegee Point, NC	U.S. Geological Survey (1949)
19	16 July 1941	Thunderstorm	Blue Ridge	Shoal Creek, NC	G. M. Clark, unpublished data
20	10 July 1942	Thunderstorm	Blue Ridge	Newfound Gap, TN/NC	Unpublished Tennessee Valley Authority report (TVA HD-976)
21	13 July 1942	Thunderstorm	Plateau	Pound, VA	G. M. Clark, unpublished data
22	15 July 1943	Thunderstorm	Blue Ridge	Pilkey Creek, NC	G. M. Clark, unpublished data
23	4–5 August 1943	Thunderstorms	Plateau	North Braxton County, WV	Erskine (1951)
24	17–18 June 1949	Cloudbursts	Ridge and Valley	Little River and Palo Alto, VA/WV	Hack and Goodlett (1960)
25	17–18 June 1949	Cloudbursts	Ridge and Valley	Petersburg, WV	Stringfield and Smith (1956); Clark (1967)
26	1 September 1951	Cloudburst	Blue Ridge	Mount LeConte-Sugarland Mountain, TN	Bogucki (1970, 1976)
27	13 June 1952	Thunderstorm	Blue Ridge	Ghormley Mountain, NC	G. M. Clark, unpublished data
28	21 June 1956	Thunderstorm	Plateau	Manchester, KY	Unpublished Tennessee Valley Authority report (TVA HD-976)
29	30 June 1956	Thunderstorm	Blue Ridge	Cove Creek, NC	Unpublished Tennessee Valley Authority report (TVA HD-976)
30	May 1959	–	Blue Ridge	Crabtree, NC	Newspaper account: Waynesville (NC) Mountaineer (4 June 1959)

TABLE 1. SELECTED MAJOR DEBRIS SLIDE/DEBRIS FLOW EVENTS IN THE APPALACHIAN HIGHLANDS
SOUTH OF THE GLACIAL BORDER (continued)

Location No. (Fig. 1)	Date as Given	Type of Storm as Reported	Geomorphic Province	Area Name as Listed	Information Source
31	29-31 July 1961	Thunderstorm	Plateau	Haysi, VA	Rostvedt (1965)
32	4-5 October 1964	-	Blue Ridge	Rosman, NC	Tennessee Valley Authority (1965) (TVA HD-1964, September-October Report A)
33	19 August 1967	Thunderstorm	Blue Ridge	Twenty Mile Creek, NC	G. M. Clark, unpublished data
34	22-23 August 1967	Frontal	Blue Ridge	Blue Ridge, GA	R.E. Mahn, Jr. (unpublished data), Tennessee Valley Authority report (TVA HD-1967 Report B)
35	July 1968	-	Blue Ridge	Big Frog Mountain, TN	G. M. Clark, unpublished data
36	19-20 August 1969	Hurricane	Blue Ridge	Upper James River drainage basin, Nelson County, VA	Williams and Guy (1971, 1973)
37	19-20 August 1969	Hurricane	Plateau	Spring Creek, WV	Schneider (1973)
38	5-6 September 1969	Thunderstorm	Plateau	Spring Creek, WV	Schneider (1973)
39	15 June 1971	-	Blue Ridge	Mount Le Conte, TN	G. M. Clark, unpublished data
40	3 August 1971	-	Valley and Ridge	Sample Branch, VA	Unpublished Tennessee Valley Authority report (TVA HD-976)
41	June 1972	Hurricane	Blue Ridge	Mount Mitchell area, NC; Waterrock Knob, NC	G. M. Clark, unpublished data
42	18 August 1972	Storm system	Plateau	Gilbert and Bens Creeks, WV	Everett (1979)
43	17 March 1973	Frontal	Blue Ridge	Foothills, TN	Newspaper account: <u>The Knoxville</u> (TN) <u>Journal</u> (17 March 1973)
44	9 July 1973	Thunderstorm	Plateau	Kanawha City area, Charleston, NC	Landers and Smosna (1973), Lessing and others (1976)
45	March 1975 through 1983	Multiple storms	Blue Ridge	Anakeesta Ridge, TN/NC	Clark (1984a), and this volume
46	19-20 July 1977	Thunderstorm or cloudburst	Plateau	Johnstown area, PA	Pomeroy (1980)
47	5-6 November 1977	Storm system	Blue Ridge	Mount Mitchell vicinity, NC	Neary and Swift (1984), and this volume
48	14-15 August 1980	Thunderstorms	Plateau	East Brady, PA	Pomeroy (1984a)
49	17 August 1982	Low-pressure trough	Valley and Ridge (Escarpment)	Southeastern TN and northwestern GA	Wilson (1983)
50	10 August 1984	Thunderstorm	Blue Ridge	Anakeesta Ridge, TN	Clark (1984b), and this volume
51	3-5 November 1985	Frontal and associated anticyclone	Ridge and Valley	Germany Valley, WV and VA	Jacobson and others (1987)

during warmer atmospheric environments. Certainly, from humid tropical mass movement studies (see Simonett, 1970; Temple and Rapp, 1972) there is ample evidence of the efficacy of catastrophic rainfall in environments that experience high humidity extremes. By contrast, even subarctic environments occasionally may contain sufficient unstable moisture columns in the summer months to provide the requisite precipitation (Rapp, 1963).

The regional literature is replete with graphic accounts of individual storms, mass movement events, and accompanying floods. Examples of modern descriptions include Allard (1951), Bogucki (1972), McCullough (1968), Neary and Swift (1984), O'Connor (1957), Riggs (1955), Scott (1972), Simpson and Simpson (1970), Stewart and others (1977), and Williams and Guy (1971, 1973).

POSSIBLE PREHISTORIC EVENTS

Increasing recognition of ancient mass movement events is reflected in recent literature. Some of the sediments recording these events may be debris flow deposits. Davies and Thomas (1984) report large deposits from the Allegheny Front southwest of Cumberland, Maryland, and from the Cumberland Escarpment in Tennessee. In the Appalachian Plateau, Davies and Obermeier (1984) observed old failures along shear surfaces seen in trenches and pipeline excavations. Some of these features may be debris slide scar surfaces seen in section, and could have been reactivated by successive mass movements since the times of their initiation.

Kite (1987) and Wilson and Kochel (1987) focused attention on the unconsolidated sediments in aprons and fans that are located next to the bases of steep slopes in the Appalachians. An exposure produced in November 1985 (Table 1, Event 51), and studied by Kite (1987), contains debris flow sediments deposited during an observed event (Table 1, Event 25). Other and older diamicta contained in this fan are grossly similar in facies to the identified historic debris fan sediment, and may be evidence of former debris flow events. Kite also noted the presence of many similar deposits in the area he studied in West Virginia and Virginia. Wilson and Kochel (1987) investigated the morphology and sedimentology of fan sediments formed by debris flow events in Tennessee, Virginia, West Virginia, New York, and New Hampshire. They concluded that most of the sediments appear to have been brought downslope by debris flows. These studies suggest that there are many sedimentary records of debris flow events in the region. Some of these sediments may be from reported or unreported events during earlier historic times. The older sediments, however, probably record prehistoric events that, if dated, could extend our knowledge of mass movements into prehistoric time.

In the Davis Creek watershed of central Virginia, at least three mass movement events have occurred since 10,650 ± 200 radiocarbon yr (Kochel and others, 1982). Geomorphic, sedimentologic, and stratigraphic evidence of past debris flows for the same general area is also reported (Kochel, 1984; Kochel and others, 1981).

Southern Blue Ridge sites may also have sediments that record prehistoric events. Gryta and Bartholomew (1977) presented evidence for late Cenozoic debris deposits in Watauga County, North Carolina. Detailed mapping in the Sherwood 7½-minute Quadrangle disclosed younger deposits overlying sediments at least several hundred years older. Mills (1982) was able to distinguish three relative degrees of weathering-rind development in clasts from foot slope deposits in the North Carolina Blue Ridge. Some of these diamicta also may be prehistoric debris fans, although a number of other origins are possible, and the fans may contain sediments of diverse modes of emplacement and would thus be polygenetic.

INTERACTIVE PRECIPITATION–MASS MOVEMENT CONSIDERATIONS

Numerous attempts have been made to determine precipitation thresholds that trigger debris slide and flow events. For specific areas, Eschner and Patric (1982), Neary and Swift (1984 and this volume), and Patric (1981) have provided rainfall data that set certain limits on total rainfall. Further advances in quantification are hampered by the low density of continuous recording rain gauges in the region, and by the notoriously spotty nature of precipitation cells in the types of storms associated with these mass movement events. Thus it is difficult to derive precise values for intensities during the short time intervals in which witnesses report hearing and seeing slope failures at and shortly after the storm peaks.

With respect to pre-storm rainfall and soil moisture conditions, differing antecedent states are reported in the surveyed literature. Torrential mass movement–triggering rains have been preceded by high soil moisture conditions, normal states, and droughts (G. M. Clark, unpublished data). For example, Bogucki (1970, p. 117–118) reported that the month of August 1951 in the Mt. LeConte area was considerably drier than normal, although the Mt. LeConte station received 1.1 in of rain on 29 August preceding the 1 September 1951 storm. It may be that storms of marginal intensities (e.g., Table 1, Events 43, 51) require pre-storm high soil moisture levels to initiate slide and flow events. However, truly intense events are demonstrably capable of producing catastrophic slope failures regardless of local soil and bedrock conditions (see Caine, 1980).

Study of precipitation events with marginal rainfall totals and/or intensities may prove to be illuminating at sites where ground conditions are constant. During the storm of November 3–5, 1985 (Table 1, Event 51), studied by Clark and others (1987), only five large debris slides and flows were triggered in one local study area with relatively uniform bedrock geology (see Jacobson and others, 1987). Precipitation received in this area ranged from approximately 200 mm to somewhat more than 250 mm, and peak rainfall intensities in the vicinity were low (7.6–38.3 mm/h). However, the authors reported an antecedent wet month and that appreciable rain fell almost continuously from midnight, November 4 to midmorning on November 5 (Jacobson and others, 1987). Associated with this storm, four of the five slides and flows began on dip slopes underlain by resistant sandstone. The fifth slide initiated on the obsequent slope at the contact between this sandstone and the underlying formation composed of interbedded sandstone, siltstone and shale.

No attempt has been made in this chapter to develop regional precipitation thresholds that would initiate pervasive debris slide–debris flow activity. Individual ground site conditions, briefly examined below, are so variable that currently, without additional specific local data and extensive analyses and hypotheses testing, there seems little use in constructing even a tentative framework. In addition, both the quality and quantity of precipitation data gathered to date (G. M. Clark, unpublished data) vary so much from event to event that standardization will be necessary to treat the data. For example. antecedent precipitation data are available only from established preexisting meteorological stations in many events, as the "storm of record" could not, of course have been anticipated. By contrast, supplemental storm data are routinely gathered after many events at locations where no antecedent information had been collected. If and when regional precipitation thresholds can be mapped and then applied to local ground site susceptibilities, it would seem logical to stratify rainfall durations and intensities on a seasonal basis. The majority of reported events (see Table 1) are in the months of June, July, and August, when deciduous vegetation is in fullleafing state in the study region. Fewer storms are recorded for the months of March, April, May, September, October, and November, when both the direct and indirect effects of vegetation in leaf on infall and ground moisture conditions would be expected to be attenuated. Although these coincidences might be used to question the efficacy of leafy vegetation in mitigating storm effects on hillslopes, other observations, discussed below, suggest otherwise. In speculation, June through August debris slide–debris flow events might be even more frequent than they are, were it not for the protection of deciduous vegetation in the green leaf time.

Long-term rainfall histories have not yet been investigated for seasonal or yearly trends in soil moisture regimes in probable failure-susceptible soils. Over even longer time intervals, the effects of climatic change on slope stability in local microclimatic areas, and over the entire region, need study to relate climatic shifts with possible changes in debris slide and flow activity.

TERMINOLOGY

The advantage of precise term definitions has been stated clearly by Varnes (1978, p. 11). The nomenclature used here was developed and modified during regional research and specific site studies to best describe the observed forms and inferred mass movements being researched. Future definition and descriptor modifications probably will prove both desirable and necessary as our knowledge of process geomorphology improves. Processes,

landforms, and earth materials in other areas often differ markedly from those observed to date in the study region (Fig. 1). For these reasons, I make no effort to promulgate use of the descriptors shown and illustrated (Fig. 2); they are simply convenient working terms for this discussion.

Debris slides (Fig. 2A, B) are rapid mass movements initiating along one or more regular to irregular, discrete movement surfaces. They involve primarily soil, vegetation, water, and entrapped air, and also upper bedrock layers. The initiating movement may be rotational, translational, or complex (Varnes, 1978). Rapp (1963, p. 196–197) provided an eyewitness account from Scandinavia, and there are several documented Appalachian sightings in unpublished reports.

Debris flows are rapid mass movements with continuous internal deformation. In the study region, debris flows often mobilize large volumes of timber, and may be fronted and possibly bordered by concentrations of tree trunks (Fig. 2C, D). Field evidence and rare eyewitness accounts suggest that at least some mass movements initiate as debris slides over a well-defined slide scar (Fig. 2A, B). They may then become transitional to debris flow in a flow track (Fig. 2A, C), possibly related to the effects of added water content, topographic constriction, and increasing velocity. Many slope failures display no definable subdivision between slide scar and flow track. For these features, and as a combination term for slide scar and flow track, the term chute is appropriate (Fig. 2A).

Water blowouts (Hack and Goodlet, 1960, p. 45–47) are rare to common features in area of intense storm damage, and have been observed to burst forth from slopes explosively. These forms (Fig. 2A) lend credence to pore water pressure (see Everett, 1979) as a slide triggering mechanism, although other forces, such as torrential rainfall impact and overland flow shear, may be involved.

Depositional features can have many forms (Williams and Guy, 1973, p. 41–44). Debris fans (Hack and Goodlett, 1960, p. 53) are spectacular and common landforms at many sites (Fig. 2A). Much rarer are untruncated debris flow deposits at hillslope bases (Fig. 3C) and large debris piles (Fig. 2D) in some channelways. More common are log jams composed primarily of trees (Bogucki, 1970, p. 53). These forms often can be seen at channelway bends (Fig. 2C). Small debris piles or debris dams (Hack and Goodlett, 1960, p. 45–47; Bogucki, 1970, p. 79–81) are usual features downslope from slide scars and water blowouts.

DRAINAGE BASIN GEOMORPHOLOGY

Introduction

Quite obviously from all reports, only certain hillslope elements fail during even the most intense precipitation events. Field localization factors are important not only in pure landscape research, but also for applied geomorphologic considerations in identifying and mapping unstable areas. In addition, if we can

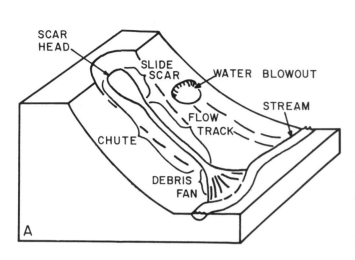

Figure 2. Terminology used in this report. A, Block diagram depicting individual slope form elements (after Clark, 1984b, p. 472). B, Typical large slide scar showing well-developed scar head from site 34 (Fig. 1). C, Flow track downslope from B with person just above photograph center as scale. Note tree trunk and other organic debris dams on both sides of channel bend, with larger deposit on outside of bend. D, Rarely preserved debris pile with large log jam at distal perimeter. Alluvial/colluvial debris slug = 1-4 m thick.

gather field data bearing on the mechanisms of slide and flow initiation and propagation, then guidance can be given to theoretical and physical modeling experiments. Realistic simulation of the complex nature of observed multiphase debris flow slurries can occur following the geotechnical studies of materials involved in these events.

Gradient, Slope Form, and Slope Position

Most recent workers have recorded slope inclinations on slide scar heads and in debris flow tracks. Slope profiles and cross profiles are especially valuable in illustrating the nature of movement surfaces. When combined with large-scale mapping, areal and volumetric calculations provide additional valuable data that shed light on denudational relationships (Ciolkosz and others, 1971).

In the Great Smoky Mountains, Bogucki (1970, 1976) reported slide scar gradients in the Alum Cave drainage basin ranging from 35 to 44°, with an average slope of 40°. R. E. Mahn, Jr. (unpublished data) recorded scar slopes averaging 31°, with a range from 18 to 38° in the Georgia Blue Ridge area (Table 1, site 34). In the foothills section of the Blue Ridge in Tennessee, Koch (1974, p. 29–30) found slide scar slopes from 32 to 43° with an average of 38°. Scott (1972, p. 131) listed scar head slope angles in North Georgia as averaging 34°, but apparently included some sites involving road construction.

In the only event reported from the northern Blue Ridge section (Table 1, site 36) Scott (1972, p. 130–131) reported average scar head slopes of 32° in the Nelson County area studied by Williams and Guy (1973), who surveyed 12 scar and hillside profiles. They reported that in each of the 12 cases, the scar head tends to be in the zone of steepest slope gradient. Theodolite slope profiles run by Bogucki (1970, 1976) in the Great Smoky Mountains, and G. M. Clark and R. E. Mann, Jr. (unpublished data) in north Georgia (Table 1, site 34) are in agreement with those from the Nelson County, Virginia, area. Wherever the initial locus or loci of movement initiation may be, fresh scar heads tend to locate at this slope break in studied Blue Ridge sites.

In an Appalachian Plateau study, pioneering work by Schneider (1973) in the Spring Creek drainage with pasture and forested slopes, the declivity on which the greatest number of slides occurred ranged from 29 to 31°, although the mean slope angle of all slides measure was 35° (Schneider, 1973, p. 47–51). Both large and small debris slides of varying geometries were included in this comprehensive study of 1,534 individual mass movements.

In Pennsylvania, Pomeroy (1980, 1984b) reported from two Ridge and Valley sites (Table 1, sites 46, 48). The average gradient of failures in the Johnstown area was just over 30°, with slopes as gentle as 20° or as steep as 40°. In the East Brady area, Pomeroy (1984b) found mass movement failures on slopes ranging from 32 to 50°, with an average grade of 38°.

With respect to slope form, the majority of slope profiles display a basal section that is slightly to moderately concave upward, with the scar head at or near the steepest part of the profile. Some profiles have an apparently planar midsection; others do not. Slope profiles carried to the hillcrest commonly show a convex upward segment. Examples of surveyed long profiles include Williams and Guy (1973, p. 23; Schneider, 1973, pl. IV; Bogucki, 1976, p. 184).

Slope position of flow tracks with certain exceptions (see Pomeroy, 1980) is strongly related to extant hillslope depressions. In western Pennsylvania and southeastern Ohio, many slope failures are not related to visually identifiable hollows, and do not have the characteristic morphology of debris slide and flow forms to the south and southeast in the remainder of the Appalachians. For these reasons, no localities have been reported from additional areas in these states. Reports of research in Pennsylvania are found in Pomeroy (1979, 1980, 1982, 1984a, b) and in Pomeroy and Popp (1982). Typical Appalachian forms show initial scar heads that do not reach the hillcrest but almost always locate at some distance downslope. Unfortunately, few published measurements exist.

Slope Orientation

At the site level, local controls often dictate preferred chute-facing directions. For example, Schneider (1973, p. 46) reported that the mean of mass movement failure faced S85°E in relation to the preponderance of small drainage basins that drain to the east in the Spring Creek drainage basin. In Nelson County, Virginia, Lisle and Kochel (1981, p. 127) related the more common north-facing chutes to the presence of smooth sheeting joints in contrast to a south-facing chute having an irregular bedrock surface developed on the locally dominant joint set. Gryta and Bartholomew (1987) analyzed chute slope–facing directions over a much wider area. They reported that the slide and flow activity associated with Hurricane Camille occurred predominantly on northeast-, east-, southeast-, and northwest-facing hillslopes.

Bogucki (1970, 1976) found a strong relationship between many chute slope–facing directions and compositional layering in the Anakeesta Formation, but there was less correspondence to structure in chutes over the thick-bedded to massive Thunderhead Sandstone. Koch (1974, p. 31–32) mapped almost three-quarters of the total of Webb Mountain chutes on the steeper south-facing slope of the east-west–trending ridge. In the areas of most intense precipitation cells, however, it is common for almost all pronounced hollow sites to fail (see Hack and Goodlett, 1960, pl. 4; Clark, 1967, pl. 1; this paper, Fig. 3).

On a regional basis, little genetic sense can be made of chute slope–facing directions in many cases, except perhaps for marginal storms over sites with high antecedent soil moisture. Pomeroy (1980, 1984b) documented movement dominance on slopes facing to the northwest, north, northeast, and east. These slope aspects are shielded from direct solar insolation, and would be expected to retain higher soil moisture levels following periods of rainfall before the main storm event.

Figure 3. Vertical aerial photograph nearly centered on area of largest and most concentrated slope mass movements of event 25 (Table 1). Original contact print scale is about 1:20,000; north is at photograph top. A, Dip slope with four large chutes extending downslope to east. B, Obsequent slope with major chute complexes north and south of letter B. C, Symmetrical ridge with chute in hollow just northeast of letter C; bedding is essentially vertical. Note round-shaped debris flow deposit north of letter C. D, Strike slope with large chute extending north in core of Wills Mountain anticlinorium to North Fork of South Branch, Potomac River. Smaller features of peripheral zone of mass movement on east portions of photograph are: E, Chute above and crossing road just east of letter E. F, Slide scars upslope of undercut bank just east of letter F. G, Minor slide scars predominantly in cleared areas east of letter G.

BEDROCK GEOLOGY AND SOILS

Blue Ridge and Ridge and Valley sites often exhibit steeply inclined structural and/or bedrock compositional surfaces exposed in chutes. Bedrock influence on movement surfaces has been inferred by Bogucki (1970, 1976) and by Lisle and Kochel (1981). Alternatively, some rainfall events may have been so intense that local structural effects were overridden (Fig. 3). In areas where bedrock is gently dipping to essentially horizontal, lithologic differences often can be related to scar head locations (Hack and Goodlett, 1960, p. 44; Pomeroy, 1980, p. 21; 1984, p. 13–14).

When the bedrock geology of more debris slide and debris flow sites is better known, relationships among lithology, structure, and mass movement location may become clearer. Gryta and Bartholomew (1987) were able to establish landslide susceptibility classes for the chutes they mapped in Nelson County, Virginia (see Table 1, Event 36), after basement rock types had been defined and mapped more rigorously. For many reported sites (Table 1), detailed lithologic study and bedrock mapping remain to be completed. Such work is often hindered by colluvial soil covers that mask the nature of underlying rock units.

Soil development on the steep hillslopes associated with Appalachian debris slide and flow movements is characteristically poor with weak horizonation. Illite and kaolinite are common clay mineral species reported by most workers, with vermiculite and chlorite often present. Clay mineral species are often moderately well crystallized. Mixed layering may be present, but commonly is barely detectable. The bedrock-soil interface is the most common detachment surface reported by most authors, although the movement base in some scar heads is within lower soil horizons. This is especially common in thicker soils.

VEGETATION AND LAND USE

Rugged terrains and soils poorly suited for tillage or pasture are predominantly forest covered in the central and southern Appalachians. Except for the most difficult terrains and isolated high mountain fastnesses, the region's forestland has been cut and/or burned at least once since the advent of European settlement, and often many times. Disregarding the higher or drier sites, rapidly reproducing hardwood species predominate on failure-susceptible slopes, and sediment yield is very low on recently undisturbed sites (Patric, 1976). Debris slide and flow events provide dramatic erosional, transportational, and depositional episodes in the region; the resultant hillslope and floodplain changes may or may not be modified by subsequent human activity. Williams and Guy (1973, p. 2) pointed out that debris fan and flood-plain deposits are often altered rapidly or destroyed after storms, and hence require immediate study before reconstruction efforts commence. Alternatively, especially in isolated or protected areas, slide scars and flow tracks often remain untouched except perhaps for minor reforestation efforts. Such sites are ideal locations for natural revegetation studies. Clark and

Kelsey (1973) reported on a number of locales where postevent changes have been recorded and are being monitored. They noted that even after 50 years of postslide history there were still marked differences between the vegetation canopy developed in slide scar heads and the forest cover outside slide scars (Clark and Kelsey, 1973).

Turning to sites where cleared land and forested areas are interspersed, it should be possible to study land use as a human factor in slide and flow occurrence. With the caveat that very few Appalachian mountain slopes are completely undisturbed, present land use has been examined by Schneider (1973, p. 92) and Pomeroy (1980, p. 21–22). Both authors observed that forest cover, or even laurel thickets, impart stabilizing influences to the underlying soils, and that slide and flow loci are less common under vegetative overstories and understories.

Human activity may also result in indirect effects on vegetation and substrates. These may translate into changes in the magnitude and frequency of mass movement events. Possible effects of airborne pollutants and introduced pests on forests, soils, and water are currently under study by a number of investigators in uplands areas in the American Southeast. For examples of such studies, see Clark (1984a), Ryan and Clark (1986), and many other reports in the same volumes. The increasing frequency and severity of slides and flows in Great Smoky Mountains areas underlain by the pyritiferous Anakeesta Formation is a case in point; these slides are currently being monitored (Clark, 1984a; Clark and Ryan, 1987). The wide range of mountain environments (Bogucki and others, 1973) and the protected nature of observation sites in the park facilitate research efforts on a variety of slope environments and processes.

SUMMARY DISCUSSION

Although available data set broad limits for precipitation thresholds (Caine, 1980) necessary for major slide and flow events, precise spot measurements of continuously incoming precipitation are needed. Such data need to be related to local bedrock, soil, soil moisture, vegetation, and land use environments to develop predictive hydrometeorologic slope-failure models. Laboratory experiments may help determine infall conditions under which rock slope covermasses fail. Experimental results could point to field observation stations where in-situ measurements are feasible. Precipitation records can and should be extended back in time to determine long-term climatic trends and associated slide and flow activity. Recent advances in dating techniques (see Pavich and others, 1984) will permit establishment of a longer absolute age chronology for mass-movement events.

Much better understanding of specific process mechanisms, rates, and triggering thresholds is needed. For example, it is not known if some previously saturated soils can give reliable indication of future slide movements. As marginal mass movement–inducing rainfalls are much more common than catastrophic events, this information would have widespread predictive value. Extraction of full geotechnical data for oriented field samples is as

Figure 4. Relations between geology and land misuse by people in peripheral mass movement zone outside locus of major storm damage (Fig. 1 and Table 1, site 43). A, Mass movement and access road failure that isolated an entire development. Note exposed bedrock fracture zone expressed as dark tonal area just left of top center below road-cut. B, Remains of club house that serviced another resort community. Sited on debris fan, unoccupied structure was demolished by debris flow that initiated at access road fill in hollow upslope.

yet rarely done. Such analyses may shed light on potential failure surfaces that are not readily visible in the field. In the most dangerous locations, field instrumentation should be installed that can respond to rapidly changing soil and rock conditions.

The large area, great volume, high velocity, and destructive rock and timber components of typical debris flows in the region render them extremely destructive (Williams and Guy, 1971; Clark, 1973). The preferred paths downslope through hollows and into valleys frequently cross access routes through which rescue personnel and emergency supplies need to pass in the event of a disaster. Figure 4A illustrates one of many slope failures that occurred during a relatively minor slide- and flow-triggering storm in March 1973, (Table 1, event 43). Poor road-alignment selection and bad construction techniques are still the rule rather than the exception in many private developments. As the region continues to experience explosions in tourism volume, transportation line construction, and the building of vacation and retirement homes (Burby, 1979), the annual mass movement damage totals and the potential for loss of human life (as seen during Hurricane Camille in 1969) will continue to grow (Williams and Guy, 1971). In the much smaller Blue Ridge storm (Clark, 1973), unoccupied buildings sited on geologically dangerous ground in channelways, at steep slope bases, and on debris fans were destroyed (Fig. 4b). A similar storm, but on a popular summer weekend evening, would likely result in tragedy.

Despite a research history spanning several human generations, central and southern Appalachian debris slide and flow knowledge is still in its infancy. The region is vast and spans several major climatic zones and many microclimatic environments. It encompasses wide varieties of bedrock lithology, structural style, soil, vegetation, and land use. After two centuries of immigration and settlement, access and logistical problems in field work still exist, especially in the terrains where these mass movements are common. Sangrey (1985) has called for a much-needed national program of landslide hazards reduction. Clearly, the Appalachian region composes a major subset of the federal problem; it deserves appropriate study, and soon.

ACKNOWLEDGMENTS

Field research was supported by U.S. Air Force Cambridge Research Laboratories, Air Force Systems Command, contract F 19628-69-C-0016, project 7529. Manuscript preparation expenses were borne by Department of Geological Sciences Discretionary Funds from the University of Tennessee. I acknowledge with thanks the contributions of Donald J. Bogucki, Carl A. Koch, Robert E. Mahn, Jr., Patrick T. Ryan, Jr., and Raymond H. Schneider; their efforts in the quantification of qualitative field relations provide data needed for knowledge advancement in both process- and applied-geomorphic research.

REFERENCES CITED

Allard, H. A., 1951, Catastrophe by deluge; A case history: Living Wilderness, v. 37, p. 12–17.

Bogucki, D. J., 1970, Debris slides and related flood damage associated with the September 1, 1951, cloudburst in the Mt. Le Conte–Sugarland Mountain area, Great Smoky Mountains National Park [Ph.D. thesis]: Knoxville, University of Tennessee, 165 p.

—— , 1972, Intense rainfall in Great Smoky Mountains National Park: Journal of Tennessee Academy of Science, v. 47, p. 93–97.

—— , 1976, Debris slides in the Mt. Le Conte area, Great Smoky Mountains National Park, U.S.A.: Geografiska Annaler, v. 58A, p. 179–191.

Bogucki, D. J., Clark, G. M., Norris, F. H., and Springer, M. E., 1973, Field conference guide for an altitudinal transect of the Great Smoky Mountains National Park: 1973 International Geobotany Conference, Knoxville, University of Tennessee, 40 p.

Burby, R. J., 1979, Second homes in North Carolina; An analysis of water resources and other consequences of recreational land development: Raleigh, Water Resources Research Institute of the University of North Carolina, North Carolina State University, 251 p.

Caine, N., 1980, The rainfall intensity-duration control of shallow landslides and debris flows: Geografiska Annaler, v. 62A, p. 23–27.

Ciolkosz, E. J., Clark, G. M., Hack, J. T., Sigafoos, R. S., and Williams, G. P., 1971, Slope stability and denudational processes; Central Appalachians, Geological Society of America Annual Meeting Guidebook, Field Trip 10: Washington, D.C., Geological Society of Washington, 31 p.

Clark, G. M., 1967, Structural geomorphology of a portion of the Wills Mountain anticlinorium, Mineral and Grant counties, West Virginia [Ph.D. thesis]: University Park, Pennsylvania State University, 165 p.

—— , 1973, Appalachian debris slide–debris flow characteristics and distribution south of the glacial border; Actualization of knowledge in mapping high risk sites: Geological Society of America Abstracts with Programs, v. 5, p. 386–387.

—— , 1984a, Debris slide/debris flow events in Great Smoky Mountains National Park, Tennessee/North Carolina; Processes, site factors, and hillslope development in selected historical events [abs.], in Wood, J. D., Jr., ed., Tenth Annual Scientific Research Meeting, Great Smoky Mountains National Park, May 24–25, 1984: Atlanta, Georgia, U.S. Department of the Interior, National Park Service, Southeast Regional Office, p. 13.

—— , 1984b, Debris slide/debris flow events in the Appalachians south of the glacial border; Processes, site factors, and hillslope development in selected historical events: Geological Society of America Abstracts with Programs, v. 16, p. 472.

Clark, G. M., and Kelsey, C. T., III, 1973, Geomorphic and forest ecologic interrelationships in debris slide scar revegetation; Appalachians south of the glacial border: Abstracts with Programs, International Geobotany Conference, 2–3 March 1973, Knoxville, University of Tennessee.

Clark, G. M., and Ryan, P. T., Jr., 1987, Debris slides and debris flows on Anakeesta Ridge, Creat Smoky Mountains National Park, Tennessee: U.S. Geological Survey Circular 1008, p. 18–19.

Clark, G. M., Jacobson, R. B., Kite, J. S., and Linton, R. C., 1987, Storm-induced catastrophic flooding and related phenomena in Virginia and West Virginia, November, 1985: Eighteenth Annual Geomorphology Symposium; Catastrophic Flooding, in press.

Clingman, T. L., 1877, Selections from the speeches and writings of Hon. Thomas L. Clingman: Raleigh, North Carolina, p. 68–77.

Davies, W. E., and Obermeier, S. F., 1984, Repetitive nature of Appalachian landslides: U.S. Geological Survey Professional Paper 1375, p. 221.

Davies, W. E., and Thomas, R. E., 1984, Large, old debris avalanches in the Appalachians: U.S. Geological Survey Professional Paper 1375, p. 221.

Davies, W. E., Bailey, J. F., and Kelley, D. B., 1972, West Virginia's Buffalo Creek flood; A study of the hydrology and engineering geology: U.S. Geological Survey Circular 667, 32 p.

Erskine, H. M., 1951, Flood of August 4–5, 1943, in central West Virginia: U.S.

Geological Survey Water Supply Paper 1134-A, 57 p.

Eschner, A. R., and Patric, J. H., 1982, Debris avalanches in eastern upland forests: Journal of Forestry, v. 80, p. 343–347.

Everett, A. G., 1979, Secondary permeability as a possible factor in the origin of debris avalanches associated with heavy rainfall: Journal of Hydrology, v. 43, p. 347–354.

Frederick, R. H., Myers, V. A., and Auciello, E. P., 1977, Five- to 60-minute precipitation frequency for the eastern and central United States: NOAA Technical Memorandum, NWS HYDRO-35, 36 p.

Gryta, J. J., and Bartholomew, M. J., 1977, Evidence for late Cenozoic debris-avalanche-type deposits in Watauga County, North Carolina: Geological Society of America Abstracts with Programs, v. 9, p. 142–143.

—— , 1987, Frequency and susceptibility of debris avalanching induced by Hurricane Camille in central Virginia: U.S. Geological Survey Circular 1008, p. 16–18.

Hack, J. T., and Goodlett, J. C., 1960, Geomorphology and forest ecology of a mountain region in the Central Appalachians: U.S. Geological Survey Professional Paper 347, 66 p.

Holmes, J. S., 1917, Some notes on the occurrence of landslides: Journal of Elisha Mitchell Society, v. 33, p. 100–105.

Jacobson, R. B., Cron, E. D., and McGeehin, J. P., 1987, Preliminary results from a study of natural slope failures triggered by the storm of November 3–5, 1985, Germany Valley, West Virginia and Virginia: U.S. Geological Survey Circular 1008, p. 11–16.

King, W. R., 1924, Record cloudburst flood in Carter County, Tennessee, June 13, 1924: U.S. Weather Bureau Monthly Weather Review, v. 52, p. 311–313.

Kite, J. S., 1987, Colluvial diamictons in the Valley and Ridge province, West Virginia and Virginia: U.S. Geological Survey Circular 1008, p. 21–23.

Koch, C. A., 1974, Debris slides and related flood effects in the 4–5 August 1938 Webb Mountain cloudburst; Some past and present environmental geomorphic implications [M.S. thesis]: Knoxville, University of Tennessee, 112 p.

Kochel, R. C., 1984, Quaternary debris avalanche frequency, sedimentology, and stratigraphy in Virginia: Geological Society of America Abstracts with Programs, v. 16, p. 562.

Kochel, R. C., Johnson, R. A., and Wayland, R. J., 1981, Geomorphic evidence for multiple episodes of debris avalanching in central Virginia [abs.]: Virginia Academy of Science, v. 32, p. 127.

Kochel, R. C., Johnson, R. A., and Valastro, S., Jr., 1982, Repeated episodes of Holocene debris avalanching in central Virginia: Geological Society of America Abstracts with Programs, v. 41, p. 31.

Landers, R. A., and Smosna, R. A., 1973, Final report on landslides of July 9, 1973, in Kanawha City area of Charleston, West Virginia: West Virginia Geological and Economic Survey, 20 p.

Lessing, P. B., Kulander, B. R., Wilson, B. D., Dean, S. L., and Woodring, S. M., 1976, West Virginia landslides and slide-prone areas: West Virginia Geological and Economic Survey Environmental Geology Bulletin 15, 64 p.

Lisle, L. D., and Kochel, R. C., 1981, Structural effects on slope failure of debris-avalanches in Nelson County, Virginia [abs.]: Virginia Academy of Science, v. 32, p. 127.

McCullough, D. G., 1968, The Johnstown flood: New York, Simon and Schuster, 302 p.

Mills, H. H., 1982, Long-term episodic deposition on mountain foot slopes in the Blue Ridge Province of North Carolina; Evidence from relative-age dating: Southeastern Geology, v. 23, p. 123–128.

Moneymaker, B. C., 1939, Erosional effects of the Webb Mountain (Tennessee) cloudburst of August 5, 1938: Journal of Tennessee Academy of Science, v. 14, p. 190–196.

Myers, E. W., 1902, A study of the southern river floods of May and June 1901: Engineering News and American Railway Journal, v. 48, p. 102–104.

Neary, D. C., and Swift, L. W., 1984, Rainfall thresholds for triggering a debris avalanching event in the Southern Appalachians: Geological Society of

America Abstracts with Programs, v. 16, p. 609.

O'Connor, R., 1957, Johnstown; The day the dam broke: Philadelphia, J. B. Lippincott Co., 255 p.

Patric, J. H., 1976, Soil erosion in the eastern forest: Journal of Forestry, v. 74, p. 671–677.

——, 1981, Soil-water relations of shallow forested soils during flash floods in West Virginia: U.S. Department of Agriculture Forest Service Research Paper, NE-469, 20 p.

Pavich, M. J., Brown, L., Tera, F., Middleton, R., and Klein, J., 1984, Dating landslides and other upper Pleistocene and Holocene features: U.S. Geological Survey Professional Paper 1375, p. 221.

Pomeroy, J. S., 1979, Storm-induced landslides in the Johnstown area, Pennsylvania, July 19-20, 1977: Geological Society of America Abstracts with Programs, v. 11, p. 49.

——, 1980, Storm-induced debris avalanching and related phenomena in the Johnstown area, Pennsylvania: U.S. Geological Survey Professional Paper 1191, 24 p.

——, 1982, Geomorphic effects of the July 19-20, 1977, storm in a part of the Little Conemaugh River area northeast of Johnstown, Pennsylvania: Northeastern Geology, v. 4, p. 1–9.

——, 1984a, Landslides caused by intense storms in Pennsylvania: U.S. Geological Survey Professional Paper 1375, p. 220–221.

——, 1984b, Storm-induced slope movements at East Brady, northwestern Pennsylvania: U.S. Geological Survey Bulletin 1618, 16 p.

Pomeroy, J. S., and Popp, J. W., 1982, Storm-induced landsliding, June 1981, in northwestern Pennsylvania: Pennsylvania Geology, v. 13, p. 12–15.

Rapp, A., 1963, The debris slides at Ulvådal, western Norway; An example of catastrophic slope processes in Scandinavia: Nachrichten der Akademie der Wissenschaften in Göttingen II. Mathematisch-Phsikalische Klasse, Nr. 13, p. 195–210.

Riggs, H. C., 1955, Floods in North Carolina; Magnitude and frequency: U.S. Geological Survey Open-File Report, 59 p.

Rostvedt, J. O., 1965, Summary of floods in the United States during 1961: U.S. Geological Survey Water Supply Paper 1810, 123 p.

Ryan, P. T., Jr., and Clark, G. M., 1986, Debris slides on Anakeesta Ridge in the GRSM, Tennessee [abs.], in Wood, J. D., Jr., ed., Twelfth Annual Scientific Research Meeting, Great Smoky Mountains National Park, May 22-23, 1986: Atlanta, Georgia, U.S. Department of the Interior, National Park Service, Southeast Regional Office, in press.

Sangrey, D. A., 1985, A national program for landslide hazards reduction: Geology, v. 13, p. 323.

Schneider, R. H., 1973, Debris slides and related flood damage resulting from Hurricane Camille, 19-20 August, and subsequent storm, 5-6 September 1969 in the Spring Creek drainage basin, Greenbrier County, West Virginia [Ph.D. thesis]: Knoxville, University of Tennessee, 131 p.

Schrader, F. E., 1945, Notable local floods of 1939; Pt. 2, Flood of July 5, 1939, in eastern Kentucky: U.S. Geological Survey Water Supply Paper 967-B, p. 41–59.

Scott, R. C., Jr., 1972, The geomorphic significance of debris avalanches in the Appalachian Blue Ridge Mountains [Ph.D. thesis]: Athens, University of Georgia, 185 p.

Simonett, D. S., 1970, The role of landslides in slope development in the high rainfall tropics: Washington, D.C., Office of Naval Research, Geography Branch, Final Report NR 389-133, 24 p.

Simpson, P. S., and Simpson, J. H., Jr., 1970, Torn land: Lynchburg, Virginia, J. P. Bell Co., 429 p.

Sitterly, P. D., 1979, Environmental geology of Hamilton County, Tennessee, in Wilson, R. L., Floyd, R. J., and Milici, R. C., coordinators, Geology of Hamilton County, Tennessee: Tennessee Division of Geology Bulletin 79, p. 47–64.

Stewart, J. M., Heath, R. C., and Morris, J. M., 1977, Floods in western North Carolina, November 1977: Raleigh, University of North Carolina Water Resources Research Institute, 23 p.

Stringfield, V. T., and Smith, R. C., 1956, Relation of geology to drainage, floods, and landslides in the Petersburg area, West Virginia: West Virginia Geological and Economic Survey Report of Investigations 13, 19 p.

Temple, P. H., and Rapp, A., 1972, Landslides in the Mgeta area, western Uluguru Mountains, Tanzania: Geografisker Annaler, v. 54A, p. 157–193.

Tennessee Valley Authority, 1940, Floods of 1940 in Tennessee River basin: Supplement to Precipitation in Tennessee River Basin, Report 0-243-67S, 337 p.

——, 1965, Floods of September-October 1964 in the upper French Broad, Little Tennessee and Hiwassee River basins: Hydrologic Data Branch Report HD-1964-A, 185 p.

Thornbury, W. D., 1965, Regional geomorphology of the United States: New York, John Wiley & Sons, 609 p.

U.S. Department of Commerce, 1969, Probable maximum and TVA precipitation for Tennessee River basins up to 3,000 square miles in area and duration to 72 hours: ESSA Hydrometeorological Report 45, 166 p.

U.S. Geological Survey, 1949, Floods of August 1940 in the southeastern states: U.S. Geological Survey Water Supply Paper 1066, 554 p.

——, 1982, Goals and tasks of the landslide part of a ground-failure hazards reduction program: U.S. Geological Survey Circular 880, 49 p.

Varnes, D. J., 1978, Slope movement types and processes, in Schuster, R. L., and Krizek, R. J., eds., Landslides—Analysis and control: National Research Council, Highway Research Board Special Report 176, p. 11–33.

Williams, G. P., and Guy, H. P., 1971, Debris avalanches; A geomorphic hazard, in Coates, D. R., ed., Environmental geomorphology: Binghamton, State University of New York, p. 24–46.

——, 1973, Erosional and depositional aspects of Hurricane Camille in Virginia, 1969: U.S. Geological Survey Professional Paper 804, 80 p.

Wilson, R. L., 1983, Debris flows resulting from the August 17, 1982, storm in southeast Tennessee and northwest Georgia: Geological Society of America Abstracts with Programs, v. 15, p. 112.

Wilson, G. C., and Kochel, R. C., 1987, Geomorphology of Appalachian alluvial fans formed by debris flows [abs.]: Geological Society of America Abstracts with Programs, v. 19, p. 137.

World Meteorological Organization, 1969, Estimation of maximum floods: Technical Note 98, 288 p.

MANUSCRIPT ACCEPTED BY THE SOCIETY DECEMBER 29, 1986

Geological Society of America
Reviews in Engineering Geology, Volume VII
1987

Holocene debris flows in central Virginia

R. Craig Kochel
Department of Geology
Southern Illinois University
Carbondale, Illinois 62901

ABSTRACT

Debris fans in low-order Appalachian Mountain drainage basins can be used to estimate the return periods between catastrophic debris flow events such as the Hurricane Camille storm of 1969 in Virginia. Debris fans in Davis Creek, Virginia, have been the sites of repeated debris flow deposition at least three times during the last 11,000 years. Debris flow frequency estimates are possible if individual events can be recognized in the fan stratigraphy. Discrimination of events is based on the recognition of paleosols, and on abrupt changes in sediment texture and in matrix composition at suspected event boundaries. Major controls on slope stability appear to include the orientation of the slope, bedrock structure, and presence of colluvial hollows at the sites prior to slope failures. Hollows are sites of between-event accumulation of colluvium, and are areas of subsurface water concentration during heavy rains. Tropical air masses seem to have been a factor in most historical Appalachian debris flows. The early Holocene initiation of debris flow activity on the central Virginia fans appears to coincide with paleoclimatic data, indicating the commencement of conditions that permitted the invasion of tropical moisture into the region at the close of Pleistocene time.

INTRODUCTION

Research on debris avalanche–debris flow processes has been designated by the U.S. Geological Survey as high priority for slope hazard studies (U.S. Geological Survey, 1982). Areas with the greatest potential hazards from debris flows include the Pacific Coast ranges, several areas of the Rocky Mountains, and the Appalachian Mountains. Alluvial fans formed dominantly by episodic deposition from catastrophic debris flows are significant piedmont landforms along Appalachian mountain fronts from Tennessee to New Hampshire. Continued urban development into these areas has increased the risk of damage by debris flow processes throughout the Appalachian region.

Few studies have focused on determinations of the frequency and controls of debris flow processes in the Appalachian region. Destruction caused by storms such as Hurricane Camille in 1969 in Virginia (Williams and Guy, 1973) have demonstrated the urgency for studies aimed at estimating the Holocene frequency of these extreme events. Studies of the sedimentology, stratigraphy, and morphology of debris fans can yield evidence of their geomorphic importance and debris flow frequency, which can be used in hazard evaluation.

This study represents a follow-up of the study of deposi-

tional and erosional effects of Hurricane Camille in Nelson County, Virginia, by Williams and Guy (1973). This discussion focuses on morphostratigraphic evidence that can be used to assess debris flow frequency and details some of the controls on debris avalanching and downstream effects of debris flows in central Virginia.

Considerable discrepancy exists in the terminology of rapid mass movements involving poorly sorted mixtures of clastic debris, organic debris, and water (Costa, 1984). For the purposes of discussion in this chapter, no distinction is attempted between debris avalanches, debris flows, and debris torrents (VanDine, 1985) in the Appalachian study sites. Investigators of debris flow processes in other regions have found it difficult to discriminate between these subtypes unless direct measurements of flow characteristics were available or unless unmodified deposits could be studied immediately after the event. Classification of flow processes is also frequently complicated by temporal variations in flow type during the event and by variations in the flow type in the downstream direction. For the most part, the flows in Virginia were dominantly of the debris avalanche category (Varnes, 1978). Sedimentologic evidence indicates that these debris ava-

TABLE 1. MAJOR HISTORICAL APPALACHIAN DEBRIS FLOWS

Date	Location	Rainfall Data			Estimated Return Period (yr)	Bedrock	Reference
		Amount (cm)	Duration (hr)	Source*			
8/20/01	Mt. Greylock, MA	--	--	--	--	Schist	Cleland, 1902
8/4-5/38	Webb Mountain, TN	28-38	4	T	--	Metasediments	Moneymaker, 1939
8/17-18/40	Watauga, TN	--	--	T-H	--	Metasediments	U.S. Geological Survey, 1949
8/17-18/40	Grandfather Mt., NC	--	--	T-H	--	Conglomerate, schist	U.S. Geological Survey, 1949
8/17-18/40	Radford, VA	--	--	T-H	--	Sedimentary rocks	U.S. Geological Survey, 1949
6/17-18/42	North-central PA	90	12	?	--	Sedimentary rocks	Eisenlohr, 1952
6/17-18/49	Little River, VA	24	3-4	T	>100	Sedimentary rocks	Hack and Goodlett, 1960
6/17-18/49	Petersburg, WV	40	24	T	--	Sedimentary rocks	Stringfield and Smith, 1956
9/1/51	Smoky Mts., NC-TN	10-20	1	T	>100	Metasediments	Bogucki, 1970, 1976
6/30/56	Cove Creek, NC	30	1	T	--	Schist, granite	Bogucki, 1970
8/19-20/69	Nelson County, VA	80	8	T-H	3,000-4,000	Granite, gneiss	Williams and Guy, 1973; Kochel and Johnson, 1984
8/19-20/69	Spring Creek, WV	10-40	8	T-H	>100	Sandstone, shale	Schneider, 1973
8/10/76	Dorset Mt., VT	10	6	T-H	--	--	Ratte and Rhodes, 1977
6/19-20/77	Johnstown, PA	25-30	--	ET	5,000-7,000	Sandstone, shale	Pomeroy, 1980
8/10-11/84	Smoky Mountains, TN	10	24	?	--	Phyllite	This study
Various dates	Adirondack Mts., NY	--	--	--	--	Granitic rocks	Bogucki, 1977
Various dates	White Mountains, NH	--	--	--	--	Granitic rocks	Flaccus, 1958

*T indicates demonstrable tropical air mass; T-H indicates hurricane; ET indicates extratropical cyclone; ? indicates difficult to determine.

lanches became debris flows farther downfan and downstream with the addition of more water and concentration into distinct channels. Radiocarbon dating of fan sediments shows that the 1969 flows were the latest of at least three catastrophic debris flow episodes in central Virginia during the last 11,000 years.

APPALACHIAN DEBRIS FLOWS

Distribution and Morphology

Historical debris flows have been reported from virtually all portions of the Appalachian Mountains between New Hampshire and Tennessee (Table 1). Appalachian debris flows normally shed sediments onto small debris fans that are significant piedmont geomorphic features along the mountains (Kochel and Johnson, 1984). Stratigraphic evidence of repeated debris flow deposition on Appalachian fans indicates that debris flows have been important geomorphic slope processes throughout the Quaternary (Mills, 1982, 1983; Kochel and Johnson, 1984).

Appalachian debris fans are typically small (<1 km²) compared to alluvial fans in most other environments (Kochel and Johnson, 1984). Most Appalachian debris fans are elongate and

have steep, segmented longitudinal profiles usually greater than 10°. Source areas for Appalachian fans are heavily forested between debris flow events. Many of the fans also have mature forest cover, indicating that debris flow recurrence intervals are great.

Triggering Mechanisms

Dominant triggering mechanisms for debris flows include intense rainfall, snowmelt, and volcanic eruptions. Volcanic processes can be ruled out for Appalachian debris flows. Snowmelt plays a minor and very localized role in the initiation of Appalachian debris flows because of the relatively low annual snowfall in the mountains (compared, for example, to the Rockies). It is unlikely that snowmelt can occur rapidly enough to mobilize debris on the densely forested Appalachian slopes. Intense rainfall appears to have been the dominant triggering process in major historical Appalachian debris flows (Table 1). In most cases, a connection with tropical air masses can be demonstrated.

Caine (1980) proposed an apparent threshold relationship between rainfall intensity and debris flow initiation for rainfall durations between 10 minutes and 10 days based on a compila-

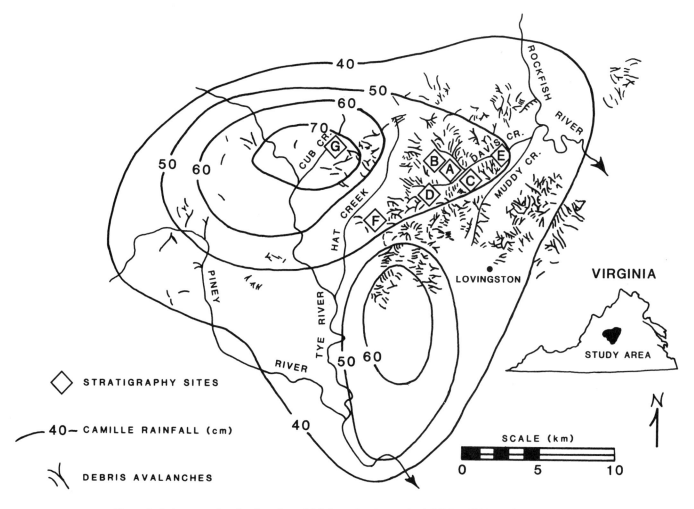

Figure 1. Index map showing location of debris avalanches and rainfall for 1969 Hurricane Camille storm. Debris avalanches mapped from aerial photographs taken one week after flood. Isohyets show cumulative rainfall between noon, August 19, and noon, August 20; however, most rain occurred during 8-hr period centered on midnight. Also shown (noted by letters) are stratigraphic sites referred to in text and other figures. Rainfall data from Camp and Miller, 1970, and National Climatic Center, n.d.

tion of worldwide data. Studies such as those of Campbell (1975) for southern California and Eschner and Patric (1982) for the southern Appalachians indicate that similar relationships can be drawn with regional applications. Most of these studies show that, although there is a lower limit of cumulative rainfall for a debris flow–producing storm, a critical rainfall intensity value must be exceeded before significant debris flow activity occurs. Studies of this type should prove valuable if combined with long-term climatic records within the region in making predictions of the risk of debris flow activity for planning purposes.

Virginia Alluvial Fans

Alluvial fans are important depositional landforms in piedmont areas of west-central Virginia (Fig. 1). Two major types of alluvial fans can be recognized on the basis of their sedimentology, morphology, dominant depositional processes, and relative age (Kochel and Johnson, 1984). Along the western flank of the Blue Ridge, an extensive apron of alluvial fan deposits has prograded westward over steeply dipping Paleozoic sedimentary rocks of the Shenandoah Valley. These Blue Ridge fans appear to have been constructed largely by water-flood processes probably associated with braided streams. No radiocarbon dates have yet been obtained from these deposits, but well-developed soils and weathering characteristics of the quartzite clasts indicate a Pleistocene or perhaps Tertiary age for these sediments. No historical activity has been recorded on these fan surfaces. Many of the fans have coalesced into a bajada along the mountain front. Incision by modern streams outlining the fans has occurred along inter-fan areas where the percentage of fine-grained sediments appears to be highest. For more detail on these pre-Holocene fans, see Kochel and Johnson (1984).

East of the Blue Ridge, hundreds of small fans occur in Precambrian crystalline rocks, which were activated by debris flows in Nelson County during Hurricane Camille in 1969. These fans are constructed solely of debris flow deposits and rarely exceed 0.5 km^2 in area. Pedogenic and radiocarbon data from these deposits indicate these fans initially became active in the early Holocene (Kochel and Johnson, 1984) and were constructed entirely by debris flows like those in 1969. These fans are the focus of the remainder of the discussion.

HURRICANE CAMILLE FLOW OF 1969

The Camille Storm

Rainfall in excess of 75 cm occurred overnight in central Virginia (Fig. 1) on August 19–20, 1969, associated with the remains of Hurricane Camille that struck the Mississippi Gulf Coast a few days earlier. Catastrophic rains occurring that night in Nelson County were the result of a combination of several factors: (1) the excessive moisture from the remains of Hurricane Camille moving into central Virginia from the southwest; (2) the orographic effects of the Blue Ridge and hills of Lovingston gneiss in Nelson County east of the Blue Ridge; (3) the collision between the tropical Camille air mass and an extratropical cyclone from the north, which acted as a lid to trap the tropical moisture; and (4) a significant influx of low-level moisture into Virginia from a tropical storm to the east off the Carolina coast.

The result of the intense rain was the occurrence of hundreds of debris avalanche–debris flows throughout a small area of central Virginia, concentrated in Nelson County (Fig. 1). Most of the debris flows were confined within the 40-cm isoheytal area that occupied a region with a radius of approximately 15 km, centered on Lovingston. Damages from the storm were extensive. Within this highly rural area, more than 100 bridges were destroyed, more than 150 lives were lost, and more than $100 million of property damage was incurred (Williams and Guy, 1973). Dramatic scour and deposition occurred on hillslopes, fans, and floodplains (Williams and Guy, 1973). Most of the rain fell during an 8-hr period centered on midnight. Eyewitnesses recall that most of the debris flow activity occurred during the peak of the rainfall between midnight and 4 A.M. This probably coincided with the latter part of the storm after the threshold of cumulative rainfall for slope failure had been exceeded and when the rainfall intensity was highest.

Debris Avalanche–Debris Flows

Debris avalanches occurred along hundreds of first-order channels and swales along upstream areas (Fig. 1). Typically, the debris avalanches were initiated by slides along the steepest portion (the inflection point) of the convex-concave slopes (Williams and Guy, 1973). The slides then rapidly disintegrated into debris

avalanches as they continued down slope toward the debris fan. Debris avalanching occurred on heavily forested slopes; thus, organic debris accounted for a significant part of the total load carried by the flows to the fans. Once on the debris fans, a large portion of the coarsest clasts accumulated as a hummocky mass at the fan apex while the remainder of the flow continued down-fan and into mainstream channels.

Controls on Slope Failure. Debris avalanches in Nelson County were of two main varieties. On several slopes, the failure plane was within colluvium or soil material. More common, however, was the failure of the hillslope at the interface between bedrock and colluvium along the zone where pore pressures were greatest. Bedrock in the region is largely Precambrian Lovingston gneiss. The Lovingston Formation exhibits a variety of facies within the study region such as granite, granite-gneiss, quartz monzanite, and schist (Bloomer and Werner, 1955), but has never been mapped in detail. Most analyses of slope stability include some kind of multivariate approach to determine the relative importance of a wide variety of factors affecting slope stability (Moser and Hohensinn, 1983; Carrara, 1983). The abundance of slope failures in a small area during the Camille flood provides an excellent opportunity to investigate how these variables may have affected stability in an area where climate and lithology are relatively constant.

The rainfall intensity was obviously a significant factor affecting the spatial distribution of debris avalanching in Nelson County during 1969. However, the lack of coincidence of debris avalanching with the highest regions of rainfall indicates that other physical factors also were important determinants of the stability of many of the slopes (Fig. 1). Williams and Guy (1973) qualitatively assessed many factors with regard to slope stability, including (1) slope aspect (orientation), (2) hillslope gradient, (3) presence of hillslope hollows, (4) basal stream action, (5) hillslope length, and (6) soil depth. They found that greater frequency of debris avalanches occurred on north- and east-slope aspects and on short, steep slopes, and where hillslope hollows were prominent.

Peatross (1986) used discriminant analysis of 23 variables related to basin morphometry and slope geometry, measured for 769 basins, to successfully classify 79 percent of the low-order basins into failed or stable sites. Measurements were all done from topographic maps and 1:6,000 scale aerial photographs taken a few days after the Camille storm. Variables most successful in producing the discriminant groupings included hillslope gradient, hillslope aspect, and horizontal curvature. Horizontal curvature is an index of the across-slope relief between slope margins and the center of the slope hollow, measured midway up the failed slope (Peatross, 1986).

Preliminary studies of field geotechnical properties of hillslope soils are currently underway at 43 failed and unfailed sites in Nelson County using the parameters in Table 2. Measurement of the relationship between bedrock jointing and foliation and debris avalanche orientation is among the factors being studied. The initial data suggest that the structural characteristics of the

TABLE 2. LIST OF PARAMETERS INCLUDED IN CURRENT FIELD STUDY
OF SLOPE STABILITY

Parameter	Style of Measurement
Lithology	Granite, granite-gneiss, schistose
Foliation	Compass bearing
Dominant joints	Compass bearing
Slope angle maxima	Maximum on failed scar or unfailed slope
Slope aspect	Compass direction of exposure
Surface etching	Relative observation
Soil thickness	Measured along midslope
Plastic limit	Measured between 0.5 and 1 m depth
Liquid limit	Measured between 0.5 and 1 m depth
Soil shear strength (i.e., angle of internal friction, cohesion)	Using Iowa borehole shear tester, done on soil along failed margins of debris avalanche
Relative permeability	Drainage character
Organic content	Combustion

bedrock (jointing, exfoliation, and foliation) exert strong control over the morphology of the debris avalanche scar (Fig. 2). Additional measurements may reveal a relationship between the incidence of failure and structural characteristics, which may explain the higher frequency of avalanches on the north- and east-facing slopes observed by Williams and Guy (1973). Preliminary results of the field studies indicate that variation in soil properties between failed and stable sites is minor (Terranova, 1987). Therefore, lithologic and structural characteristics of the bedrock, in combination with local slope geometry, may be more important controls on slope stability than soil properties where shallow (<2 m) debris avalanche failures occur with slip planes within the bedrock or at the soil-bedrock boundary.

The field observations of this study concur with Williams and Guy (1973) in that almost all failures occurred at sites of hillslope hollows. This was also supported in the work of Peatross (1986) and appears to hold true for many Appalachian debris avalanches I have inspected between New England and North Carolina. An important question is whether the hollows existed prior to the avalanching in 1969. Figure 3 shows a close-up of a typical avalanche scar in Nelson County with significant solution-etched microrelief developed on the granite-gneiss. Solution rills are common at most sites. Bedrock surfaces at all failed sites have been etched or pitted by solution, allowing orthoclase phenocrysts to stand 1 to 2 m high in relief. Twidale (1976) described similar pitting in granitic rocks in Australia, which were produced by solution in rillen and in soils adjacent to the footslope of large granite outcrops. The most common type of pitting recognized by Twidale (1976) is where feldspar and biotite have been weathered, leaving quartz standing in relief. However, Twidale (1976) noted that in coarse-grained or porphyritic granites, orthoclase phenocrysts stand in relief similar to those observed in the coarse facies of the Lovingston Formation in Virginia. Twidale (1976) showed that pitting developed below the surface with the aid of ground water. Once pitted surfaces were exposed by erosion of the soil cover, subaerial weathering processes rapidly destroyed the pitting, and smooth bedrock surfaces were formed. The ob-

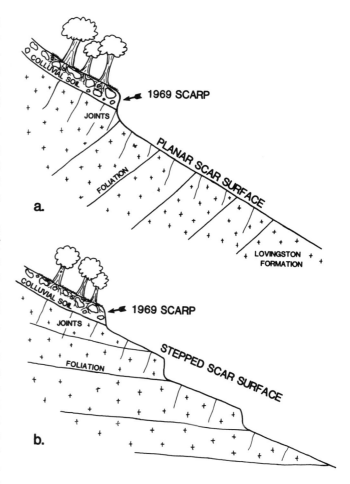

Figure 2. Schematic cross sections showing influence of bedrock structural characteristics on debris avalanche scar morphology. a, Planar surfaces, where foliation and hillslope orientation are nearly normal. In these cases, failures were characterized by spalling of thin layers of bedrock along joint surfaces normal to slope. b, Stepped surfaces, where foliation planes intersected hillslopes at small acute angles. These differences can be seen along the track of a single avalanche scar if its trend changes significantly downslope.

Figure 3. Microrelief on bedrock surfaces at debris avalanche sites indicates that hillslope hollows were there prior to 1969. a, Solution rillen developed by ground-water drainage below thin, colluvial soils prior to 1969 failure (photo by Thomas Terranova). b, Close-up of pitting (etching) on granite-gneiss surfaces at failed sites. Orthoclase phenocrysts stand high in relief, as do quartz veins.

served intensity of pitting and rillen development in the Lovingston Formation at failed sites could not have occurred since 1969 on the gneiss. This suggests that the failure sites were active zones of subsurface flow concentration for long periods in hollows that existed prior to the avalanching. Pitting is insignificant on other bedrock surfaces not related to debris flows observed in the Lovingston gneiss.

Recognition of colluvial hillslope hollows may be valuable in predicting sites of future debris avalanche hazards. Surveys using geophyiscal techniques could be useful in mapping subsurface topography on colluvial slopes in these regions. Shallow soils and colluvium accumulate on these steep slopes (Fig. 4) between successive debris avalanches at a site, gradually filling the hollows prior to the next failure. A significant period of time is required before enough colluvium can accumulate to provide the source debris necessary for the next major debris avalanche. My observations of debris avalanche scars 15 years after the Camille flood indicate that the recovery process varies between sites, depending primarily on the location of the failure plane within the regolith. Failure within colluvium leaves soil available for immediate revegetation. Bedrock scars revegetate slowly because they must collect colluvium before vegetation can be reestablished. Sites

with failure planes within the colluvium have undergone rapid recovery since 1969. Trees in these sites are already well established, so that, within another 10 to 20 years, locating the avalanche scars will be very difficult. Avalanche scars with failure planes in the bedrock or at the bedrock-colluvium interface are recovering at a much slower rate. Complete recovery will likely require hundreds of years. On these scars, revegetation and accumulation of colluvium are occurring in patches. The areas of most rapid recovery on bedrock failure sites occur along major joint faces and upslope from small patches of colluvium that did not fail in 1969. The stepped failure surfaces on slopes where foliation parallels slope show accelerated recovery rates of colluvium and vegetation.

Debris Fan Deposits

Fan Morphology. Debris fans in Nelson County are typically small, segmented, and steep, with gradients averaging between 40 and 100 m/km (Fig. 5). Debris fans observed in other areas of the Appalachians, such as in the Delwood–Maggie Valley area of North Carolina and in the Smoky Mountains, have similar steep gradients. Most of the fans are elongate and irregular in plan view due to valley wall confinement in first-order basins.

Figure 4. View of thin, colluvial soil along margin of debris avalanche scar in Davis Creek (Fig. 1, site a). Poorly sorted colluvium typically is <1 m thick and exhibits little or no pedogenic development except for thin accumulation of organics in upper few centimeters. Vertical bar at left = 1 m. Photograph taken in 1980.

The well-established relationship between fan area and drainage basin area established for fans in arid areas (Bull, 1962) does not occur for these fans due to their confinement. Fan areas remain small over a wide range of contributing basin areas.

Thickness of Nelson County debris fans is generally between 5 and 20 m, where it was measured by augering and study of cuts along stream cuts incised into the fans. The thin nature of Nelson County fans is similar to the values estimated by Mills (1983) for debris fans in the Roan Mountain area of North Carolina. Thick fan deposits are probably uncommon for a number of reasons, including (1) the limited supply of debris from small low-order basins with thin colluvial soils; (2) transportation of the debris over the fans and exportation to downstream areas because of the steep fan gradients; (3) the low frequency of deposition on these fans; and (4) the coincidence of debris flow activity with peak-flow stage in the mainstream at the distal edge of the fans. Eye-witnesses of the Camille flood recall that debris avalanching was concentrated in the early morning hours of August 20 when the streams were in peak flood. Aerial photographs taken immediately after the flood support this observation because debris flow deposits rarely extended beyond the limit of stream flooding on fans, and the loci of debris flow deposition on many of the fans was deflected in the downstream direction.

Sedimentology and Stratigraphy

Deposits from 1969 Debris Flows. These deposits are generally lobate and restricted to less than 50 percent of the fan areas (Fig. 5). In most cases in Davis Creek, the 1969 deposits are concentrated in areas where channels had incised into fans prior to the flood. The deposits are very poorly sorted mud matrix–supported gravels ranging in size as large as 5 m in maximum dimension. Deposit thickness was extremely variable on the fans studied in Davis Creek but showed no distinct variations in the downfan direction, with the exceptions of hummocky accumulations of the coarsest debris at the hillslope base (Fig. 6a). Similarly, no downfan trends in grain size could be discerned.

Basal contacts of the 1969 deposits were uneven and erosional in all cases. At several sites a distinct coarsening-upward trend of inverse grading was observed, as was a tendency for imbrication of coarse clasts (Fig. 6b). Clasts were dominantly unweathered, although there were occasional rotted boulders that probably were weathering in situ on slopes before they were incorporated into the flow. No soil development has occurred on the deposits except for a thin organic horizon under the grass and young forest cover that developed since 1969.

Older Debris Flow Sediments

Augering and hand-trenching of several debris fans in Davis Creek indicated that repeated debris flows have occurred on these fans throughout their aggradational history (Fig. 7a). The irregular nature of these units indicates that earlier deposits were prob-

Figure 5. Aerial photograph of debris fan in Nelson County after Camille storm. About half of fan surface received deposits from debris flows originating as hillside debris avalanches in forested slopes. This fan occurs in downstream portion of basin where not constrained by valley walls. Most fans are elongate where confined by narrow valleys in headward regions of basins. Photo courtesy of the Virginia Division of Mineral Resources, Charlottesville.

ably lobate and areally restricted on the fans like those in 1969. Correlations between trenches and auger sites across the fans were based on the recognition of erosional surfaces, paleosols, texture, and matrix mineralogy (Fig. 7b).

Recognition of multiple events at a site is important in the analysis of debris flow hazards on these fans. Figure 8 shows the distinct contact between older debris flow sediments and overlying 1969 sediments on Fan D (Fig. 1) in Davis Creek. Morphostratigraphic criteria useful in distinguishing events in the Davis Creek fans included recognition of eroded paleosols on former fan surfaces at depositional contacts and abrupt changes in sedi-

ment characteristics (e.g., texture, induration, clast weathering, and mineralogy of matrix materials altered as a function of weathering) across unit boundaries. Table 3 illustrates these differences between the 1969 deposits and the older sediments immediately underlying them in Davis Creek fans. Using these techniques either three or four debris flow events can be recognized in most Davis Creek fans.

FREQUENCY OF DEBRIS FLOWS

Investigations of the return periods between debris flow

Figure 6. Debris flow deposits near apex of typical debris fan in Davis Creek (Fig. 1, site c). a, Most of coarsest material accumulated at slope base in hummocky zone. b, Imbrication of boulders near the fan apex in upper few meters of deposit.

events are critical for environmental planning in mountainous areas affected by debris flows such as the Appalachian Mountains. Most studies of debris flow frequency have used one or a combination of the following techniques to estimate average return periods: (1) dendrochronology, using ages of tilted trees, ages since tree scarring, and adventitious roots; (2) lichenometry; (3) radiocarbon dating of organic materials incorporated in the debris flow deposits; and (4) analysis of meteorologic data when an approximate regional threshold rainfall intensity for debris flow initiation is known for the region. Costa (1984) has provided a summary of the studies and techniques employed.

Radiocarbon dating was used in estimating the ages of debris flows prior to 1969 on the Nelson County fans because the other techniques could not be applied. No historical records of earlier flows existed in the area, particularly during the life span of the trees. Lichen growth curves are not well established in the Appalachians and also cannot be successfully applied because subsequent flows normally bury earlier deposits entirely. Finally, meteorological records are short, and data collection points are widely distributed in the mountainous areas.

Prehistoric debris flow deposits have been radiocarbon-dated in several Davis Creek fans (Fig. 1, sites a, b, and d). All of the samples dated were from either organic-rich paleosols or

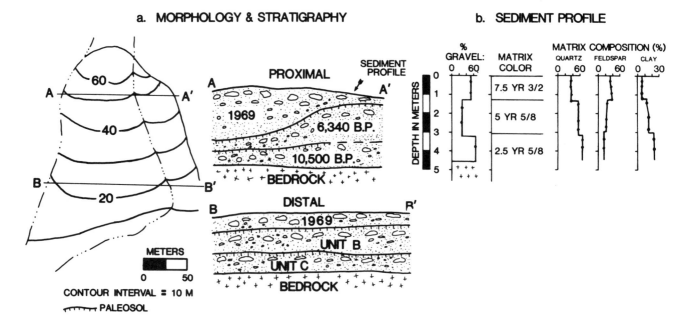

Figure 7. Stratigraphy and sedimentology of a debris fan along the North Prong of Davis Creek (Fig. 1, site b). a, Cross sections show irregular nature of recent deposits across fan, resulting from shifting loci of depositional lobes. Cross sections were measured along section lines at stream banks and in two trenches dug midway between two streams. b, Variations in texture and matrix composition with depth useful in determining boundaries between debris flow events.

TABLE 3. DAVIS CREEK DEBRIS FLOW DEPOSITS

	1969 Deposits	Older Deposits
Coarse clasts	Coarser	Finer
Sorting	Very poor	Very poor
Matrix mineralogy	Low-quartz/feldspar rock fragments	Quartz-dominant, minor feldspar and rock fragments
Matrix texture	Higher sand/mud	Lower sand/mud
Color	Brown	Reddish-brown
Soils	Entisols Incipient A horizon	Well-defined A and B horizons Buried soils
Clast weathering	Variable--fresh and weathered	Clay coats, clast ghosts, all weathered

dispersed charcoal fragments within the matrix of the debris flow deposits. The radiocarbon dates on the paleosols represent mean residence times (Geyh and others, 1971) or a minimum age between the deposition of the successive deposits between which it occurs. For a more detailed discussion of the possible errors and range of ages of these samples, see Kochel and Johnson (1984).

Basal debris flow deposits are correlatable between at least two sites (Fig. 1, sites a and b) at approximately 11 ka. These data indicate that there have been either three or four debris flow events there during the last 11,000 yr (Fig. 7a). Hence, an average at-a-site return period of between 3,000 and 4,000 yr can be assumed.

There are several sources of potential problems with estimates made from this type of data. First, this technique assumes that the observed stratigraphic section contains evidence of each of the debris flow events that have occurred on that fan. The described sections were in the proximal area of these fans; thus, it is likely that every flow would have deposited sediment on these sites because there is limited area for avulsion. However, the possibility that earlier units may have been eroded by succeeding flows cannot be ruled out.

Another possible complication with frequency analyses of debris avalanches is that there is a period of recovery required between successive events for the accumulation of colluvium on failed slopes to supply subsequent debris flows. If the time between events was short, a second rainfall event may result in a water-flood without significant debris flow at those sites. Evidence of this kind of relationship was suggested by a study of hillslope failures in Great Britain by Newson (1980). Regardless of the problems, the radiocarbon dates provide a reasonable estimate of the magnitude of the recurrence interval of debris flows at the Davis Creek sites. Improvements of these estimates will be possible with additional radiocarbon dates and also by the correlation of debris flow activity on upstream fans with the downstream flood-plain record.

DOWNSTREAM RESPONSE DURING DEBRIS FLOWS

Downstream Flows and Channel Response

Events large enough to generate significant debris avalanching in headwater basins undoubtedly result in large-magnitude floods in downstream regions of the basins such as Davis Creek and the Rockfish River. Even though the rainfall area of Hurricane Camille was extremely localized, the runoff from the Rockfish and Tye Rivers in Nelson County produced the third highest flood on the James River at Scottsville, Virginia, in the last 190 yr. Slightly higher flood stages were caused by Hurricane Agnes in 1972 and Hurricane Juan in 1985.

In the Nelson County area, tremendous floods occurred on all major streams affected by the Camille rains (Williams and Guy, 1973), resulting in catastrophic erosion and deposition of channels and flood plains. Considerable debate has ensued concerning the geomorphic effects of large, infrequent floods since the issue was raised by Wolman and Miller (1960). The effects of catastrophic floods vary significantly with climate, topography, channel geometry, and sediment load, among other factors (Kochel, 1987). The magnitude-frequency controversy is beyond the scope of this paper. However, some important insights into the factors controlling channel response were gained by a study of aerial photographs taken immediately after the flood in Nelson County (Johnson, 1983), in particular, the importance of debris flows. Johnson used stepwise multiple regression to show that the amount of channel widening was dependent primarily on the percentage of area affected by debris avalanching upstream from the site of channel measurements (Fig. 9). Secondary factors affecting the amount of width increase were channel gradient and basin shape in the equation:

$$CW = 8.2DA + 4592CG - 126K + 93$$

where CW is channel width increase in percent; DA, the percentage of upstream area affected by debris avalanching; CG, the channel gradient; and K, the basin shape expressed as a lemniscate. Significant channel change did not occur unless there was a supply of large amounts of coarse debris and steep channel gradients on which to transport this material. It was interesting that of the 17 morphometric parameters Johnson (1983) used in his analysis, estimated peak flow discharge ranked 14th, accounting for less than 4 percent of the variation. These results demonstrate the importance of the linkage between slope processes and

Figure 8. View of trench cut into proximal portion of fan in upper Davis Creek (Fig. 1, site d) showing contact between dark, organic-rich sediments from 1969 flows and older, oxidized deposits from prehistorical flows.

downstream channel processes in determining the geomorphic response of a particular large rainfall event. Engineering design of hydraulic structures should be undertaken cautiously in areas where stream headwaters are subject to debris flows. Channel response to large floods may be much more catastrophic than for rivers in similar regions in which coarse sediment is not readily supplied to downstream channels during floods (Kochel, 1987).

Flood-Plain Sediments in Davis Creek

Channelization efforts following the Camille flood drastically altered most of the flood plains in the areas most affected by the flood. However, observations of aerial and ground photographs taken immediately after the flood, observations of Williams and Guy (1973), and studies of undisturbed segments of the flood plains provide some idea of the nature of the flows that

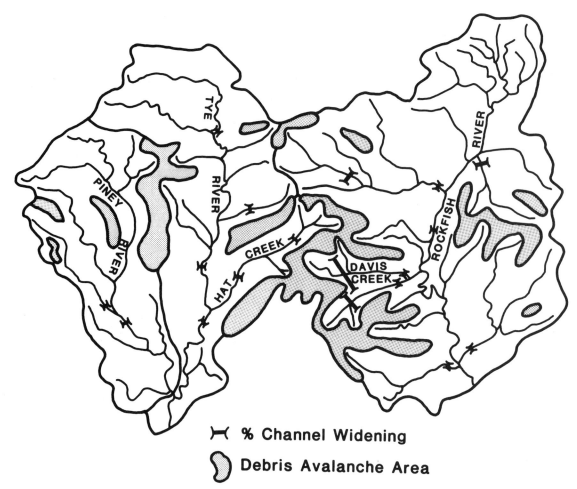

⊢⊣ **% Channel Widening**

🫘 **Debris Avalanche Area**

Figure 9. Schematic map of relationship between areal extent of debris avalanching and channel width increase in Nelson County area during Camille flood. Bar length at study sites is proportional to percentage of channel width increase observed (after Johnson, 1983).

affected downstream areas of Davis Creek. Figure 10 shows examples of the flood-plain stratigraphy near the mouth of Davis Creek. Characteristics indicative of debris flow, rather than water-flood, origin of these sediments, in accord with criteria outlined by Costa and Jarrett (1981), include: (1) extremely poor sorting, (2) sharp erosional contacts between units, (3) lack of cross-bedding and other bedforms, (4) occasional inverse grading, (5) uniform nature of deposits over broad areas of the flood plain (Fig. 10a), and (6) transport of delicate clasts such as soil materials (Fig. 10b) and weathered boulders. In addition, some of the observations from photographs indicate that boulder levees were sometimes found along channel margins on the flood plain.

In Figure 10c, three distinct flood events can be discussed. Each of the two deposits below the 1969 layer have well-developed paleosols that are partially preserved at this site. Most of the A-horizon was stripped off of the intermediate unit during the emplacement of the 1969 sediments. However, a 45-cm-thick

buried textural B horizon remains. Significant portions of the buried A and B horizons are visible in the lower unit exposed at this site. Considerable time had elapsed between the occurrence of the three floods at this site in order to permit the pedogenesis observed on these former flood-plain surfaces. These three floods recorded in the downstream flood-plain stratigraphy of Davis Creek may correlate with the three fan units observed, but have not been radiocarbon dated at this time.

Regional versus at-a-Site Frequency

Care should be taken when interpreting the significance of recurrence intervals of debris flows at-a-site for application to environmental planning. While the average return period for flows on Davis Creek fans may be 3,000 to 4,000 yr, the return periods for similar events over a state-wide region or over the central and southern Appalachians may be considerably lower. For example, Table 1 shows numerous debris avalanche events reported in the Appalachians over the last 100 years alone.

Figure 10. Downstream flood-plain sediments near mouth of Davis Creek (Fig. 1, site e). a, In this area, nearly uniform deposit of poorly sorted debris was deposited during flood. Note thick, organic A-horizon buried by gravel marking 1969 flood-plain surface. b, Close-up view of delicate clasts of soil transported in Camille sediments. Survival of these clasts and fragile weathered granites argues for laminar flow conditions during some of downstream flows. c, Stratigraphy of cut bank showing three major flood events. Uppermost unit deposited by Camille flood over buried B-horizon developed in earlier unit. Basal unit contains portion of buried A-horizon and thicker buried B-horizon.

Future research on the frequency of catastrophic events like debris flows needs to focus on this problem of regional recurrence intervals. One likely approach to the problem would be through the analysis of meteorological records that have exceeded estimated thresholds for initiating debris flows. The major hurdle in this investigation, however, is the density of official weather stations and the length of their records. In a recent discussion of intense Appalachian rainstorms, referred to informally as "Appalachian convective complexes," Michaels (1985) noted that they may be considerably more frequent than official meteorological records indicate. Although these intense rains are infrequent, they are usually too small to encounter the network of official rain gauges. There seems to be a need to establish a more systematic gathering of climatological data related to these problems and associated catastrophic floods.

PRE-HOLOCENE FAN DEPOSITS

The extensive alluvial fan deposits along the western flank of the Blue Ridge Mountains in west-central Virginia described by Kochel and Johnson (1984) are interpreted to be dominantly pre-Holocene in age. Age estimates are based on the lack of evidence of historical deposition on the fans and the extensive soils developed on these fan surfaces. In addition, a major paleosol occurs a few meters below the fan surfaces, which separates relatively fresh clasts of resistant Antietam quartzite from totally

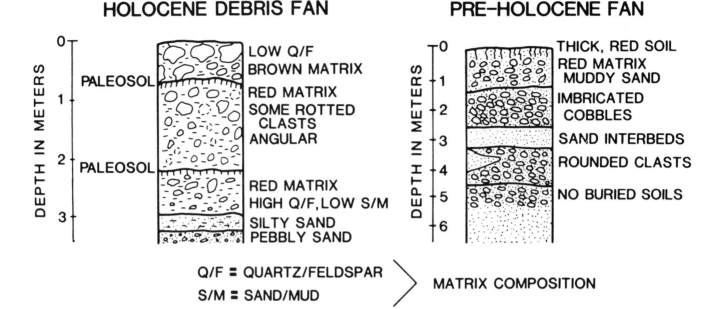

Figure 11. Stratigraphy of Holocene and pre-Holocene fans at Ginseng Hollow (Fig. 1, site f) in Hat Creek. a, Holocene fan composed of two debris flow units characterized by mud matrix, poorly sorted gravels similar to those described in Davis Creek. b, Pre-Holocene fan contains strongly developed surface soil and is dominated by sand matrix gravels that appear to be well imbricated. A few thin, mud-rich lenses occur in section.

disintegrated quartzite clasts below. Estimates on the age of these Blue Ridge fans are imprecise, ranging from Pleistocene to Tertiary.

The sedimentology of the fans west of the Blue Ridge indicates that depositional processes were dominated by braided streams rather than by debris flows characteristic of the Holocene fans east of the Blue Ridge. The apparent lack of coordination with modern Holocene processes in the area lends support to the idea that the Blue Ridge fans are relict from an earlier, different climate.

At a few locations in Nelson County, Holocene debris fans are incised into older fan sediments. A good example of this relationship occurs at Ginseng Hollow in the drainage of Hat Creek (Fig. 1, site f). Figure 11 illustrates the sedimentological differences between the Holocene debris fan sediments and the sediments of the older fan remnant along the east side of Ginseng Hollow. Older sediments are composed dominantly of clast-supported gravels that appear to be better sorted, more rounded, and well imbricated compared to the Holocene debris flow sediments. The older Ginseng Hollow sediments are similar to the sediments west of the Blue Ridge, described by Kochel and Johnson (1984), that are suggestive of braided stream deposition. The well-developed soils and intense weathering of the older Ginseng Hollow sediments in the fan remnant indicate a considerable time gap between these periods of fan construction. In addition, there has been enough time elapsed for incision by Ginseng Hollow

such that the Holocene fan base level is 4 to 5 m below the older fan surface. Similar pre-Holocene fans occur throughout Nelson County. Most of these fans are covered by orchards and have thick, well-oxidized soils developed on their surfaces. Mills (1982) described two distinct ages of fan development in the southern Appalachians similar to that observed in Virginia. The older fans, however, seem less common in Virginia than in North Carolina and Tennessee.

BEGINNING OF DEBRIS FAN DEPOSITION IN CENTRAL VIRGINIA

The date of the basal debris flow deposits on bedrock in the Davis Creek debris fans appears to be approximately 11 ka, coinciding with the start of the Holocene in Virginia. Organic-rich fine-grained sediments have been observed immediately underlying the basal debris flow deposits in fans at site g (Fig. 1) along Cub Creek (A. Howard, personal communication, 1984) and at sites a and b in Davis Creek. These fine-grained sediments also contain angular fragments of bedrock and in places are finely laminated. The deposit at the base of the Cub Creek sequence has a radiocarbon age of 13,170 ± 190 yr B.P. This clearly brackets the beginning of Holocene debris flow activity in central Virginia between 13,170 and 10,800 yr B.P. These deposits are interpreted as late Pleistocene slope deposits of probable solifluction origin.

The combination of basal debris flow deposits dated at 11

ka, and the apparent change in depositional processes on older fans like those at Ginseng Hollow and west of the Blue Ridge suggests that the onset of Holocene climatic conditions dramatically altered dominant slope denudational processes in central Virginia. Most historical debris flows in the Appalachians have been triggered by the incursion of tropical storms and/or hurricanes into these temperate regions (Table 1). Therefore, the initiation of significant debris flow activity on Appalachian alluvial fans may reflect the response of the geomorphic system to conditions permitting the ready influx of tropical moisture concurrent with the retreat of the polar front at the close of the Pleistocene.

Michaels (1985) noted that the key ingredient required to produce heavy rainstorms such as those associated with catastrophic "Appalachian convective complexes" is an uninterrupted influx of warm, tropical air. The most common source of tropical moisture in the Appalachians, other than weak easterly surface flows, is tropical cyclones. Excessive rains produced in the Virginia mountains in recent years have been from tropical systems, including Hurricanes camille (1969), Agnes (1972), Chris (1982), and Juan (1985).

Support for this model of debris flow coincidence with the retreat of the polar front can be drawn from palynologic data (Fig. 12). Delcourt and Delcourt (1981) have shown that vegetational zones that correlate today with the approximate summer position of the polar front occurred along a narrow band across central Virginia about 11 ka (shaded bands in Fig. 12). Studies of paleocirculation systems by Bryson and others (1970) indicate that the approximate location of the summer polar front was in the central Virginia latitude at about the same time. This coincidence with the start of debris flow activity on these fans may reflect the first time since the Pleistocene that tropical moisture could successfully invade the mountains of central Virginia and Nelson County to trigger the intense rainfalls required for extensive debris avalanching.

If this model is correct, then we may see a systematic decrease in the age of initiation of debris flow activity northward along the Appalachians from the North Carolina–Tennessee area to New England. This range would be expected to coincide with the gradual retreat of the polar front from maximum Pleistocene conditions in the late Wisconsinan as it retreated northward to its present position. This span of time is probably in the range of 5,000 to 7,000 yr, based on the palynologic information (Watts, 1979; Delcourt and Delcourt, 1981). I am currently conducting a pilot study to test the potential of this model.

SUMMARY

Significant progress is being made in attempts to delineate controls on slope stability in areas of central Virginia affected by debris avalanching and debris flows that occurred in 1969. The primary criteria relating to slope stability include slope aspect (orientation), bedrock structure (foliation and joints), and the preexistence of hillslope hollows that were filled with a thin mantle of colluvium. Although slope steepness is a significant

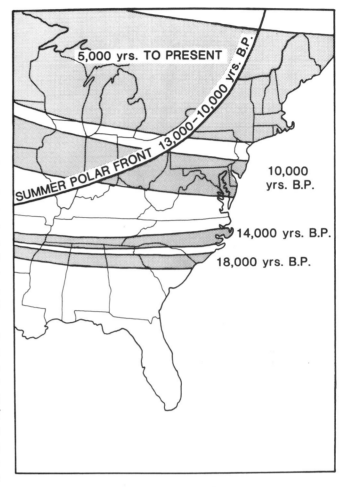

Figure 12. Approximate locations of mixed conifer–northern hardwood forest vegetation zones (shaded areas) over past 18,000 yr (modified from Delcourt and Delcourt, 1981). Approximate summer polar front position from Bryson and others (1970) tends to correspond with this vegetation zone. This zone, based on the vegetation relationships, was probably at latitude of central Virginia 11,000 yr B.P., which corresponds to beginning of debris flow activity in Davis Creek, and may reflect approximate northern limit of incursion of significant tropical moisture important in triggering Appalachian debris flows.

factor, its utility in hazard assessment is best when combined with other morphometric lithologic, and/or geotechnical parameters of the site. Continuing field research is expected to focus on these relationships.

The influence of tropical air systems can be demonstrated in almost all instances of widespread debris flows in the Appalachians. Conditions required for the intense rains needed to trigger debris avalanches on forested slopes generally cannot be met without either a strong easterly surface flow or the influence of tropical cyclones, or both. Negligible sedimentation and erosion occurs on slopes and debris fans between major Appalachian debris flow events. Once forested, these slopes remain fairly stable, except during catastrophic rainfalls such as those associated with tropical systems. This association between tropical moisture and debris flows may be reflected in the sedimentary record of debris fans. The apparent initiation of debris flow processes in central Virginia about 11 ka coincides with palynologic data that indicate that the approximate location of the summer polar front was in the same area during that time. Frequent excursions of tropical moisture would have suddenly become possible as the summer polar front position retreated northward across Virginia during the earliest Holocene.

Debris avalanches and debris flows represent a major hazard in piedmont regions of the Appalachian Mountains. Stratigraphic and sedimentologic studies of debris fan sediments such as those in central Virgina can yield data on the frequency of debris flows. Individual events can be recognized by the observations of paleosols, abrupt changes in sediment texture, and abrupt changes in matrix composition at suspected event boundaries in fan strata. In many cases, organic debris and/or paleosol organics can be sampled for radiocarbon dating to estimate flow frequencies. Return period estimates for debris flows within a drainage basin can be strengthened in many cases by correlating fan stratigraphies with flood-plain stratigraphy at downstream sites.

Estimates of debris flow return periods at-a-site in Virginia are typically long, in the range of thousands of years. Conversely, there have been numerous episodes of widespread debris flows in the Appalachians during the last 100 years, and thus the frequency of Appalachian debris flows may be much greater when considered on a regional scale. More research is needed to define this relationship between local and regional debris flow frequency if intelligent hazard assessments are to be made. Recognition of hazards in many local areas is exacerbated by the lack of historical events owing to long at-a-site return periods.

ACKNOWLEDGMENTS

Numerous persons have assisted me in the field over the past few years. In particular, I thank Robert Johnson, David Simmons, Greg Wilson, and Thomas Terranova for their help. Partial support for field work has been provided by the Office of Research and Development Administration and the Department of Geology at Southern Illinois University. In addition, William Odum and the Department of Environmental Sciences of the University of Virginia graciously provided me with office space during part of the field work. I thank Sam Valastro of the Radiocarbon Laboratory of the University of Texas for performing the radiocarbon analyses. Discussions with Judith Peatross and Thomas Terranova have contributed to the ideas expressed concerning slope stability. Thanks also to DeAnn Kirk and Andy Mason for drafting the figures and to Betty Atwood for the word processing assistance.

REFERENCES CITED

Bloomer, R. O., and Werner, H. J., 1955, Geology of the Blue Ridge region in central Virginia: Geological Society of America Bulletin, v. 66, p. 579–606.

Bogucki, D. J., 1970, Debris slides and related flood damage associated with the September 1, 1951, cloudburst in the Mt. Le Conte–Sugarland Mountain area, Great Smoky Mountains National Park [Ph.D. thesis]: Knoxville, University of Tennessee, 165 p.

—— , 1976, Debris slides in the Mt. Le Conte area, Great Smoky Mountains: Geografiska Annaler, v. 58A, p. 179–192.

—— , 1977, Debris slide hazards in the Adirondack province of New York State: Environmental Geology, v. 1, p. 317–328.

Bryson, R. A., Baerreis, D. A., and Wendland, W. M., 1970, The character of late-glacial and post-glacial climatic changes, *in* Pleistocene and Recent environments of the central Great Plains: Lawrence, University of Kansas Press, p. 53–74.

Bull, W. B., 1962, Relations of alluvial fan size and slope to drainage basin size and lithology in western Fresno County, California: U.S. Geological Survey Professional Paper 450-B, p. 51–53.

Caine, N., 1980, The rainfall-duration control of shallow landslides and debris flows: Geografiska Annaler, v. 62A, p. 23–27.

Camp, J. D., and Miller, E. M., 1970, Flood of August 1969 in Virginia: U.S. Geological Survey Water Resources Division Open–File Report, 120 p.

Campbell, R. H., 1975, Soil slips, debris flows, and rainstorms in the Santa Monica Mountains, Southern California: U.S. Geological Survey Professional Paper 851, 51 p.

Carrera, A., 1983, Multivariate models for landslide hazard evaluation: Mathematical Geology, v. 15, p. 403–426.

Cleland, H. F., 1902, The landslides of Mt. Greylock and Briggsville, Massachusetts: Journal of Geology, v. 10, p. 513–557.

Costa, J. E., 1984, Physical geomorphology of debris flows, *in* Costa, J. E., and Fleisher, J. P., eds., Developments and applications of geomorphology: New York, Springer-Verlag, p. 268–317.

Costa, J. E., and Jarrett, R. D., 1981, Debris flows in small mountain stream channels of Colorado and their hydrologic implications: Association Engineering Geologists Bulletin, v. 18, p. 309–322.

Delcourt, P. A., and Delcourt, H. R., 1981, Vegetation maps for eastern North America; 40,000 yr B.P. to the present, *in* Romans, R. C., ed., Geobotany II: New York, Plenum Press, p. 123–157.

Eisenlohr, W. S., Jr., 1952, Floods of July 18, 1942, in north-central Pennsylvania: U.S. Geological Survey Water Supply Paper 1134-B, p. 59–158.

Eschner, A. R., and Patric, J. H., 1982, Debris avalanches in eastern upland forests: Journal of Forestry, v. 80, p. 343–347.

Flaccus, E., 1958, White Mountain landslides: Appalachia, v. 24, p. 175–191.

Geyh, M. A., Benzler, J. H., and Roeschmann, G., 1971, Problems of dating Pleistocene and Holocene soils by radiometric methods, *in* Yaalon, D. H., ed., Paleopedology; Origin, nature, and dating of paleosols: Jerusalem, Israel University Press and International Society of Soil Scientists, p. 63–75.

Hack, J. T., and Goodlett, J. C., 1960, Geomorphology and forest ecology of a mountain region in the central Appalachians: U.S. Geological Survey Professional Paper 347, 66 p.

Johnson, R. A., 1983, Channel response to extreme rainfall events, Hurricane Camille storm in central Nelson County, Virginia [M.S. thesis]: Charlottesville, University of Virginia, 109 p.

Kochel, R. C., 1987, Geomorphic effects of floods; Revisiting the magnitude-frequency problem, *in* Baker, V. R., Kochel, R. C., and Patton, P. C., eds., Flood geomorphology: New York, Wiley (in press).

Kochel, R. C., and Johnson, R. A., 1984, Geomorphology and sedimentology of humid-temperate alluvial fans, central Virginia, *in* Koster, E. H., and Steele, R. J., eds., Sedimentology of gravels and conglomerates: Canadian Society Petroleum Geologists Memoirs 10, p. 109–122.

Michaels, P. J., 1985, Virginia climate advisory: Charlottesville, University of

Virginia, v. 9, no. 2, 30 p.

Mills, H. H., 1982, Long-term episodic deposition on mountain foot-slopes in the Blue Ridge province of North Carolina; Evidence from relative age dating: Southeastern Geology, v. 23, p. 123–128.

——, 1983, Piedmont evolution at Roan Mountain, North Carolina: Geografiska Annaler, v. 65A, p. 111–126.

Moneymaker, B. C., 1939, Erosional effects of the Webb Mountain Tennessee cloudburst of August 5, 1938: Journal Tennessee Academy Science, v. 14, p. 190–196.

Moser, M., and Hohensinn, F., 1983, Geotechnical aspects of soil slips in alpine regions: Engineering Geology, v. 19, p. 185–211.

Newson, M., 1980, The geomorphological effectiveness of floods; A contribution simulated by two recent events in mid-Wales: Earth Surface Processes and Landforms, v. 5, p. 1–16.

Peatross, J. A., 1986, Morphometric analysis of slope stability controls during the Hurricane Camille storm in Virginia [M.S. thesis]: Charlottesville, University of Virginia, 185 p.

Pomeroy, J. S., 1980, Storm-induced debris avalanching and related phenomena in the Johnstown area, Pennsylvania, with references to other studies in the Appalachians: U.S. Geological Survey Professional Paper 1191, 24 p.

Ratte, C. A., and Rhodes, D. D., 1977, Hurricane-induced landslides on Dorset Mountain, Vermont: Geological Society America Abstracts with Programs, v. 9, no. 3, p. 311.

Schneider, R. H., 1973, Debris slides and related flood damage resulting from Hurricane Camille, 19-20 August, and subsequent storm, 5-6 September, 1969, in the Spring Creek drainage basin, Greenbriar County, West Virginia [Ph.D. thesis]: Knoxville, University of Tennessee, 131 p.

Stringfield, V. T., and Smith, R. C., 1956, Relation of geology to drainage, floods, and landslides in the Petersburg area, West Virginia: West Virginia Geological and Economic Survey Report of Investigations 13, 19 p.

Terranova, T., 1987, Multivariate analysis of geological, hydrological, and soil mechanical controls on slope stability in central Virginia [M.S. thesis]: Carbondale, Southern Illinois University, 89 p.

Twidale, C. R., 1976, Origin and significance of pitting on granite rocks: Zeitschrift für Geomorphologie, v. 20, p. 405–416.

U.S. Geological Survey, 1949, Floods of August 1940 in the southeastern states: U.S. Geological Survey Water Supply Paper 1066, 554 p.

——, 1982, Goals and tasks of the landslide part of a ground-failure hazards reduction program: U.S. Geological Survey Circular 880, 48 p.

VanDine, D. F., 1985, Debris flows and debris torrents in the southern Canadian Cordillera: Canadian Geotechnical Journal, v. 22, p. 44–68.

Varnes, D. J., 1978, Slope movement types and processes, *in* Schuster, R. L., and Kreisich, R. J., eds., Landslides; Analysis and their control: Washington, D.C., National Academy of Sciences, Transportation Research Board, Special Report No. 176, p. 11–33.

Watts, W. A., 1979, Late Quaternary vegetation of the central Appalachians and the New Jersey coastal plain: Ecological Monographs, v. 49, p. 427–469.

Williams, G. P., and Guy, H. P., 1973, Erosional and depositional aspects of Hurricane Camille in Virginia, 1969: U.S. Geological Survey Professional Paper 804, 80 p.

Wolman, M. G., and Miller, J. P., 1960, Magnitude and frequency of forces in geomorphic processes: Journal of Geology, v. 68, p. 54–74.

Manuscript Accepted by the Society December 29, 1986

Geological Society of America
Reviews in Engineering Geology, Volume VII
1987

Dating and interpretation of debris flows by geologic and botanical methods at Whitney Creek Gorge, Mount Shasta, California

W. R. Osterkamp
C. R. Hupp
U.S. Geological Survey
MS 413, National Center
Reston, Virginia 22092

ABSTRACT

Debris flow activity in the Whitney Creek basin of Mount Shasta is caused by incisement of soft pyroclastic beds in upper fan areas, and is the dominant late Holocene geomorphic process. A variety of geologic and botanical techniques permit the dating of many debris flows. These methods aid in the interpretation of recent denudation rates and late Quaternary geomorphic changes at Whitney Creek gorge. Geologic techniques used for dating and interpreting debris flows included carbon-isotope analyses of wood and charcoal samples, stratigraphic relations, analysis of aerial photography, and particle-size analyses of sediment deposits. Relatively recent debris flows were dated dendrochronologically using tree ages, eccentric growth-ring patterns following tree tilting by a debris flow, suppression and release sequences, and corrasion scars caused by debris flow impacts on tree trunks. Results indicate intense debris flow activity along upper Whitney Creek during recent centuries; a minimum of 10 debris flows are identified for the last 420 yr.

Sediment yields and denudation rates estimated from debris flow frequency and volume data suggest that activity has been most intense in the last five centuries. Sediment thicknesses on lower parts of the Whitney Creek fan appear sufficient to account only for deposition rates during late Holocene time. If present rates of deposition had prevailed throughout Holocene time, the average thicknesses of the lower fan deposits would be at least eight times greater than they are.

INTRODUCTION

Mount Shasta, about 65 km south of the Oregon-California border (Fig. 1), is the largest stratovolcano of the southern Cascade Range. The mountain is formed predominantly of basaltic andesite flows and basalt flows which are covered, over large areas of the mountain, by fans consisting of poorly indurated pyroclastic flows and associated debris flow and fluvial sediments. The fans in many places on the lower slopes of the mountain do not exceed several meters in thickness, but locally at elevations of 2,500 to 3,000 m above sea level on the 4,317-m peak, the fans are as thick as 250 m. Six glacial meltwater streams deeply incise the pyroclastic and related flow deposits of the upper fan areas, forming narrow gorges that commonly have highly unstable and barren walls. During periods of high streamflow, the unstable valley walls are easily undercut, leading to slope failures and stream damming. Debris flows often form from the failed material as it becomes saturated with continued streamflow. Thus, the upper fan areas are eroding rapidly, whereas large parts of the lower fan areas are highly aggradational due largely to debris flow and fluvial deposits of reworked pyroclastics.

Whitney Creek, discharging from Whitney Glacier, has cut down as much as 100 m into the fan material over which it flows. A unique variety of geologic and botanical evidence, including

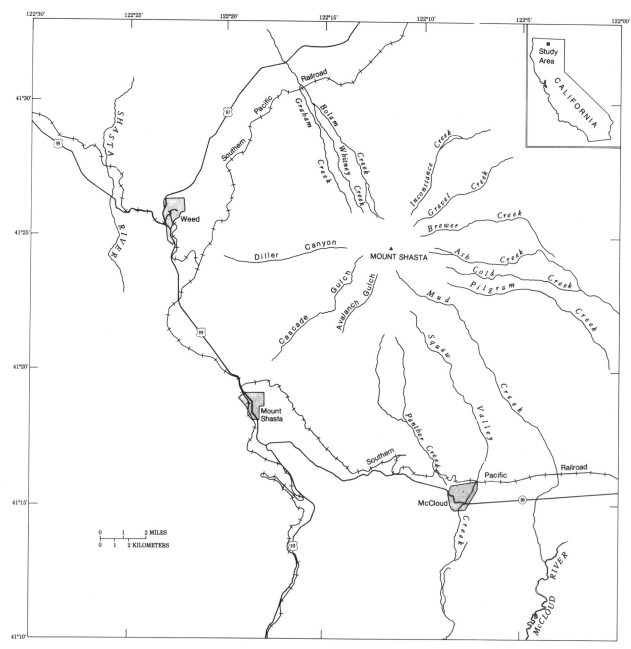

Figure 1. Map of Mount Shasta area, showing glacial meltwater streams, rivers, and towns.

terraces that were preserved following incision of debris flow deposits in a lower reach of Whitney Creek gorge (Fig. 1) permits a partial reconstruction of the Holocene history of that part of the gorge. The techniques used to date events in the gorge have wide application to other forested areas experiencing debris flow activity on Mount Shasta, as well as to mountainous terrains in general.

This chapter elaborates the techniques employed to deduce the recent geologic history of the Whitney Creek gorge area. Geologic and botanical methods are described, but emphasis is placed on the lesser known botanical techniques that lead to a

chronology of recent debris flow activity. Results are summarized and used to interpret geomorphic processes on Mount Shasta in general.

DATING METHODS

The investigation at Whitney Creek gorge was designed to: (1) gain an understanding of the late Quaternary history of the area, (2) date relatively recent debris flows of the area, and (3) evaluate late Holocene rates of erosion and deposition on fan areas by identifying magnitudes and frequencies of debris flow activity. Techniques used to date geomorphic events and processes provided both absolute and relative ages.

Geologic Techniques

Carbon-isotope analyses of wood and charcoal (Miller and Crandell, 1975; Christiansen and others, 1977; Miller, 1980) indicated dates of pyroclastic flow activity at Whitney Creek gorge, as well as the age of a basaltic andesite flow on the fan surface immediately adjacent to the gorge. Radiocarbon dating also suggests a minimum age for fluvial deposition on the fan surface that preceded the present incisement. This date supports several flow-event dates determined by botanical methods. Inspection of aerial photographs and field observations of neoglacial features and stratigraphic relations, coupled with the carbon-isotope data, permitted the determination of relative ages of various pyroclastic, fluvial, and debris flow deposits.

Particle-size analyses of sediment samples suggested the probable mode of deposition—whether fluvial or debris flow—of unconsolidated material within the gorge (Scott, 1985). Refractograms of pyroclastic and debris flow samples confirmed the origin of debris flow material.

Data collected from Whitney Creek gorge were supplemented with stratigraphic observations and carbon-isotope analyses of wood and charcoal samples from the lower part of the Whitney Creek debris fan (Fig. 1). Samples from six pits dug at various places in the lower fan provided information on magnitudes and frequency of debris flow deposition that could be compared directly to dates obtained from the gorge area.

Botanical Techniques

Dendrochronology—the study of annual growth rings of trees—was used extensively to date geomorphic events of the past five centuries in Whitney Creek gorge (Hupp, 1984). Two basic types of dendrochronologic data were collected: tree ages, to provide a minimum age of a surface or event; and times of tree deformations, which yield absolute ages of the events causing the damage.

The age of a single tree, determined from the number of growth rings in an increment core taken from the base of the tree, gives a minimum age of the surface upon which the tree grows (Sigafoos, 1964). Ages of Jeffrey pines (*Pinus jeffreyi*) part way up the steep right wall of the study reach of Whitney Creek gorge showed that that part of the incisement has been relatively stable more than 430 years. Normal depths below the soil surface of root collars at the bases of these trees showed that little slope erosion or deposition has occurred during that period. Trees on the opposite side of the gorge grow on nearly barren and highly unstable slipfaces. Nowhere are they older than several decades, indicating that recent erosion has been concentrated along the left wall. A minimum but reasonably accurate age for a debris flow is indicated by the age of a cohort of trees growing on its terrace surface, assuming the trees began growing soon after the time of

deposition. The ages of two prominent terraces were determined by tree-ring analysis to be 145 and 315 yr (the years 1840 and 1670, respectively). These dates are based on an assumed ecesis period of 1 to 3 yr, the time required for the woody plant species to become established. In Figure 2, a cohort of young trees has developed on the lobate terminus of a debris flow (A). The accompanying representation of an increment core indicates that the trees are 5 yr old; thus, the debris flow occurred 6 to 8 yr ago.

Debris flows and a variety of other geomorphic and hydrologic events often cause deformations of those trees surviving the event. The number of annual growth rings added after the deformation gives a nearly exact date for the debris flow. On Mount Shasta, tree deformations are generally of three types: eccentric annual growth, suppression and release sequences, and corrasion scars. One or all of the deformations can be preserved in surviving trees.

If the pressure of a viscous debris flow on a tree results in abrupt tilting, eccentric annual growth occurs. Eccentric growth is a compensation to tilting (B, Fig. 2) and, in coniferous species, results from a greater production of stem wood on the underside of the trunk than on the topside. Thus, growth rings on the underside are measurably wider than are the same rings on the upper side. When this pattern appears after years of relatively concentric ring growth, the date of disturbance and tilting is generally indicated within 1 yr. The stagnation of a large debris flow lobe in Whitney Creek gorge, as illustrated in Figure 2, resulted in tilting and eccentric-growth patterns in six ponderosa pines (*Pinus ponderosa*) in 1840. Similar tilting of pines in Whitney Creek gorge occurred at the edges of a terminal lobe in 1804.

A suppression-and-release sequence (C, Fig. 2) is a succession of relatively narrow, older rings followed by an abrupt shift to a succession of wide, younger rings. Suppression generally is the result of competition between the specimen tree and its neighboring trees. Should these competitors be removed, the specimen tree is said to be released and a period of greater growth with wider rings follows. The growth of trees adjacent to the path of a debris flow that removed neighboring trees may be released following the debris flow. Following a period of normal growth rates, suppression may also occur if a debris flow partially inundates a trunk without killing the tree. The reduced supplies of water and oxygen available to the more deeply buried root system may cause abrupt growth retardation. Dates based on suppression-and-release sequences are sometimes conjectural and should be used with caution. If replication of the date from other specimens is available, and if climatic responses can be ruled out, the technique provides accurate, dependable dates. In Whitney Creek gorge, for example, most ponderosa pines that date the 1670 debris flow surface show suppression sequences for the period 1830 to 1840. Suppression-and-release sequences also date a minor debris flow of Whitney Creek in 1977.

Corrasion and resultant scarring of surviving tree trunks by moving debris (Hupp, 1983) probably is the most common and diagnostic botanical method available to date debris flows accurately on Mount Shasta. During a debris flow, corrasion damages

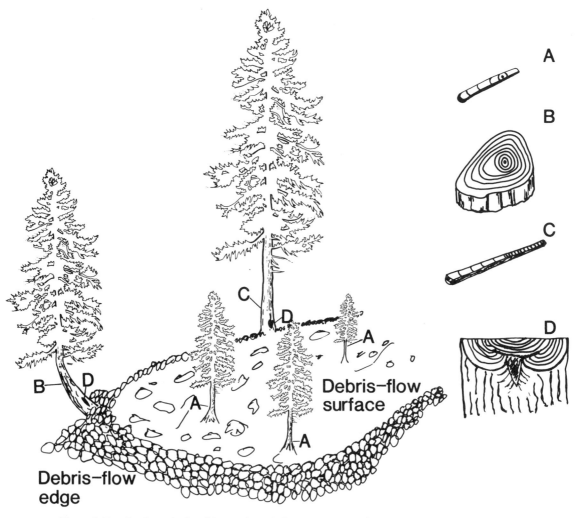

Figure 2. Dendrochronologic evidence of debris flows. (Modified from Hupp, 1984.) Increment cores from cohort of young trees (A) give similar ages and date debris flow surface. Tilting of tree by advancing lobe of debris flow causes eccentric growth rings (B). Reduction of competition, the result of destruction of vegetation by debris flow, causes suppression-release sequence (C). Impacts of debris flow clasts on tree trunks produce scars preserved in the wood of trunk (D).

the cambium, or wood-producing tissue, on the upstream side of tree stems in the flow path. This deformation terminates radial growth where the tree was damaged (D, Fig. 2), and therefore, growth rings are not added to the scarred area of the tree. During subsequent years, however, the scar is increasingly covered by callus tissue until the damaged area is again completely enveloped by a continuous cambial layer around the trunk. Thus, evidence of relatively recent debris flows is often apparent by observation of scars, and the date of the damaging event is determined by counting the discontinuous growth rings added after the damage occurred. Corrasion evidence of older debris flows may be available only by sectioning a tree or by taking increment cores at various angles to find completely covered scars within the tree trunk. Partial sectioning, the cutting of a small wedge of wood from the upstream side of a tree or on either side of an observable

scar often provides debris flow dates without destroying the tree. Among the Whitney Creek events for which abundant corrasion-scar dates are available are debris flows that occurred in 1868, 1919, and 1935.

SUMMARY OF LATE QUATERNARY GEOLOGIC HISTORY

The following summary of the geologic history of Whitney Creek gorge is largely an interpretation of late Pleistocene and Holocene events. In general, it appears that significant geomorphic changes occurred in late Pleistocene time and late Holocene time, but not in earlier parts of the Holocene Epoch. Few data suggesting landscape modification are available for most of Holocene time in the Whitney Creek gorge area.

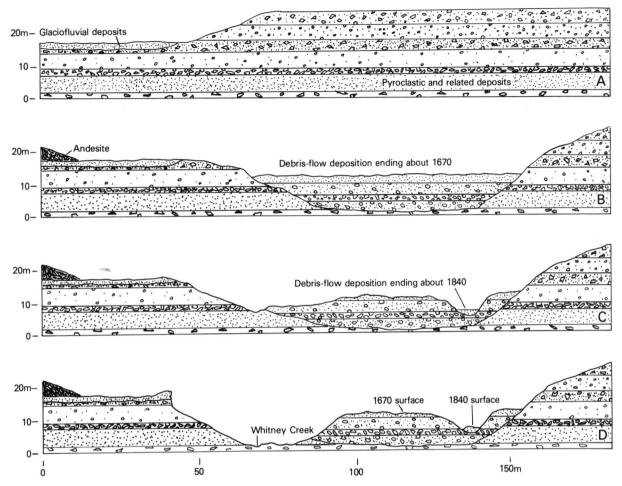

Figure 3. Cross sections at Whitney Creek gorge, showing sequence of incisements and deposition of fluvial and debris flow sediments. A, Incisement of fan deposits and partial refilling by glaciofluvial deposits in late Pleistocene time. B, Incisement of fan deposits in late Holocene time and partial refilling by series of debris flows ending about 1670. C, Continuing erosion of pyroclastic and debris flow beds, and partial refilling by a series of debris flows ending about 1840. D, Shifting of Whitney Creek channel to left and continuing escarpment retreat of west wall to their present positions.

The fan deposits into which Whitney Creek is incised are associated with eruptive events probably ranging in age from about 12,000 to 9,400 radiocarbon yr (Christiansen and others, 1977; Miller, 1980). Fluvial erosion, possibly by glacial melt-water, incised about 10 m of the fan surface at the Whitney Creek gorge area. This broad, shallow incisement was partially refilled with several meters of silt, sand, and fine gravel, presumably as glaciofluvial deposition (Fig. 3A). Examination of aerial photographs shows that the channel near Whitney Creek gorge was but one of several dissecting the upper fan surface. The late Pleistocene channel flowed in a more northerly direction than does Whitney Creek, and represents a drainage network that appears to have little or no relation to the present drainage system of the northwest side of Mount Shasta.

Late Pleistocene drainage of the Whitney Creek gorge area was disrupted by andesite flows that are dated by carbon-isotope

analyses at about 9,300 yr (Miller, 1980). One of these flows overlies the fluvial deposits that are exposed on the left wall at Whitney Creek gorge (Fig. 3B). The andesite largely controls the position of upper Whitney Creek, which presently incises fan deposits along the eastern edge of the andesite flow.

Following the extrusion of andesite flows, a poorly integrated drainage system may have resulted in limited fluvial erosion for an extended portion of Holocene time. On the lower part of the Whitney Creek debris fan, there is significant evidence only of geomorphically recent fluvial and debris flow deposition. Seven carbon-isotope analyses of wood and charcoal samples collected from soil pits dug on the lower aggradational part of the debris fan (Fig. 1) gave ages ranging from about 1,800 yr to modern. The oldest samples were associated with a widespread pyroclastic layer that may be the base of late Holocene deposition on lower Whitney Creek fan. The 1,800-yr pyroclastic event may also be recorded by preserved roots collected from the fluvial deposits above Whitney Creek gorge (Fig. 3A) that gave a similar radiocarbon age. No evidence of pyroclastic deposition within the last 1,800 yr has been found in Whitney Creek gorge. Hence, it is inferred that most or all of the incisement of the present gorge occurred during the last 1,800 yr, and that the incision may have been a response to increased runoff of glacial meltwater by warming of neoglacial temperatures.

Late Holocene debris flow activity as early as 1,200 yr B.P. has been recorded for other glacial meltwater basins of Mount Shasta (Dickson and Crocker, 1953), but no dates for the Whitney Creek basin previous to the year 1565 are presently available. Suppression-and-release sequences in Jeffrey pines older than 430 yr suggest a possible debris flow at that time. The pines survive on the right escarpment of Whitney Creek gorge several meters above the upper limit of the 1670 deposition (B, Fig. 3). These trees indicate that, prior to their ecesis, channel degradation occurred along the right side of the present incisement, and that the depth of incision then may have been about half the present depth of the lower gorge reach. No later than 420 yr ago (the year 1565), the erosive effects of Whitney Creek shifted to the left, and virtually no slope erosion has occurred on the right wall of the gorge section since that time.

Net erosion continued during the century after 1565, followed by a series of debris flows during a period of possibly several years or more that culminated in 1670 (Fig. 3B). The 1670 surface was fluvially dissected during the next 160 yr, and the position of Whitney Creek during that period became generally entrenched on the left side of the remaining 1670 surface. Debris flow lobes that were formed in 1804 about 100 m upstream from the study reach, for example, separate the 1670 deposits from the present channel of Whitney Creek. Starting about 1830 and ending in 1840, another series of debris flows partially filled incisements of the 1670 surface (Fig. 3C). Because these flows did not destroy evidence of the earlier 1804 event, it is possible that they were locally restricted to the right side of the gorge.

Since 1840, most active erosion at the study reach of Whitney Creek gorge has been along the left escarpment (Fig. 4). Botanical evidence was found of at least six debris flows that occurred after 1840; others for which evidence is lacking probably occurred. The largest of those flows, and the one that probably determined the present position of Whitney Creek (Fig. 3D), occurred in 1935. That debris flow scarred numerous trees, some as high as 7 m above the present stream bed, and probably caused measurable channel scour. Debris of the 1935 event was spread over an 8-km^2 area of the lower Whitney Creek fan, up to 12 km downslope from the Whitney Creek gorge site (Osterkamp and others, 1986).

Until July 1985, the last documented debris flow of Whitney Creek was a minor event in 1977. The most recent debris flows along Whitney Creek and in other basins of Mount Shasta have occurred in the summer season following several weeks or more of anomalously warm air temperatures. During the 8-yr

Figure 4. Left wall of Whitney Creek gorge. View is west showing 1670 surface in foreground. Whitney Creek, not visible, is beyond vegetated terrace and in front of bare, unstable escarpment of valley side. Andesite flow represented in Figure 3 lies atop escarpment.

period since the 1977 flow, no anomalously warm summers have occurred at Mount Shasta to cause rapid and sustained runoff of glacial meltwater. Renewed debris flow activity along Whitney Creek and other glacial meltwater streams of the mountain may be likely if unusually warm summer temperatures again occur.

GEOMORPHIC PROCESSES AND EROSION RATES

Recurring debris flows are the dominant late Holocene geomorphic process in the Whitney Creek basin of Mount Shasta. The principal sediment sources of the debris flows are the upper fan deposits, for which denudation rates are among the highest that have been recognized worldwide (Osterkamp and Costa, 1986). Almost all of the debris flow sediment is redeposited on the lower fan areas, causing abnormally high aggradation rates. Magnitude and frequency data of debris flows collected from Whitney Creek gorge and similar parts of Mount Shasta suggest that the prevailing geologic and hydrologic conditions are unique. The high degradation rates caused by these conditions will persist as long as rapid melting of stored glacial ice and snow periodically releases large amounts of summer streamflow to Whitney Creek.

Assessment of recent erosion rates in the upper Whitney Creek basin supports the inference that late Holocene frequencies of debris flows on Mount Shasta are greater than in earlier parts of the Holocene. Based on area of deposition and average thickness calculated from stream-bank exposures and soil pits, the estimated volume of the 1935 Whitney Creek debris flow was 8×10^6 m^3. From porosity estimates and recent flow histories on Mount Shasta, an assumed bulk density of the deposit of 2.0 and a recurrence interval of 50 yr leads to an estimated average annual sediment yield of 3×10^4 Mg/km^2. This yield corresponds to a denudation rate for the upper basin of Whitney Creek of about 11,000 mm per 1,000 yr; if only the specific contributing areas for sediment are considered, the denudation rate is roughly 20 times greater. In addition, this estimate may be highly conser-vative because it is based largely on one debris flow; earlier poorly documented debris flows and other modes of sediment transport were not considered. Sediment yields and denudation rates calculated for other glacial meltwater basins of Mount Shasta, for which more reliable frequency and volume data are available (Osterkamp and others, 1986), give results in the same orders of magnitude.

The lower Whitney Creek debris fan covers an area of about 20 km^2. Had the present estimated sediment yields prevailed throughout Holocene time, the average depth of burial by debris flow and fluvial deposits over the 20-km^2 area would exceed 80 m. Observations of stream incisements, outcroppings of Pleistocene and early Holocene volcanic rocks, soil pits, and water-well logs suggest that the average depth of burial may be less than 10 m. It is inferred, therefore, that late Holocene rates of sediment transport by debris flows along Whitney Creek are unusually high, and that these rates could not have persisted throughout Holocene time.

REFERENCES CITED

Christiansen, R. L., Kleinhampl, F. J., Blakely, R. J., Tuchek, E. T., Johnson, F. L., and Conyac, M. D., 1977, Resource appraisal of the Mt. Shasta Wilderness Study Area, Siskiyou County, California: U.S. Geological Survey Open-File Report 77-250, 53 p.

Dickson, B. A., and Crocker, R. L., 1953, A chronosequence of soils and vegetation near Mt. Shasta, California; I. Definition of the ecosystem investigated and features of the plant succession: Journal of Soil Science, v. 4, p. 123–141.

Hupp, C. R., 1983, Geo-botanical evidence of late Quaternary mass wasting in block field areas of Virginia: Earth Surface Processes and Landforms, v. 8, p. 439–450.

—— , 1984, Dendrogeomorphic evidence of debris flow frequency and magnitude at Mount Shasta, California: Environmental Geology and Water Science, v. 6, no. 2, p. 121–128.

Miller, C. D., 1980, Potential hazards from future eruptions in the vicinity of Mount Shasta volcano, northern California: U.S. Geological Survey Bulletin 1503, 43 p.

Miller, C. D., and Crandell, D. R., 1975, Postglacial pyroclastic–flow deposits and lahars from Black Butte and Shastina, west of Mt. Shasta, California: Geological Society of America Abstracts with Programs, v. 7, no. 3, p. 347–348.

Osterkamp, W. R., and Costa, J. E., 1986, Denudation rates in selected debris-flow basins: Proceedings, Fourth Federal Inter-Agency Sedimentation Conference, Las Vegas, Nevada, v. 1, p. 91–99.

Osterkamp, W. R., Hupp, C. R., and Blodgett, J. C., 1986, Magnitude and frequency of debris flows, and areas of hazard on Mount Shasta, Northern California: U.S. Geological Survey Professional Paper 1396-C, 21 p.

Scott, K. M., 1985, Lahars and lahar-runout flows in the Toutle-Cowlitz River system, Mount St. Helens, Washington: U.S. Geological Survey Open-File Report 85-500, 202 p.

Sigafoos, R. S., 1964, Botanical evidence of floods and flood-plain deposition: U.S. Geological Survey Professional Paper 485-A, 35 p.

MANUSCRIPT ACCEPTED BY THE SOCIETY DECEMBER 29, 1986

Printed in U.S.A.

Geological Society of America
Reviews in Engineering Geology, Volume VII
1987

The importance of hollows in debris flow studies; Examples from Marin County, California

Steven L. Reneau
William E. Dietrich
Department of Geology and Geophysics
University of California at Berkeley
Berkeley, California 94720

ABSTRACT

Hollows are the concave-out portions of hillslopes not occupied by channels. The topographic convergence in hollows forces colluvial debris to accumulate and causes shallow subsurface runoff to be concentrated during storms. Consequently, hollows are more susceptible to landsliding than side slopes and constitute important mappable source areas of debris flows. Hollows can be extremely subtle topographic features that require recognition in the field; these subtle hollows are commonly tributary to larger hollows, and greatly increase the density of mappable debris flow sources. In a study area in Marin County, California, hollows are spaced 20 to 60 m apart along the slope, resulting in a density of 25 to 35 km of hollow axis per km^2. Even the subtle hollows can produce debris flows capable of destroying houses, particularly when large trees are carried by a flow. Mitigation measures that focus on draining the main hollow axis may be inadequate because of the destructive ability of debris flows shed from small tributary swales and from side slopes. Road runoff discharged onto hollows can trigger landsliding and gullying, but this problem can be prevented by extending culverts downslope to stream channels. Along the drainage network, from subtle tributary hollows to major hollows, and to first-order channels where many additional hollows enter, the recurrence interval of debris flow events probably systematically decreases as the number of upslope sources increases, perhaps reaching the lowest recurrence interval on second-order channels. Farther downstream, debris flows may occur less frequently. A greater emphasis on hollows as debris flow source areas and as paths for flows from upslope should make a significant contribution toward identifying the hazard to existing structures and toward improved siting of new development.

INTRODUCTION

The importance of hollows as mappable sources of debris flows on steep, soil-mantled hillslopes is becoming increasingly recognized in many regions where land-use pressures are leading to housing construction in narrow river valleys and on the surrounding slopes. The debris flows are generally produced during high-intensity rainstorms by the rapid mobilization of shallow landslides in colluvial soils (Fig. 1). Hollows are sites of long-term accumulation of colluvial debris and of convergence of shallow ground water during storms (e.g., Dietrich and Dunne, 1978; Okunishi and Iida, 1981), both of which contribute to the high susceptibility of these sites to failure. Here we briefly review

research that has demonstrated the significance of hollows as sources of debris flows, and discuss research concerned with quantification of the debris flow hazard. Three case studies are then presented that address several aspects of debris flow hazards and that illustrate the importance of identifying even the subtlest hollows on hillslopes. Finally, some of the practical implications of our review and case history analyses are discussed.

HOLLOWS AND DEBRIS FLOWS

Hack and Goodlett (1960) and Hack (1965) proposed a three-fold division of hillslopes into hollows, noses, and side

Figure 1. Landslide scar in grassy hollow at head of Bootjack Creek, Mount Tamalpais, Marin County, California. Landslide occurred during January 1982 storm, mobilizing as a debris flow; margins of debris flow path are visible in foreground. Scar is 55 m long, 1.0 to 2.5 m deep; ground slope is 27°; arrow points to lower end of landslide scar. Bedrock is greenstone of Franciscan assemblage.

slopes, and we have adopted their terminology here. A hollow is "any area on the slope in which the contours are concave outward away from the ridge," and they "generally occur in the valley axis at the stream head as a sort of extension of the channel" (Hack, 1965, p. 20). A nose is "the area on the interfluve in which the slopes are convex outward toward the valley" (Hack, 1965, p. 21), and side slopes are areas with straight contours located between noses and either hollows or channels. Examples of hollows in several landscapes are shown in Figure 2. A hollow can be a concave slope of any size, and can occur as an isolated area on a side slope, as shown in valleys A and B of Figure 2B. The examples shown by Hack (1965) in Figure 2B illustrate the fact that hollows can form a branching drainage network above the channel head. In this chapter, the term "swale" is used interchangeably with hollow.

There is considerable variation between workers in different areas and with different backgrounds in the terminology used to describe hillslopes. For example, Jacobson (1985) stated that the local usage of the term "hollow" in parts of the Appalachians refers to first- and second-order valleys, whereas the term "cove" refers to unchanneled basins. In forested areas of Oregon, hollows are referred to as "headwalls" (F. J. Swanson, personal communication). In Japan, Tsukamoto (1973) introduced the term "zero-order basin" to refer to unchanneled basins; these basins include the noses and side slopes draining into hollows in addition to the axial region, and are the main source areas for debris flows in parts of Japan (e.g., Tsukamoto, 1973; Tsukamoto and others, 1982; Oyagi, 1984). We prefer the terminology of Hack to the term zero-order basin because it implies a finer scale examination of hillslopes, and, in describing the processes acting at each point on a hillslope, the fundamental differences are whether flow lines

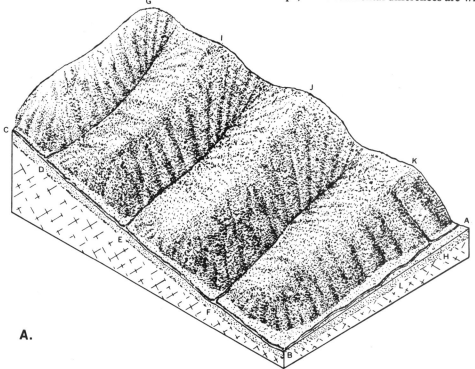

A.

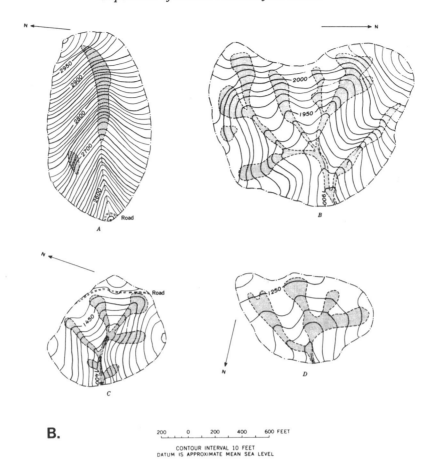

B.

200   0   200   400   600 FEET

CONTOUR INTERVAL 10 FEET
DATUM IS APPROXIMATE MEAN SEA LEVEL

Figure 2 (this and facing page). Examples of landscapes that are regularly divided into hollows and noses. A, Idealized drawing of hillslopes in Shenandoah Valley of Virginia and West Virginia; from Hack (1965, Fig. 4). Hollows drain sides of each valley; channel occurs where slope from ridge crest to stream channel becomes sufficiently long, as at H near right side of figure. B, Topographic maps of four valleys in areas of different relief, Shenandoah Valley; from Hack (1965, Fig. 9). Hollows indicated by stippled pattern. Valley A underlain by sandstone; valley B, by carbonate rocks; valleys C and D, by shale. C, Photograph of clearcut slopes, Mt. Peter and Cedar Creek drainage, Siuslaw River basin, central Oregon Coast Range. Bedrock is Eocene Tyee Sandstone. Hollows are primary source of debris flows in this area (Swanson and others, 1981). D, Oblique aerial photograph of grassy slopes of Bolinas Ridge, Marin County, California; San Francisco Bay in background. Bedrock beneath ridge is greenstone of Franciscan assemblage.

of water and colluvial debris are convergent, parallel, or divergent; these distinctions formed the basis for Hack's definitions of hollows, side slopes, and noses. This terminology has also received wide usage in geomorphic literature.

Prior to 1960, the landslide literature contains rare reference to topographic concavities as preferred sites of failure. Our present understanding of the importance of hollows as sources of debris flows originates with the work of Hack and Goodlett (1960) in the Appalachian Mountains of Virginia. The importance of hollows in the Appalachians and the Adirondacks has been confirmed by many other workers, including Williams and Guy (1971, 1973), Woodruff (1971), Clark (1973), Bogucki (1976, 1977), Lessing and others (1976), and Pomeroy (1984). Much of this work was spurred by the widespread landsliding from Hurricane Camille in 1969 and the consequent recognition that debris flows or debris avalanches are a major geologic hazard in eastern North America.

Similar understanding of the importance of hollows as debris flow sources in western North America developed from research on landslide problems on logged and unlogged slopes in coastal Alaska (Swanston, 1967, 1969), British Columbia (O'Loughlin, 1972), and the Oregon Coast Range (Pierson, 1977; Dietrich and Dunne, 1978; Swanson and others, 1981; Swanson and Roach, 1985), on chaparral slopes in southern California (Kojan and others, 1972; Hollingsworth and Kovacs, 1981), and in coastal scrub and grasslands in central California (Lehre, 1981, 1982). Much attention has recently been focused on hollows as debris flow source areas since a major, destructive storm in the San Francisco Bay area in January 1982 (Smith and Hart, 1982; Shlemon and Wright, 1983; Reneau and others, 1984; Sitar and Johnson, 1984; Smith, 1984; Reneau and Dietrich, 1985, 1987; Johnson and Sitar, 1986; Shlemon and others, this volume; Ellen and Wieczorek, 1987), and since the destructive pulses of debris flows in Utah in 1983 (e.g., Anderson and others, 1985; Keaton and others, 1985).

The studies cited above clearly establish that, where shallow landslides in colluvium occur, hollows can be the primary sources for debris flows. The importance of hollows may vary, however, as a function of the geologic and climatic setting in different areas, and may show variations within a given region. Numerous studies have documented the tendency of rapid debris flows to be produced by shallow landslides in cohesionless, sandy, or gravelly soils, and of slower earthflows to be produced by landslides in clay-rich soils. In addition, in areas where debris flows occur, significant variations in fine-scale texture of the topography may exist that influence the relative importance of hollows in comparison to other topographic positions. In general, it appears that the greater the area of a hillslope or an unchanneled valley occupied by side slopes, the less important hollows are as sources of debris flows. A few examples are given below that illustrate how the importance of hollows as sites of debris flow initiation may vary in different areas.

In Marin County, California, Ellen and others (1987) have reported that hollows are relatively more important as debris flow sources in terrain characterized by massive bedrock and a regular division of the topography into drainages and interfluves, and less important where the bedrock is less uniform and the topography is correspondingly less regular. In interbedded flows, tuffs, and volcanic breccias of the central Oregon Cascade Range, Marion (1981) found that side slopes are more frequent sites of landslide initiation than hollows, perhaps due to these slopes occupying a higher percentage of the total landscape. On stratified sandstone and shale bedrock in the Appalachian Plateau of West Virginia, Jacobson (1985) found that shallow landslides in colluvium tend to initiate along benches on side slopes, and not along hollow axes. Along the slopes of river valleys in the Appalachian Plateau of Pennsylvania, also with stratified sandstone and shale bedrock, Pomeroy (1981, 1982) found that the topography lacks a regular division into hollows and noses, and that hollows are correspondingly of little importance as debris flow source areas. Nearby, however, where the slopes are steeper and sandstone predominates, hollows are the most important source (Pomeroy, 1984).

Much progress has been made toward understanding the debris flow hazard and toward reducing the destruction caused by these flows. On a regional level, the relative hazard from debris flows on different slopes can be identified based on studies that correlate the location of previous landslides with soil and topographic factors. For example, Hollingsworth and Kovacs (1981) have proposed that the finer the soil texture, the gentler the slope on which debris flows are initiated in the Santa Monica Mountains of southern California. For portions of Marin and Sonoma Counties in central California, Ellen and others (1983) have prepared a regional map delineating slopes susceptible to debris flows. They used interpretation of aerial photographs to divide the region into different terrain types, and used detailed field studies of selected areas to document the types of shallow landslides in each unit (e.g., debris flows versus earthflows); they believe that debris flows are most common in areas of massive, resistant bedrock, where there is a regular division of hillslopes into drainages and interfluves.

Important research is being conducted by Japanese workers to allow the prediction of potential failure sites on a given hillslope. A recent summary of this research is provided by Oyagi (1984), and two examples from Japan are mentioned here. Okimura (1983) has used a two-dimensional stability analysis to predict the least-stable portion of a slope, incorporating longitudinal variations in slope gradient and soil thickness. Potential landslide size can be predicted with this method. Okimura and Kawatani (1987) coupled a three-dimensional ground-water-flow model with an infinite slope stability analysis to predict the relative stability of 10- by 10-m square units of hillslope; soil thickness and hydraulic conductivity were held constant in this method. Despite the numerous assumptions inherent in such models, both analyses showed reasonable correspondence between the predicted sites of lowest stability and observed landslide scars. Models of this kind should eventually prove to be of great value in predicting the stability of individual hillslopes in developed areas.

Within areas that are susceptible to debris flows, possibly the most important task is to identify the paths that these flows will follow. It is widely recognized that debris flows propagate down existing drainages. The hazard is least on divergent and planar slopes, and increases in areas of topographic convergence and down-channel on alluvial fans. Even subtle hollows can effectively funnel flows. For example, Hollingsworth and Kovacs (1981) recognized that very subtle swales have a greater risk of experiencing a debris flow than planar slopes, and that these subtle features require recognition in the field.

The debris flow hazard is perhaps greatest along second-order (as defined by the Strahler [1952] method) channels, with these channels receiving debris flows from multiple first-order basins upslope, which in turn are fed by numerous hollows. The hazard generally declines farther downstream as the drainage area increases. As flows propagate downstream, they should tend to slow down with decreasing channel gradient, and to thin and spread out with increasing valley-floor width, eventually stopping once the yield strength of a flow is no longer exceeded (e.g., Johnson, 1970, 1984; Costa, 1984). Debris flows may also become diluted downstream by the addition of flood waters, decreasing the density and possibly the destructiveness of flows (e.g., Benda, 1985). Benda (1985) studied debris flows in the central Oregon Coast Range, and found that they typically terminated at the junction of second-order and higher order channels; relatively few flows propagated down fourth-order channels. Similarly, one debris flow that was studied in detail on Inverness Ridge in Marin County, California, became nonerosive where a second-order channel entered a third-order channel, and where the channel gradient dropped from 6° to 4° (Ellen, 1987). Two houses built along a second-order channel nearby were destroyed in the same storm by another debris flow. In the Wasatch Range of Utah, Lips and others (1984) have also predicted runout distances for debris flows based on channel gradient and the volume of potential debris flows.

This chapter presents three case studies from sites of recent debris flow and gullying problems in Marin County, California; site locations are shown in Figure 3. These erosional events were mainly associated with the storm January 3–5, 1982, during which 36-hr rainfall totals reached 300 to 400 mm for much of Marin County, and locally exceeded 600 mm in the Santa Cruz Mountains to the south (Smith and Hart, 1982; Ellen and Wieczorek, 1987). In comparison, the mean annual rainfall in Marin County is about 600 to 900 mm (Rantz, 1971). These case studies address several aspects of debris flow hazards in this region, and attempt to illustrate the importance of mapping the finest detail of the topography to develop methods of hazard reduction in developed areas.

CASE STUDIES

Madrone Park Circle, Mill Valley

At a house along Madrone Park Circle in Mill Valley, a debris flow struck during the night of January 4, 1982, sweeping

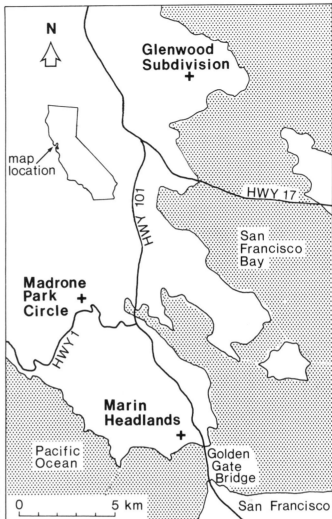

Figure 3. Location map of Marin County, California, case studies.

the house from its foundation and depositing it 45 m downslope in a narrow second-order valley, effectively blocking the flow; this obstruction may have prevented damage to other houses directly downstream that were built on the valley floor (Ellen, 1987). Miraculously, the woman and her daughter in the house when the debris flow hit were not killed.

The landslide that mobilized into a debris flow occurred within a dense hardwood forest, dominated by California laurel (*Umbellularia californica*) and coast live oak (*Quercus agrifolia*), on a 30° hillslope, shown in Figures 4 and 5. The headscarp was located 95 m below the ridge crest in a subtle colluvium-mantled hollow, and the failure plane was 1 to 2 m below the ground surface, generally within a reddish soil horizon; the majority of the roots are restricted to the upper 80 cm here. Sand cone tests provided dry bulk densities of 1.20 to 1.35 g/cm^3 for the upper

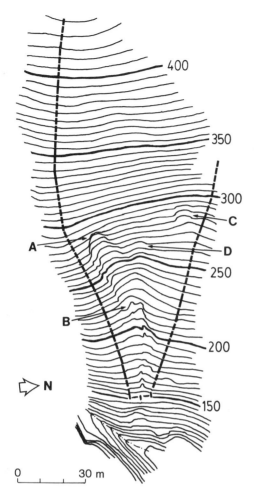

Figure 4. Topographic map of hillslope above Madrone Park Circle, Mill Valley, where debris flow in 1982 destroyed house built in axis of subtle hollow. Foundation of house shown as three solid black lines along 150-ft contour, and drainage area above house shown by dashed lines. Ridge crest is at top of map. A indicates headscarp of 1982 landslide scar, within very subtle topographic concavity; B, point where debris flow banked into swale, producing some erosion of ground surface; C, old, vegetated landslide scar with distinct scarps; D, very degraded landslide scar bowl at head of swale. Contour interval = 5 ft; datum is arbitrary; 100-ft contour approximately 300-ft elevation. Area surveyed by Moran Engineering, Berkeley.

Figure 5. Photograph of Madrone Park Circle landslide scar. Person is at point B in Figure 4.

root-permeated horizon, and 1.60 to 1.75 g/cm^3 for the lower horizons (A. Kropp and Associates, Berkeley, California). The colluvium is derived from graywacke sandstone of the Franciscan assemblage, and consists of roughly 45 percent sand, 40 percent silt, 10 to 15 percent clay, and minor gravel. No bedrock was exposed in the landslide scar, and an auger hole in the axis reached weathered sandstone bedrock at a depth of 3.5 m below the original ground surface.

During the initial landslide, about 300 m^3 of colluvium and the overlying forest was mobilized. The mass of trees and satu-rated colluvium banked into the main swale, incorporating more trees, and causing minor erosion of the surface. Several trees along the perimeter of the debris flow path withstood the flow, and mudlines across them provided valuable information about the thickness and velocity of the flow. A detailed reconstruction of the debris flow has been attempted to understand its character-istics when it reached the house.

The approximate surface of the Madrone Park Circle debris flow was reconstructed along six cross sections surveyed perpen-dicular to the center line of the flow path, using the elevation of each edge of the path and mudlines on standing trees to estimate depth (Figs. 6, 7). The average depth of the flow at each tree was determined as the midpoint between mudlines on the upslope and downslope sides. The depths on individual trees sometimes agreed well with a straight-line approximation between one edge of the path and either the opposite edge or another tree, while at others the flow surface apparently bulged upward. The flow wid-ened from 13 m at Section 5, at the base of the scar, to 22 m at

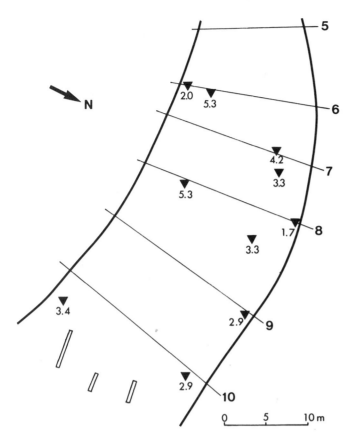

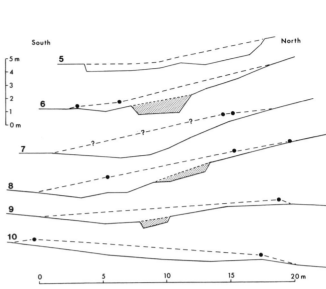

Figure 6. Map of Madrone Park Circle debris flow path, showing surveyed cross sections and flow velocities calculated from mudlines on standing trees. Trees indicated by inverted triangles, with calculated velocity given in meters per second. Centerline of Section 5 is at 223-ft contour; foundation of house shown below Section 10.

Figure 7. Cross sections across debris flow path, showing estimated flow surface and superelevation of flow around bend in swale. Solid dots indicate flow depths determined from mudlines on standing trees on or near each section. Eroded areas shown by stippled pattern. South side of Section 5 includes lower end of 1982 landslide scar; older landslide scar bowl present on north side. Apparent cross-sectional area of Section 7 is anomalously large; flow depth here may be overestimated.

Section 10, and thinned from a possible maximum thickness of about 1.7 m at Section 7 to only about 0.8 m at Section 10, immediately above the house.

Measurements of the elevation difference of the mudlines between the upslope and downslope sides of the trees were used to calculate velocity for 10 trees along the debris flow path; the location of these trees is shown in Figure 6. We used the equation and pressure coefficient employed by Wigmosta (1983) to map the velocity field of a mudflow generated during the 1980 Mt. St. Helens eruption:

$$V = (C g h)^{1/2}, \qquad (1)$$

where C is the pressure coefficient, taken as 1.21; g is gravitational acceleration; and h is the difference in mudline elevation. Figure 8 shows a composite velocity profile across the debris flow path between Sections 6 and 7, at approximately the 210-ft contour. The maximum velocity in the center of the flow was at least

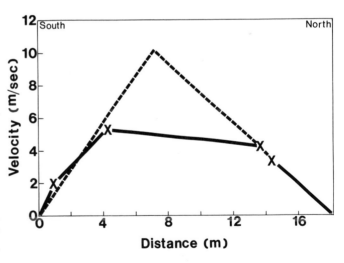

Figure 8. Composite velocity profile across 1982 debris flow path between Sections 6 and 7. Each point is vertically averaged velocity calculated using mudlines on standing trees. Lower curve drawn assuming that maximum vertically averaged velocity is 5.3 m/sec; used to calculate minimum average velocity for entire flow. Upper curve drawn assuming that velocity increased linearly from margins, providing maximum possible average velocity.

TABLE 1. VEGETATION TRANSECT DATA, MADRONE PARK CIRCLE

Tree weight (lbs)	1	2	3	4	5	6	7	All Transects
0-200	6	2	–	6	2	1	1	18
200-500	1	–	–	3	2	3	5	14
500-1,000	–	1	4	–	2	2	1	10
1,000-2,000	–	–	1	–	3	2	2	8
2,000-3,000	–	–	1	1	–	2	–	4
3,000-4,000	–	1	1	–	–	–	–	2
4,000-5,000	1	–	–	–	–	–	–	1
Total Weight	5,391	3,862	10,045	3,599	6,564	9,679	4,665	43,805
Area (m²)#	87	87	87	91	94	87	84	617

*Multiple laurel stems growing from a single base were counted as one tree.
#5- by 20-m belt transect on slope converted to horizontal area.

5.3 m/sec, and possibly as high as 10 m/sec. The velocity of the flow in the center undoubtedly varied more gradually than inferred from the fitted lines to the data, perhaps having a constant velocity "plug" as predicted in Bingham materials (e.g., Johnson, 1970, 1984). Integration of the curves in Figure 8 across Sections 6 and 7 yielded a minimum average velocity for the entire flow of about 4 m/sec, and a maximum average velocity of about 6 m/sec.

The curvature of the debris flow path produced a superelevation of the flow surface at Sections 5 through 9, as shown in Figure 7, and we used this to provide an additional estimate of the average flow velocity, as described by Johnson (1984):

$$V = (r\,g\,\cos\theta\,\tan\alpha)^{1/2}, \qquad (2)$$

where r is the radius of curvature of the bend, α is the cross-flow slope, and θ is the channel slope. This yielded a mean velocity for the entire flow of 4.7 to greater than 10 m/sec, depending on how the radius of curvature was measured. We found equation (2) difficult to employ because of the rapidly varying radius of curvature; hence the velocity estimate from equation (1) based on the mudlines around trees is probably more accurate. As discussed by Costa (1984), neither method of back-calculating debris flow velocities has yet been verified with measured velocities, although it is encouraging that both methods provided roughly similar estimates here.

The flow carried woody debris removed from about 600 m² of forest: 60 percent of the area constituted the landslide scar and 40 percent the central portion of the debris flow path. Vegetation measurements were made to estimate the nature and weight of this component of the flow. An examination of aerial photographs taken before and after the storm, both 1:20,000 scale stereopairs and high-quality 1:1,000 scale enlargements, indicated that the forest composition within the scar and debris flow path was comparable to that remaining in the adjacent forest. In order to quantify the forest composition, the heights and diameters of all trees larger than 5 cm in diameter were measured in seven 5- by 20-m belt transects in the undisturbed forest; for each tree the approximate weight was determined using equations derived for estimating standing tree biomass (Pillsbury and Stephens, 1978; N. H. Pillsbury, unpublished data). These equations exclude below-ground biomass and branches smaller than 5 cm in diameter, and as such provide conservative estimates of total woody debris weight.

From the vegetation transect data, we estimate that about 44,000 lb, or 20 metric tonnes, of woody debris is present in a roughly 600-m² area of this hardwood forest, as summarized in Table 1. California laurels provide 65 percent of this weight, and coast live oaks the remaining 35 percent. In the transects, single laurels and oaks reach an estimated 2,155 and 3,765 lb, respectively, and one clump of three laurel stems growing from a single base has a combined weight of 4,645 lb. The largest trees are 50 cm in diameter; the maximum height, 19 m.

The number and weight of trees carried by this debris flow were clearly substantial, and despite the short distance traveled, these trees likely played a major role in damaging the house. This is also indicated by scars on standing trees 4 m above the ground, resulting from the impact of trees either carried or toppled by the flow. The house was elevated above the ground on stilts, and it may well have been the force of the trees rather than the flow itself that dislodged the house.

This debris flow is especially illustrative of the subtleties of the topography that need to be recognized in order to decrease the hazard that these flows present to development. In our review above, we emphasized that recognition of potential source areas and delineation of probable debris flow paths are the two most practical needs to minimize the debris flow hazard. The house on Madrone Park Circle was built with considerable care given in order to avoid disruption of the slope; no road was excavated, and a small tram was used to reach the house from the road

Figure 9. Oblique aerial photograph of western portion of Glenwood subdivision, San Rafael, on floor of fourth-order valley.

below. Unfortunately, the house was built directly in the axis of a small but distinct swale that could both produce a debris flow and serve as the path for any debris flow off the upper slope (Fig. 4). Developed areas in southern Marin County had been damaged by debris flows on many occasions in the last several decades (Rice and others, 1976), and the susceptibility of this specific slope to shallow landslides in the colluvium could be seen by the presence of two much older landslide scars nearby, distinguishable on the detailed topographic map (Fig. 4). The swale is not shown on the 1:24,000-scale U.S. Geological Survey topographic map, and neither the swale nor the older scars would be visible through the dense forest canopy if standard aerial photographs were employed to map the most hazardous areas. Clearly, for purposes of mapping, aerial photographs in forested areas are inadequate, and the hillslopes surrounding potential developments must be carefully inspected on the ground to identify subtle topographic concavities that may be source areas or paths for debris flows.

Glenwood Subdivision, San Rafael

During the January 1982 storm, the drainage basin above the Glenwood subdivision in eastern San Rafael experienced abundant shallow landsliding, as discussed by Smith and Hart (1982). Two houses built along a third-order channel were destroyed by a debris flow at a site where damage from another flow had occurred in 1973. The 1973 flow is discussed by Johnson (1984). As at the Mill Valley site, a dense hardwood forest obscures the finest detail of the topography, although a regular division of the topography into drainages and interfluves is clear, as shown in Figure 9. The landslide scars in this area are being studied in detail to document their distribution and characteristics, and to determine the depositional history of colluvium in hollows (Reneau and others, 1986; Reneau and Dietrich, 1987). Significantly, only about one-third of the 1982 landslides originated along the axes of major hollows that could be recognized on the 1:24,000-scale U.S. Geological Survey topographic maps. One-half the remainder originated along the axes of subtle hollows, comparable to the swale above the Mill Valley house or the even subtler concavity where the Mill Valley scar is located (Fig. 4), and the rest originated from side slopes.

Figure 10 is a plan map of a relatively large unchanneled basin above the Glenwood subdivision that intersects a first-order channel, showing a branching network of hollows and the location of landslide scars of varying age. The bedrock is sandstone and shale of the Franciscan assemblage. The lower portion of the

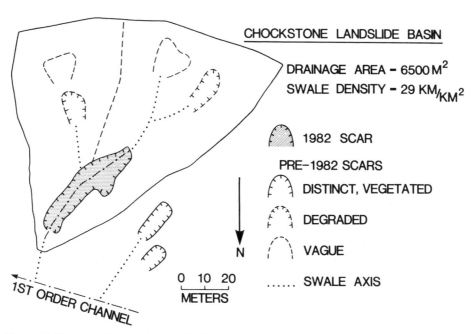

Figure 10. Plan map of an unchanneled basin in watershed above Glenwood subdivision, San Rafael, that produced a debris flow in 1982, showing drainage boundary, swale axes, and landslide scars. Scars are grouped into different age classes based on scarp degradation: youngest pre-1982 scars are vegetated yet retain vertical scarps; intermediate age scars have distinct margins although no vertical scarps remain; oldest scars have vague margins and scarps are reduced to rough slope breaks.

main hollow failed in January 1982, mobilizing about 550 m^3 of colluvium as a debris flow. The failure at this site may have been strongly influenced by the colluvial stratigraphy, with prominent textural variations existing both longitudinally and vertically. At the headscarp of this scar, the failure plane was 2.7 m deep and the total colluvium thickness was about 5.5 m, consisting of a 3-m-thick layer of coarse openwork gravel overlain by a denser, finer textured colluvium with matrix-supported gravel. The lower gravel layer pinched out downslope. Subsurface flow within the gravel, derived from the bedrock (e.g., Wilson and others, 1984; Wilson and Dietrich, 1985) or perched on the bedrock-colluvium interface, may have produced excessive pore pressures at the base of the denser, upper colluvium, and may have been responsible for failure. Similarly, Hayes (1985) has measured excessive pore pressures in a hollow in the Santa Cruz Mountains within a discontinuous basal sand of relatively high hydraulic conductivity. Such coarse basal layers often do not exist, but where present they could play a major role in determining the stability during storms.

In the basin shown in Figure 10, there are two subtle swales tributary to the main hollow, and all of the swales contain pre-1982 landslide scars. These older scars can be seen only by direct field observation. As shown at the Mill Valley site, the older scars further demonstrate the recurrent nature of landsliding from these slopes and the importance of the smaller swales as source areas for debris flows. Although the density of scars in this basin is high compared to most in the area, it is rare to find a basin of similar size without any scars. The presence of scars at different longitudinal positions along a single hollow (Fig. 10) indicates that, for purposes of stability evaluations, hollows should be envisioned as consisting of multiple potential debris flow sources. Failure along a portion of a hollow does not preclude subsequent failure elsewhere in the basin.

In the Glenwood area, extensive areas of side slope are rare, and instead most hillslopes are interrupted by hollows spaced about 20 to 60 m apart. For example, the maximum spacing in the Chockstone basin (Fig. 10), measured near the ridge crest, is about 40 m. Casual observations elsewhere in Marin County suggest that a fairly regular spacing between hollows is common. Documentation of a characteristic hollow spacing in an area may provide a useful measure of the topography to guide the location and mapping of potential debris flow source areas. An additional measure of the topography is the swale density, which we define as the total length of hollow axes in a basin divided by the total catchment area. This is analogous to standard drainage densities that measure the length of stream channels in an area. For selected unchanneled basins in the Glenwood area, we have measured swale densities of 25 to 35 km/km^2, with the 29 km/km^2 density of the Chockstone basin (Fig. 10) being typical. These densities provide a quantitative measure of the extent of potential debris flow sources in this area.

As discussed earlier, the recurrence interval for a debris flow event should decrease as upslope catchment area increases, being lower at the base of a large unchanneled basin than along a tributary hollow, and even lower along a first-order channel, perhaps reaching a minimum along second-order channels. This is shown schematically in Figure 11. A recurrence interval can also be expressed as the relative probability of a site experiencing a debris flow in any year, with the probability, P, being the inverse of the recurrence interval, R.I. ($P = 1/\text{R.I.}$). If landslide events in a catchment are independent of each other and are randomly distributed through time, the probability of debris flow occurrence for catchments of varying size can be estimated by determining the number of upslope source areas and the probability of failure in each. The probability is given by:

$$P = 1 - (1 - s_1)(1 - s_2) \ldots (1 - s_n), \qquad (3)$$

where s_i is the probability of a debris flow from source i, and n is the total number of sources in the catchment. If each source has the same R.I., then equation (3) reduces to:

$$P = 1 - (1 - s)^n. \qquad (4)$$

Where n is much smaller than the R.I., equation (4) can be closely approximated by:

$$P = s\,n. \qquad (5)$$

The recurrence interval for landslide initiation from a portion of a hollow can be estimated by dating colluvium that is involved in landsliding. Radiocarbon dates have been obtained from basal colluvium exposed in landslide scars in the San Rafael hardwood forests (Reneau and others, 1986), providing preliminary estimates of at-a-site recurrence intervals of on the order of 10,000 yr ($s = 0.0001$). Basal dates do not always record the last landslide event at each site, and landslides may therefore be more frequent.

The number of discrete sources in large unchanneled basins is uncertain. At a minimum, if each hollow comprised one source area, then the Chockstone basin (Fig. 10), with two tributaries to the main hollow, would contain three discrete sources. The presence of five recognizable scars in this basin suggests that this estimate is low, and that the number of potential sources is actually greater than five. As an upper limit, the number of possible sources is constrained by the length of landslides. Average landslide length in this area is about 20 m (Reneau and Dietrich, 1987), and if we consider that this approximates the length of discrete source areas within a long hollow, the Chockstone basin, with 190 m of hollow axis, can then contain roughly 10 source areas.

An estimate of the probability of a failure somewhere in the Chockstone basin (Fig. 10), using equation (5) and an average R.I. of 10,000 yr, is 10×0.0001, or 0.001. This provides an average recurrence interval of about 1,000 yr. For a first- or second-order channel with five basins of this size upslope, the probability of a debris flow entering the channel from these basins is 5×0.001, or 0.005, and the recurrence interval is approxi-

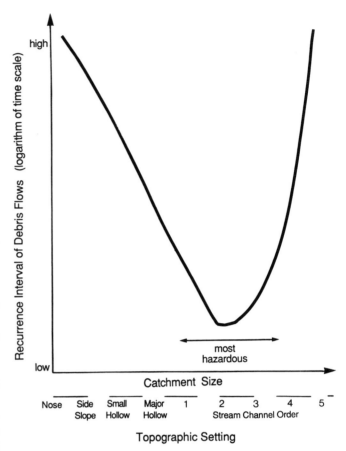

Figure 11. Hypothetical relationship of recurrence interval of debris flows and catchment size, showing topographic setting.

mately 200 yr. The presence of smaller unchanneled basins tributary to the stream channel, and the possibility of failures on side slopes, increases the number of sources and further decreases the recurrence interval of a debris flow event.

The probabilities presented here should be considered rough preliminary estimates due to the simplified form of this analysis. Debris flows would be more frequent if the average recurrence interval for landslide initiation in a portion of a hollow is less than 10,000 yr. The frequency would be overestimated by this method if the number of discrete source areas in a large unchanneled basin is less than our estimate, or if the failures are not independent of each other, such as where secondary failures are triggered within a debris flow path (e.g., Reneau and Dietrich, 1987; Ellen, 1987). These calculations also assumed that each discrete source has approximately the same R.I., while the at-a-site R.I. may vary between different sites in an area, possibly as a function of the strength of topographic convergence (Reneau and Dietrich, 1985, 1986). In addition, the minimum possible recurrence interval for debris flows is limited by the return period of a hydrologic event

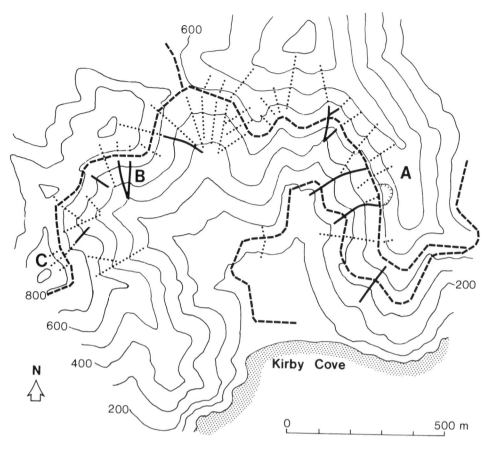

Figure 12. Topographic map of part of Marin Headlands, immediately north of Golden Gate Bridge. Dashed lines indicate main roads; dotted lines, hollow axes; heavy solid lines, gullies; hachured line, landslide scarp. Hollow axes mapped using 1:24,000-scale San Francisco North 7.5-min Quadrangle, supplemented by available roadcut exposures of colluvial deposits; many hollows not crossed by roads are probably not shown; lower end of each hollow could not always be determined. Gullies mapped from 1982 aerial photographs. Contour interval = 100 ft. A indicates location of Figure 13; B, location of Figure 14; C, location of Figure 15.

sufficient to trigger failure. Despite the uncertainties involved, the increasing frequency of debris flows with increasing catchment size for low order catchments (Fig. 11) is clearly shown by these calculations, and the order-of-magnitude estimates are probably accurate. L. E. Benda and T. Dunne (personal communication) are also using a similar probabilistic approach to calculate the frequency of scouring events in channels in the Oregon Coast Range. To predict the decreasing frequency along higher order channels, factors such as channel gradient, valley floor width, debris flow volume, and tributary junction angles need to be addressed (e.g., Lips and others, 1984; Benda, 1985).

Marin Headlands

Over at least the last 30 yr, but particularly since the January 1982 storm, road runoff has produced extensive gullying in colluvial deposits below the main road along the Marin Head-

lands just north of the Golden Gate Bridge (Figs. 12, 13, 14). Exceptional exposures of colluvium, some exceeding 5 m in thickness, are located along this road beneath topographic concavities (Fig. 15). These deposits were partially mapped by Schlocker and others (1958) and described by Schlocker (1974). The exposures are all on slopes that feed into first- or higher order channels, and are located a horizontal distance of roughly 30 to 180 m below the ridge crest. The colluvium is predominantly unstratified angular gravel set in a finer textured matrix, derived from well-bedded chert and greenstone of the Franciscan assemblage. In at least one hollow, the basal colluvium near the channel head is cemented to the underlying bedrock. A gully has formed above the road in one hollow, cutting a notch into the underlying bedrock. Farther north along the road, a similar notch-shaped cut is exposed at the base of a colluvial deposit, suggesting that fluvial incision of bedrock when a colluvial fill is absent has probably been an important process eroding the bedrock.

Figure 13. Photograph of hillslopes in Marin Headlands (location A in Fig. 12). Golden Gate Bridge and San Francisco in upper right. Areas of darker vegetation crudely correspond to areas of thick colluvium, and grassy slopes are underlain by relatively thin soil. Arrows point to two gullies in colluvium below road.

Figure 14. Deep gullies in colluvial deposits below main road in Marin Headlands (location B in Fig. 12). Note culvert to left of main gullies, where road runoff is discharged onto slope; roadcut above culvert exposes colluvial deposit beneath subtle hollow.

The gullying downslope of the road has developed in response to runoff discharged from culverts that terminate a short distance below the road, as shown in Figure 14. It is common practice in road construction to direct road runoff to natural drainage ways under the reasonable assumption that the natural drainage path will transmit the water with a minimum amount of damage. This road, and many roads like it in soil-mantled landscapes, however, are generally well above stream channels and instead hollows are the natural drainage ways. The colluvium mantling the hollows often responds to the greatly increased input of water by either gullying or failing as a landslide, and the scars can continue enlarging for years. The potential for gullying in these deposits was described much earlier by Schlocker and others (1958), but apparently little was done to address this problem. Along a 2-km stretch of road in Figure 12, roughly 25 colluvium-mantled hollows are exposed, and 10 gullies are present below the road, some probably initiating as landslide scars. In addition, at least three landslides involving colluvium and road fill have directly affected the road. A similar problem exists in gravel-rich colluvium near a ridge crest in the Berkeley Hills, 20 km to the east (Reneau and others, 1984), and landslide studies elsewhere have often noted the role of road runoff in triggering failure (e.g., Sidle and others, 1985).

A practical solution to this problem is to extend the pipes containing the road runoff downslope to the nearest stream. Typically, low-order streams in mountainous or hilly areas flow on bedrock, such that the localized increase in flow would have a minimal effect on erosion. Figure 16 is a graph plotting the distance from channel heads upslope to ridge crests as a function of the average hollow gradient for a sample of Marin County hollows. For the hollows in the Marin Headlands, with an average

Figure 15. Colluvial deposit exposed in roadcut, roughly 75 m below ridge crest, Marin Headlands (location C in Fig. 12). About 3 m of colluvium underlies subtle topographic concavity. Contact with underlying bedrock of Franciscan chert is outlined.

gradient of roughly 50 percent, this graph predicts that the natural channel heads will be located 100 to 200 m below the main ridge crest, allowing an estimate of the pipe length and cost of this kind of mitigation work. Although more costly than short pipes, the savings in repair costs would have been substantial. Both empirical and theoretical analyses (Dietrich and others, 1985, 1986) indicate that the relationship between hollow length or catchment area and average hollow gradient will vary with climate and bedrock. Hence, separate graphs like Figure 16 should be constructed in different areas.

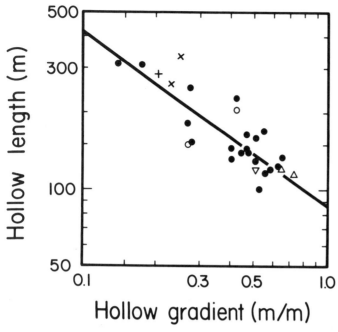

Figure 16. Graph of maximum hollow length versus average hollow gradient, from Dietrich and others (1986, Fig. 5). Solid circles indicate hollows in Marin County, and remaining symbols indicate hollows in other areas described in Dietrich and others (1986).

DISCUSSION AND CONCLUSION

It is well documented that, in many areas, hollows are the most important sources for debris flows. In parts of the San Francisco Bay area, for example, studies by several workers indicate that about two-thirds of failures initiate within hollows (Smith and Hart, 1982; Smith, 1984, 1987; Reneau and Dietrich, 1987; Ellen and others, 1987), demonstrating that hollows should be given the most emphasis in identifying debris flow source areas in this region. In some other areas, hollows appear to occupy a smaller portion of the total landscape, perhaps due to differences in the geologic and climatic setting, and consequently they are less important as sources of debris flows. In order to provide a regional basis for hazard evaluation, studies are clearly needed that systematically identify the location of past failures and the relative susceptibility of different bedrock types, slope gradients, and topographic positions in each region. The recent studies of Hollingsworth and Kovacs (1981) and Ellen and others (1983) are useful steps in this direction.

In urbanized areas, mitigation techniques are being developed and applied to protect existing structures from debris flows (e.g., Hollingsworth and Kovacs, 1981; Smith and Hart, 1982; Baldwin and others, this volume). The subtlety of many hollows, their close spacing, and the common occurrence of failures on side slopes lead to important implications for mitigation measures. In hilly areas susceptible to debris flows, few sites except ridge crests can be considered completely safe from this hazard;

the relative risk increases as the catchment area above individual structures increases, as illustrated in Figure 11. Although trenching and draining major swales may be an effective technique to stabilize specific deposits, the subtle swales and side slopes feeding into these hollows remain possible source areas.

Hollows are important not only as sources of debris flows, but also as conduits that funnel flows off the upper slopes, regardless of where the failure is located. Identification of natural drainages thus forms the basis for the debris flow susceptibility maps of Smith (1984, 1987). As shown in the Mill Valley and San Rafael case studies, and also noted by Hollingsworth and Kovacs (1981), these concavities can be extremely subtle features identified only by careful inspection in the field; identification relying on standard topographic maps or using aerial photography, particularly where a forest canopy exists, is inadequate.

Setbacks from channels need to be adequate to accommodate flows that may reach 20 m or more in width, as demonstrated by the Mill Valley debris flow. In addition, two debris flows in first- and second-order channels that are described in detail in Ellen (1987) also locally exceed 20 m in width. Smith and Hart (1982) noted that the tendency of flows to bank around bends and produce a superelevation of the flow surface, as seen at the Mill Valley site, widens the hazardous zone. The height of this superelevation increases with increasing flow velocity and is greatest at the sharpest bends in debris flow paths. As a possible extreme example, one flow on Inverness Ridge in January 1982 was directed perpendicular to a second-order channel and rode directly up the opposite slope, rising 10 m in elevation; this provided a minimum velocity of 14 m/sec for the flow (Ellen, 1987). In a separate study, we have prepared a debris flow susceptibility map for a proposed subdivision in San Rafael using previously calculated velocities of debris flows to estimate the superelevation that could occur at channel junctions where the curves in potential debris flow paths were greatest. This procedure identified a broad area of relatively gentle slope set above a stream channel as being a potentially hazardous site for development; this area extended for up to 50 m away from the channel, and erroneously would have been considered safe if the hazard zone was delineated as a 20-m-wide strip centered on the stream.

In forested areas, the importance of the woody debris content of debris flows cannot be overemphasized where mitigation measures are being planned. Channels or basins designed to contain a given volume of debris may become blocked by an irregular mass of trees, resulting in an overtopping of the structure and diversion of the flow. In the Mill Valley example, although the flow had traveled only a short distance from the landslide scar, the number and the weight of trees were substantial and may have been of primary importance in destroying the house.

The diversion of drainage from roads onto swales has been repeatedly shown to trigger landslides and gullying, and deserves greater attention in urbanized and developing areas. Actively eroding scars below roads can require expensive maintenance, as along the Marin Headlands, and road runoff can significantly increase the debris flow hazard to development downslope. The extension of culverts downslope beyond the colluvial deposits to natural stream channels is a relatively simple and effective method to alleviate this problem. Compared to the potential for loss of life and destruction of houses in developed areas, the cost of installing and maintaining such culverts is minor.

Much progress has been made in recent years toward understanding the origin and characteristics of shallow landslides and resultant debris flows; this should lead to improved siting of new development. In particular, more emphasis must be given to potential hazards upslope and beyond the property boundaries of individual tracts of land. This emerging understanding of debris flow hazards also needs to be better communicated to people presently living in hazardous areas in hollows and along stream channels. Clearly, much remains to be accomplished to allow development to exist in steep terrain with the minimum of risk from this hazard.

ACKNOWLEDGMENTS

This study was partially supported by National Science Foundation grant EAR-84-16775. The field work included in the case studies was aided by numerous people who gave freely of their time and ideas, including D. Chambers, L. Dingler, E. Hughes, D. Marron, S. Raugust, P. Whiting, and C. Wilson. Soil analyses were provided by A. Kropp and Associates, and unpublished tree biomass equations were generously provided by N. Pillsbury.

REFERENCES CITED

Anderson, L. R., Keaton, J. R., and Brooks, R. K., 1985, Swale formation, soil development and variation in hydraulic conductivity at a landslide site in the Wasatch Range near Farmington, Utah [abs.]: EOS American Geophysical Union Transactions, v. 66, p. 900.

Benda, L. E., 1985, Delineation of channels susceptible to debris flows and debris floods, *in* Takei, A., ed., Proceedings, International Symposium on Erosion, Debris Flow and Disaster Prevention, Tsukuba, Japan: Tokyo, Erosion Control Engineering Society, p. 195–201.

Bogucki, D. J., 1976, Debris slides in the Mt. Le Conte area, Great Smoky Mountains National Park, U.S.A.: Geografiska Annaler, v. 58A, p. 179–191.

—— , 1977, Debris slide hazards in the Adirondack province of New York state: Environmental Geology, v. 1, p. 317–328.

Clark, G. M., 1973, Appalachian debris slide-debris flow characteristics and distribution south of the glacial border: Actualization of knowledge in mapping high risk sites: Geological Society of America Abstracts with Programs, v. 5, p. 386–387.

Costa, J. E., 1984, Physical geomorphology of debris flows, *in* Costa, J. E., and Fleisher, P. J., eds., Developments and applications of geomorphology: Berlin, Springer-Verlag, p. 268–317.

Dietrich, W. E., and Dunne, T., 1978, Sediment budget for a small catchment in mountainous terrain: Zeitschrift fur Geomorphologie, suppl. 29, p. 191–206.

Dietrich, W. E., Reneau, S. L., and Wilson, C. J., 1985, The geomorphology of "zero order basins" [abs.]: EOS American Geophysical Union Transactions, v. 66, p. 898.

Dietrich, W. E., Wilson, C. J., and Reneau, S. L., 1986, Hollows, colluvium, and landslides in soil-mantled landscapes, *in* Abrahams, A. D., ed., Hillslope processes, Sixteenth Annual Binghamton Symposia in Geomorphology: Boston, Allen and Unwin, p. 361–388.

Ellen, S., 1987, Debris flows and related phenomena in the storm, *in* Ellen, S., and Wieczorek, G. F., Landslides, floods, and marine effects of the storm of January 3–5, 1982, in the San Francisco Bay region, California: U.S. Geological Survey Professional Paper 1434 (in press).

Ellen, S., and Wieczorek, G. F., 1987, Landslides, floods, and marine effects of the storm of January 3–5, 1982, in the San Francisco Bay region, California: U.S. Geological Survey Professional Paper 1434 (in press).

Ellen, S., Peterson, D. M., and Reid, G. O., 1983, Map showing areas susceptible to different hazards from shallow landsliding, Marin County and adjacent parts of Sonoma County, California: U.S. Geological Survey Miscellaneous Field Studies Map MF-1406.

Ellen, S., Cannon, S. H., and Reneau, S. L., 1987, Distribution of debris-flow phenomena in Marin County, *in* Ellen, S., and Wieczorek, G. F., eds., Landslides, floods, and marine effects of the storm of January 3–5, 1982, in the San Francisco Bay region, California: U.S. Geological Survey Professional Paper 1434 (in press).

Hack, J. T., 1965, Geomorphology of the Shenandoah Valley, Virginia and West Virginia, and origin of the residual ore deposits: U.S. Geological Survey Professional Paper 484, 84 p.

Hack, J. T., and Goodlett, J. C., 1960, Geomorphology and forest ecology of a mountain region in the central Appalachians: U.S. Geological Survey Professional paper 347, 66 p.

Hayes, J., 1985, Hydrologic behavior of a colluvium-filled bedrock hollow [abs.]: EOS American Geophysical Union Transactions, v. 66, p. 897.

Hollingsworth, R., and Kovacs, G. S., 1981, Soil slumps and debris flows: Prediction and protection: Bulletin of the Association of Engineering Geologists, v. 18, p. 17–28.

Jacobson, R. B., 1985, Spatial and temporal distributions of slope processes in the upper Buffalo Creek drainage basin, Marion County, West Virginia [Ph.D. thesis]: Baltimore, John Hopkins University, 484 p.

Johnson, A. M., 1970, Physical processes in geology: San Francisco, Freeman, Cooper and Company, 577 p.

—— , 1984, Debris flow, *in* Brunsden, D., and Prior, D. B., eds., Slope instability: New York, John Wiley & Sons, p. 257–361.

Johnson, K. A., and Sitar, N., 1986, Techniques for identification of source areas for debris flows: Berkeley, Department of Civil Engineering, University of California, Report No. UCB/GT/86-01, 38 p.

Keaton, J. R., Anderson, L. R., and Brooks, R. K., 1985, Geomorphology, geometry and evidence for recurrence of slope failures in steep swales in metamorphic rock filled with colluvial and residual soil debris in the Wasatch Range near Farmington, Utah [abs.]: EOS American Geophysical Union Transactions, v. 16, p. 900.

Kojan, E., Foggin, T. G., III, and Rice, R. M., 1972, Prediction and analysis of debris avalanche incidence by photogrammetry, Santa Ynez Mountains, California, *in* 24th International Geological Congress, Section 13, p. 124–131.

Lehre, A. K., 1981, Sediment budget of a small California Coast Range drainage basin near San Francisco, *in* Davies, T.R.H., and Pearce, A. J., eds., Erosion and sediment transport in Pacific Rim steeplands: International Association of Hydrological Sciences Publication no. 132, p. 123–139.

—— , 1982, Sediment mobilization and production from a small mountain catchment: Lone Tree Creek, Marin County, California [Ph.D. thesis]: Berkeley, University of California at Berkeley, 320 p.

Lessing, P., Kulander, B. R., Wilson, B. D., Dean, S. L., and Woodring, S. M., 1976, West Virginia landslides and slide prone areas: West Virginia Geological and Economic Survey Environmental Geology Bulletin 15, 64 p.

Lips, E. W., Ellen, S., and Wieczorek, G. F., 1984, Identifying debris flow and debris flood potential along the Wasatch Front between Salt Lake City and Willard, Utah: Geological Society of America Abstracts with Programs, v. 16, p. 576.

Marion, D. A., 1981, Landslide occurrence in the Blue River drainage, Oregon [M.S. thesis]: Corvallis, Oregon State University, 114 p.

Okimura, T., 1983, A slope stability method for predicting rapid mass movements on granite mountain slopes: Natural Disaster Science, v. 5, p. 13–30.

Okimura, T., and Kawatani, T., 1987, Mapping of the potential surface-failure sites on granite mountain slopes: Proceedings of First International Geomorphology Conference, Manchester, England, September 1985 (in press).

Okunishi, K., and Iida, T., 1981, Evolution of hillslopes including landslides: Japanese Geomorphological Union Transactions, v. 2, p. 291–300.

O'Laughlin, C. L., 1972, A preliminary study of landslides in the Coast Mountains of southwestern British Columbia, *in* Slaymaker, H. O., and McPherson, H. J., eds., Mountain geomorphology: Geomorphological processes in the Canadian Cordillera: Vancouver, Tantalus Research, p. 101–111.

Oyagi, N., 1984, Landslides in weathered rocks and residual soils in Japan and surrounding areas: A state-of-the-art report: Proceedings of IVth International Symposium on Landslides, Toronto, v. 3, p. 1–31.

Pierson, T. C., 1977, Factors controlling debris-flow initiation on forested hillslopes in the Oregon Coast Range [Ph.D. thesis]: Seattle, University of Washington, 166 p.

Pillsbury, N. H., and Stephens, J. A., 1978, Hardwood volume and weight tables for California's central coast: Sacramento, California Department of Forestry, 54 p.

Pomeroy, J. S., 1981, Storm-induced debris avalanching and related phenomena in the Johnstown area, Pennsylvania, with reference to other studies in the Appalachians: U.S. Geological Survey Professional Paper 1191, 22 p.

—— , 1982, Geomorphic effects of the July 19-20, 1977, storm in a part of the Little Conemaugh River area, northeast of Johnstown, Pennsylvania: Northeastern Geology, v. 4, p. 1–9.

—— , 1984, Storm-induced slope movements at East Brady, northern Pennsylvania: U.S. Geological Survey Bulletin 1618, 16 p.

Rantz, S. E., 1971, Precipitation depth-duration-frequency relations for the San Francisco Bay region, California: U.S. Geological Survey Basic Data Contribution 25.

Reneau, S. L., and Dietrich, W. E., 1985, Landslide recurrence intervals in colluvium-mantled hollows, Marin County, California [abs.]: EOS American Geophysical Union Transactions, v. 66, p. 900.

—— , 1986, Landslide recurrence intervals from debris flow source areas, central California Coast Ranges: Abstracts and Program, Association of Engineering Geologists, 29th Annual Meeting, San Francisco, p. 61.

—— , 1987, Size and location of colluvial landslides in a steep forested landscape, *in* Proceedings, Symposium on Erosion and Sedimentation in the Pacific Rim, Corvallis, Oregon, 3-7 August, 1987: International Association of Hydrological Sciences Publication (in press).

Reneau, S. L., Dietrich, W. E., Wilson, C. J., and Rogers, J. D., 1984, Colluvial deposits and associated landslides in the northern San Francisco Bay area, California, USA: Proceedings of IVth International Symposium on Landslides, Toronto, p. 425–430.

Reneau, S. L., Dietrich, W. E., Dorn, R. I., Berger, C. R., and Rubin, M., 1986, Geomorphic and paleoclimatic implications of latest Pleistocene radiocarbon dates from colluvium-mantled hollows, California: Geology, v. 14, p. 655–658.

Rice, S. J., Smith, T. C., and Strand, R. G., 1976, Geology for planning, central and southeastern Marin County, California: California Division of Mines and Geology Open File Report OFR 76-2 SF, 103 p.

Schlocker, J., 1974, Geology of the San Francisco North quadrangle, California: U.S. Geological Survey Professional Paper 782, 109 p.

Schlocker, J., Bonilla, M. G., and Radbruch, D. H., 1958, Geology of the San Francisco North quadrangle, California: U.S. Geological Survey Miscellaneous Geologic Investigations Map I-272.

Shlemon, R. J., and Wright, R. H., 1983, Soil-stratigraphic dating of colluvial-filled gullies, Pacifica, California: Geological Society of America Abstracts with Programs, v. 15, p. 328.

Sidle, R. C., Pearce, A., and O'Loughlin, C. L., 1985, Hillslope stability and land use: American Geophysical Union Water Resources Monograph 11, 140 p.

Sitar, N., and Johnson, K. A., 1984, Identification of potential source areas for debris flows using color, black and white, and black and white infra-red photography: Geological Society of America Abstracts with Programs, v. 16, p. 658.

Smith, T. C., 1984, Delineating areas susceptible to debris avalanches and debris flows near Pacifica, California: Geological Society of America Abstracts with Programs, v. 16, p. 661.

—— , 1987, A method for mapping relative susceptibility to debris flows, with an example from San Mateo County, California, *in* Ellen, S., and Wieczorek, G. F., eds., Landslides, floods, and marine effects of the storm of January 3-5, 1982, in the San Francisco Bay region, California: U.S. Geological Survey Professional Paper 1434 (in press).

Smith, T. C., and Hart, E. W., 1982, Landslides and related storm damage, January 1982, San Francisco Bay region: California Geology, v. 35, p. 139–152.

Strahler, A. N., 1952, Hypsometric (area-altitude) analysis of erosional topography: Geological Society of America Bulletin, v. 63, p. 1117–1142.

Swanson, F. J., and Roach, C. J., 1985, Frequency of debris avalanches from clearcut hollows, Siuslaw River basin, Oregon [abs.]: EOS American Geophysical Union Transactions, v. 66, p. 900.

Swanson, F. J., Swanson, M. M., and Woods, C., 1981, Analysis of debris-avalanche erosion in steep forest lands: An example from Mapleton, Oregon, USA, *in* Davies, T.R.H., and Pearce, A. J., eds., Erosion and sediment transport in Pacific Rim steeplands: International Association of Hydrological Sciences Publication no. 132, p. 67–75.

Swanston, D. N., 1967, Soil-water piezometry in a southeast Alaska landslide area: U.S. Forest Service, Pacific Northwest Forest and Range Experiment Station Research Note PNW-68, 17 p.

—— , 1969, Mass wasting in coastal Alaska: U.S. Forest Service, Pacific Northwest Forest and Range Experiment Station Research Paper PNW-83, 15 p.

Tsukamoto, Y., 1973, Study on the growth of stream channel; (1) Relation between stream channel growth and landslides occurring during heavy storm: Shin-sabo, v. 25, p. 4–13.

Tsukamoto, Y., Ohta, T., and Noguchi, H., 1982, Hydrological and geomorphological studies of debris slides on forested hillslopes in Japan, *in* Walling, D. E., ed., Recent developments in the explanation and prediction of erosion and sediment yield: International Association of Hydrological Sciences Publication no. 137, p. 89–98.

Wigmosta, M., 1983, Rheology and flow dynamics of the Toutle River debris flows from Mount Saint Helens [M.S. thesis]: Seattle, University of Washington, 184 p.

Williams, G. P., and Guy, H. P., 1971, Debris avalanches—A geomorphic hazard, *in* Coates, D. R., ed., Environmental geomorphology: Binghamton, State University of New York Publications in Geomorphology, p. 25–46.

—— , 1973, Erosional and depositional aspects of Hurricane Camille in Virginia, 1969: U.S. Geological Survey Professional Paper 804, 80 p.

Wilson, C. J., and Dietrich, W. E., 1985, Lag in the saturated zone and pore pressure development after peak runoff in hollows [abs.]: EOS American Geophysical Union Transactions, v. 66, p. 898.

Wilson, C. J., Reneau, S. L., Dietrich, W. E., and Narasimhan, T. N., 1984, Modelling the generation of excessive pore pressures in debris flow susceptible deposits [abs.]: EOS American Geophysical Union Transactions, v. 65, p. 889.

Woodruff, J. F., 1971, Debris avalanches as an erosional agent in the Appalachian Mountains: Journal of Geography, v. 70, p. 399–406.

MANUSCRIPT ACCEPTED BY THE SOCIETY DECEMBER 29, 1986

Geological Society of America
Reviews in Engineering Geology, Volume VII
1987

Anatomy of a debris flow, Pacifica, California

Roy J. Shlemon
Roy J. Shlemon and Associates, Inc.
P.O. Box 3066
Newport Beach, California 92663

Robert H. Wright
David R. Montgomery
Harlan Miller Tait Associates
1269 Howard Street
San Francisco, California 94103

ABSTRACT

A major debris flow occurred on January 4, 1982, in the Oddstad Boulevard area of Pacifica, California. The flow emanated from a previously unrecognized colluvium-filled swale (one of many making up first-order drainages in the region), moved down a 21°, 172-m-long slope, and extended into an urban area. The failure involved the upper 4.5 m of a 6.1-m-thick colluvial section in the upper of two bedrock basins underlying the swale. Soil-stratigraphic measurements show that upper-basin colluvium accreted slowly to form a cumulic soil profile, characterized by thick surface (mollic epipedon) and subsoil (argillic) horizons. An approximately 500-yr-old mean residence time (MRT) radiocarbon date from the prefailure mollic epipedon indicates that the average sedimentation rate was about 0.6 m/1,000 yr and, accordingly, that colluviation began at least 8,000 to 10,000 yr ago. In contrast, the lower basin is characterized by at least four pre-1982 slide deposits. These deposits emanated almost wholly from within the lower basin, and are distinguished by clast lithology and angularity, and by the local presence of capping buried paleosols.

Radiocarbon MRT dates of approximately 2 to 3 ka for the upper, older debris flows, and the presence of a moderately developed argillic horizon on an underlying flow, suggest that lower basin failure recurrence is on the order of 1,000 to 4,000 yr.

A simple, three-stage evolutionary model for the Oddstad swale is postulated for engineering-geologic comparisons with swales elsewhere: (1) initial basin incision by fluvial processes in late Pleistocene time; (2) change of climatic regime and resultant colluvial filling of the upper basin in Holocene time; and (3) exhumation and renewed fluvial incision of the upper basin following the 1982 debris flow.

INTRODUCTION

On January 4, 1982, an intense rainstorm triggered thousands of shallow landslides in the central Coast Ranges of California. In the San Francisco Bay area, landslides resulted in 24 fatalities and millions of dollars in property damage (Smith and Hart, 1982; Brown and others, 1984). Almost 500 landslides occurred within the city of Pacifica, resulting in the deaths of three persons, the destruction of four homes, and an estimated $6 million in damages (Howard-Donley Associates, 1982).

One of the largest and most destructive landslides in Pacifica occurred in the 1200 block of Oddstad Boulevard (Fig. 1). Here, late in the evening of January 4, a debris flow emanated from near the crest of a hill, destroying two houses, killing three children, and damaging several other houses (Figs. 2, 3). Investigations following this tragedy provided a unique opportunity to study the debris flow and prefailure hillslope.

Initial assessments (Shlemon and Wright, 1983, 1984) re-

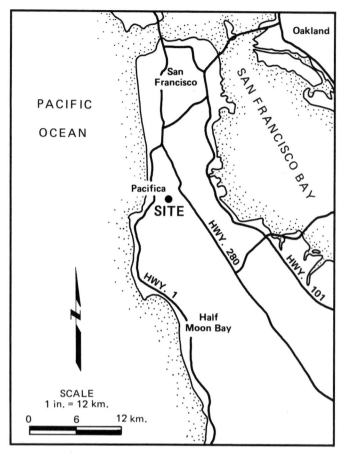

Figure 1. Location map of Oddstad debris flow, Pacifica, California.

vealed that the Oddstad failure emanated from a colluvium-filled swale, topographically expressed as a subtle "crenulation." Such features were not only previously unrecognized in Pacifica, but also, with few exceptions, elsewhere in northern and central California (see, for example, Schlocker and others, 1958; Marron, 1982; Dietrich and Dorn, 1984; Dietrich and others, 1984; Reneau and others, 1984). In the 1960s, when accelerated residential development began in the inland valleys in Pacifica, colluvium-filled swales were not being mapped as discrete geologic units nor were they recognized as potential sources of debris flows by any workers. As late as the early 1970s, these features were not recognized or mapped on geologic and landslide maps of the Pacifica area (see, for example, Brabb and Pampayen, 1972a, b).

Colluvium-filled swales have variously been called "soil wedges" (Dietrich and Dunne, 1978), "bedrock hollows" (Reneau and others, 1984; Marron, 1985), and "colluvial-filled gullies" (Shlemon and Wright, 1983). Here, we use the term "colluvium-filled swale" to designate the source of the Oddstad debris flow, a notation that best describes the prefailure topography. We also employ the term "first-order drainage" in its

classical descriptive sense, that is, as the most upstream, field-discernible depression that conducts water and sediments to lower parts of a watershed (Horton, 1945; Strahler, 1964).

This chapter presents the results of our detailed investigations as a case study in engineering geology. First we describe the occurrence and geomorphic setting of the January 4, 1982, Oddstad debris flow. Second, we point out various investigation techniques employed at the site. Third, we describe the debris flow and preexisting colluvium-filled swale. Fourth, we illustrate how soil-stratigraphic techniques are used to date the colluvium and to identify pre-1982 debris flows. Finally, we offer a model to explain the evolution of the Oddstad swale, the general applicability of which may be "tested" by comparison with colluvium-filled swales elsewhere.

OCCURRENCE AND GEOMORPHIC SETTING

The Oddstad debris flow occurred about 11:00 PM on January 4, 1982, near the end of an intense 30-hr rain storm that dumped as much as 22 cm on the slope, superimposed on about 58 cm of antecedent seasonal rainfall (Fowler, 1984). The failure originated from near the head of a broad, colluvium-filled swale on a natural, coyote brush– and poison-oak–covered, east-facing hillslope in the upper portion of the North Fork San Pedro Creek drainage basin. This swale is one of numerous first-order drainages that, like others in the North Fork San Pedro Creek drainage basin (Fig. 4) is steep (15 to 40°), and, as now recognized on color-infrared photography, was filled with colluvium. Almost 50 shallow failures occurred in the upper portion of the drainage basin during the storm of January 3–5, 1982. Some failures resulted in debris flows that funneled into third- and fourth-order drainages where they eventually reached developed areas as mudflows.

Some swales, however, were free of colluvium, owing either to nonfilling or to previous debris flows. Why some colluvium-filled swales failed and others did not remains an enigma, particularly since the general geologic, geomorphic, vegetation, and climatic setting is similar. Undoubtedly, each swale is unique, although obviously local geomorphic thresholds were reached during the Jaunary 3–5, 1982, storm; failure of the Oddstad colluvium-filled swale is a case in point.

INVESTIGATIVE TECHNIQUES

The main emphasis of the initial investigation was to document existing conditions and obtain samples prior to the forthcoming winter rains (1982–1983) and/or to repair the slope (completed by others during 1983). A detailed (1 in = 10 ft; 1-ft contour interval) topographic map of the area was completed in June 1982 (Fig. 5), and field work continued through November 1982. All field locations and samples were located with respect to a surveyed and staked axial centerline so that any point on the topographic map could be identified by a centerline station number (in feet, from the base of the slope), and a left or right

Figure 2. Oblique aerial photograph of Oddstad debris flow taken March 2, 1982 (Pacific Aerial Surveys, SMT-C15-7).

(looking upslope) number (in feet); e.g., Station 0+50 L 10. In this paper, all units are given in metric, except for topographic contour intervals and station numbers.

Field work consisted of the detailed mapping of (1) slide boundaries; (2) distribution of slide features and deposits; (3) remaining (unfailed) slope deposits; and (4) bedrock materials. Thirty-six seismic refraction survey lines, totaling 1,188

m, were run on a rough grid pattern on the slope (see Fig. 5) to provide subsurface data. Some 106 hand-auger holes were excavated to determine depth of slide deposits; to determine the depth of colluvial deposits/depth to bedrock; to obtain samples for laboratory analyses; and to provide calibration for seismic refraction survey lines. Detailed logs were made of three exposures in the upper part of the landslide scar. Here also, detailed soil (pedo-

Figure 3. Photograph, January 4, 1982, Oddstad debris flow taken from Oddstad Boulevard on January 9, 1982, 5 days after failure.

genic) profiles were measured, described, and sampled. In the lower part of the landslide scar, an exploratory trench approximately 4.9 m deep (see Fig. 5) was excavated, logged, and sampled to determine the nature of sediments underlying this part of the hillslope. A detailed soil profile was also measured and described, and samples were collected for radiocarbon dating. Finally, a 12.2-m hollow-stem auger hole was drilled, logged, and sampled near the edge of Oddstad Boulvevard (see Fig. 5) to determine the depth to, and the thickness of, fill and colluvium at the base of the hillslope.

Sixty laboratory tests were performed to determine engineering properties, including moisture content, particle size (sieve and hydrometer), Atterberg limits, and triaxial shear. Soil laboratory tests, including chemical and particle-size analyses, were performed on an additional 22 samples, and radiocarbon dates (^{14}C) were obtained from three samples.

CHARACTERISTICS OF THE DEBRIS FLOW AND PREFAILURE SWALE

January 4, 1982, Oddstad Debris Flow

The failure occurred near the head of a broad first-order drainage swale on an east-facing hillslope above the 1200 block

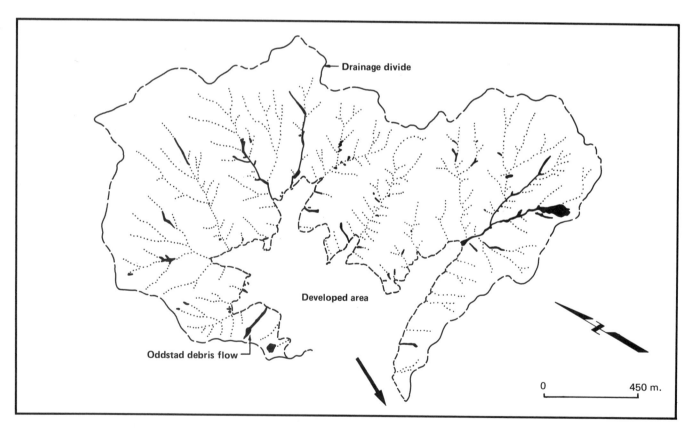

Figure 4. Map of upper portion of North Fork, San Pedro Creek drainage basin, Pacifica, showing drainage swales and channels (dotted lines), and locations of January 4, 1982, slope failure (heavy solid lines).

of Oddstad Boulevard. The scar extended some 230 m from near the top of the headscarp to the slope base. The runout area extended across the building pads at the base of the slope and into Oddstad Boulevard. The failure consisted of a source area and a main track (Fig. 6).

Source Area. The source area extended from about elevation 195 m downslope to about elevation 168 m, and was about 56.4 m long, 24 m wide at the maximum, and as deep as 4.6 m. Scarp height ranged from about 2.4 m at the crown to about 3.7 m along lateral scarps near the toe. The failure surface was irregular, but generally U-shaped in cross section and concave in longitudinal section (Fig. 7). The failure surface slope ranged, in a downslope direction, from 40 to 30° in the upper portion of the source area, and decreased downslope to 20 to 12° near the toe.

The source area contained at least an estimated 2,477 m³ of material, the majority of which reached the base of the slope below. The failed material consisted entirely of colluvium that had underlain the prefailure, natural 25° slope; no bedrock was exposed in the source area scar. The debris, exposed in scattered deposits in the source area and as levee deposits along the margins of the main track, consisted of dark yellowish-brown (10YR 4/2; dry) to moderate brown (5YR 3/4; wet) silty sand, with 20 ± percent low to medium plastic fines, and 80 ± percent fine- to coarse-grained, poorly graded, angular to subangular sand, and less than 2 percent angular Franciscan greenstone fragments as much as 0.1 m in diameter.

Some debris remained in the source area scar and upper part of the main track. This material originated from a slump-failure on the right side (looking upslope) of the source area shortly after the initial failure. This failure locally produced multiple, superimposed flow lobes that repeated the prefailure, near-surface colluvial stratigraphy. At Station 8+00 to 8+12 (Fig. 8), five "stacked" flow lobes were recognized. These lobes were distinguished by their distinctive, dark-colored organic horizons (topsoil). This exposure was particularly instructive, for initial inspection suggested that the repeated stratigraphy might be evidence of pre–January 4, 1982, slope failures; accordingly, detailed mapping was undertaken.

Main Track. The main track extended some 172 m downslope, where the debris reached building pads at the base of the slope. The main track was roughly hourglass-shaped, flaring from about 10.7 m wide in the center to about 21.3 m wide at both the top and bottom (see Fig. 6). The majority of the slide debris flowed on the average 21° ground surface of the main track, locally stripping vegetation to the roots and removing near-surface topsoil. Elsewhere, delicate grasses were flattened, but not

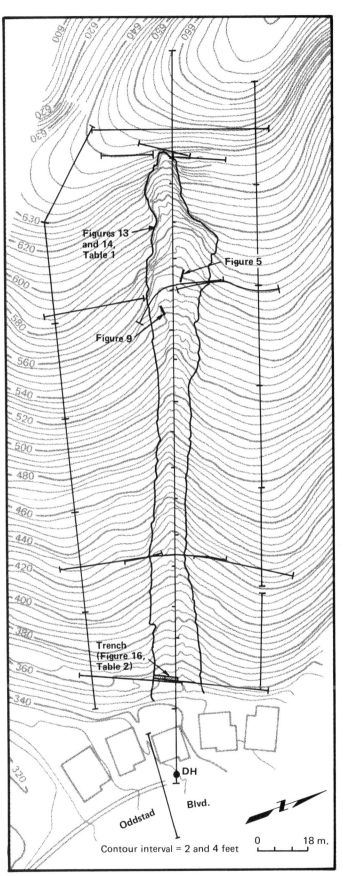

Figure 5. Map of Oddstad slope showing simplified postfailure topography (June 1982); scar of January 4, 1982, debris flow; seismic refraction survey lines; deep drill hole (DH); exploratory trenches; and locations discussed in text.

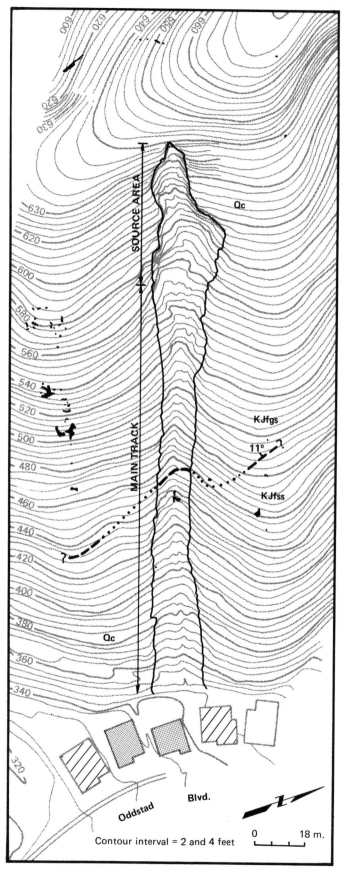

stripped or buried, suggesting that the debris flow was fluidized and rapid, perhaps "cushioned" by air. Along the margins of the main track, debris was deposited as linear levees, locally exceeding 0.61 m thick, on the prefailure ground surface (Fig 9). Later runoff eroded an axial channel, locally about 1.0 m deep, in the main track, removing debris flow deposits and underlying colluvium, and exposing sheared shale in the vicinity of the bedrock high (see Fig. 7).

The Oddstad failure probably initiated as slump-translational sliding of the saturated colluvium in the lower third of the source area. This apparently resulted in loss of support and near-simultaneous, progressive upslope failure of the remaining two-thirds of the source area. As noted previously, an area on the right side (looking upslope) of the source area failed as a slump sometime after the initial failure, and much of its debris was deposited within the source area scar and upper part of the main track.

Pre-Failure Swale

The natural configuration of the Oddstad slope is shown by the prefailure topography (Fig. 10). The east-southeast–facing slope consisted of a broad, linear, first-order drainage between two parallel spur ridges. The distance between the crests of the ridges was about 76.2 m, and the local topographic relief in the upper swale was about 18 m. The overall axial slope was about 25°.

Stereographic aerial photography extending back to 1941 confirms that the slope was in a natural state, and that no failure had occurred since at least 1941. Pre-late 1960s aerial photography shows that, prior to development in the late 1960s, the swale merged downslope into a fluvial terrace bordering the North Fork of San Pedro Creek. Development essentially buried the terrace and the lower part of the slope beneath fill (see Fig. 7).

Comparison of pre- and postfailure topography (see Fig. 5, 10) and photographic interpretation indicate that bedrock was not exposed in the swale prior to failure. Scattered outcrops on spur ridges and in the eroded axial channel of the main track scar (see Fig. 6) show that the upper half of the slope is underlain by Franciscan greenstone; the lower half is underlain by Franciscan sandstone and shale. The two units are separated by a north-south–trending, gently west-dipping (11°) bedrock fault (see Figs. 7, 10).

The greenstone is intensely to closely fractured, hard, moderately strong to strong, and deeply weathered. The sandstone is generally intensely to closely fractured, hard, strong, and moder-

←

Figure 6. Map of Oddstad slope showing postfailure topography (June 1982) and scar of January 4, 1982, debris flow. Underlying bedrock consists of Franciscan greenstone (KJfgs) and Franciscan sandstone (KJfss), separated by a north-striking, gently west-dipping (11°) shear zone. Solid black areas indicate bedrock outcrops; dot pattern, location of destroyed houses; line pattern, damaged houses.

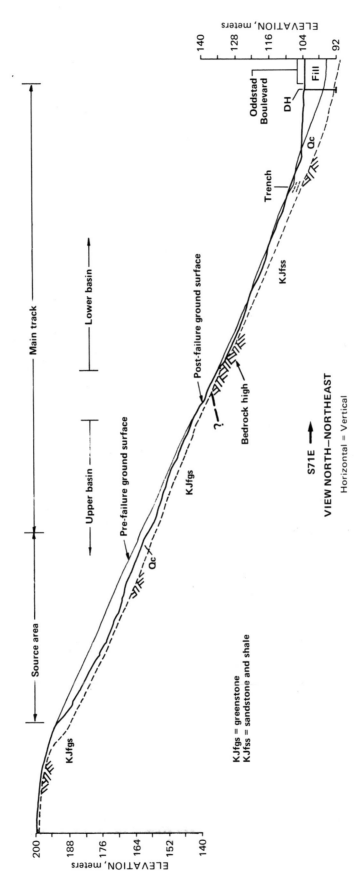

Figure 7. Simplified axial cross section, January 4, 1982, Oddstad debris flow showing prefailure topography; postfailure topography; and approximate colluvium-bedrock contact.

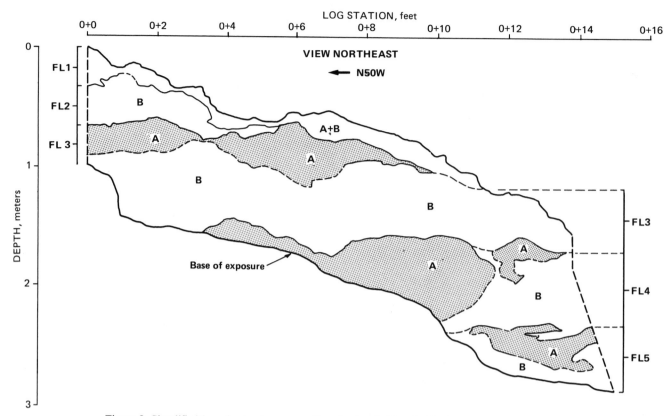

Figure 8. Simplified log of natural exposure (Log Station 8+00 – 8+12), January 4, 1982, Oddstad debris flow showing multiple flow lobes (FL1 – FL5) of slide. Unit A (patterned) is topsoil (organic horizons); unit B subsoil (cambic and argillic horizons). See Figure 5 for location of exposure.

Figure 9. Simplified log of natural exposure (Log Station 7+55 – 7+59), January 4, 1982, Oddstad debris flow showing 1982 debris and underlying (unfailed) colluvium. Unit A (patterned) is topsoil (organic horizons); unit B, subsoil (cambic and argillic horizons). C^{14} sample yielded date of 490 ±60 yr (MRT) BP. See Figure 5 for location of exposure.

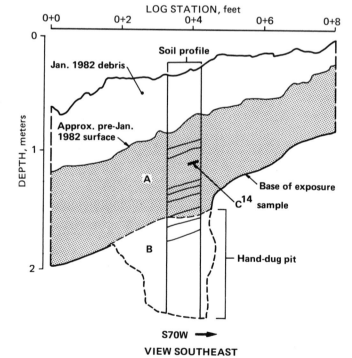

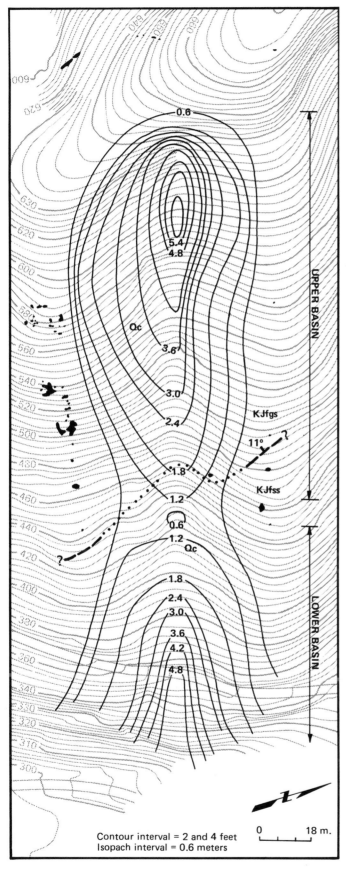

Contour interval = 2 and 4 feet
Isopach interval = 0.6 meters

0   18 m.

ately to little-weathered. The shale below the bedrock fault (topographically and structurally) is intensely fractured (sheared and foliated), moderately strong, and moderately to little-weathered.

The configuration of the bedrock topography underlying the slope is reconstructed from outcrops, hand-auger holes, seismic refraction survey lines, and comparison of pre- and postfailure topography. Such reconstruction (Figs. 7, and 10) shows that the bedrock topography defines two distinct subsurface basins. The upper basin is a closed, elongate trough, concave in longitudinal section, that extends from almost the ridge crest to midslope, just above the bedrock fault. This basin is asymmetric: the right (looking upslope) flank is somewhat steeper than the left, and the "deepest" part of the basin is located in the upper part. The axis of the upper basin is coincident with the axis of the prefailure swale. The concavity of the upper basin bedrock subsurface is similar to the January 4, 1982, failure surface; namely, ranging from about 43° in the upper part, and decreasing to 24 to 21° in the lower part.

The lower basin is downward-opening trough, extending from midslope—below the bedrock fault—downslope and beneath the fill of the developed area (see Fig. 10). The bedrock fault and underlying shale essentially form a relatively resistant bedrock high, separating the two basins.

Following the January 4, 1982, failure, colluvium was exposed everywhere in the source area scar, or upper Oddstad basin. Lateral scarps locally exposed up to 3.7 m of colluvium, generally characterized by grayish-brown (5YR 3/2) to dusky-brown (5YR 2/2) sandy clay topsoil (organic horizons) and moderately yellowish-brown (5YR 5/4) to moderate-brown (5YR 4/4) sandy clay and gravelly clay subsoil (cambic and argillic horizons). Colluvial exposures, together with hand-auger holes, seismic reflection survey lines, and comparison of pre- and postfailure topography permit construction of an isopach map showing the original thickness of upper basin colluvium (Fig. 10). These data indicate that the prefailure thickness of colluvium in the upper basin ranged from more than 6.1 m in the upper part to about 0.61 m over the bedrock high (see Figs. 7, 10).

In addition to distribution and thickness of colluvium, measurements of in-situ dry density and shear test results provide some information about engineering properties (summarized on Figs. 11, 12).

Density of the upper basin colluvium does not progressively increase with depth (see, for example, Reneau and others, 1984), but rather is "scattered." Samples taken from just below the 1982 failure surface show a wide range of densities (Fig. 11). Consoli-

Figure 10. Map of Oddstad slope showing prefailure topography (pre-1970) and isopachs of original colluvium thickness that define two distinct basins. Bedrock units are same as in Figure 6; solid black areas indicate bedrock outcrops. Isopachs based on exposures, auger holes, and seismic refraction survey lines (see Fig. 5).

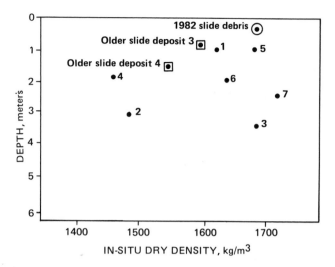

Figure 11. In-situ dry density data from Oddstad colluvium (upper basin: seven samples), derived from Franciscan greenstone; 1982 debris, derived from Franciscan greenstone; and (3) older slide deposits (3 and 4, lower basin), derived from Franciscan sandstone and shale. Upper basin colluvium samples plotted with respect to prefailure ground surface: samples 1 through 3 from just below basal failure surface; sample 4 from lateral scarp; samples 5 through 7 from headscarp.

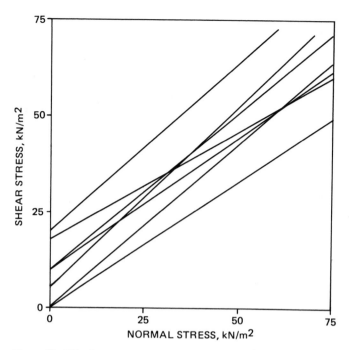

Figure 12. Effective stress failure envelopes derived from consolidated undrained, multistage triaxial shear test data from unfailed Oddstad colluvium (upper basin: seven samples), derived from Franciscan greenstone on undisturbed samples saturated by back pressure. Cohesion ranges from cohesionless to 19.6 kN/m^2; friction angles range from 29 to 43°.

dated, undrained, multistage triaxial shear tests on undisturbed samples of unfailed colluvium saturated by back pressure yield cohesion values from 0 to 1,953 kg/m^2, and angles of internal friction range from 29 to 43° (Fig. 12).

Mechanical analysis and soil stratigraphic data also show that the upper basin colluvium was essentially homogeneous; that is, there were no distinct zones of roots, pedogenic clay, or gravels that might have given rise to distinct permeability contrasts, as has been reported elsewhere (Reneau and others, 1984). Thus, why failure in the Oddstad upper basin swale occurred above the base of the colluvium, rather than at the colluvium-bedrock contact (Fig. 7), remains enigmatic.

SOIL-STRATIGRAPHIC AGE ASSESSMENTS

Soil-stratigraphic techniques are being increasingly applied to engineering-geologic investigations, particularly to reconstruct local geomorphic history, to date last displacements of faults, and, in some cases, to determine the recurrence intervals of mass movements (Shlemon, 1985). Soil stratigraphy includes the field of paleopedology, and generally employs the terms and concepts of the soil scientist. Soil (pedologic) units particularly applicable to the Oddstad debris flow are the organic (A) horizons of the modern solumn and of buried paleosols, frequently containing sufficient organic matter (mollic epipedon) for radiocarbon dat-

ing; and the cambic or argillic (B) horizons, subsoil units indicative of relative soil (pedogenic) age. A total of four representative soil profiles were measured and described from headscarp, lateral scarp, and main track exposures in the upper basin, and from the east wall of an approximately 4.9-m-deep trench excavated in the lower basin. Soil-stratigraphic terminology and field procedures follow those of Soil Survey Staff (1951, 1975) and Birkeland (1984).

Upper Basin Soil Stratigraphy

A soil profile from the south lateral scarp (Station 8+64; Figs. 13, 14) is representative and illustrates the unusual thickness of colluvium filling the upper basin. Here, some 7 organic (A_{11} through A_{17}; mollic epipedon) and 11 argillic horizons (B_{11} through B_{110}) composed a more than 3.7-m-thick soil-stratigraphic section (Table 1). The mollic epipedon contained about 5 percent organic matter, and was thus amenable to radiocarbon dating. The subsoil argillic horizons were slightly developed and generally typified by weak, coarse, subangular-blocky structure, reddish-brown colors (Munsell 7.5YR 4/4 = 5YR 4/2), and common, thin clay films filling tubular pores and lining ped faces.

The argillic horizons were particularly instructive, for their "abnormal" thickness in this Mediterranean climatic regime did not result from residual weathering, but rather from pedogenesis

Figure 13. Photograph of lateral scarp of January 4, 1982, Oddstad debris flow taken from source area looking southeast downslope. Ladder and flagging are at soil profile location (Log Station 8+64; see Fig. 5 for location of profile; see Fig. 14 for detail).

Figure 14. Photograph of Log Station 8+64, south lateral scarp of January 4, 1982, Oddstad debris flow. See Figure 5 for location; see Table 1 for soil profile, measurement, and description; see Figure 15 for soil profile data.

keeping pace with slow sideslope and headwall accretion. The thick soil in the upper basin is thus a cumulic profile ("cumula-tive" of Birkeland, 1984).

Slow colluvial filling of the upper basin is also substantiated by laboratory mechanical and chemical analyses (Fig. 15). In particular, organic matter decreases uniformly from about 5 per-cent at the surface to less than 1 percent at depth. These data support field observations that no buried organic horizons, indica-tive of significant unconformities, occurred in this section.

In addition, particle-size distribution remains relatively con-stant with depth. This is seen well by the almost uniform distribu-tion of clay in the soil column (see Fig. 15). There were, however, some minor changes in colluvial sedimentation rates as indicated by the presence of weak stonelines in the A_{14} and B_{13} horizons,

and by local abrupt and smooth lower boundaries of some soil horizons (see Table 1).

The lack of significant unconformities in the upper basin colluvial section is also shown by the general vertical distribution of sodium and pH at the measured profile. The influx of sodium, presumably eolian-derived from nearby ocean source areas, may cause dispersal of illuvial clays, accelerate soil profile develop-ment, and thus give rise to a buried paleosol inherently indicative of an unconformity (Shlemon and Hamilton, 1978). Accordingly, minor breaks in the colluvial section may be recorded by the slight sodium increase in the A_{14} and B_{13} horizons (see Fig. 15).

Soil pH usually reflects contemporary weathering environ-ments, although abrupt changes with depth may well indicate unconformities in a soil-stratigraphic section. However, the cu-

TABLE 1. SOUTH LATERAL SCARP, SURFACE SLOPE 31°, SOIL PROFILE MEASUREMENT AND DESCRIPTION, NATURAL EXPOSURE, STATION 8+64, JANUARY 4, 1982, ODDSTAD DEBRIS FLOW*

Horizon	Depth (m)	Description
O	0.00-0.09	Very dark gray (10YR 3/1) to very dark grayish-brown (10YR 3/2) when moist, silty clay loam; strong, fine granular to moderate fine subangular blocky structure; slightly hard firm, very slightly sticky, nonplastic; many medium to coarse random roots, locally forming organic mat; common, medium vertical roots; common fine pores; gradual wavy to gradual smooth boundary
A_{11}	0.09-0.18	Very dark grayish-brown (10YR 3/2) to very dark brown (10YR 2/2) when moist, silty clay loam; moderate, medium subangular blocky structure; hard to very hard, very firm, non-sticky and non plastic; common, medium vertical roots; common fine pores; gradual wavy to gradual smooth boundary
A_{12}	0.18-0.27	Very dark brown (10YR 2/2); dry and moist, pebbly silty clay loam; hard to very hard, firm, slightly sticky and nonplastic; common fine to medium vertical roots; common fine pores; approx. 10-15 percent angular clasts to 5 mm in diameter, gradual smooth to abrupt smooth boundary
A_{13}	0.27-0.37	Very dark grayish-brown (10YR 3/2) to very dark brown (10YR 2/2) when moist, silty loam; moderate, medium angular blocky to columnar structure; slightly hard, friable to slightly firm, nonsticky and nonplastic; few medium vertical roots; common fine pores; approx. 5 percent angular clasts to 5 mm in diameter, locally, lower boundary typified by few angular clasts to 1-in diameter, forms weak stoneline and unconformity parallel to modern slope; abrupt smooth boundary
A_{14}	0.37-0.55	Very dark gray (10YR 3/1) to very dark brown (10YR 3/2) silty clay; moderate medium to coarse subangular blocky structure; slightly hard, firm, slightly sticky and slightly plastic; few fine and coarse vertical roots; common fine pores; few angular fragments scattered throughout horizon; gradual wavy boundary
A_{15}	0.55-0.67	Very dark grayish brown (10YR 3/2) dry and moist, pebbly silty clay; weak, medium to coarse angular blocky structure; slightly hard, firm slightly sticky and slightly plastic; few fine random roots; few fine pores; approx. 5 percent angular clasts to 5 mm in diameter, gradual wavy to gradual diffuse boundary
A_{16}	0.67-0.79	Very dark grayish-brown to brown (10YR 3/2-7.5-7.5YR 4/2) to very dark grayish-brown (10YR 3/2) when moist, silty clay to silty clay loam; moderate fine to medium angular and weak coarse angular blocky structure; slightly hard, friable, nonsticky and nonplastic; few fine random roots; common, thin, black (10YR 2/1) organic stains on ped faces; approx. 5-8 percent angular clasts to 8 mm in diameter, increasing to approx. 10 percent near base; abrupt smooth boundary
A_{17}	0.79-0.91	Very dark grayish-brown to dark brown (10YR 3/2-7.5YR 3/2) to very dark grayish-brown (10YR 3/2) when moist, silty loam; weak medium angular blocky structure; slightly hard, firm nonsticky and nonplastic; few fine to coarse random roots; common fine pores; few to common, thin, black (10YR 2/1) organic stains on ped faces; common manganese staining within root tubules; approx. 5-8 percent angular clasts to 5 mm in diameter, gradual wavy to gradual diffuse boundary
A-B	0.91-1.16	Brown (7.5YR 4/2) to dark brown (7.5YR 3/2) when moist, silty clay; weak medium angular blocky structure; hard, firm, slightly sticky and slightly plastic; common fine pores; few thin organic stains forming "tongues" on ped faces grading downward into dark brown (7.5YR 3/2), few, moderately thick clay films on ped faces and filling old vertical root tubules; few angular clasts to 5 mm in diameter, gradual smooth boundary
B_{11}	1.16-1.83	Brown (7.5YR 4/2) dry and moist, light silty clay; moderate medium angular blocky structure; slightly hard to hard, firm, sticky and plastic; few to common fine roots; few fine pores; 5-6 stratified illuvial clay lenses to 5-mm thickness superimposed on weakly stratified colluvial parent material; few, moderately thick dark reddish-brown (5YR 3/2) clay films on ped faces; stratified colluvial units with apparent dip of 18-20° downslope; horizon is cumulic, weakly stratified silty clay-silty clay loam; clay films concentrated in old root tubules and channels; approx. 5 percent angular clasts, random, to 5 mm in diameter, gradual wavy boundary
B_{12}	1.83-2.04	Brown (7.5YR 4/4) to brown (7.5YR 4/2) when moist, sandy clay loam; moderate medium angular blocky structure; hard, firm, sticky, slightly plastic to plastic; common fine to coarse vertical roots; common, thin clay films bridging mineral grains, and common, thin dark brown (7.5YR 3/2) clay films lining root tubules; approx. 5 percent very angular clasts to 10 mm in diameter, gradual smooth boundary
B_{13}	2.04-2.25	Brown (7.5YR 4/2) dry and moist, pebbly sandy loam; moderate medium to coarse subangular blocky to weak medium to coarse columnar structure; hard, firm, slightly sticky and slightly plastic; few medium random roots; common, moderately thick dark reddish brown (5YR 3/2) clay films on ped faces, and common, thin, illuvial clay lining root tubules; approx. 15 percent angular clasts to 8 mm in diameter, horizon delimiting weakly stratified colluvial parent material; gradual smooth to gradual wavy boundary

TABLE 1. SOUTH LATERAL SCARP, SURFACE SLOPE 31°, SOIL PROFILE MEASUREMENT AND DESCRIPTION,
NATURAL EXPOSURE, STATION 8+64, JANUARY 4, 1982, ODDSTAD DEBRIS FLOW* (continued)

Horizon	Depth (m)	Description
B_{14}	2.25–2.50	Brown (7.5YR 4/4) to brown (7.5YR 4/2) when moist, silty clay loam; weak to moderate angular blocky structure; slightly hard, firm, slightly sticky and slightly plastic; few medium random roots; common, moderately-thick dark reddish gray (5YR 4/2) clay films bridging mineral grains and lining ped faces; few angular clasts near horizon base with few moderately thick illuvial clay coating on pebble faces; gradual wavy boundary
B_{15}	2.50–2.74	Brown (7.5YR 4/4) dry and moist, silty clay; weak, moderate subangular blocky structure; slightly hard to hard, firm, slightly sticky and slightly plastic; very fine to fine random roots; common, moderately thick, dark reddish-gray (5YR 4/2) clay films bridging mineral grains and lining ped faces; approx. 5 percent angular clasts near top of horizon to 10 percent angular clasts near base to 5 mm in diameter, gradual smooth to abrupt smooth boundary
B_{16}	2.74–2.86	Brown (7.5YR 4/4) to brown (7.5YR 4/2) when moist, heavy pebbly silty clay; weak, fine subangular blocky structure; hard, firm, slightly sticky and slightly plastic; few fine vertical roots and few to common old root channels; common, moderately thick clay films lining ped faces and coating clasts; approx. 30 percent, highly weathered angular clasts; gradual wavy to gradual smooth boundary
B_{17}	2.86–3.14	Brown (7.5YR 4/4) dry and moist, pebbly silty clay; weak, medium angular blocky structure; hard, firm, slightly sticky and slightly plastic; many fine old root channels, reticulate form; common, moderately thick, dark reddish-brown (5YR 3/2) clay films lining root tubules; local manganese staining bordering few, medium modern roots; illuvial clay films increasing toward base of horizon; horizon weakly stratified colluvial unit; gradual smooth boundary
B_{18}	3.14–3.26	Brown (7.5YR 4/2) to dark reddish-gray (5YR 4/2) when moist, silty loam; weak, fine subangular blocky structure; slightly hard, friable, slightly sticky and slightly plastic; common, old root channels, reticulate form; common, moderately thick, dark reddish-brown to weak red (5YR 3/2–2.5YR 4/2) clay films lining ped faces and filling old root tubules; local manganese staining; approx. 5 percent fine, weathered angular clasts; gradual wavy boundary
B_{19}	3.26–3.41	Similar to B_{18} in color, texture, structure, plasticity, and consistency; many very fine old root channels with reticulate form; common, moderately thick to thick, weak red (2.5YR 4/2) illuvial clay films filling root channels; gradual wavy boundary
B_{110}	3.41–3.65+	Similar to B_{18} in color, texture, structure, plasticity, and consistency; many fine pores; common fine old root channels; random with reticulate form; approx. 15 percent angular clasts to 5 mm in diameter, base of exposure

*See Figure 5 for location of profile; see Figure 15 for soil profile data.

mulic, upper basin soil displays no major breaks in pH gradient, but rather decreases gradually with depth, most likely reflecting the distribution of subsoil organic acids (see Fig. 15).

An upper basin soil-stratigraphic section was also described from an exposure along the eroded axial channel just below the source area (Station 7+57; see Fig. 9). Here measurements were made and samples collected from the natural exposure and from a 0.9-m-deep hand-dug pit. At this locality, between 0.3 and 0.9 m of 1982 slide debris (levee deposits) overlay organic horizons developed on older colluvium. About 1.7 m of buried organic and underlying argillic horizons were exposed here; an additional 2.6 m of colluvium underlay this section, and more than 6.1 m was present in the deepest part of the upper basin (see Fig. 10). The colluvium here was comparable to that in the headscarp and lateral scarp areas; namely, silty and clayey sand bearing several black (10YR 2/2) to dark gray (10YR 3/1) organic horizons overlying dark reddish-brown (5YR 3/2), slightly developed, argillic horizons.

Field measurements and laboratory data indicate that no buried paleosols or unconformities were present in this section. This, together with the relatively homogeneous grain-size distribution, suggests that here sediments slowly filled the upper basin. An approximate sedimentation rate is provided by a radiocarbon date of 490 ± 60 yr (Beta-5054), obtained at about 0.45 m below the prefailure ground surface, from the organic horizon buried by the January 4, 1982, debris flow (A_{14b}; see Fig. 9). The radiocarbon age is minimal, for it is a mean residence time date, derived from a bulk sample with 4.9 percent organic matter. Such near-surface samples are inherently contaminated by modern organic acids, but nevertheless, with appropriate corrections, have proven useful to estimate colluvial sedimentation rates (Yaalon, 1971). The almost 500-yr-old MRT age, dating the upper 0.45 m of an approximately 6.1-m-thick total cumulic section, yields an average sedimentation rate of about 0.61 m/1,000 yr, thus suggesting that fluvial incision on the Oddstad swale ceased, and that colluviation began some 8,000 to 10,000 yr ago (Shlemon and Wright, 1983).

Lower Basin Soil Stratigraphy

A representative soil stratigraphy for the lower basin was measured on the east wall of an approximately (maximum) 4.9-m-deep trench exposure (Station 3+26; see Fig. 5). Here, including the January 4, 1982, deposits, five debris flow deposits were identified (Fig. 16). The deposits were distinguished by lithology, angularity of clasts, and capping buried paleosols. In contrast to the homogeneous colluvium of the upper basin, these deposits and soils indicate that at least four debris flows had occurred in the lower basin prior to the January 4, 1982, event. Moreover, based on clast lithology (sandstone and shale) and size, the flows emanated almost wholly from within the lower basin, apparently originating at or downslope from the bedrock high (see Fig. 7).

Debris Deposit 1. Levee deposits of the January 4, 1982, debris flow up to 0.24 m were present at the trench site. The deposits (1) consisted of moderate brown (5YR 3/4) silty sand containing approximately 20 percent low plastic fines, 75 to 80 percent fine- to coarse-grained sand, a trace to 5 percent fine gravel. Up to 50 percent plant debris was layered at the base of the deposit.

Older Debris Deposit 2. Of the four older debris flow deposits beneath the January 4, 1982, debris, three were present at the measured profile. An older debris flow deposit (2) was encountered within 0.3 m of the surface (Table 2). This deposit bears a slightly developed paleosol. The now-buried organic horizons (A_{11} through A_{13}) were very dark brown (10YR 2/2 – 3/2) in color, and silty clay to pebbly loam in texture. Field observations showed that an apparent abrupt increase in clay content between the A_{11} and A_{12} horizons, indicated by laboratory mechanical analyses data (Fig. 17), was not pedogenic in origin, but rather the result of parent-material stratification.

The subsoil was a cambic horizon (B), distinguished mainly by its reddish-brown (5YR 5/6) color. A few thin clay films lined ped faces and bridged mineral grains, but were insufficient to classify the horizon as argillic. An abrupt wavey lower boundary marked the unconformity with the underlying buried paleosol (see Table 2).

Laboratory data showed that soil organic matter decreased with depth. However, the A_{11} horizon contained about 4 percent organic matter (see Fig. 17), adequate to yield an MRT date of 1950 ± 170 yr (Beta-6023). This date indicates that slide debris in the lower basin had not failed nor had been capped by upslope sediments for at least the last 2,000 yr.

Older Debris Deposit 3. A third, older debris flow deposit (3), approximately 1.4 m thick, was also exposed in the trench (Fig. 16). This deposit was likewise capped by a buried paleosol, here typified by approximately 0.61- and 0.91-m-thick organic

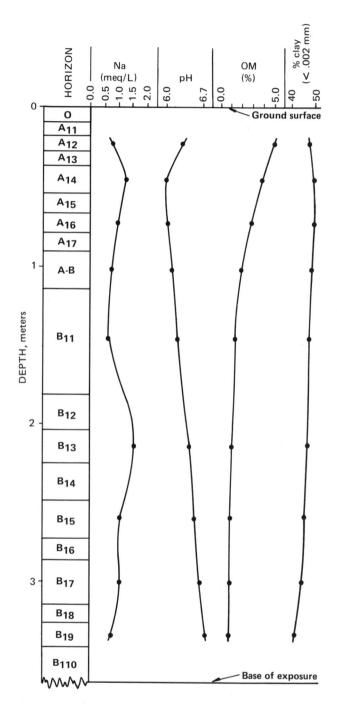

Figure 15. Soil profile data, natural exposure (Log Station 8+64), unfailed colluvium in lateral scarp of January 4, 1982, Oddstad debris flow, showing sodium (Na) content in milliequivalents per liter; pH; percentage of organic matter (OM); and percentage of clay content. See Figure 5 for location of profile.

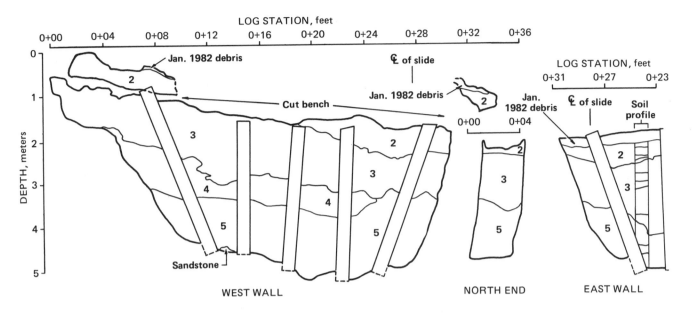

Figure 16. Simplified log of trench exposure, January 4, 1982, Oddstad debris flow showing 1982 slide debris overlying superimposed older debris deposits (2 through 5) of lower basin. C^{14} samples from deposits 2 and 3 yielded dates of 1,950 ± 170 yr (MRT) BP, and 2,910 ± 80 (MRT) BP, respectively. See Figure 5 for location of trench; see Table 2 for soil profile measurement and description; see Figure 17 for soil profile data.

($11A_{11b}$ through $11A_{13b}$) and cambic ($11B_{11b}$ through $11B_{12b}$) horizons, respectively (see Table 2).

The buried organic horizons contained up to 3 percent organic matter (horizon $11A_{11b}$; see Fig. 17), and yielded an MRT radiocarbon date of 2,910 ± 80 yr (Beta-6024). Soil textures ranged from clay loam to pebbly clayey loam; but angular clasts of sandstone and shale, derived wholly from the lower basin, were common throughout the unit. An approximately 5 to 8 percent increase in subsoil clay (see Fig. 17) was essentially pedogenic in origin, indicated by thin clay films lining ped faces and filling tubular pores (see Table 2).

Older Debris Deposit 4. A fourth, older debris flow deposit (4), approximately 0.6 m thick, was exposed in the left end (looking upslope) of the trench (Fig. 16). It was not present at the measured profile, and was either not originally deposited at this location or was eroded prior to deposition of older debris deposit 3. This deposit consisted of moderate yellowish-brown (10YR 4/4) sandy clay with approximately 60 percent medium plastic fines, 40 percent fine- to coarse-grained, poorly graded, subangular sand, and 2 percent subangular gravel up to 13 mm in maximum dimension.

Older Debris Deposit 5. A still older debris deposit (5) and capping buried paleosol was encountered in the trench at a depth of 1.9 m (see Table 2). Only the buried argillic horizon was preserved: the organic horizons typically were either mechanically eroded or chemically oxidized. The argillic horizon was a dark reddish-brown (5YR 3/4 – 4/4) gravelly sandy clay, with

moderate medium- to coarse-angular blocky structure, and common, moderately thick clay films lining ped faces (IIIB$_{2b}$; see Table 2). This soil was moderately developed, and, by comparison with the overlying radiometrically dated, slightly developed buried paleosols, probably represented some 2,000 to 4,000 yr of weathering. It therefore appears that the four pre-1982 buried debris deposits and their capping soils in the lower basin trench probably formed over a several-thousand-year period. Accordingly, episodic debris flows apparently occurred in the lower basin about every 1,000 to 4,000 yr. The deposits exposed in the trench thus record an almost complete history of lower basin slide occurrence from early Holocene and perhaps even from late Pleistocene time.

EVOLUTION OF THE COLLUVIUM-FILLED SWALE

The Oddstad swale is one of hundreds in the Pacifica area in which at least some colluvium failed during the January 3–5, 1982, storm. However, many more did not fail. Based on our site-specific information, and on reconnaissance in the San Francisco Bay area, we propose a general three-stage evolutionary model for the Oddstad colluvium-filled swale. This swale may be unusual, for it contains two distinct basins, an upper and a lower, each of which had a different history of colluvial filling and failure. Nevertheless, because similar swales may occur in a wide variety of geomorphic and geologic environments, and the processes are applicable to all swales, we present the Oddstad case as

TABLE 2. SOIL PROFILE MEASUREMENT AND DESCRIPTION, TRENCH EXPOSURE,
STATION 3+26, JANUARY 4, 1982, ODDSTAD DEBRIS FLOW*

Horizon	Depth (m)	Description
		Debris Flow of January 1982: very dark brown (10YR 2/2) to pinkish-gray (7.5YR 6/2) when moist; mixed organic sediments and colluvium with common angular clasts; many large horizontal roots at base; deposits contorted; 0.5-0.6 m of debris flow at measured locality; abrupt wavy boundary (unconformity)
A_{11}	0.00-0.09	**Older Debris Deposit 2:** Very dark brown (10YR 2/2) to dark brown (7.5YR 2/2) silty clay loam; weak, fine angular blocky structure; slightly hard, friable, sticky and plastic; many fine vertical roots; few coarse roots; approx. 5 percent angular pebbles to 3 mm in diameter, gradual smooth boundary; C^{14} date of 1950±170 yr (MRT) BP
A_{12}	0.09-0.30	Very dark brown (10YR 2/2) to very dark brown (7.5YR 3/2) sandy clay loam; weak, medium subangular blocky structure; hard, firm, slightly sticky and slightly plastic; few fine roots; few coarse roots with thin manganese stains; approx. 5 percent reddish, angular sandstone clasts to 51 mm in diameter, slickensided shale fragments to 51-mm-long diameter, gradual smooth boundary
A_{13}-B	0.30-0.40	Very dark grayish-brown (10YR 3/2) to dark brown (7.5YR 3/2) pebbly silty loam; weak, medium subangular blocky structure; hard to very hard, slightly sticky and slightly plastic; few medium and few coarse random roots; few thin clay films in root tubules; approx. 5 percent angular clasts to 3 mm in diameter, gradual wavy boundary
B	0.40-0.52	Dark brown (7.5YR 3/2) to reddish-brown (5YR 4/4) pebbly silty clay loam; common fine to medium subangular blocky structure; hard, firm, sticky and plastic; few fine vertical roots with manganese stains; few thin clay films on ped faces and bridging mineral grains; approx. 10 percent very angular shale and red sandstone clasts concentrated near base; horizon lenticular increasing to 0.6 m+ laterally; lower boundary relief to 76 mm, abrupt wavy boundary (unconformity)
$11A_{11}b$	0.52-0.73	**Older Debris Deposit 3: Buried Paleosol:** Very dark brown (10YR 2/2) silty clay loam; weak fine to dark medium subangular block structure; slightly hard, firm, sticky and plastic; few fine vertical roots; common fine pores; approx. 5 percent very angular reddish sandstone and volcanic clasts; gradual smooth boundary; C^{14} date of 2,910±80 yr (MRT) BP
$11A_{12}b$	0.73-0.88	Dark yellowish-brown (10YR 3/4) silty clay; weak to moderate fine angular blocky structure; hard, firm, sticky and plastic; few fine roots; common, fine pores; few coarse roots with manganese stains; approx. 5 percent angular reddish volcanic clasts to 3 mm in diameter, gradual smooth boundary
$11A_{13}$-B_b	0.88-1.06	Dark yellowish-brown (10YR 3/4) to dark brown (10YR 3/4) to dark brown (7.5YR 3/2) silty clay; moderate, medium subangular blocky structure; very hard, firm, sticky and very plastic; few fine roots; few very fine pores; few thin clay films bridging mineral grains and filling tubular pores; gradual smooth boundary
$11B_{11}b$	1.06-1.62	Dark yellowish-brown (10YR 3/4) pebbly silty clay loam; moderate medium to coarse subangular blocky structure; hard to very hard, firm, sticky and plastic; few coarse old root casts with manganese stains; few thin clay films filling tubular pores and lining ped faces; approx. 5-10 percent angular clasts; continuous wavy boundary
$11B_{12}b$	1.62-1.89	Dark brown (10YR 3/3) silty clay; moderate to strong, medium to coarse angular blocky structure; hard to very hard, very firm, sticky and very plastic; common, fine old root casts; few thin clay films on ped faces; common pressure faces; abrupt wavy to abrupt irregular boundary (unconformity)
$111B_1b$	1.89-2.38	**Older Debris Deposit 5: Buried Paleosol:** Dark reddish-brown (5YR 3/4) pebbly silty clay; moderate medium to coarse angular blocky structure; hard to very hard, very firm, sticky and very plastic; few common clay films (thin) bridging mineral grains and filling tubular pores; approx. 10 percent highly weathered clasts to 3 mm in diameter at top of horizon increasing to approx. 25-30 percent shale clasts to 51-mm diameter near base; gradual wavy boundary
$111B_2b$	2.38-2.74	Reddish-brown (5YR 4/4) gravelly sandy clay loam; moderate medium angular blocky structure; hard, firm, sticky and plastic; few fine old root casts; few to common thin to moderately thick clay films on ped faces; approx. 50-60 percent very angular shale clasts from upslope fault zone (bedrock) to 76-mm diameter, resistant unit to base of trench

*See Figure 5 for location of profile; see Figure 17 for soil profile data.

a comparative model to understand better the engineering geology of such features.

Stage 1: Fluvial Incision

The initial highland topography of the San Pedro basin had greater relief than the present. First-order drainages, as now, probably extended to ridge lines, but were essentially devoid of colluvium. Fluvial incision, rather than channel filling, was the dominant slope-forming process. Here, both the upper and lower Oddstad basins were formed, with bedrock relief reflecting differential erosion across a bedrock fault and various lithologic units comprising the underlying Franciscan Formation. Based on radiocarbon, soil-stratigraphic and palynologic dating of swales in California, such fluvial incision most likely took place during the late Pleistocene, a time of different climatic, vegetative, and hydrologic regimes (Shlemon and Wright, 1983; Dietrich and Dorn, 1984; Reneau and others, 1984; Marron, 1985).

Stage 2: Swale Filling

With the onset of the Holocene, changing environments apparently led to accumulation of colluvium in formerly incised low-order drainages. As shown by the Oddstad swale, the filling history was likely very complex. For example, in the upper basin, colluvium slowly accumulated. No buried paleosols, stonelines, or other evidence of significant unconformities were present to indicate possible episodic colluvial filling and flushing. Colluvial accretion here occurred for at least the last 8,000 to 10,000 yr. In contrast, the lower basin was filled and partially emptied several times. Here, the presence of multiple debris flow deposits, some capped by slightly to moderately developed buried paleosols, attest to episodic filling and failure. Radiocarbon dates and relative soil profile development suggest that lower basin debris flows occurred in intervals of about 1,000 to 4,000 yr. This frequency may be the geologic "norm," for comparable filling and failure frequency has been reported for swales in northwestern California (Marron, 1985) and elsewhere in the San Francisco Bay area (Reneau and others, 1984).

Stage 3: Failure and Swale Exhumation

With slope failure occasioned by long and intense precipitation, the upper Oddstad basin became partially exhumed, and, but for subsequent slope repairs, would have left a complex stratigraphic legacy. For example, although much of the upper basin colluvium was removed during the January 4, 1982, failure, some remained in the source area, either in place or locally slumped or overriding other slump blocks. This added to stratigraphic complexity by apparent "stacking" of soil organic horizons (see Fig. 8). Superficially, these organic horizons resembled multiple buried paleosols. Only detailed mapping showed that these were but remnants of prefailure near-surface materials. If left unrepaired, the remaining slide debris and unfailed colluvium

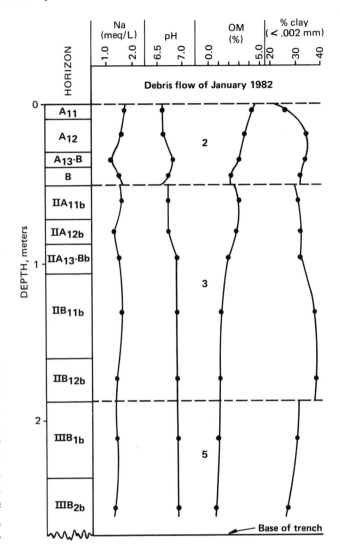

Figure 17. Soil profile data, trench exposure (Log Station 3+26), January 4, 1982, Oddstad debris flow, showing: sodium (Na) in milliequivalents per liter; pH; percentage of organic matter; and percentage of clay content. Unconformities (dashed lines) separate older debris deposits 2, 3, and 5 of lower basin. See Figure 5 for location of trench; see Figure 16 for trench log; see Table 2 for soil profile measurement and description.

in the upper basin would have failed over time, essentially exhuming the upper basin. In time, the upper basin would again slowly fill with colluvium.

The final, exhumed stage of swale evolution in the lower Oddstad basin was precluded by urban development along the base of the slope in the 1960s. During the 1982 event, near-surface sediments were locally scoured by the passing debris flow and by later runoff that eroded gullies down the center of the main track. Elsewhere, as in the vicinity of the trench, debris was deposited as levees. If the slope had been left unrepaired and the debris not removed by subsequent erosion, the deposits would have added to the late Pleistocene and Holocene stratigraphic record of debris flows in the lower basin.

In sum, although only a single topographic feature, the two colluvium-filled subsurface basins underlying the Oddstad swale evolved differently, providing contrasting models of fluvial incision, episodic filling, and exhumation.

SUMMARY AND CONCLUSIONS

Of the many shallow slope failures in Pacifica during the storm of January 3–5, 1982, the Oddstad debris flow was the most destructive, producing loss of life and substantial property damage. Later detailed investigations provided special opportunities to analyze the anatomy of the debris flow, to determine the age and recurrence of prior failures, and to reconstruct the evolution of the prefailure slope.

The Oddstad debris flow emanated from a first-order drainage, a complex two-basin, colluvium-filled swale that previously had been manifested only by a small topographic "crenulation." The January 4, 1982, debris flow originated in an upper basin filled with at least 6.1 m of colluvium. The flow essentially passed over the lower basin, and into the developed area downslope.

Soil-stratigraphic measurements and descriptions show that the upper basin colluvium accumulated very slowly such that a more than 3.7-m-thick cumulic soil profile had developed. This colluvium was internally free of buried paleosols, stonelines, and other unconformities, indicating that colluviation essentially continued until the January 4, 1982, failure.

The mollic epipedon of the upper basin cumulic soil contained about 5 percent organic matter, and yielded an MRT radiocarbon date of about 500 yr. This date, although inherently minimal, provides an average sedimentation rate of about 0.61 m/1,000 yr, suggesting that colluviation here began about 8,000 to 10,000 yr ago.

In contrast, the lower basin contained evidence of several older debris flows. Here, a 4.9-m-deep trench exposed five distinct debris flow deposits, including those of January 4, 1982. The older debris flow deposits were distinguished mainly by clast lithology and angularity, and by the presence of capping buried paleosols. MRT radiocarbon dates of approximately 2 and 3 ka provided minimum ages for the upper two deposits underlying

the January 4, 1982, debris. A stratigraphically lower and older deposit was capped by a moderately developed argillic horizon that, when compared in morphology to the overlying, dated paleosols, probably formed in about 2,000 to 4,000 yr. Accordingly, debris flows originating in the lower basin recurred episodically about every 1,000 to 4,000 yr.

A generalized three-stage model is proposed to explain the contrasting evolution of the upper and lower basins. Initially, first-order drainages were incised by fluvial processes, presumably under climatic, vegetative, and hydrologic conditions of the late Pleistocene. With onset of the Holocene, a second stage of evolution began when colluvium began to fill the upper basin. Such colluviation continued essentially uninterrupted until a local geomorphic threshold was reached, and failure ensued on January 4, 1982. In contrast, the lower basin was, in part, episodically filled and flushed. Each debris flow on the lower slope remained sufficiently stable such that a soil profile formed, eventually to be buried by younger deposits. The third stage of slope evolution was attained by the upper basin on January 4, 1982, when failure occurred and exhumation began. Here, fluvial incision would likely again have taken place had not slope repairs been made. In contrast, slope evolution in the lower basin was essentially aborted in the 1960s. Locally it received sediments from upslope on January 4, 1982, and was, in essence, still in a stage of filling, albeit episodic, prior to being repaired.

The Oddstad debris flow is but one of many that occurred in the central Coast Ranges of California. Its anatomy and evolution are complex; nevertheless, the case study data obtained may prove beneficial to engineering geologists who encounter colluvium-filled swales elsewhere.

ACKNOWLEDGMENTS

We gratefully acknowledge the support of R. Burford, F. Latimore, and J. McKibben for authorizing this investigation. Additionally, we thank P. Frame and P. Shires for field assistance, specifically for carrying out mapping and geophysical surveys, respectively. Our appreciation also extends to T. Camara for preparation of illustrations, to J. Costa and G. Wieczorek for review, to M. Vail for word processing services, and to Harlan Miller Tait Associates for use of laboratory facilities.

REFERENCES CITED

Birkeland, P. W., 1984, Soils and geomorphology: New York, Oxford University Press, 372 p.

Brabb, E. E., and Pampeyan, E. H., 1972a, Preliminary geologic map of San Mateo County, California: U.S. Geological Survey Miscellaneous Field Studies Map MF-328.

—— , 1972b, Preliminary map of landslide deposits in San Mateo County, California: U.S. Geological Survey Miscellaneous Field Studies Map MF-344.

Brown, W. M., III, Sitar, N., Saarinen, T. F., and Blair, M. L., 1984, Debris flows, landslides, and floods in the San Francisco Bay region, January 1982; Overview and summary of a conference held at Stanford University, August

23–26, 1982: Washington, D.C., National Research Council and U.S. Geological Survey, 83 p.

Dietrich, W. E., and Dunne, T., 1978, Sediment budget for a small catchment in mountainous terrain: Zeitschrift für Geomorphologie, Supplement Bd. 29, p. 191–206.

Dietrich, W. E., and Dorn, R., 1984, Significance of thick deposits of colluvium on hillslopes; A case study in the coastal mountains of northern California: Journal of Geology, v. 92, p. 133–146.

Dietrich, W. E., Reneau, S. L., and Wilson, C. J., 1984, Importance of colluvium-filled bedrock hollows to debris flow studies: Geological Society America Abstracts with Programs, v. 16, p. 488.

Fowler, W. L., 1984, Potential debris flow hazards of the Big Bend Drive drainage basin, Pacifica, California [master's thesis]: Stanford, California, Stanford University, 101 p.

Horton, R. E., 1945, Erosional development of streams and their drainage basins: Hydrophysical approach to quantitative morphology: Bulletin of the Geological Society of America, v. 56, p. 275–370.

Howard-Donley Associates, 1982, Geological investigation, landslide type and distribution, and mechanics details of nine representative failures, January 1982 rainstorms, city of Pacifica, California: Consultant's Technical Report, Job No. 834-01A, 108 p.

Marron, D. C., 1982, Hillslope evolution and the genesis of colluvium in Redwood National Park, northwestern California; The use of soil development in their analysis [Ph.D. thesis]: University of California at Berkeley, 187 p.

—— , 1985, Colluvium in bedrock hollows on steep slopes, Redwood Creek drainage basin, northwestern California, *in* Jungerius, P. D., ed., Soils and geomorphology: Catena, suppl. 6, p. 59–68.

Reneau, S. L., Dietrich, W. E., Wilson, C. J., and Rogers, J. D., 1984, Colluvial deposits and associated landslides in northern San Francisco Bay area, California, USA: Proceeding of the Fourth International Symposium on Landslides, Toronto, Canada, p. 425–430.

Schlocker, J., Bonilla, M. G., and Radbruch, D. H., 1958, Geology of the San Francisco north quadrangle, California: U.S. Geological Survey Miscellaneous Geologic Investigations Map I–272.

Shlemon, R. J., 1985, Application of soil-stratigraphic techniques to engineering geology: Association of Engineering Geologists Bulletin, v. 22, no. 2, p. 129–142.

Shlemon, R. J., and Hamilton, P., 1978, Late Quaternary rates of sedimentation and soil formation, Camp Pendleton–San Onofre State Beach coastal area, southern California, USA: Tenth International Congress on Sedimentology, Jerusalem, Israel, p. 603–604.

Shlemon, R. J., and Wright, R. H., 1983, Soil-stratigraphic dating of colluvial-filled gullies, Pacifica, California: Geological Society of America Abstracts with Programs, v. 15, no. 5, p. 328.

—— , 1984, Soil-stratigraphic dating of debris flows: Geological Society of America Abstracts with Programs, v. 16, no. 6, p. 654.

Smith, T. C., and Hart, E. W., 1982, Landslides and related storm damage, January 1982, San Francisco Bay region: California Geology, v. 35, p. 139–152.

Soil Survey Staff, 1951, Soil survey manual: Washington, D.C., U.S. Government Printing Office, U.S. Department of Agriculture Agricultural Handbook 18, 754 p.

—— , 1975, Soil taxonomy: Washington, D.C., U.S. Government Printing Office, U.S. Department of Agriculture, Soil Conservation Service Agricultural Handbook 436, 754 p.

Strahler, A. N., 1964, Quantatitive geomorphology of drainage basins and channel networks, *in* Chow, V. T., ed., Handbook of applied hydrology: New York, McGraw-Hill, section 4-11.

Yaalon, D. H., ed., 1974, Paleopedology: Jerusalem, Israel Universities Press, 350 p.

MANUSCRIPT ACCEPTED BY THE SOCIETY DECEMBER 29, 1986

Geological Society of America
Reviews in Engineering Geology, Volume VII
1987

Debris flow defenses in British Columbia

Oldrich Hungr
G. C. Morgan
Thurber Consultants, Ltd.
Suite 200, 1445 West Georgia Street
Vancouver, British Columbia V6G 2T3
Canada

D. F. VanDine
VanDine Geological Engineering Services
#3 - 159 Clarence Street
Victoria, British Columbia V8V 2H9
Canada

D. R. Lister
British Columbia Ministry of Transportation and Highways
940 Blanshard Street
Victoria, British Columbia V8W 3E6
Canada

ABSTRACT

A considerable amount of experience with engineering control of debris flow hazards has been gathered in British Columbia, Canada. A summary of this experience encompasses the entire spectrum of possible defensive measures. Passive measures include hazard mapping and zoning, the basic techniques of which are briefly described, and various types of warning systems that have been used with mixed success. Active defensive measures have been applied in the source areas, transportation zones, and deposition zones of debris flow–prone creek basins. The primary measures being applied at present in the source areas concentrate on controlling timber harvesting methods and encouraging reforestation. Engineered erosion control devices such as check dams and channel linings have thus far received limited use in British Columbia. In the transportation zone, design methods have been developed for training chutes and channels, deflecting dikes, diversions, adequate bridge openings and clearances, and overhead debris chutes. The most widespread designs of defensive measures relate to the deposition zone (debris fan) of mountain streams and include inexpensive "open" deposition basins, as well as more sophisticated "closed" structures incorporating a controlled discharge section and a spillway. A number of examples of completed or proposed structures are described and discussed from the point of view of design methodology.

INTRODUCTION

Debris flow activity has in recent years caused substantial property damage as well as loss of life in Canada's westernmost province. In response, engineering geologic studies have been undertaken in some localities, and defensive measures implemented to reduce future losses. This chapter reviews the technical aspects of this response and describes the range of remedial measures currently available for the defense of settlements and transportation routes against debris flows.

We have used the general term "debris flow" (Varnes, 1978), although most of the described cases occur along the

Pacific Coast where "debris torrent" (Swanston, 1974; VanDine, 1985) is a preferred regional designation for flows using established drainage channels.

Until the end of 1984, 43 debris flow events had been documented in western Canada. General reference has been made to numerous others. More than half of these documented events have occurred since 1980; most are located within the Coast Mountains and interior Columbia Mountains of British Columbia (Fig. 1). These regions have high relief, high annual precipitation, and high rainfall intensity.

The 43 events have resulted, either directly or indirectly, in 17 deaths. Many highways, railways, and logging roads have been blocked or severed. More than 50 bridge structures have been damaged or destroyed. Buildings and houses have been flooded, displaced from their foundations, or demolished. A conservative estimate of the structural and property damage caused by debris flows in British Columbia over the past 20 years exceeds $100 million (VanDine, 1985). Although high, these losses are probably disproportionately small relative to the extent of the affected regions and the frequency of debris flow occurrence. It is certain that continuing development and settlement of Canada's mountain regions will bring about even higher tolls in the future.

Debris flows in this area are composed primarily of coarse-grained inorganic and organic debris that may include boulders up to several meters in diameter and whole logs up to several tens of meters long. A fine-grained component, made up of soil ranging from clay to gravel and wood mulch, accompanies the coarse fraction. The organic content (i.e., wood remains) can form as much as 60 percent by volume in both the coarse- and fine-grained components, although in typical cases inorganic earth materials predominate.

Debris flows form in the headwaters or steep middle reaches of mountain creeks by means of several alternate triggering mechanisms. The most common appear to be slumping of over-steepened banks and spontaneous instability of loose creek-bed deposits. A debris flow "event" typically consists of several surges of concentrated high-discharge, high-density flow, separated and followed by more diluted "afterflow" and water flooding. The flows usually occur in response to major rainstorms accompanied by rapid snowmelt. A detailed discussion of the climatic aspects of the coastal British Columbia debris flows has been compiled by Church and Miles (this volume). Events triggered by glacial outbursts, glacial lake drainage, icefall, and major rockfall have also been described (e.g., Jackson, 1979; Hungr, 1985; Clague and others, 1985).

A detailed description of the nature of debris flows in western Canada has been provided in several case histories (e.g., Broscoe and Thompson, 1969; Nasmith and Mercer, 1979; Evans and Lister, 1984; Lister and others, 1984), in engineering reports (Thurber Consultants, 1983, 1985) and in a summary paper (VanDine, 1985).

Because of the destructive effects of debris flows on the provincial highway system (Evans and Lister, 1984; Lister and others, 1984), the British Columbia Ministry of Transportation

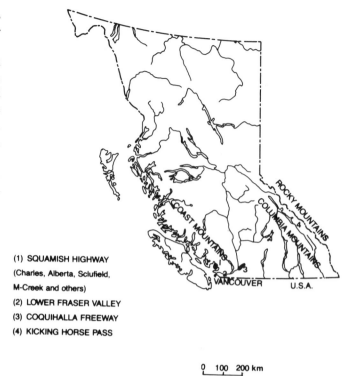

(1) SQUAMISH HIGHWAY
(Charles, Alberta, Sclufield,
M-Creek and others)
(2) LOWER FRASER VALLEY
(3) COQUIHALLA FREEWAY
(4) KICKING HORSE PASS

0   100   200 km

Figure 1. Map showing locations of major debris flow activity in southern British Columbia.

and Highways has been primarily responsible for the development and construction of debris flow defenses. Such measures have been constructed along British Columbia Highway 99 (Squamish Highway) north of Vancouver and the new Coquihalla Freeway between Hope and Merritt. Other groups interested in debris flow defenses include the Ministries of Environment and Forests, three major railways, the British Columbia Hydro and Power Authority (whose transmission lines are affected), and several pipeline and forestry companies.

The main parameters of debris flow relevant to the design of remedial measures include magnitude (the volume of material delivered to the deposition area during a single event), maximum flow discharge and velocity, point of deposition, runout distance, behavior at channel bends, run-up against barriers and obstructions, and impact stresses and forces. A summary of some of the current approaches toward evaluating these parameters has been provided in Hungr and others (1984) and VanDine (1985). As interpretation and design techniques are rapidly developing at present, both in British Columbia and elsewhere, no review can claim to thoroughly cover the subject.

A CLASSIFICATION OF DEFENSIVE MEASURES AGAINST DEBRIS FLOWS

A response to a natural hazard can be either passive or active. Passive measures involve avoiding the threatened area,

TABLE 1. CLASSIFICATION OF DEFENSIVE MEASURES AGAINST DEBRIS FLOW

Measure	Purpose
Passive Measures	
Hazard mapping and zoning	Restrict use of endangered areas
Warning systems: advance, during event, or post-event	Facilitate evacuation at times of danger
Active Measures	
A. In source area	
Reforestation/controlled harvest	Reduce debris production due to logging or natural loss of forest cover
Forest road construction control	Eliminate unstable cuts and fills that could act as debris sources or initiation points
Stabilization of debris sources (channel linings or check dams)	Stabilize channel bed and side slopes in source reaches
B. In transporation zone*	
Training by chutes, channels, and deflecting walls or dikes	Ensure passage of debris surges down a predetermined path, without blockage or overflowing (branching)
Channel diversion	Change the path of debris flow away from endangered areas
Bridges designed for passage	Protect traffic on bridge and prevent channel blockage due to bridge obstruction
"Sacrificial" bridges or fords	Prevent channel blockage due to the obstruction of a bridge with inadequate clearance
Bypass tunnels beneath creek bed	Protect transportation route without modifying stream channel
C. In deposition zone*	
Open debris deposition basins; dikes or walls	Control the extent of a natural deposition area by shaping and diking
Closed retention barriers and basins: full or partial volume	Create a controlled deposition space fronted by a straining structure and a spillway
Bridges or other structures designed for burial	Prevent damage to structure during burial by debris flow
Debris sheds (galleries) or cut-and-cover tunnels	Place transportation route beneath deposition area

*The limits of transporation and deposition zones are understood as those applicable after the defensive measures are in place. Channels and chutes will move the point of deposition downstream, barriers and basins upstream.

either permanently or at the time of imminent danger, without changing the hazard phenomenon. Active measures require modifying the phenomenon (the debris flow and its path) and its impact so that possible damage can be controlled.

Table 1 lists the principal means of protecting structures and linear developments against debris flow damage. The two types of passive measures rely on delineating the extent of danger in space and time. Active measures represent the larger group. They are divided into three subgroups, depending on the location along the flow path where treatment is implemented.

Active measures applied in the source areas of debris flows, such as high gullies and steep erodible reaches of a creek, are intended to reduce the volume of unstable material available to generate debris flows. An associated benefit is the reduction in the number and activity of potential points of initiation. These mea-

sures can be counted on to reduce the magnitude and frequency of debris flow events. Since they can rarely eliminate the hazard altogether, they are generally used in conjunction with some other measures. For example, a scheme typical in European practice utilizes a series of check dams to stabilize erodible reaches in conjunction with a retention basin located at the head of the fan (e.g., Eisbacher and Clague, 1984).

Active measures used in the transportation zone concentrate on improving the ability of the channel to pass the debris surges downstream. Blockage or overflowing could cause avulsion (uncontrolled branching) of subsequent surges of coarse material, or the fine afterflow and flood water. The protected area extends on both sides of the channel, above it (such as a bridge deck), or beneath it (a tunnel). Confined channelization can be used to extend the limits of the transportation area downstream, and thus to protect structures located at the apex of the original deposition area. This is the principle of the *Schusrinne* (shooting channel) as used in the European Alps.

Of special importance is the design of deflecting walls or dikes required to prevent overtopping of the channel on the outside of bends. Deflecting dikes used in the deposition zone to constrain the lateral extent of deposits are covered under open deposition basins below.

The purpose of defense measures in the deposition zone is to control the areal extent of deposition and to design any structures located there so that damage is controlled when deposition takes place. Closed debris basins are intended to retain a predetermined volume of debris while straining the associated water flow through a discharge section and passing any excess debris or water over a specially designed spillway. Such structures can be used to create a deposition area at a location that was formerly part of the transportation zone, upstream of the fan.

A less elaborate type of retention structure uses designed earthworks to limit the extent of an existing deposition area. In other words, grading and diking is used to encourage deposition to take place on a specific part of the fan. This is called an open deposition basin. No straining structure or spillway is provided, only a gap in the terminal dike to pass the afterflow and flood in a desired direction.

Examples of almost all of the types of remedial measures shown in Table 1 have either been built, designed, or at least seriously considered at various sites in British Columbia. The following text contains selected examples to illustrate each type, and provides a brief discussion of the design principles and problems.

HAZARD MAPPING AND ZONING

Definition of Hazard Zones

A debris flow can cause damage in three ways:

A. Rapidly moving high-discharge ("climax") surges in and immediately downstream of the transportation zone can destroy objects by violent dynamic thrust and impact;

B. In the distal parts of the deposition zone, discharges and velocities are relatively low and impact loads are reasonably small; yet, large volumes of moving debris can bury areas and objects. Also, the liquid afterflow and flood discharges, being forced out of the normal channel by depositing surges, travel over and erode unprotected surfaces and deposit gravel and other fine debris.

C. Downstream of the deposition zone, there is a relatively large area endangered by flooding when the intersurge or post-event flood travels down some unexpected path (often multiple) away from the regular channel.

High- and low-velocity impact zoning was introduced in a Colorado study by Mears (1977). In the Squamish Highway Debris Torrent and Flooding Hazard Study (Thurber Consultants, 1983), three hazard zones were used: direct impact, indirect

TABLE 2. DEFINITION OF HAZARD ZONES
FOR DEBRIS FLOW HAZARD MAPPING*

Category	Description
Td	Direct impact zone of debris torrent: Zone through which the high-energy debris front may travel; thus the risk of impact damage from one or more surges is high. Material transported through this zone could include boulders and rock fragments as much as several meters in diameter and logs tens of meters long
Ti	Indirect impact zone of debris torrent: Zone through which later surges may be potentially diverted and/or through which afterflow may travel; thus the risk of impact damage is lower. Material could include large rock and log debris, but is more likely to contain rock of less than 1 meter to fine-grained material and organic mulch
Tf	Flood zone due to debris torrent: Zone that is potentially exposed to flooding as a result of blockage of the main channel by debris torrent deposit. The risk of impact damage is low. Fine-grained material and mulch could be contained in the flood water

*From Thurber Consultants, Ltd. (1983).

impact, and flood zone, corresponding to the hazard descriptions given under points A through C above. The precise definitions of the zones are given in Table 2, and a sample hazard map is shown in Figure 2.

Delineation of Hazard Zones

To map the three hazard zones, it is first necessary to delineate the deposition area. The highest point upstream at which deposition can begin is referred to here as the "point of deposition." "End of runout" is defined as a line skirting the lowermost limits of possible debris surge travel. This limit is somewhat gradational, as a flood discharge proceeding downstream of the deposition area may still be heavily charged with bedload and floating debris. It is assumed, however, that no large-scale debris movements will take place downstream of the end of runout. The lateral extent of the deposition area is controlled by the topography.

The point of deposition is located where the channel slope angle falls below a certain limit and/or where lateral confinement of the channel is lost. Hungr and others (1984) reported a limiting angle of 8 to 12° with continuing channel confinement, and 10 to 14° in its absence. Subsequent experience with debris flow events in the lower Fraser Valley indicates that the latter limit may be as high as 16 to 20° on certain creeks. Even higher angles apply in cases where a large part of the debris flow volume originates spontaneously in rockfall or icefall (Hungr, 1985). For example,

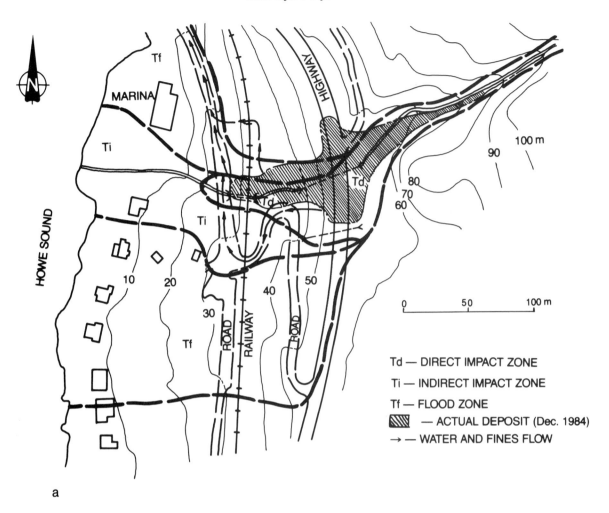

b

Figure 2. Sclufield Creek debris flow of December 4, 1984. a, Comparison of predicted (Td) and actual runout areas. b, Photograph of deposition area.

icefall–debris flow deposits on Mt. Stephen in the Kicking Horse Pass, (Fig. 9), have a deposition angle of 22°.

The presence of channel confinement is more crucial to the maintenance of flow than channel slope angle, provided that it is below about 18°. As shown by our experience, a confined channel is that which carries a debris surge peak discharge with a width-to-depth ratio of less than approximately 5.

The end of runout can be outlined by first estimating the design debris flow magnitude, then assuming an average thickness of the deposits. The deposit area thus obtained can then be distributed over a portion of the fan surface downstream of the point of deposition, using judgment to account for the influence of topographic relief. Lacking adequate mapping, a ratio of 1 (width) to 2 (length) can be assumed. The distal limits of the deposits define the end of runout. This method was used for the Squamish Highway mapping (Thurber Consultants, 1983).

In our experience, a mean deposit thickness of between 1.0 and 1.5 m is reasonable for magnitudes ranging from 10,000 to 50,000 m^3. A formula derived by Innes (1983) from a correlation of volumes and plan dimensions of a number of surveyed debris flow lobes, gives a thickness estimate in the range of 1.1 to 1.7 m for the same magnitude limits. However, this involves extrapolation from smaller deposits.

The runout formula of Takahashi and Yoshida (1979), adapted by Hungr and others (1984) and based on momentum conservation principles, can be used as an additional guide. The formula calculates runout distance downstream of the point at which the channel angle first drops below 10°, and requires the knowledge of peak discharge and flow depth at that point. The formula is applicable only to events with relatively coarse, non-plastic debris material that quickly gains strength by means of drainage when mixing due to rapid motion ceases. Such materials are characteristic of the British Columbia coast. Debris with a substantial fine fraction is capable of slow, oozing movement the runout of which should probably be analyzed by means of a Bingham model. While appropriate analytical techniques exist (e.g., Jeyapalan and others, 1983), the selection of realistic Bingham parameters for application to actual cases is currently a major difficulty (Hungr, 1981).

Empirical formulas for the delineation of runout have also been developed in Japan (e.g., Ikeya, 1981; Takahashi, 1981b), but as yet they have not been adequately tested in British Columbia.

The limits of the smaller direct impact zone are highly dependent on topography. In a situation where the surface of the deposition area approximates an ideal cone, one could use the velocity formulation of the runout equation (Hungr and others, 1984). In the more normal circumstances of complex topography of channels, scarps, forest, and other obstructions, there is little choice but to outline the direct impact limits by means of experienced judgment. The direct impact zone, of course, encompasses the stream channel itself and its immediate vicinity. Consideration must be given to a reactivation of former channels, which often happens during debris flow events.

The flood hazard zone is outlined by assuming that the flood discharge can cross the deposition area boundary at any point of its perimeter and travel down the fall of the land from there.

Figure 2 is an example of a debris flow–hazard map from the Squamish Highway. Sclufield Creek was subject to a debris flow event in December 1984, a year after the mapping. The actual debris deposit and drainage paths are superimposed on the predicted zone limits. There is an approximate coincidence between the direct impact zone and the actual deposit outline, except that the ability of the debris to run up an embankment was underestimated. The lower part of the indirect impact zone was saved by the presence of several cross ditches, which contained much of the debris, diverting flood flow to the right. The actual event magnitude was close to the predicted value. This case history illustrates the importance of topographic details in drawing a hazard zoning map. The analytical tools referred to above represent only an aid to the use of experience and judgment.

Development Restrictions as a Defense Measure

Historically in British Columbia, debris fans have been sites for small communities, mining and logging camps, mills, and even towns such as Port Alice on Vancouver Island (Nasmith and Mercer, 1979). Generally the return intervals of the debris flows or floods (for which the debris flows have often been mistaken) have been sufficiently long relative to the settlement of the area so that the hazard was not perceived.

For most areas of the province, hazard mapping has not yet been carried out to a level that would specify that certain channels have the potential for debris flows, let alone identify the hazard to the extent described above. Legislation and administration programs developed for natural hazards have tended to focus on a response rather than on a planned approach to management (Buchanan, 1983).

Currently the methods by which development can be restricted in areas subject to debris flows are by community planning and zoning or by land subdivision approval. Community plans may designate hazardous areas, or such areas may be given some kind of designation that does not allow for intensive settlement land use, such as park land or agricultural land. A municipal council may prohibit particular uses in areas subject to natural hazards by means of zoning.

The subdivision of land under the Land Titles Act must be approved by an official known as the approving officer (Lister, 1980). Within municipalities this is a senior municipal employee, but in unorganized areas (about 99 percent of the province by area, representing 20 percent of the population) this approving function is performed by the Ministry of Transportation and Highways. When a subdivision application is received for an area subject to a geologic hazard, the ministry requires that the area be investigated by a geotechnical engineer. If a hazard exists, approval may be withheld or a restrictive covenant may be entered against the title so that certain portions of the property must be avoided for construction of dwellings.

WARNING SYSTEMS

Advance Warning

The most commonly discussed pre-event warning systems use correlations of rainfall data with debris flow occurrence (e.g., Ikeya, 1976; Caine, 1980; Takahashi, 1981a).

In British Columbia, however, preliminary research indicates that rainfall or rainfall intensity cannot be used as the sole basis of a debris flow warning system (Miles and Kellerhals, 1981; Thurber Consultants, 1983; Church and Miles, this volume). Other factors that have been found to influence the occurrence of debris flows are snow melt and the amount of antecedent rainfall in the drainage area. One other reason why prediction of debris flows from rainfall data has not been successful is the scarcity of weather records from high altitudes, and, in particular, from the headwaters of debris flow–prone streams where important orographic effects are known to influence the weather patterns.

In 1983, the Ministry of Transportation and Highways located five automated weather stations in an area subject to debris flows along the east side of Howe Sound, immediately north of Vancouver. The stations are located in the middle reaches and headwaters of active debris flow drainages at altitudes ranging up to 1,500 m. They are equipped with continuous-tipping bucket rain gauges and instruments recording wind speed and direction, relative humidity, and temperature. Propane catalytic heaters are used to collect snow precipitation. Data are transmitted continuously at 1-hr intervals using radio transmitters, and, in two cases, the GEOS satellite system. Data processing is automated, based on a microcomputer.

No doubt data from this sophisticated weather observation system will eventually provide a basis for prognosis of debris flow activity. Allowing for a period of debugging, however, there is at present only one season of data available. This was a quiet season, with only one recorded debris flow event (Sclufield Creek, December 14, 1984). The instruments recorded a 24-hr precipitation total of 41 mm, accompanied by a sharp rise in temperature and substantial snowmelt (G. Bonwick, Snow Avalanche Section, British Columbia Ministry of Transportation and Highways, personal communication).

The current contingency plans used by the Ministry stress the role of highway patrols. In 1981, following the death of nine people during the M-Creek event, the Ministry reinforced the patrol system on the Squamish Highway, to the extent that some creek crossings are under full-time surveillance during periods of extreme weather. The patrols observe water discharge changes and flow discoloration. Bridges with insufficient clearance have been provided with lights.

Event Warning Systems

The purpose of an event warning system is to provide an alarm when a debris flow event is already in progress. The only device of this type to have been used in British Columbia is described by Strilaeff (1984). It was installed on Alberta Creek following a February 1983 disaster that caused two deaths and demolished or damaged five houses in the village of Lions Bay, north of Vancouver.

The warning device was commissioned by a resident of one of the remaining houses adjacent to the creek. It consists of two trip-wire sensors with radio transmitters, located in the middle reaches of the creek, and a receiving unit in the protected dwelling. The location of the sensors is 1.7 km distant from the area of the houses. Thus, considering a typical average flow velocity of a major surge, the system could provide a warning period of the order of 3 min.

The sensors consist of a steel cable anchored in bedrock and stretched 1.5 m above the creek bed in a relatively stable reach. The alarm was designed to be triggered by pulling a switch. The transmitter, located at a safe height on the bank, is equipped with a timer device sending a daily test signal to the receiver unit.

The system was never tested by a debris flow. The two trip-wire sensors were disconnected by a deadfall and a minor rockfall from the stream banks within the first winter of their operation. It would appear that more sturdily designed sensors are needed, possibly placed within specially constructed protective structures.

The effectiveness of such a system in protecting dwellings is questionable. Hasty evacuation of a home near a debris flow stream, unless perfectly organized, can cause loss of life rather than prevent it. For example, on Charles Creek in 1981, a person was swept away by flood waters while attempting to flee an endangered dwelling; the house remained undamaged.

Warning systems could be valuable in protecting bridges carrying frequent traffic, where warning lights could be activated with an instantaneous effect. Such systems are in use in Japan. Highway and railway officials are reluctant to use them, however, due to their unreliability and the traffic disruption caused by false alarms. Clearly, development of more reliable systems is needed.

Post-event Warning Systems

Post-event warning systems are simple to provide and can be invaluable on transportation routes, where they warn of a disruption such as burial of road surface by debris, or a bridge collapse.

The British Columbia Railway, whose track follows the Squamish Highway, has for a number of years maintained the practice of checking the track using "speeders" immediately prior to the passage of trains. The major purpose for this is to check for rocks that have fallen on the track.

With higher traffic intensity, an automatic warning device is desirable, and is used at several locations on the major railways. An example of a "slide warning fence" used in the deposition area of the Cathedral Mountain debris flow in the Kicking Horse

Figure 3. Debris flow warning fence along Canadian Pacific Rail track, Cathedral Mountain, Kicking Horse Pass.

suspended from a horizontal wire connected to the controller box. The switch is triggered by the increased tension as the debris flow lifts the fence panels to pass underneath them. The advantage of this arrangement is that it is easy to restore after an event. Other, simpler devices use a weak copper link in the wire to interrupt the current, instead of the controller box system. However, frequent false alarms make these devices unpopular with railway maintenance personnel.

FOREST MANAGEMENT PRACTICES RELATED TO DEBRIS FLOW MITIGATION

Logging operations can be an important contributor to the initiation of debris flows. As well as increasing the volume of debris available in the channel, clear-cut logging causes a delayed loss of root strength and an increase in average pore water pressures (e.g., Wu and Swanston, 1980). Both can lead to more frequent debris flow initiations. Failures of logging road fills and backslopes and plugging of culverts are other important causes of debris flows (e.g., Evans and Lister, 1984).

The British Columbia Ministry of Forests has set guidelines for logging and forest road construction. In addition, each cutting permit contains site-specific requirements. Although the present guidelines do not refer to mass movement specifically, various sections are implicitly relevant to debris flow mitigation.

Sufficient buffer is to be left to protect water courses, although this is usually enforced only with regard to the larger fish-bearing streams. The plan and shape of clear cuts should consider soil protection and water quality, among a number of other factors. The cut areas should be replanted. The impact of roads should be reduced by such measures as locating away from streams, canyons, and slide areas; adapting design specifications to local slopes and soil conditions; building culverts and troughs to handle 25-yr runoff; and preventing drainage from flowing over unstable fills. A maintenance program is required, with drains and water bars constructed to direct runoff away from creeks. Roads should be "retired" when no longer used by removal of culverts and building of cross drains to reestablish natural drainage courses.

These guidelines could go a long way in minimizing the debris flow hazard. They are, however, quite general and open to differences of interpretation. The economics of logging and the health of the forest industry play an important role in determining the extent to which they are followed. The guidelines are presently being rewritten.

A joint task force of the Ministry of Forests and the Ministry of Transportation and Highways is investigating the protection forest concept for use along the Coquihalla Freeway. Such a forest is managed to ensure that there are always healthy trees in place near the creek channels. The stands are unevenly aged; mature trees can be selectively cut, and replanting takes place. This concept is used in the European Alps to reduce the hazards of debris flows and snow avalanches. It does, however, require government subsidization.

Pass since 1965 is shown in Figure 3. The device consists of two lengths of thick wire mounted on wooden posts to form a 1.2-m-high fence. Each wire connects to a "controller box" containing a spring and latch switch that closes when the pre-set wire tension either increases or drops.

The fence illustrated in Figure 3, located along the highest of three levels of track, actuated a stop signal ahead of the middle track crossing during the September 6, 1978, debris flow event (Jackson, 1979). However, the locomotives of a freight train had already passed the signal location. They collided with the debris of the first surge, and were partly buried by the second.

Similar warning devices protect some 20 locations on the western part of the Canadian Pacific Railway system, mostly with regard to rockfall but also against debris flow. Some debris flow fences used consist of chain-link fencing reinforced with slats and

STABILIZATION OF DEBRIS SOURCES

Check Dams

Scour of loose material in the creek bed and undercutting of unstable creek banks are two of the most important processes of debris flow surge growth. Both can be arrested, or reduced, by construction of a series of check dams in the unstable reaches.

The construction of check dams along a steep channel can be quite difficult and expensive, although such dams are used extensively in Europe and Japan. Their construction in these areas relies to a great extent on innovative construction methods using manual labor (Thurber Consultants, 1984). Sometimes, the construction period takes a decade or more.

On Alberta Creek, 17 reinforced concrete check dams, nominally 2.5 m high and 30 m wide along the crest, were considered to protect a 210-m-long reach of a creek at a gradient of 20°. The check dams would hae been constructed in a relatively accessible area, but the estimated price per dam exceeded $50,000 Canadian. Because of the expense, a decision was made to use a concrete lining instead.

A slide deposit of more than 1,000 m^3 of debris in the upper channel of Alberta Creek has been stabilized temporarily by a steel cable net attached to rock anchors and backed by logs. Rockbolts have been used elsewhere to retain large, unstable boulders in a creek channel (Martin and others, 1984).

Creek Channel Linings

Stabilization of the creek bed and protection of the toe of the banks can also be achieved by lining the channel. A short lined section of channel on Charles Creek along the Squamish Highway survived three major debris flow events (Fig. 4). This lining was built to maintain channel alignment upstream of a bridge and protect the abutments. Its performance illustrates the possibility of controlling channel erosion by this means. The lining consisted of riprap with a modal rock diameter of approximately 0.5 m, slush-grouted by concrete to a depth of 0.2 to 0.5 m. The underlying material is coarse, bouldery debris. The channel cross section was a trapezoid 4.5 m deep with side slopes of nearly 45°. The bed-slope angle was 15°. During the November 1983 event, the channel carried a maximum debris flow discharge estimated by eyewitnesses as 295 m^3/sec. The lining suffered only localized damage (as seen in Fig. 4), while a similar unlined cross section 100 m upstream was subject to scour as much as 4 m deep (VanDine, 1985). A lower velocity low-discharge event in 1981 caused no damage at all to the lining.

To stabilize source reaches, however, a lining would need to be installed over long distances at very steep slopes. This introduces three potential problems:

1) The lining may be prone to damage from bank slumps and debris slides, unless these are stabilized to a reasonable degree. In reaches of very unstable banks, check dams are likely to be safer, as they can be made strong and well keyed into the banks.

Figure 4. Grouted riprap lining of Charles Creek channel, shortly after passage of debris flow event. Notice damaged bridge beams.

2) The relative smoothness of a lined channel will induce instability in flood-water flow, creating excessive velocities and slugging or roll waves (Brock, 1969). However, it is unlikely that the smooth channel surface would seriously affect debris surge motion, which is laminar and already in the form of a roll wave (Hungr and others, 1984). Given the fact that a channel designed for passage of debris flow has a discharge capacity many times exceeding that required by flood flow, instability phenomena connected with the latter are of little consequence.

3) Abrasion may create serious maintenance problems for such steep channel linings, even if it affects only the interstitial concrete in grouted riprap.

The Europeans use masonry linings of cut stone. In British Columbia two types of lining have been constructed recently: intact rounded boulders embedded in steel fiber–reinforced concrete in which the projecting boulders have the secondary purpose of dissipating energy of large water flows; and smooth liners

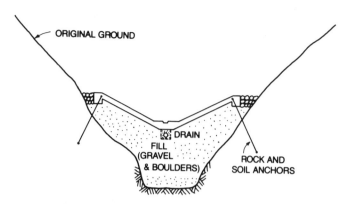

Figure 5. Design concept for gorge stabilization on Alberta Creek, incised in glacial till and outwash deposits. (Based on drawing by Ker Priestman Associates, Ltd., Victoria, and Thurber Consultants, Ltd., Vancouver.)

of concrete, which are hardened with a silica fume additive. As yet, we have no significant operating experience with these liners.

Figure 5 shows a design that is being considered to stabilize a reach on Alberta Creek, immediately upstream of the debris fan apex. Fill placed in the channel invert will provide a firm, well-drained base for the lining, while serving to stabilize shallow bank slumps by means of toe surcharge. The lining will consist of abrasion-resistant, silica fume–hardened concrete anchored to resist uplift. The smoothness of the lining is considered acceptable, due to the high-discharge capacity of the channel planned further downstream. A reduction in design debris flow magnitude of approximately 5,000 m³ is expected to result from stabilizing this 210-m-long reach. Furthermore, housing located along the crests of the channel slopes will be protected against erosion.

CHUTES AND CHANNELS

A debris flow surge moves in the form of a roll wave of relatively uniform velocity but varied discharge (Hungr and others, 1984). Its front rises steeply in an accumulation of bouldery material. Subsequent peak and tail regions are finer and more dilute. The flow resistance is greatest in the coarse frontal region. On slope angles flatter than approximately 16°, the front is propelled forward by the thrust of the more liquid material traveling behind it. This mode of motion is totally dependent on lateral confinement. Should the confinement be lost due to an increase in channel width, the surge peak would collapse, the tail would overtake the frontal accumulation, and deposition would begin.

With regard to the debris flows of the British Columbia coast, it appears that a sufficient confinement exists when the mean width-to-depth ratio of the peak flow cross section is less than approximately 5. The channel cross-section design must take account of the range of surge discharges that can occur even

within a single event. For example, in a rectangular channel 10 m wide at 15° angle, a discharge of 300 m³/sec would flow approximately 3 m deep and would therefore be confined. Conversely, a discharge of 50 m³/sec would have a peak depth of only 1 m and could be expected to begin depositing within the channel. To avoid deposition in the channel, the design cross sections can be tapered toward the base. Cross sections approximating a semi-ellipse can be seen in Europe.

Another consideration is the danger of timber jamming, which dictates that the channel should not be made too narrow and that the side walls should not be vertical.

Well-designed channels normally have a nearly constant cross section without sharp bends, a uniform slope, and a stable lining. Such channels can reduce the potential for blockage by debris and a subsequent avulsion. They extend the transportation zone of a creek into what would otherwise be the deposition area.

A rigid liner such as concrete or grouted riprap will prevent erosion that can be so severe as to prevent the channel from carrying out its function. Channels lined with heavy riprap have been used in British Columbia. However, there is no guideline for selecting a stable particle size. The use of ungrouted riprap can at best be considered as a pragmatic attempt to achieve the most under a given budget. Permanent stability from debris flow erosion can hardly be ensured.

Figure 6 shows a concrete-lined channel planned to pass debris flow through a distance of approximately 500 m down the fan of Alberta Creek. The fan is occupied by the community of Lions Bay, whose houses stand as close as 10 m to the edge of the existing channel.

The new channel has a trapezoidal base part, only wide enough at the bottom to permit equipment to travel on it. The lower parts of the side walls are built at two horizontal in one vertical, the steepest slope at which concrete can be placed without forming. The upper side walls are built as retaining walls, sloping at one-third horizontal in one vertical to discourage debris jamming. The steep walls allow obtaining the required freeboard without encroaching too far into residential properties surrounding the stream.

The channel was designed using the laminar Newtonian flow formula described by Hungr and others (1984). The cross section is intended to have a maximum discharge capacity of 350 m³/sec with 1-m additional freeboard. The required 5:1 width-to-depth ratio is satisfied for all discharges greater than 50 m³/sec. Freeboard in the channel bends was designed using the forced vortex superelevation equation, with a multiplier of 5.0 to account for any lateral rigidity of the debris tongue, as well as possible shock waves.

CHANNEL DIVERSIONS

Diversions of debris flow creeks to more favorable alignments are practicable in the transportation zone where there is no evidence of any blockages or avulsions having occurred. The diversion must be designed to provide not only adequate free-

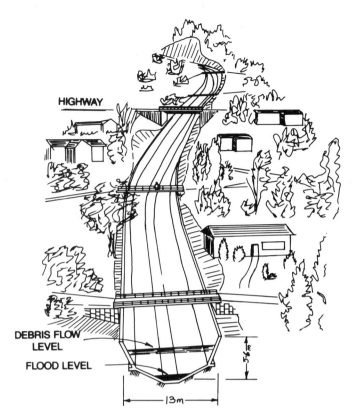

Figure 6. Design concept for debris chute on Alberta Creek fan. (Based on drawing by Ker Priestman Associates and Thurber Consultants).

board to pass the design event, but also to cope with the possibility of slow-moving, smaller flows coming to a temporary halt in the channel.

One noteworthy side-benefit of a diversion is that it can reduce the magnitude of the future debris flows. Commonly, there are several sources of debris along a creek where a flow can be initiated or can grow by picking up debris. A diversion will channel water away from the downstream debris sources. Taking this to the extreme, if it was possible to bleed water from a creek at sufficiently closely spaced locations, then the chance of a debris flow could be completely removed, irrespective of the accumulation of debris in the channel (M. Quick, personal communication).

An early concept for controlling future debris flows on Alberta Creek was to construct a lined diversion channel across the hillside above the community of Lions Bay into an existing debris basin on neighboring Harvey Creek some 600 m away. The design of the channel used a constant grade equal to the average creek slope angle (20°), and a constant trapezoidal cross section with a minimum depth of 10 m. The capacity of this diversion, as estimated by comparison to the mudline cross sections of the existing channel, was three times the design discharge of 300 m³/sec. Notwithstanding this conservative design approach and

the benefit of keeping future debris flows from passing through the community, the proposed diversion was perceived to impose an added risk on some residents who did not live on the creek. Consequently, construction of the diversion did not proceed.

Small-scale diversions have been used in several locations along the Coquihalla Highway to change the course of the creek on the debris fan. Since such diversions involve changes to the deposition area, not the transportation zone, they are discussed together with "open" debris basins.

BRIDGES DESIGNED FOR PASSAGE

Bridges crossing a debris flow path are now normally designed to allow free passage of the design debris discharge. In the transportation zone, where sufficient slope and confinement exist to ensure deposition-free flowage, it is simply necessary to provide sufficient minimum clearance above the design flow depth. In other cases, an additional allowance must be made for the building up of stagnant deposits within the channel.

Design discharge is perhaps the single most difficult parameter of debris flow hydraulics to determine. Observations of peak discharges of debris surges at various sites in British Columbia yielded values more than 10 times as great as the predicted 200-yr maximum instantaneous discharge of water flood on the same creek (e.g., Thurber Consultants, 1983). This contrasts with "bulking rates" measured by the Los Angeles County Flood Control District, which range only up to 2.0 (see Costa, 1984, p. 303).

Hungr and others (1984) showed that the bulking rate approach, based on scaling up a predicted water flood discharge in proportion to the added volume of transported solids, cannot account for the high debris discharges observed in this region, as it neglects the important effects of surge growth. They suggested two methods of discharge prediction, one of which relies on a necessarily crude correlation between peak discharge and event magnitude. The other assumes that the peak discharge originates by the spontaneous failure of a debris dam and uses an idealized formulation for discharge derived from the dam-break theory. Both methods can be regarded merely as first-order approximations, since the factors responsible for the formation of debris surges and their short-lived peaks are at present largely unknown, apart from the highly idealized studies of Takahashi (e.g., 1978). No other published practical means of discharge prediction have been noted.

It should be pointed out that the peak discharge is not a constant, but can vary in the course of a surge's descent down the channel. For example, peak discharge estimates made from superelevation observations after the December 1984 event on Sclufield Creek ranged from 390 m³/sec at the base of a steep reach to 280 m³/sec on a flatter reach 100 m downstream, to 180 m³/sec at the crest of a waterfall 100 m farther downstream. It appears that the surge contracted in length at a reduction in the slope angle, producing a higher peak, then spread out again at a convex channel reach. Such behavior can be expected, given the highly unsteady nature of surge flow.

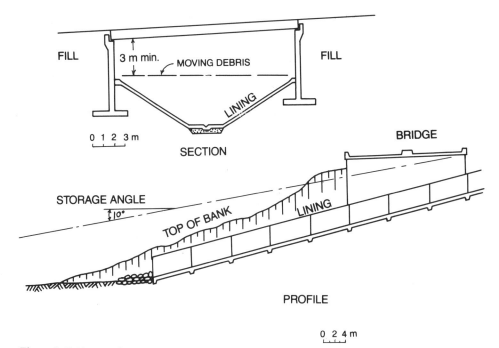

Figure 7. Bridge on Coquihalla Highway, designed for debris passage. Channel must be capable of storing entire design debris flow magnitude below storage line. (Based on design drawing by Ker Priestman Associates.)

Fortunately, however, flow depth is highly insensitive to discharge in laminar flow, no matter which of the several established rheologic flow models is used. For example, assuming a simple Newtonian flow, depth is a third root function of discharge. Given this, an order of magnitude discharge estimate is sufficient to dimension bridge openings. The Newtonian model, calibrated against mud-line observations from several local events (Hungr and others, 1984), was used to design bridges on the Squamish and Coquihalla Highways. The bridge openings were made 3 m higher than the theoretical peak-flow depth, to allow for tumbling logs and waves and to provide a margin of safety. Most of the bridges so designed have clear heights of between 6 and 8 m.

Aside from a sufficient clear height, the bridge design should avoid creating any sudden change in channel cross section or gradient that could promote the onset of deposition. In particular, drop structures located beneath or just upstream of bridges have been avoided, as it was noted that areas at the toe of falls often invite the deposition of boulder pockets.

Often, sufficient clearance cannot be obtained by raising the bridge. For example, in case of railway bridges it is very difficult and expensive to change the rail grade. In such cases, the channel may be subexcavated beneath the bridge by steepening the gradient upstream. Unless the excavated channel can be continued for a long distance downstream, however, a reduction in creek gradient at some point downstream of the bridge occurs, causing deposition. A gradual build-up of deposits under the bridge deck

results, reducing the clear height available to later-arriving debris surges. As illustrated in Figure 7, the important parameter in this situation is the mean slope angle of the surface of the deposits, referred to as the "storage angle." Assuming that the point of deposition will lie initially at the break of the slope, the entire magnitude of the design debris flow event should be capable of being stored within the channel beneath a line inclined at the storage angle, without affecting the bridge.

Obviously, an upper limit estimate of the storage angle is needed in this case, as the available storage volume downstream of the bridge increases with lower storage angles. For coastal British Columbia creeks, this upper limit has been assumed to be 10°, because deep, confined surges have always been observed to flow freely on this slope angle.

SACRIFICIAL BRIDGES OR FORDS

In cases of infrequently traveled or minor roads, the destruction of a bridge may not in itself be cause for serious concern. However, the bridge deck must not cause deposition or an avulsion, or join the debris surge to travel downstream and serve as a battering ram, aggravating the destructive power of the flow. Both of these undesirable circumstances have been known to happen on the Squamish Highway.

Of particular concern is the behavior of a minor subdivision road bridge during the 1981 event on Charles Creek. The bridge consisted of two steel I-beam stringers approximately 0.75 m

Figure 8. M-Creek bridge on British Columbia Rail line north of Vancouver, being excavated following burial by debris flow.

high, covered by timber planking. The bridge had a maximum clearance of only 1.5 m. It was located 20 m downstream from a concrete highway bridge with a 6-m clearance, both being located a short distance downstream of the fan apex, where the channel slope was approximately 14°.

The event was composed of many small surges, with estimated maximum discharge of less than 100 m³/sec. The surges failed to displace the low subdivision road bridge and began depositing behind it, quickly filling in the available channel freeboard. It is assumed that the resulting loss of channel confinement caused further progressive deposition upstream of the small bridge, until the 6-m clearance of the large highway bridge was infilled. The remainder of the debris flow event, amounting to at least 20,000 m³, then deposited above the highway bridge and on top of it, covering the highway to a depth of 6 m. The post-event flood flow was diverted along the highway ditch and caused severe damage to residential properties 500 m distant from the creek.

Sacrificial bridges should be designed so as not to present an obstacle to the debris flow motion when impacted. The above example indicates that even a relatively light bridge structure can cause the deposition of small surges. Based on our knowledge of the behavior of debris flows on the British Columbia coast, light bridges can be considered as "sacrificial" only if they have a fairly high clearance (minimum, approximately 4 m). Such bridges can be expected to pass minor surges with low velocities. Large, rapidly moving surges will destroy them without losing momen-

tum. The bridges could be anchored at one abutment by a flexible anchor, such as a cable loop. Thus the stringers would be thrown to one side by a passing surge, but would not join the flow.

Similar lightweight, medium-clearance bridges are intended for the three subdivision roads that cross the designed channel on Alberta Creek, as described in a previous section.

Fords, or low fills capable of being easily washed away by a debris flow or flood, can serve a similar purpose in the transportation zone. The so-called "Squamish Culvert," used on many local logging roads north of Vancouver, is simply a ford, improved by a low fill of cobbles and boulders. Low summer discharges seep through the fill; winter floods and debris flows wash it out. Good lateral control of the channel is needed to prevent an avulsion.

STRUCTURES DESIGNED FOR BURIAL

In the natural deposition zone of a debris flow stream, it may be possible to accept the eventuality of a structure being buried by a debris flow. The structure should then be designed to withstand the debris flow impact, so as to be serviceable immediately upon re-excavation.

The low-massive bridges used by the British Columbia Railway on its line following Howe Sound are a good example of such structures, although we have no knowledge that they were designed with an awareness of any specific parameters of debris flow dynamics. Figure 8 shows one of the bridges being excavated following the 1981 M Creek debris flow event.

Figure 9. Artist's concept of proposed snow/debris shed on Mount Stephen, Kicking Horse Pass. Deposition area of icefall-triggered debris flows will be on shed roof.

The bridges consist of short, massive box girder reinforced concrete spans about 80 tons in weight, keyed into heavy concrete abutments. The keys are of reinforced concrete, 15 cm wide. They have resisted the impact of an approximately 300-m³ discharge on M Creek in 1981 and Alberta Creek in 1983, although the concrete of the abutment keys cracked in the latter event. The 295-m³/sec discharge of the November 1983 event on Charles Creek, however, succeeded in shearing off one of the keys. The bridge deck was then twisted out of the other abutment, lifted by the debris flow surge, and hurled into Howe Sound some 100 m downstream.

Thrust forces developed by rapidly moving debris surges can be considerable, and can be estimated by methods suggested by such authors as Mears (1977) and Hungr and others (1984). For example, the horizontal thrust applied by a 300-m³/sec debris

discharge on a bridge deck 10 m long by 1 m deep could be as large as 500 tons. This estimate is made accounting for bulk momentum transfer only. Additional structural allowance must be made for point loads created by the impact of large boulders.

DEBRIS SHEDS

Sheds or galleries are a proven device for protection of transportation routes crossing snow avalanche or rockfall paths. In numerous places where debris flows are active on avalanche slopes, the avalanche sheds double as debris sheds and serve to pass debris surges over the road or railway.

As an exceptional case, the avalanche shed being designed at Mt. Stephen, Kicking Horse Pass (Fig. 9), is specifically intended to provide protection against debris flows as well. The debris flows are of an unusual nature, triggered by large-scale icefalls from the Mt. Stephen glacier. As a result, these unusually sluggish flows are often associated with no observable water discharge, depositing to form a cone with a 22° slope angle. Due to this low mobility, the debris is expected to deposit on the roof of the avalanche shed. Maintenance will be required to remove the accumulated debris from the shed and to maintain the high dike freeboard required to channel powder snow avalanches away from the shed portals.

Figure 10 shows a small debris shed used to convey a minor stream across the CN Rail track in the Fraser Canyon. Such narrow debris sheds can be used in a well-confined and stable sector of the transportation zone of a debris flow stream.

OPEN DEBRIS DEPOSITION BASINS

The principle of open basins is to constrain a natural deposition area of a debris flow to predetermined limits laterally, upstream, or downstream. Using a variety of simple provisions, this method is one of the most practical and effective means of controlling the debris flow hazard. Of course, continuing maintenance and removal of deposits is required.

Lateral dikes are constructed parallel to, or nearly parallel with, the flow direction; they should be high enough to contain the expected maximum thickness of deposits in addition to the flow depth and a safety freeboard. If such dikes are needed to deflect debris flow away from a given area, they must also be designed for runup or superelevation of the design discharge. Lateral dikes should always be protected against erosion, preferably by a grouted lining or at least heavy riprap.

Terminal dikes are used to limit the downstream extent of debris deposition and to deflect the debris flow at a sharp angle away from its original path. Usually the reduction in slope resulting from such change in direction will cause bulk deposition behind the terminal dike.

To extend a deposition area artificially upstream, the channel is levelled and widened to promote spreading out of the debris surge and a loss of confinement. A reduction in flow velocity can also be expected to result from this action.

A number of open basins have now been designed in British Columbia using various combinations of the above elements. The earliest large-scale debris flow defense scheme in the province uses series of double lateral dikes to deflect depositing debris away from the town of Port Alice on Vancouver Island (Nasmith and Mercer, 1979). Figure 11 shows the results of a scaled physical model test used to dimension the dikes. Debris flows were modeled by means of a bentonite slurry, its water content calibrated to obtain runout similar to that observed in an actual event. The model tests indicated the need for doubling the dike, to avoid overtopping by depositing debris.

Another open basin was used to protect a prison in the Fraser Valley (Martin and others, 1984). As shown in Figure 12, this consists of a short lateral dike used to direct the debris flow into a wide deposition area inclined at 10° and ending at a

Figure 10. Small debris shed on Canadian National rail line in Fraser Canyon.

massive terminal dike with a 7-m-high crest, aligned obliquely across the fan slope. The dike is riprap-protected. The basin overflow is directed to an insensitive area (parking lot) east of the protected structures.

Both of the above examples involved designs with balanced cut-and-fill quantities. This is not always economically advantageous, however. On road projects, open debris basins can sometimes be easily constructed in conjunction with the required borrowing of gravel from debris fans. Figure 13 shows a basin on the Trans-Canada Highway in the lower Fraser Valley near Chilliwack, created by shaping of a large gravel pit so as to intercept the outlet of a debris channel. The gradual widening and gradient reduction within the pit are intended to achieve the maximum spreading of debris deposits, so that the volume capacity of the pit, being several times larger than the design debris flow magnitude, can be fully utilized to reduce maintenance. The inlet channel of the basin is protected by grouted riprap.

At another site near Chilliwack, a series of lateral and terminal dikes have been designed as 100 percent fill structures, making use of a large surplus of earth and rockfill material from the adjacent road excavation.

Figure 11. Marginal dikes deflecting depositing debris from community of Port Alice—a physical model test. (After Nasmith and Mercer, 1979; reproduced by permission.)

Figure 12. Terminal dike protecting Agassiz correctional institution. (Courtesy of D. Martin, Piteau Associates, Ltd., Vancouver.)

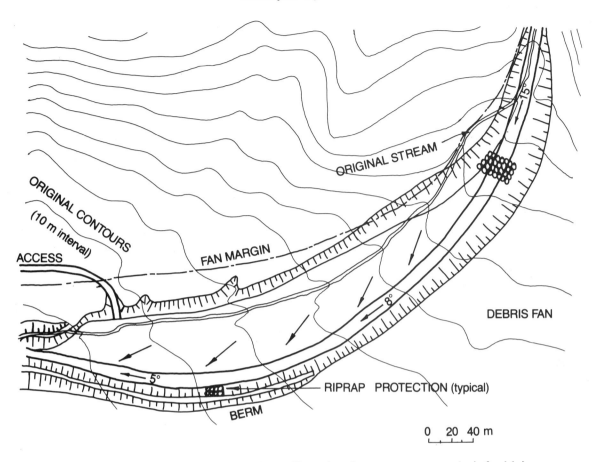

Figure 13. Gravel borrow pit on Ted Creek near Hope, shaped to act as open storage basin for debris flow. Design event magnitude is 60,000 m³. (Design drawing by Ministry of Transportation and Highways, based on concept by Thurber Consultants.)

In laying out open debris basins, it is advantageous to utilize as much of the original natural deposition area as possible. Often, the diking constraints are used merely to prevent future expansion of the deposits in a certain direction. Similar methods are used in dimensioning basins as those described in connection with mapping of the runout zone, except that in this case there are attempts to modify the existing topography and provide suitable constraints. A method for estimating runup against terminal dikes, as a function of flow velocity and depth, was suggested by Hungr and others (1984).

CLOSED DEBRIS BARRIERS AND BASINS

Siting and Dimensioning of Debris Barriers

Closed barriers need not be located in the deposition zone or on the debris fan. A suitable location is chosen along the lower part of the debris flow path, a barrier is erected across it and a basin is created behind. The barrier is provided with both a straining outlet to pass water discharges and a spillway to handle

emergency debris overflow. Access for removal of debris from the basin is required.

In British Columbia, the storage capacity of debris basins has been designed to contain the full "design event magnitude," that is, the estimated maximum volume of debris that can be transported in a single event. No safety factor or multiplier has been used on magnitude estimates; overflow spillways are relied upon to pass possible excess volumes safely over the barriers.

The means of estimating design magnitude used—as briefly described elsewhere (Hungr and others, 1984; VanDine, 1985)—have now been further developed. They are based on a detailed inspection and description of the entire length of the debris flow path, which notes factors such as the width, slope, and particle size of the creek bed, height, angle, and degree of stability of the banks. The design debris flow magnitude is estimated from these parameters by empirical means, taking into account any documented events in the drainage under consideration.

The depth of the basin storage space is measured from the crest of the emergency spillway. The space available behind the barrier is a function of the vertical angle of the surface of the

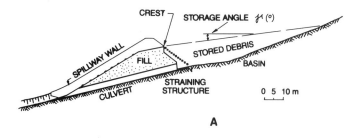

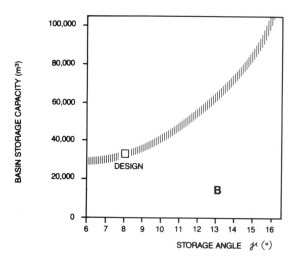

Figure 14. a, Storage angle definition. b, Storage angle relationship with basin capacity.

debris, referred to as the "storage angle" (Fig. 14). This same angle is used in estimating storage beneath bridges, although conservative design in the present case requires a lower limit estimate of its value. This is well illustrated by Figure 14b, which shows the storage volume–storage angle function of a debris basin similar to that shown in Figure 15. For a given design volume, a very great reduction in crest height of the barrier could be accepted, if a greater storage angle could be relied upon. The overall cost of the structure reflected in the volumes of material placed and moved is strongly related to the crest height. Therefore, a good estimate of the storage angle is very important to the economy of the structure.

The approach taken in the design of three barriers along the Squamish Highway and several on the Coquihalla Freeway was to assume a storage angle only so great that the last surge of a debris flow event, traveling over the surface of a basin full of debris, would achieve a complete runout before reaching the barrier. The runout equation of Takahashi and Yoshida (1979), adapted by Hungr and others (1984), was used to make the runout estimate.

The important assumption implicit in this approach is that the debris deposited in the basin rapidly attains a sufficient amount of shear strength to support the adopted storage angle (ranging between 4 and 8°). There is little doubt that this condition is satisfied in case of the coastal debris flows, the material of which has little or plastic fines and drains relatively rapidly on deposition. Where finer debris exists, however, plastic yielding of the highly surcharged debris mass in the basin may cause gradual leveling of the deposit's surface and extrusion of material through the emergency spillway. A reduction in the assumed storage angle would be necessary to avoid this, resulting in a greater basin depth. No practical means of predicting the storage angle now exists for this type of debris. The problem involves a complex interplay of time, discharge, drainage, and shear strength.

The height of the spillway crest is also designed to resist runup by the first-arriving surges. The runup equation (Hungr and others, 1984) has been used to check that the spillway entry cannot be reached by debris surges whether the basin is empty, full, or filled to an intermediate level.

It must be assured that, in the event of an overflow, the discharge will pass over the spillway rather than over the wing of the barrier, especially for earthfill barriers which could be destroyed by uncontrolled overflow. The crest of the barrier is therefore sloped toward the spillway, typically at an angle similar to the original slope of the stream at the barrier location.

Closed basins can be designed as balanced structures, using material excavated from the basin space to build the barrier. Where a natural storage area is available, a barrier can be built with little or no excavation. Alternatively, a basin can be excavated below the existing creek-bed level, and the narrow outlet of the excavation is spanned by a small barrier structure (Fig. 16). Such design alternatives are selected to make the best use of available site conditions. In one example, rockfill obtained from the excavation of a basin on one creek was used to construct a barrier on another, under a single contract.

Other Design Considerations

Most debris barriers in British Columbia have been designed as earthfill structures. This is a design well suited to the use of large earthmoving equipment, which is preferred by local contractors and is consequently economical. In contrast, concrete and masonry gravity or arch dam designs are prevalent in Europe.

An example of an earthfill structure completed recently on Harvey Creek, Squamish Highway, is shown in Figure 15. It consists of an excavated basin fronted by an earthfill embankment that incorporates a double central drainage culvert, a slotted straining structure, and a debris spillway. The embankment is designed as a water-retaining structure with a low-permeability filtered upstream core. This is to prevent failure of the embankment, founded on a steep slope, in the event that the straining structure becomes obstructed by debris.

The straining structure consists of an oblique, concrete-lined shaft supported by fill, the upstream side of which is covered by a series of removable reinforced concrete beams. The beams are placed in hard rubber seats and are designed to resist point im-

a

b

Figure 15. Debris barrier on Harvey Creek, Squamish Highway. a, Downstream face and spillway, with basin in background. b, Straining structure and culvert.

Figure 16. Excavated debris basin on Magnesia Creek, Squamish Highway.

pact. They can be lifted out to gain access into the structure during cleaning. A standard precast double box culvert connects from the base of the structure to the downstream toe of the embankment. It is designed to carry the 200-yr flood discharge.

The emergency debris spillway is dimensioned to carry the full maximum estimated discharge of the design event without undue constriction. This has been necessitated by the requirement that the barrier should remain undamaged, even when subjected to a design event while full of debris. Large concrete ribs placed across the spillway are intended to prevent the debris flow from accelerating excessively on the steep spillway slope. The barrier face is protected by a grouted riprap lining on the upstream side and adjacent to the spillway.

Figure 16 shows a basin created by rock excavation below the original creek grade. A straining structure very similar to that described above spans the narrow opening of the rock excavation in the form of a buttress dam. No spillway is provided, as debris

can safely flow over the massive crest beam of the barrier and remain contained in the rock gorge downstream.

The two structures described were built in sensitive, inhabited areas, and, consequently, comprise a high degree of conservatism to ensure continuing safe performance. In less critical locations, considerably less sophisticated and more economical designs have been used. Figure 17 is an example of a simple earthfill barrier designed to protect a culvert on the Coquihalla Freeway. Similar principles are applied here as on the Harvey Creek structure described above. The embankment is not zoned but incorporates a rockfill toe drain. Water drainage is provided by three corrugated steel pipe culverts placed at different levels and protected by simple debris racks. The culverts provide drainage in turn as the basin fills up, until in the final instance, drainage can occur over the shaped spillway. The spillway is protected by grouted riprap. The central culvert rack is removable for cleaning.

CONCLUSIONS

A variety of engineering concepts have been developed recently in British Columbia as a response to debris flow hazards. Two broad types exist: active and passive measures. Because response has been required to specific sites that have incurred damage, active measures have been used. A systematic preventive approach toward debris flow has only begun to be developed in this province. Undoubtedly continued pressures for development of potentially hazardous sites will lead to further research and improvement in the procedures described in this chapter. Research is required particularly with regard to estimating debris discharge, erosiveness, and storage angle and runout for debris containing fine grain sizes.

ACKNOWLEDGMENTS

The majority of the work described herein was initiated and supported by the British Columbia Ministry of Transportation and Highways. The ministry's active interest in debris flow protection has brought about significant advances in this branch of civil engineering.

We are grateful to G. F. Buck and G. Bonwick, D. Martin, H. W. Nasmith, and J. Price for providing information and graphic material, and to M. Church and J. E. Costa for critical reviews of the manuscript.

REFERENCES CITED

Brock, R. R., 1969, Development of roll-wave trains in open channels: American Society of Civil Engineers Journal of the Hydraulics Division, v. 96, no. HY 4, p. 1401–1427.

Broscoe, A. J., and Thompson, S., 1969, Observations on an alpine mudflow, Steele Creek, Yukon: Canadian Journal of Earth Sciences, v. 6, p. 219–229.

Buchanan, R. B., 1983, An assessment of natural hazards management in British Columbia [M.A. thesis]: University of Victoria, 260 p.

Caine, N., 1980, The rainfall intensity-duration control of shallow landslides and debris flows: Geografiska Annaler, v. 62A, no. 12, p. 23–27.

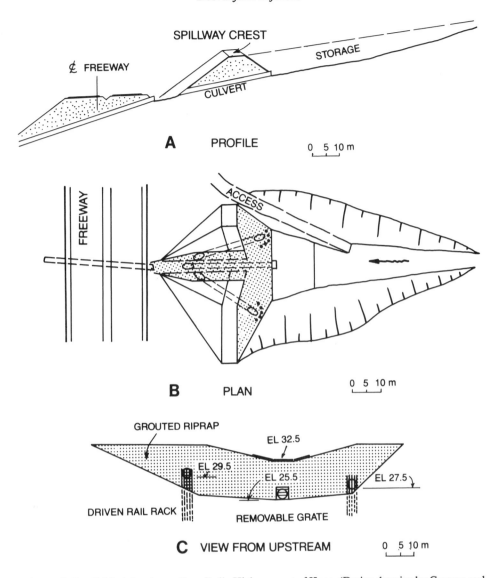

Figure 17. Small debris barrier on Coquihalla Highway east of Hope. (Design drawing by Graeme and Murray, Ltd., Victoria, based on concept by Thurber Consultants.)

Clague, J. J., Evans, S. G., and Blown, J., 1985, A debris flow triggered by the breaching of moraine-dammed lake, Klattasine Creek, British Columbia, Canadian Journal of Earth Sciences, v. 22 (in press).

Costa, J. E., 1984, Physical geomorphology of debris flows, *in* Costa, J. E., and Fleisher, P. J., eds., Developments and applications in geomorphology: Berlin, Springer-Verlag, p. 269–317.

Eisbacher, G. H., and Clague, J. J., 1984, Destructive mass movements in high mountains; Hazard and management: Geological Survey of Canada Professional Paper 84-16, 230 p.

Evans, S. G., and Lister, D. R., 1984, The geomorphic effects of the July 1983 rainstorms in the southern Cordillera and their impact on transportation facilities: Geological Survey of Canada Professional Paper 84-1B, p. 223–235.

Hungr, O., 1981, Dynamics of rock avalanches and other types of slope movements [Ph.D. thesis]: Edmonton, University of Alberta, 500 p.

——, 1985, Transport mechanisms in debris flows of the Canadian Cordillera: Geological Society of America Abstracts with Programs, v. 17, p. 362.

Hungr, O., Morgan, G. C., and Kellerhals, R., 1984, Quantitative analysis of debris torrent hazards for design of remedial measures: Canadian Geotechnical Journal, v. 21, p. 663–677.

Ikeya, H., 1976, Introduction to sabo works; The preservation of land against sediment disaster: Tokyo, Japan Sabo Association, 168 p.

——, 1981, A method of designation for area in danger of debris flow, *in* Erosion and sediment transport in Pacific Rim steeplands: Christchurch, New Zealand, International Association of Hydrological Sciences, no. 132, p. 576–587.

Innes, J. L., 1983, Lichenometric dating of debris-flow deposits in the Scottish Highlands: Earth Surface Processes and Landforms, v. 8, p. 579–588.

Jackson, L. E., Jr., 1979, A catastropic glacial outbrust flood *(jokulhlaup)* mechanism for debris flow generation at the Spiral Tunnels, Kicking Horse River

Basin, British Columbia: Canadian Geotechnical Journal, v. 16, p. 806–813.

Jeyapalan, J. K., Duncan, J. M., and Seed, H. B., 1983, Analyses of flow failures of mine tailings dams: American Society of Civil Engineers Journal of Geotechnical Engineering, v. 109, no. GT 2, p. 150–171.

Lister, D. R., 1980, Geotechnical studies and land subdivision in British Columbia, *in* Proceedings, Specialty Conference on Slope Stability Problems in Urban Areas: Toronto, Canadian Geotechnical Society Paper 12, 14 p.

Lister, D. R., Morgan, G. C., VanDine, D. F., and Kerr, J.W.G., 1984, Debris torrents in Howe Sound, British Columbia: Proceedings, 4th International symposium on landslides, Toronto, v. 1, p. 649–654.

Martin, D. C., Piteau, D. R., Pearce, R. A., and Hawley, P. M., 1984, Remedial measures for debris flows at the Agassiz Mountain Institution, British Columbia: Canadian Geotechnical Journal, v. 21, p. 505–517.

Mears, A. I., 1977, Debris-flow hazard analysis and mitigation; An example from Glenwood Springs, Colorado: Denver, Colorado Geological Survey Information Series 8, 45 p.

Miles, M. J., and Kellerhals, R., 1981, Some engineering aspects of debris torrents: Fredericton, New Brunswick, 5th Canadian Hydrotechnical Conference (unpublished).

Nasmith, H. W., and Mercer, A. G., 1979, Design of dykes to protect against debris flows at Port Alice, British Columbia: Canadian Geotechnical Journal, v. 16, p. 748–757.

Strilaeff, P. W., 1984, Debris torrent alert system for Alberta Creek at Lions Bay: British Columbia Professional Engineer, v. 35, no. 2, p. 14–16.

Swanston, D. N., 1974, Slope stability problems associated with timber harvesting in mountainous regions of the western United States: U.S. Department of Agriculture, Forest Service, Pacific Northwest Forest and Range Experimental Station General Technical Report PNW-21, 14 p.

Takahashi, T., 1978, Mechanical characteristics of debris flow: American Society of Civil Engineers Journal of the Hydraulics Division, v. 104, p. 1153–1169.

—— , 1981a, Debris flow: Annual Review of Fluid Mechanics, v. 13, p. 57–77.

—— , 1981b, Estimation of potential debris flow and their hazardous zones; Soft countermeasures for a disaster; Journal of Natural Disaster Science, v. 3, p. 57–89.

Takahashi, T., and Yoshida, H., 1979, Study on the deposition of debris flows; Pt. 1, Deposition due to abrupt change of bed slope: Japan, Kyoto University, Annals, Disaster Prevention Research Institute, v. Z2, p. B-2.

Thurber Consultants, 1983, Debris torrent and flooding hazards, Highway 99, Howe, Sound: Victoria, British Columbia, Ministry of Transportation and Highways, 25 p., (unpublished).

—— , 1984, Debris torrents; A review of mitigative measures: Victoria, British Columbia, Ministry of Transportation and Highways, 32 p., (unpublished).

—— , 1985, Debris torrent assessment, Wahleach and Floods, Highway 1, Hope to Boston Bar Creek Summit, Coquihalla Highway: Victoria, British Columbia, Ministry of Transportation and Highways, 27 p., (unpublished).

VanDine, D. F., 1985, Debris flows and debris torrents in the southern Canadian Cordillera: Canadian Geotechnical Journal, v. 22, p. 44–68.

Varnes, D. J., 1978, Slope movement types and processes, *in* Schuster, R. L., and Krizek, R. J., eds., Landslides; Analysis and control: Washington, D.C., National Academy of Sciences Transportation Research Board Special Report 176, p. 11–33.

Wu, T. H., and Swanston, D. N., 1980, Risk of landslides in shallow soils and its relation to clearcutting in southeastern Alaska: Forest Service, v. 26, p. 495–510.

MANUSCRIPT ACCEPTED BY THE SOCIETY DECEMBER 29, 1986

Geological Society of America
Reviews in Engineering Geology, Volume VII
1987

On debris flow/avalanche mitigation and control, San Francisco Bay area, California

Joel E. Baldwin II
Baldwin-Wright, Inc.
P.O. Box 1272
Pacifica, California 94044

Howard F. Donley
609 Price Avenue, Suite 102
Redwood City, California 94063

Terry R. Howard
Department of Geology
University of Idaho
Moscow, Idaho 83843

ABSTRACT

A storm that occurred January 3–5, 1982 in the San Francisco Bay area precipitated a host of mitigation schemes to provide protection against the now-perceived widespread debris flow/avalanche hazard. These procedures are now being designed and constructed in the Bay area. Removal of colluvium and loose bedrock in the source area mitigates the hazard of debris flows—a costly measure requiring access for equipment. Reinforcement of oversteepened slopes with rock riprap has proven to be an economical and expeditious means of supporting the oversteepened head scarp and flanks of a source area scar. In seismically active regions, the use of riprap for repair of source areas should be carefully scrutinized, especially when considered for critical structure sites.

Retaining walls are in common use to support unstable slopes in the source area. Their design is based on at-rest earth pressures that can range from an equivalent fluid pressure of 7,070 N/m^3 to as much as 12,570 N/m^3. Free-standing baffles of timber or steel, embedded in the main track of a confined debris flow/avalanche, reduce velocity but allow deposition to occur in an area accessible to maintenance equipment. Baffles can be spanned by heavy-gauge chain-link or gabion wire to provide a similar effect.

Impact walls capable of arresting and containing more than 150 m^3 of debris, after sustaining an instantaneous impact load of at least 19,640 N/m^3, are constructed on or at the hillside base. Deflection walls can be designed to direct flows to a specified depositional area. Sites positioned on fans or within drainages of limited area are protected by earthern basins designed for impact and containment of debris. Free drainage of a portion of the downstream face mitigates potentially adverse conditions that can develop due to captured runoff. The embankments are designed for an impact force of at least 19,640 N/m^3, unless constructed with an upstream baffle system.

Lessons learned since 1982 in the San Francisco Bay area have changed the thinking of geotechnical consultants on new hillside development. Numerous sites have been protected by one or more of these engineered mitigation schemes. Thousands of hazardous sites remain, however, that are likely to be impacted by future debris flows/avalanches.

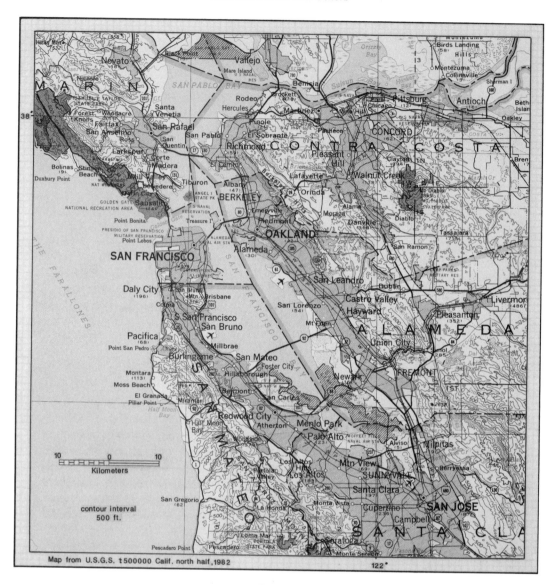

Figure 1. Map showing San Francisco Bay area.

INTRODUCTION

Landslide hazards in the San Francisco Bay area, mostly posed by large-scale landslides, have been recognized for quite some time (Brabb and others, 1972; Brabb and Pampeyan, 1972; Nilsen and others, 1979). Nevertheless, the winter of 1982 established a new awareness in the Bay area for a particular, catastrophic type of landslide known as a debris flow/avalanche (Varnes, 1978).

In the winter of 1982, the Bay area was subject to one or several storms with prolonged and intense rainfall that triggered thousands of debris flows/avalanches. Although many individual landslides had local dimensions of modest proportions, the widespread distribution and devastating effect to the region was enormous (Smith and others, 1982). For example, the 35-km² coastal hillside city of Pacifica, California (Fig. 1), suffered more than 475 slope failures of this type, mostly on the evening of January 4, 1982. Thousands of other debris flows/avalanches occurred during the same 20- to 36-hr storm event (January 3–5) throughout the Bay area, contributing to a loss of 33 lives, and damaging or destroying more than 7,000 structures of one kind or another, for a real cost totaling more than $280 million (Brown, 1984).

Aside from the associated widespread physical losses, a tragic aspect of this event is that the regional hazard from debris flows had gone essentially unrecognized prior to 1982. As a result, pre-1982 site engineering geologic characterization, for the most part, failed to recognize debris flow/avalanche processes, leaving hillside structures unprotected. In fact, many sites were developed within drainage basins or at the foot of hillsides susceptible to debris flow/avalanche failure.

Since 1982, recognition, evaluation, and mitigation of the perceived debris flow/avalanche hazard has been a principal occupation of private consulting firms, as well as local, state, and federal governmental earth science and engineering agencies within the San Francisco Bay area. This concentrated effort has led to a confident and aggressive approach to implementing debris flow/avalanche mitigation measures for sites with obvious defects.

This chapter describes the general geologic and soil engineering state-of-practice considerations that form the basis for debris flow/avalanche hazard mitigation design in the San Francisco Bay area. We describe design parameters and illustrate a representative sample of mitigation devices from case histories.

DESIGN CONSIDERATIONS

Engineering Geology

Engineering geologic site characterization is probably the most important factor in designing and positioning one or more effective debris flow/avalanche mitigation devices. This characterization allows a determination of whether a slope has a potential for failure, whether the hazard can be mitigated, and onto what segment of the slope a proposed mitigation device would be most effectively positioned. Campbell (1975) offered a good understanding of the debris flow/avalanches, and defined the most susceptible terrain. With his contribution, coupled with the experience gained locally from the 1982 storm, we soon realized that a debris flow/avalanche can occur on virtually any soil-mantled hillside subject to at least 25 mm of antecedent rainfall, and then to prolonged, intense rainfall (i.e., 6.25 mm/hr over a 3- to 4-hr period; Campbell, 1975); this is regardless of slope aspect and underlying lithology, provided that runoff is concentrated, that the slope gradient ranges from 50 to 100 percent, and that the soil mantle is generally cohesionless (Howard and others, 1987). Wieczorek and Sarmiento (1983) and Dietrich and others (1987) have worked extensively with debris flow/avalanche processes in the San Francisco Bay area and have delineated additional hydrologic and geologic factors that contribute to debris flow/avalanche initiation.

We have learned that the most common site for debris flow/avalanche initiation is in the headward reach of first-order drainages (Reneau and others, 1984), although other geomorphic sites experienced failure. Examples include artificially oversteepened colluvial slopes; preexisting, steep landslide scarps; and, to a lesser extent, uniform, planar slopes. In all cases, however, concentrated surface runoff and/or perched ground water (probably both, acting simultaneously) were primary factors of initiation (Dietrich and others, 1987; Wieczorek and Sarmiento, 1983).

For a mitigation device to be effective, it must be positioned with respect to the appropriate segment of a debris flow/ava-

Figure 2. Southeasterly view of drainage basin in Pacifica, California, illustrating components of debris flow/avalanche; source area, main track, and depositional area. This photograph demonstrates how natural revegetation can reduce recognition of potential slope hazard.

lanche. Following Campbell (1975), we characterize three segments: source area; main track; and depositional area (Fig. 2):

Source Area. This is the region where the regolith detaches as a slide, commonly at preexisting, mappable tension cracks or microscarps (Fig. 3a) that commonly extend downward through the soil to or near the bedrock contact. Downslope from the source area, the saturated "soil" mass experiences an instantaneous loss of strength and transforms into a debris flow/avalanche (Fig. 3b). The soil and water slurry then completely evacuates the source area, leaving a "spoon-shaped" scar on the hillside.

Main Track. This is the commonly scoured, original ground surface over which the debris flow/avalanche descends the slope, with gradually increasing velocity to a terminal velocity dependent on steepness, channel width, and effective viscosity of the flowing mass (Figs. 3c, d). Frictional contact between the flow and slope surface allows the debris flow/avalanche to scour vegetation and the upper few to tens of centimeters of colluvium from the slope. As the flow incorporates additional mass, the momentum of the flow increases along the main track.

Depositional Area. Once the debris flow/avalanche encounters a marked decrease in slope gradient (i.e., base of slope or through impact with obstructions) deposition begins to occur

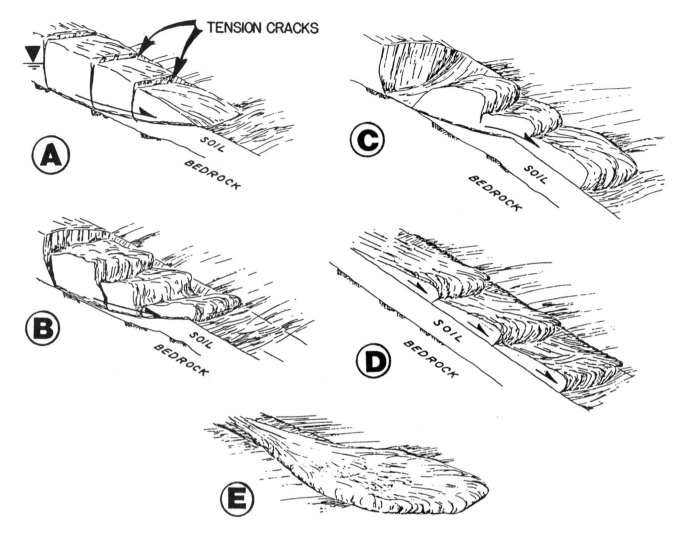

Figure 3. Sequence of failure and mode of transport of a debris flow/avalanche. A, Initiation of failure by slippage of coherent slab of soil in source area along rupture surface in soil or colluvium or at contact of soil or colluvium and bedrock, with detachment occurring along preexisting tension cracks. B, Agitation of saturated soil mass causes instantaneous reduction of strength and initiation of flowage within source area. C, Evacuation of source area by "liquified" soil mass, and downslope descent over original ground surface (main track). D, Progressive acceleration of debris flow/avalanche in main track, stripping vegetation and surficial soil as it proceeds. E, Deposition of debris flow/avalanche at slope base of (fan).

(Fig. 3e). The limits of the debris flow/avalanche depositional area are difficult to characterize, although Campbell cited slopes of about 20 percent and less as common for deposition. However, where appreciable solid material is incorporated into the flow in the main track, and/or for debris flows in well-drained granular soil, deposition can occur not far from the source area, well up on the slope. Conversely, debris flows that occur in highly confined drainage channels can accommodate higher runoff flows (even if ephemeral), thereby generating a more fluidized flow, with much greater runout, far beyond the expected area of deposition.

Geotechnical Engineering

Design of debris flow/avalanche mitigation devices over the past three years in the San Francisco Bay area is based principally upon an empirical approach; it utilizes an ultimate impact force of 19,640 N/m^3 of equivalent fluid pressure suggested by Hollingsworth and Kovacs (1981) following their experience with debris flows during the winter of 1975 in southern California.

The ultimate design force of 19,640 N/m^3 is utilized when positioning a device at right angles to the anticipated debris flow/

avalanche path. In principle, by orienting the device at an angle to the flow path, the ultimate design force can be reduced proportional to the sine of the acute angle between the device and the flow path.

Design pressure also varies when considering slope position of the device with respect to the location on the slope profile (Fig. 4). For example, if a device is to provide support to a source area scarp underlain by sandy colluvium, then an active pressure as low as 7,070 N/m³ might be used for design. A finer grained material at the same position may require a higher at-rest pressure.

The design active force increases exponentially away from the source area head scarp, 7,070 N/m³ to the ultimate value of 19,640 N/m³ near the transition zone between the source area and the main track. This design value is maintained along the main track, and extended for an "estimated" distance beyond the transition zone into the depositional area; it can be based upon slope angle and length, and upon an estimate of thickness of the debris flow. The distance within the depositional area for application of an impact force of 19,640 N/m³ should be considered a function of the expected runout; this depends, in turn, on a variety of factors, including composition, volume of flow, channel, and fan geometry. In principle, therefore, a mitigation device can be designed for different impact force values, depending on its position relative to the source area and its orientation relative to the expected debris flow/avalanche path.

Retaining walls have been constructed to support the oversteepened slopes within the source area; baffles in the main track to control the velocity with which the debris flow descends the slope; walls and baffles in the main track or depositional area to deflect the debris flow to a safe area for clean-out, and/or to sustain the full impact force, usually at the base of the slope. The generally preferred design goal is to control the velocity and course of descent, and to provide containment and clean out at a safe location at the base of the slope or slope segment. However, we have encountered drainage-basin conditions that limit this goal, and which require other more creative designs.

SOME MITIGATION DEVICE DESIGN AND CONSTRUCTION DETAILS

Source Area Mitigation

Slope Modification. Retrogressive landslide events on oversteepened slopes composing the source area scar of a debris flow can present a hazard equal to the event that formed the scar. This applies not only to recent debris flow scars, but also to revegetated, subdued, older debris flow scars that formed during historic events. The general consensus among practitioners is that control of subsurface drainage and diversion of surface drainage, although important components, fall short of providing a comprehensive hazard mitigation scheme. Grading the source area scar to a uniform slope, thus having a finished surface gradient equal to or less than the adjacent slopes, is a common means of

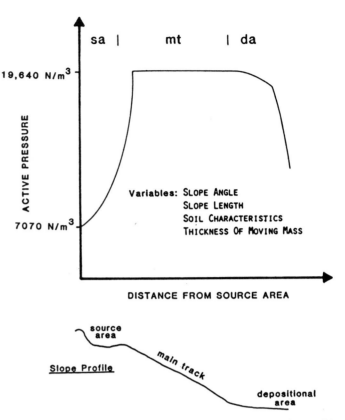

Figure 4. Diagram and slope profile illustrating state-of-practice considerations for design of mitigation devices relative to source area; sa refers to source area, mt to main track, da to depositional area.

mitigating potential hazards. This can be accomplished where clear access to the source area by excavation equipment is provided, and where the cost of trucking the spoil offsite is not prohibitive. Figure 5 illustrates a dissected drainage basin where colluvium was removed from the entire unstable portion of the slope.

An important consequence of this grading for mitigation is the removal of soil-supporting vegetation; in turn, this allows severe erosion on the slope and siltation at the base of the slope. It is therefore imperative that comprehensive erosion and sediment control form an integral part of the mitigation. Amimoto (1981) offered a wide variety of ways to reduce slope erosion. It is recommended that grading take place in the spring or early summer months, to allow ample time for revegetation of the denuded slope. Hydromulching is a common way to apply seed and fertilizer, and to promote accelerated growth of ground cover.

Lateral surface drains, extending across the graded drainage basin, have been constructed in many cases. Construction of surface drainage facilities on a graded slope, however, requires a well-coordinated maintenance program to assure that the drains do not become clogged, thereby causing concentrated runoff to

Figure 5. Southeasterly view of slope in Pacifica, California, where soil removal (arrows) within source areas and along main track of debris flows mitigated debris flow/avalanche hazard to residential sites at toe of slope.

spill onto the slope and result in renewed debris flow/avalanche initiation. This was a common occurrence on numerous, older engineered slopes during the 1982 event that resulted in significant slope failures. In fact, the locality of Figure 5 has experienced some flooding at the toe of the graded slope due to failure of the surface drainage system by increased runoff and siltation.

Riprap. Oversteepened slopes forming the source area scar have been successfully supported by installing riprap (Fig. 6). This measure requires clear-grading equipment access unless the work can be accomplished by hand. The principal component is a keyway that is graded near the toe of the scar to resist sliding of the riprap (Fig. 7). The keyway base usually extends a minimum depth of 1 m into bedrock, and should have a minimum 2 percent base gradient into the slope to provide appropriate subdrainage control. The riprap is composed of angular, resistant rock, commonly having a maximum dimension no less than 18 in. The riprap is separated from the underlying soil by a drainage filter fabric to mitigate the potential for piping or erosion of the soil foundation. The finished slope of the riprap is generally recommended to be no steeper than 50 percent, especially in tectonically active regions. If the finished riprap slope is steeper, it is generally recommended that the surface be covered with chain-link fence, securely anchored to the slope, and that a chain-link

fence be constructed at the toe of the riprap to contain fugitive boulders (see Fig. 6b).

Retaining Walls. A retaining wall is an effective measure for supporting oversteepened slopes in the source area. The most common type employed in the San Francisco Bay area is a soldier pile retaining wall. Depending on the earth material being supported and the ground-water conditions upslope from the source area, the wall is designed for an active equivalent fluid pressure that can range from 7,070 N/m^3 to as much as 12,570 N/m^3. The foundation for the wall generally comprises drilled or hand-dug, cast-in-place, reinforced concrete piers that are founded in bedrock and typically spaced 2 m. The reinforcement for the piers is generally steel I-beams spanned by treated timber lagging to support the soil. Depending on the upslope conditions, retaining walls are provided with at least 0.5 m of freeboard to reduce the potential of overtopping by soil failures originating farther upslope. Tie-backs are generally required if the wall exceeds 3 m in height.

Main Track and Depositional Area Mitigation

Baffles. A baffle system can be constructed across the potentially unstable drainage basin downslope from the source area to deflect, check, or regulate the flow of a potential debris flow/avalanche. The baffles can be constructed of treated timber or steel, having dimensions capable of resisting bending or breakage by an advancing flow. Baffles can be emplaced in staggered, upstream-downstream rows having a typical spacing of 2 to 3 m. The configuration and number of baffles and their spacing is generally governed by channel characteristics and mitigation requirements, and must be designed with respect to eventual debris clean-out. Baffles have also been designed for "sacrificial" utilization where the perceived flow force is expected to exceed cost-effective or practical installation. This type of system is expected to fail following impact, and simultaneously offer some resistance to flow advance. In this case, baffles can be placed in foundation holes filled with sand or soil rather than concrete to allow for easy removal and replacement.

Baffle systems can be designed as isolated posts, or they can be spanned by heavy-gauge chain-link or gabion wire (debris fences, Fig. 8). Use of chain-link or gabion wire as a component of the baffle system should offer free drainage for the accumulated debris. Keep in mind, however, that spanning isolated baffles with material such as chain-link or filter fabric (see Fig. 8) develops a catchment, and thereby creates an impoundment of material for removal.

Deflection Devices. A deflection device is usually made up of pier-supported walls (Fig. 9) or a series of baffles or debris fences having design similar to those mentioned earlier; or gravity structures. They are emplaced within the main track or depositional area to control the direction and reduce the velocity of flow. For example, gabions have been designed to act as a gravity deflection device within broad drainage basins, or at the base of uniform slopes subject to debris flow (Fig. 10a). They are con-

b

a

Figure 6. a, Northeasterly view of hillside in Pacifica, California, where rock riprap was added above high school building to mitigate potential debris flow/avalanche. b, Steepness of slope (100 percent) necessitated use of heavy-gauge chain-link fence to cover riprap surface, and construction of heavy-gauge chain-link fence at toe to capture fugitive rocks.

structed on a limited, graded pad, and consist of stacked, resistant, rock-filled heavy-gauge galvanized wire baskets (Fig. 10b). The basal gabion unit is generally founded on a bedrock surface having a slight inclination into the slope to allow for back drainage. To resist sliding, the basal unit is keyed into bedrock, and/or is supported on the downslope side by compacted fill.

The advantages of a gabion gravity diversion wall over a rigid structure are that: (1) the baskets are capable of sustaining the ultimate impact force of 19,640 N/m^3, (2) they can be deformed without appreciable reduction of efficiency, and (3) they are easily replaced. Gabions can be cheaper to install than drilled foundation systems but do require access for equipment to be cost-effective.

Deflection devices are capable of soil retention, and therefore pose maintenance considerations. When emplaced, they can offer protection to structures over a wide area (Fig. 11).

Impact Walls. Impact walls are designed and constructed to sustain an instantaneous force of 19,640 N/m^3 while containing the soil and vegetation debris until it can be removed. A variety of designs and construction techniques have been employed. Their limitations are based principally on the position of the impact wall on the slope and on access to maintenance construction equipment. From the standpoint of effective and lower cost maintenance, impact walls are generally considered for emplacement within the depositional area, at the base of the slope.

Concrete walls, soldier pile walls, and soil and/or rock gravity walls (including gabions) have been employed for impact and

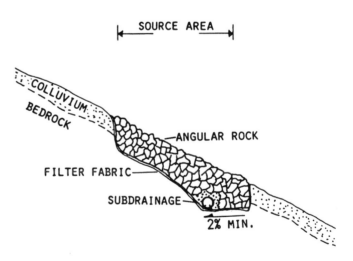

Figure 7. Typical design considerations for riprap repair scheme within source area of debris flow.

containment. The most common type of wall constructed in the San Francisco Bay area is the soldier pile system, which has a design similar to the retaining wall mentioned earlier. Pile spacing is commonly 2 m. The configuration of the wall should suit the site requirements. For example, Figure 12 illustrates a segmented wall in a highly confined residential area, between a public street and slope. The wall segments overlap at the ends to offer effective

Figure 8. Westerly view of slope in Pacifica, California, where baffles spanned by heavy chain-link fence were installed in main track of recent debris flow/avalanche to reduce flow velocity of potential, secondary debris flow/avalanche. Filter fabric installed on uphill side of chain-link fence to reduce downslope siltation has impounded some debris.

a

b

Figure 9. a, Easterly view of slope in Pacifica, California, uphill from condominium complex where soldier pile walls were constructed (arrows) to divert potential 3,800-m^3 debris flow/avalanche to common lawn area between buildings. b, Close-up view of soldier pile diversion wall.

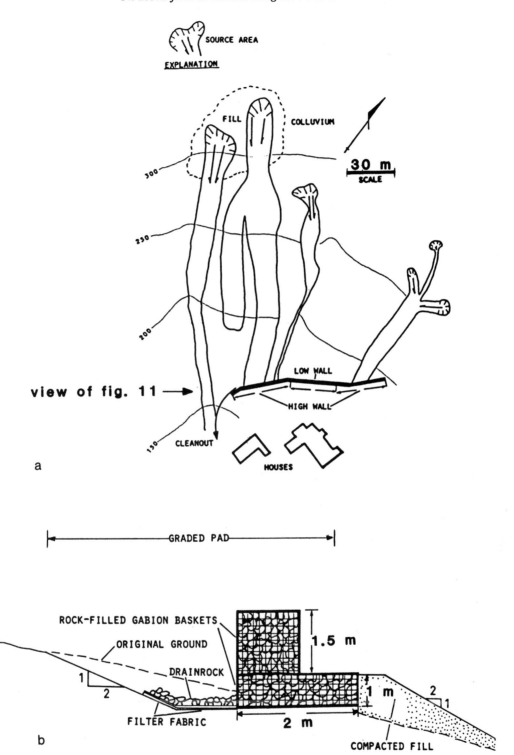

Figure 10. a, Gabion deflection wall constructed at base of uniform slope subject to debris flows in Tiburon, California. Wall has been constructed with high segments, which sustain impact and mitigate potential for overtopping, and low segment, which provides channellization of flow to desired depositional area for subsequent clean-out. b, Typical design for gabion deflection wall. (From file of Donald Herzog & Associates.)

Figure 11. Northeasterly view from depositional area of as-built gabion deflection wall illustrated in Figure 10.

Figure 12. Northeasterly view of segmented soldier pile impact wall constructed in Pacifica, California. End of wall segments overlap. Spacing between wall segments of 2 to 3 will allow clean-out by grading equipment (i.e., Bobcat or D-3).

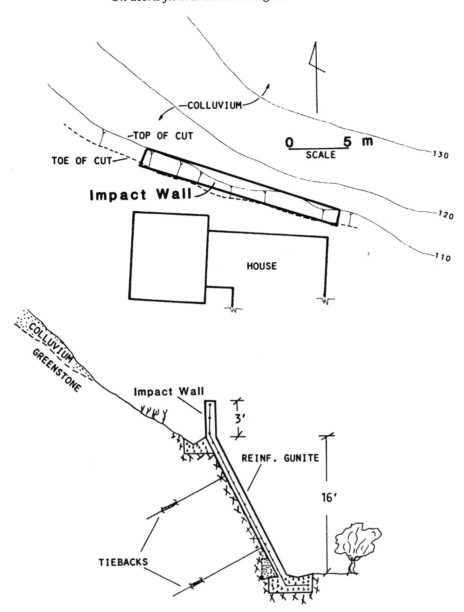

Figure 13. Illustration of highly confined residential site in Pacifica, California, where impact wall was constructed less than 3 m away from house to support rock-cut slope and to mitigate potential hazard by debris flow/avalanche occurring within colluvium upslope. Tie backs were constructed to resist wall overturning during impact. (From file of Donald Herzog & Associates.)

protection for the entire length, while the distance between the segments allows access from the street for clean-out by a small piece of grading equipment.

Figure 13 illustrates a wall intended to provide protection to a house graded into a debris flow–prone slope, while at the same time providing support to the cut slope. This creative alternative was employed because of the inaccessibility to the upper reaches of the unstable colluvial slope and because of the close proximity of the house to the cut slope, which also required support. Surface drainage behind the wall is an important component of this system or any other mitigation device that may impound runoff.

Debris Basins. A debris basin is designed to contain a single debris flow/avalanche event, or multiple events, until removal, commonly scheduled for the end of summer, when the impounded material is capable of supporting equipment loads. Considerations that must be incorporated into design of a debris basin include anticipated temporary impoundment requirements, not only of soil and vegetative material, but also of drainage basin

Figure 14. Easterly view of earthern debris basin constructed at base of hillside in Pacifica, California. Debris basin was designed to contain an estimated 2,300-m³ debris flow that may originate from oversteepened slopes of recent debris flow/avalanche source area. Note free-draining face of angular concrete riprap constructed in downstream corner (upper right) of earthern berm. Drainage standpipes were not used in this design because of potential for clogging due to expectation of high annual siltation.

runoff, expected impact force, drainage of impounded runoff, and maintenance. Debris basins are best suited for the base of a slope, in the depositional area, principally because of the intensive maintenance factors. Construction material most often used is on-site earth that has accumulated on the fan at the base of the slope. The perimeter berm, commonly rectangular in plan, is constructed on the original ground surface, or on a graded, level pad by compacting successive lifts of soil (minimum of 90 to as high as 95 percent of maximum dry density of the soil) to the design height (Fig. 14). Slopes of the berm are generally recommended to be no steeper than 50 percent for stability purposes. Having relatively gentle slopes on the upstream-side of the berm poses a potential hazard of runup and overtopping. Steeper berm slopes should be supported by an engineered retaining wall, or an upstream baffle system can be constructed to reduce the flow of an advancing debris flow/avalanche in order to resist overtopping of the berm having lower angle slopes (Fig. 15).

Comprehensive drainage is an important aspect of debris basin design. Standpipe drains within the basin can be clogged by debris deposition. Where this is a problem, a segment of the debris basin can be constructed with a free-draining face to reduce the hazard related to impounded runoff.

DISCUSSION AND CONCLUSION

We are now aware that any hillside subjected to prolonged, intense rainfall, particularly those having slopes 50 to 100%, may pose a potential hazard by debris flow/avalanche to structures located downslope. Construction in hillside areas is therefore severely limited by this potential hazard. While evaluating the foundation conditions of a particular hillside site, it is now becoming a standard that an equally important aspect of hillside geotechnical investigations, especially for sites positioned at the base of a slope, is to assess the potential for debris flow/avalanche initiation for a variety of drainage basin and hillside morphologic conditions. In most cases, this means that the investigation will extend beyond the limits of the site proposed for development.

We have defined a suite of basic mitigation devices that have been designed and constructed for San Francisco Bay area hillside sites to reduce this hazard. Certainly, there are many more possible designs that can be employed to protect structures from the ravages of debris flow/avalanche hazard. The imperative is that the hazard be recognized and appropriately mitigated.

We now realize that the essence of debris flow mitigation is to try to recognize the potential hazard and correct it in the source

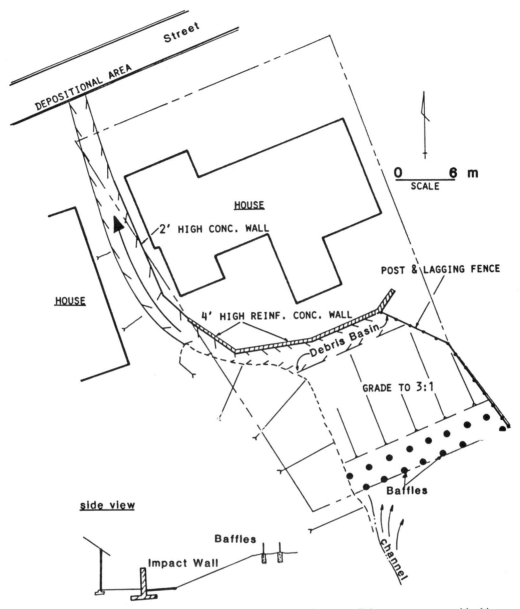

Figure 15. Combination of upstream baffles, debris basin, and impact wall that were constructed in this highly confined site in San Mateo, California. Baffles were designed to reduce flow velocity, and were spaced at 2.5-m centers to allow for access of maintenance equipment. Slope angle downslope from baffles was minimized to further reduce flow velocity after impact. Debris basin and impact wall, designed to contain an estimated 75-m^3 debris flow/avalanche, was constructed at base of hill at fan apex. Drainage provision from basin to street offers additional area for deposition in street, should design volume be exceeded.

area. If this is deemed impractical, after detailed geotechnical studies of the respective drainage basin, the procedure should be to control the course and reduce the velocity of a perceived debris flow within the main track, and to provide containment in a predetermined "design" depositional area. Devices proposed for the source area and main track do require maintenance and should be critically evaluated so that their effectiveness will not be lost with time.

ACKNOWLEDGMENTS

The many geologists and engineers throughout the Bay area, as well as southern California, deserve recognition for their creative and expeditious efforts in providing debris flow hazard mitigation since the winter of 1982. We thank Gerald Wieczorek for reviewing the manuscript and offering many constructive comments. Our gratitude is also extended to Chuck Traversy for his help with the manuscript.

REFERENCES CITED

Amimoto, P. V., 1981, Erosion and sediment control handbook: California Department of Conservation Resources Agency, 198 p.

Brabb, E. E., and Pampeyan, E. H., 1972, Preliminary map of landslides in San Mateo County, California: U.S. Geological Survey Miscellaneous Field Studies Map MF–344, 1 sheet, scale 1:62,500.

Brabb, E. E., Pampeyan, E. H., and Bonilla, M. G., 1972, Landslide susceptibility in San Mateo County, California: U.S. Geological Survey Miscellaneous Field Studies Map MF–360, 1 sheet, scale 1:62,500.

Brown, W. M., III, 1984, Summary of the conference, proceedings, debris flows, landslides, and floods in the San Francisco Bay region, January 1982; Overview and summary of a conference held at Stanford University, August 23-26, 1982: Washington, D.C., National Academy Press, p. 1.

Campbell, R. H., 1975, Soil slips, debris flows, and rainstorms in the Santa Monica Mountains and vicinity, southern California: U.S. Geological Survey Professional Paper 851, 51 p.

Dietrich, W. E., Wilson, C. J., and Reneau, S., 1987, Hollows, colluvium, and landslides in soil mantled landscapes, *in* Abrahams, A., ed., Hillsope processes: Allen and Unwin, 140 p. (in press).

Hollingsworth, R., and Kovacs, G. S., 1981, Soil slips and debris flows; Prediction and protection: Association of Engineering Geologists Bulletin, v. 18, no. 1, p. 17–28.

Howard, T. H., Baldwin, J. E., II, and Donley, H. F., 1987, Landslides in Pacifica, California, *in* Ellen, S., and Wieczorek, G. F., eds., Landslides, floods and

marine effects of the storm of January 3-5, 1982, in the San Francisco Bay Area: U.S. Geological Survey Professional Paper 1434, Chapter 9 (in press).

Nilsen, T. H., Wright, R. H., Vlasic, T. C., and Spangle, W. E., 1979, Relative slope stability and land-use planning in the San Francisco Bay region, California: U.S. Geological Survey Professional Paper 944, 29 p.

Reneau, S. L., Dietrich, W. E., Wilson, C. J., and Rogers, J. D., 1984, Colluvial deposits and associated landslides in the northern San Francisco Bay Area, California, USA, *in* Proceedings, 4th International Symposium on Landslides: Toronto, Canada, p. 425–430.

Smith, T. C., Hart, E. W., Baldwin, J. E., and Rodriques, R. J., 1982, Landslides and related storm damage, January 1982, San Francisco Bay region, California Geology: California Division of Mines and Geology, v. 35, no. 7, p. 137–164.

Varnes, D. J., 1978, Slope movement types and processes, *in* Schuster, R. L., and Krizek, R. J., eds., Landslides analysis and control: Washington, D.C., National Academy of Sciences, Transportation Research Board, Special Report 176, p. 11–33, 1 Pl.

Wieczorek, G. F., and Sarmiento, J., 1983, Significance of storm intensity; Duration for triggering debris flows near La Honda, California: Geological Society of America Abstracts with Programs, v. 15, no. 5, p. 289.

Manuscript Accepted by the Society December 29, 1986

Index

[Italic page numbers indicate major references]

precipitation
  Appalachian Mountains, 82, 86, 88, 126, 140
  British Columbia, 64, 67, 68, 69, 70, 72
  North Carolina, 93
  prior to debris flows, 93, 140
prehistoric events, 130, 147
pseudoplastic fluid, 2
Purisma Formation, Tahana Member, 94
pyroclastic events, Mount St. Helens, 52

Quaternary, 140, 158

rainfall, antecedent to debris flows, 93, 130
  See also precipitation
recurrence intervals of mass movements, 175, 190
Ridge and Valley Province, Appalachian Highlands, 126, 133, 135
rill networks, 108, 113
road runoff, as cause of landslides, 177
Roan Mountain, North Carolina, debris fans, 145
rock avalanches, *41*
  Alberta, 41, 42
  Washington, 42
  See also landslides
rock pitting, Australia, 143
Rockfish River, Virginia, floods, 149
Rocky Mountain Front Ranges, Canada, 116, 122
  See also Canadian Rocky Mountains
Rocky Mountain Main Ranges, Canada, 116, 122
  See also Canadian Rocky Mountains

San Dimas Experimental Forest, California, 106
San Francisco Bay region

debris avalanche mitigation, *223*
debris flows, *31*, 93, 94, 96, 168, 178, *181*, *223*
San Gabriel Mountains, California, fire at, 106
San Lorenzo Formation, 95
San Pedro basin, California, 197
San Rafael, California, landslide, 173, 178
Santa Cruz Mountains, California, *93*, 169, 174
Santa Monica Mountains, California, 168
Scandinavia, debris slides, 131
Schusrinne, 204
Sclufield Creek, British Columbia, 206, 207, 211
Scottsville, Virginia, flood, 149
shear stress, 2, 4, 10
Sherman rockfall, 42
Shoestring Glacier, Washington, 55
Siadmarreh, Iran, landslip, 41
side slopes, defined, 166
Silverhope Creek, British Columbia, 65
slickensides, 8
slides, 8, 31
  debris flow, 98, 99
slope failures, Pennsylvania, 133
slope modification, 227
slumps, debris flow, 98
slurry flow, 4, 7, 8, 133
slurry strength, 33
Smoky Mountains, debris fans, 144
soil slip/debris flows, 31, 33, 38
  See also debris flows
soil slips, 31
soil stratigraphy, 194
solifluction, 3, 10
Sonoma County, California, 168
South Fork Toutle River, Washington, 52, 53, 54, 55, 61
Spring Creek, Appalachian Plateau, 133
storms. *See* precipitation
streamflow, 3, 8
  hyperconcentrated, 9, 10
sturzstroms, 8, 10, 41

See also debris avalanches, rock avalanches
swales, 166, 182, 184, 195
See also hollows

Tennessee, debris flows, 130
terminology, *1*, 131, 139, 166
Tertiary, 141, 152
thixotropic, defined, 2
Thunderhead Sandstone, 133
Toutle River, Washington, 51, 60
  See also North Fork Toutle River; South Fork Toutle River
Transverse Ranges, California, dry ravel, 108
Turtle Mountain, Canada, 41
Tye River, Virginia, flood, 149

Utah, debris flows, 168

Vancouver, British Columbia, 202, 206, 213, 215
velocity, 4, 19
  of debris flow, 171, 172
Virginia
  debris avalanches, *139*
  debris fans, 144, 145, 147, 150, 152
  debris flows, 130, 139, 145, 168
  floods, 149
viscosity, fluid, 2, 7, 18
volcanic processes, 42, 52, 140

Wahleach, British Columbia, 68, 72
warning systems, 207
Wasatch Range, Utah, 169
Washington, debris flows, 4
Watauga County, North Carolina, debris flow deposits, 130
water blowouts, defined, 131
Webb Mountain, Tennessee, 133
West Virginia, debris flows, 130, 168
Whitney Creek gorge, Mount Shasta, California, *157*
Whitney Glacier, California, 157
Wisconsinan, 116

yield strength, 2, 7, 8

Typeset by WESType Publishing Services, Inc., Boulder, Colorado
Printed in U.S.A. by Malloy Lithographing, Inc., Ann Arbor, Michigan